Professional Sitecore 8 Development

A Complete Guide to Solutions and Best Practices

Phil Wicklund

Jason Wilkerson

Apress®

Professional Sitecore 8 Development: A Complete Guide to Solutions and Best Practices

Phil Wicklund
Minneapolis, Minnesota, USA

Jason Wilkerson
Minnetrista, Minnesota, USA

ISBN-13 (pbk): 978-1-4842-2291-1
DOI 10.1007/978-1-4842-2292-8

ISBN-13 (electronic): 978-1-4842-2292-8

Library of Congress Control Number: 2016959582

Managing Director: Welmoed Spahr
Acquisitions Editor: Susan McDermott
Developmental Editor: Laura Berendson
Technical Reviewer: Kamruz Jaman, Mike Reynolds, Nick Wesselman
Editorial Board: Steve Anglin, Pramila Balen, Laura Berendson, Aaron Black, Louise Corrigan, Jonathan Gennick, Robert Hutchinson, Celestin Suresh John, Nikhil Karkal, James Markham, Susan McDermott, Matthew Moodie, Natalie Pao, Gwenan Spearing
Coordinating Editor: Rita Fernando
Copy Editor: Kezia Endsley
Compositor: SPi Global
Indexer: SPi Global
Cover Image: Selected by Freepik

Distributed to the book trade worldwide by Springer Science+Business Media New York, 233 Spring Street, 6th Floor, New York, NY 10013. Phone 1-800-SPRINGER, fax (201) 348-4505, e-mail orders-ny@springer-sbm.com, or visit www.springer.com. Apress Media, LLC is a California LLC and the sole member (owner) is Springer Science + Business Media Finance Inc (SSBM Finance Inc). SSBM Finance Inc is a Delaware corporation.

For information on translations, please e-mail rights@apress.com, or visit www.apress.com.

Apress and friends of ED books may be purchased in bulk for academic, corporate, or promotional use. eBook versions and licenses are also available for most titles. For more information, reference our Special Bulk Sales–eBook Licensing web page at www.apress.com/bulk-sales.

Any source code or other supplementary materials referenced by the author in this text is available to readers at www.apress.com. For detailed information about how to locate your book's source code, go to www.apress.com/source-code/.

Printed on acid-free paper

I dedicate this book to my mother, who unceasingly drilled into me:
"If there's a will, there's a way!"

—Phil

I dedicate this book to my wife, Anna. Without you, I could never have
accomplished this. For real. Also, to the Sitecore Community;
your passion and excitement is infectious and it drives me.

—Jason

Contents at a Glance

Contents

Foreword

Since the dawn of Sitecore, developers have needed introductory orientation as well as clear, comprehensive answers to their burning technical questions about the world's leading ASP.NET web content and experience management platform. But as with many emerging platforms, information lagged behind enthusiasm. In the beginning, there was disassembly, with most Sitecore solutions entirely dependent on the pioneering work of our original savior, Lutz Roeder.

Next came the Sitecore Developer Network forums and the advent of Sitecore developer documentation in PDF format, largely and somewhat unfortunately contributed by yours truly, the former @sitecorejohn. It is not even worth mentioning that those 500 pages of marketing fluff later written by someone with a name similar to mine who worked at their kitchen counter for three months in the fall of 2011. Today, there are so many sources of information about Sitecore that just identifying them can be a full-time job, with many of the most justified and valiant voices lost in the cacophony of distraction.

These are some of the reasons why I welcome *Professional Sitecore 8 Development* as a means to restore sanity to an increasingly disjointed archipelago of information. This book provides the best starting point available today for developers new to Sitecore technologies, including the web Content Management System (CMS) and Experience Platform (XP).

For anyone unfamiliar with the platform, this book covers all of the fundamentals that a developer new to Sitecore needs to understand from the beginning. For those familiar with Sitecore, it provides a wealth of information that even seasoned software engineers should find invaluable.

In particular, this book outlines core concepts about developing with Sitecore and demonstrates how to incorporate modern design patterns into projects in order to deliver high-quality, scalable, and testable solutions. The book shows how to apply Helix design and development principles, a set of overall objectives and conventions from Sitecore itself that support the objective of achieving optimal and maintainable solutions. On top of this, it demonstrates the strongest aspects of development as implemented in the Habitat project also provided by Sitecore. This type of foundation becomes more critical as the complexity, importance, and interconnectedness of WCM continues to increase in order to enable the next generation of digital marketing practices.

As the former Chief Technology Officer for Sitecore, I have known the authors of this new work, Jason and Phil, since they appeared in the community years ago. To his tremendous credit, Jason has rapidly achieved the coveted Sitecore Most Valuable Professional (MVP) status, while Phil manages an entire engineering team responsible for implementing solutions based on Sitecore digital marketing technologies. Phil previously wrote the *Practical Sitecore 8 Configuration and Strategy* book published in 2015. The insights in this new work come from their real-world experiences implementing advanced solutions for Sitecore customers in North America.

I continue to be impressed with the Sitecore software and ecosystem and was delighted when Jason requested that I write the forward for this volume. This book makes a significant and important contribution that is now available to the entire Sitecore community, which I have watched grow, evolve, and progress at an ever-increasing rate as the software cadence and feature set has accelerated. This book may just be the best starting point for implementing what I still consider to be the best Web Content Management System available today.

I have an additional reason to be thankful for such a book. In my new role as senior vice president of experience platforms for POSSIBLE at @cmsvortext, I now benefit from these efforts as would any consumer rather contributing to them as a producer. As I continue to develop in my own career, reading draft chapters of this book has rewarded my time investment by providing a valuable training resource.

Regardless of your background, whether with or without Sitecore, I am confident that you will benefit from this well-structured and researched volume. As a final word, I would like to personally thank all of you for being members of the Sitecore community!

—John West
Senior Vice President, Experience Platforms, POSSIBLE
Former Chief Architect and CTO, Sitecore

About the Authors

Phil Wicklund is the manager of digital technology services at RBA, Inc.—a digital and technology consultancy.

His passion is leadership. It sounds simplistic, or worse, cliché, but his passion runs deep and no other word hits closer to the mark. He loves leadership because he loves casting a vision for a better future; a future of personal growth, betterment of the human condition, ways to create future value for companies, and a future of shared accomplishment with his teammates. Such a future is one worth fighting for, and he has never been afraid to take the path of maximum resistance to make a goal a reality.

He has led and managed countless large-scale, enterprise projects as a project manager and/or technical lead. He also has experience managing a staff of 36+ consultants. Additionally, he's been blessed with countless opportunities to interface with and advise CXO-level customers on creating value for their companies.

He has also written three technology books; teaching is his second passion. He loves the feeling at the end of a day when he has been able to apply his expertise to help someone in need. He sincerely hopes this book helps a lot of people learn a tool that isn't always the easiest to learn.

He is currently in his third year of doctoral studies at the University of St. Thomas. Learning, you could say, is his third passion. He is working to extend his studies in technology and business by deepening his understanding of organizational leadership, working toward a dissertation that combines the three disciplines.

Jason Wilkerson is the Discipline Lead of the Sitecore practice at RBA, Inc., a Sitecore Platinum Partner. In 2016, he had the honor of being selected as a Sitecore Technology MVP, primarily due to his commitment to the Sitecore community as a speaker, blogger, and thought leader.

Jason's passions lie deep in architecture and technology. With an unrivaled eye toward quality and elegance, he strives to make every customer's solution the most intuitive and maintainable it can possibly be—not only from a technical standpoint, but also from the user's perspective.

With almost two decades of experience building enterprise-class software, as well as leading teams of developers, project managers, business analysts, and quality assurance testers, he's been able to assemble an impressive list of successful projects, leaving nothing but satisfied customers behind him.

In his free time, Jason is also an avid singer, guitar player, and bassist. From a very early age, the same passion that has driven him in technology has driven his love for music and the honing of his talents.

It is this creative outlet, he believes, that provides a unique perspective in the realm of technology. His training and education in computer science provides the foundation for the engineering side of software, but his creative nature serves as the backdrop for creating intuitive, user-centric customer solutions.

About the Contributor

Michael West (author of Chapter 10) is a passionate technologist and Application Architect at Concentra—a national healthcare company in Dallas, Texas. In his roles as developer, manager, designer, and innovator, he begins with empowering others and ends by helping them succeed. During Michael's time working in IT, he has taken on responsibilities in UX design, UX development, DevOps, environment governance, and release management. He enjoys taking on new challenges and is known for bringing innovative solutions to the software industry. Michael received the 2015 and 2016 Sitecore Technology MVP award in recognition of his active contribution to the Sitecore community. He is a key contributor to the popular open source module Sitecore PowerShell Extensions (SPE), found on the Sitecore marketplace. Teaching others is another passion of his. Many of his thoughts and ideas are shared with the community through user groups, video tutorials, and written material.

About the Technical Reviewers

Kamruz Jaman is an independent Sitecore specialist and four-time Sitecore MVP. Kamruz has over 15 years of development and architecture experience using the Microsoft technology stack, having spent the majority of his career in industries such as finance, technology, ecommerce, pharmaceuticals, distribution, insurance, and travel. Having worked exclusively with Sitecore for the past seven years, Kamruz is heavily involved in the Sitecore community and has spoken at user groups and conferences. He also likes to blog and share his knowledge with the community via Slack, Stack Overflow, and the Sitecore forums.

Mike Reynolds is a Sitecore MVP with over eight years of Sitecore architecture and development experience and is an independent consultant with a proven track record of pushing the envelope of the Sitecore platform to deliver best-of-breed solutions for clients. A well-known thought leader in the Sitecore community, Reynolds was recognized as a Sitecore Technology MVP in 2014, 2015, and 2016 for his community contributions.

Nick Wesselman is a four-time Sitecore MVP and manages product development for Active Commerce, "Sitecore ecommerce done right." Nick has been developing content management and ecommerce applications for over 15 years and has contributed to Sitecore modules such as WeBlog and Sitecore PowerShell Extensions

Acknowledgments

We would first like to acknowledge the support and help we received from our technical editors—Kamruz Jaman, Mike Reynolds, and Nick Wesselman—as well as our contributing author, Michael West. The impact of their feedback, support, and guidance over the past six months cannot be understated. Gentlemen, you have our sincerest thanks!

Additionally, we wish to offer our thanks to the Apress team, most notably Susan McDermott and Rita Fernando. Susan, thank you for giving us the opportunity to write this book and partner with such a reputable brand, Apress, once again. Rita, thank you for your patience, guidance, and help these past months as we slogged through the material together. Apress is truly a best-in-class publisher, and we're honored to continue our partnership.

Lastly, we wish to thank the Sitecore community itself. The community is large and robust, filled with thousands of thought leaders who really deserve the credit for this book. Everybody knows you can find whatever you need online these days. This book is really an assemblage of all the great materials and best practices championed by so many fine, hard-working individuals. We raise our glass to YOU!

Introduction

We believe this book represents the most foundational, core aspects of Sitecore that every Sitecore developer needs to understand. The goal of this book is to take developers who are new to Sitecore all the way from setting up their local development environment to more advanced topics, such as pipelines or extending the Experience Editor, and many things in between.

The earlier chapters focus on an introduction to the platform, including its core capabilities and features, as well as getting started with development. Later chapters start layering in "best practices" that even seasoned Sitecore veterans will find beneficial.

Chapters toward the end of the book start to home in on key capabilities, such as search and the marketing features, where you will really start to dive into the particulars.

Again, our goal is to lay a foundation of "core" Sitecore development concepts. Many of these are for beginners, but many are still quite advanced. The Sitecore platform is sooooo big, there are just too many nooks and crannies; we could never hope to cover all of them. Literally an entire book of just "Advanced Sitecore Development Techniques" could be written if ever that were to be attempted (any takers?). Hopefully you agree that the following 11 chapters represent the most important topics each and every Sitecore developer should understand and master. Beyond these, we look to the Sitecore community to fill the gaps with blog posts or future books.

Note This book isn't meant to provide production-ready code samples, but rather it teaches the patterns for successfully building quality, testable, maintainable code. Our goal is to teach you how to fish, so to speak.

How This Book Is Structured

- Chapter 1, "Introduction to Sitecore," will answer the question, "what is Sitecore?" Additionally, the chapter quickly gets pragmatic by showing you, step-by-step, how to set up your development environment.

- Chapter 2, "Building your First Component," helps you do just that, build your first component. Components are the most basic building block of any page within Sitecore. This chapter shows you how to do the stereotypical "hello world" example.

- Chapter 3, "Data Templates and Content," extends component development by focusing on the core foundational aspects of any Sitecore deployment: templates. Templates are the basis of everything in Sitecore, and you need a solid understanding of them before you advance in the book.

- Chapter 4, "Back-End Dev Architectures," extend that first "hello world" example you wrote in Chapter 2 by discussing common patterns for Sitecore development, such as MVC and modular architectures.

- Chapter 5, "Improving the Design with Patterns," extends Chapter 4's discussion around back-end techniques by adding many best practices, such as ORMs, dependency injection, and abstracting through patterns.

- Chapter 6, "Front-End Dev Techniques," focuses on the front-end developer a bit by discussing layouts, placeholders, CSS, and JavaScript.

- Chapter 7, "Unit Testing Sitecore," walks you through the ins and outs of unit testing in and around Sitecore, including popular tools such as AutoFixture, Moq, and FakeDb.

- Chapter 8, "Search-Driven Solutions," focuses on Search: how to index, search, and refine content.

- Chapter 9, "Programming the Customer Journey," focuses on the marketing capabilities of Sitecore and how to develop and customize them.

- Chapter 10, "Sitecore PowerShell Extensions," shows you how automation helps with many of the administrative capabilities within Sitecore, as well as how to program Sitecore with PowerShell.

- Chapter 11, "Extending the Experience Editor," explains how to customize the Experience Editor to make it friendlier for content authors and marketers.

Contacting the Authors

Phil Wicklund:

- phil@sitecoreconfig.com
- http://sitecoreconfig.com
- https://linkedin.com/in/philwicklund
- Twitter: @philwicklund

Jason Wilkerson:

- jasonmwilkerson@gmail.com
- http://citizensitecore.com
- Twitter/Slack: @longhorntaco
- https://linkedin.com/in/jasonmwilkerson

CHAPTER 1

■ ■ ■

Getting Started

What do you need to know about Sitecore before getting your hands on the code? Whenever I read development books, I always want to get into the code as quickly as possible. Sure, there's always tons of great background information that helps you understand the code better. Sitecore is no exception. In fact, that's part of the problem with writing a Sitecore book—it's just such a huge platform!

Critics of this chapter might comment that we've skipped too much introductory material for a first chapter. This chapter is really NOT an introduction to Sitecore. This chapter is an introduction to Sitecore development. As such, we'll cover some of the most fundamental aspects of Sitecore, but just enough to get you to a point that you can understand the code, what it's doing, and how it's working.

This means answering the "What is Sitecore" question from a high-level perspective. The goal here is to give you a 30,000-foot view of Sitecore's capabilities, its server roles, and how data flows in Sitecore. Additionally, we'll introduce you to Sitecore's administrative user interface, the Launchpad. Finally, we'll discuss Sitecore features in relation to previous versions of Sitecore to give you a view back.

Next we'll cover the Sitecore hierarchy. Namely, you need to know the core "building blocks" of Sitecore. You'll create data templates, layouts, placeholders, and components during the course of building out your Sitecore digital properties. Understanding these four building blocks represents the most foundational knowledge you need to have before you see a single line of code. Without that backdrop, the code won't make sense.

With that foundation laid, the next step will be to set up your development environment. This includes setting up a local SQL server, installing Sitecore, and getting the necessary tools in place, most obviously Microsoft Visual Studio.

With all that under your belt, you can finally start building something! However, we're going to save that for Chapter 2.

What Is Sitecore?

Sitecore is HUGE, Huge, huge! Where do you even start? You could literally write an entire book on just the features and capabilities of Sitecore without ever seeing a single line of code. Oh wait, I did that; it's called *Practical Sitecore 8 Configuration and Strategy* (Apress, 2015), to be specific (#shamelessplug).

Most of the features and capabilities discussed in that book are there to help the marketer and/or content administrator do their job, create great user experiences for their customers, and manage their campaigns. This book, however, is geared toward the developer, not the marketer per se. The best place to start, in that case, is with a gross oversimplification of Sitecore to ensure we're all on the same page.

Electronic supplementary material The online version of this chapter (doi:10.1007/978-1-4842-2292-8_1) contains supplementary material, which is available to authorized users.

Sitecore is a Web Content Management (WCM) solution on steroids. You could argue that Sitecore is really a Customer Experience Platform (CXP, or better yet WCM 2.0). However, arguing that would be going down the rabbit hole I just argued we shouldn't go down. Given that, Sitecore is two things at its core: 1) a web site you build and 2) a database within which you can manage content. The most simplistic Sitecore architecture diagram you could ever create is shown in Figure 1-1.

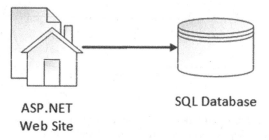

**ASP.NET
Web Site**

SQL Database

Figure 1-1. Sitecore, at its most basic definition, is a web site with a database

You'll see in Figure 1-2 that Sitecore itself isn't even depicted in Figure 1-1; however, that requires more explanation that is best saved for later. The point, fundamentally, is that a Sitecore site is just an ASP.NET web site that connects to a database. Sitecore helps you manage the data in that database; Sitecore is not the web site your customers will experience—that is something you build yourself.

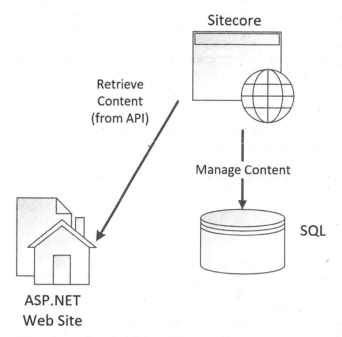

Sitecore

Retrieve
Content
(from API)

Manage Content

SQL

**ASP.NET
Web Site**

Figure 1-2. Sitecore really is a web site within your web site that's used to manage content

Confused? You might be. Many people bring a lot of expectations and baggage to Sitecore. Namely, that Sitecore comes with a "bag of tricks" such as widgets, page templates, etc., that you can just drag and drop and in five minutes have a site, WordPress-style. For better (not really worse), Sitecore is just about the opposite of WordPress as you could ever get. To help explain the difference, let's compare the two types of solutions next: developer platforms versus portal/web solutions.

Developer Platforms versus Portal Solutions

Sitecore is a developer platform, not a canned "portal solution" such as many popular horizontal portal solutions out there, such as SharePoint, WebSphere or Liferay. Some of those products make claims to be a platform, but you'll see in a bit why Sitecore stands out as unique in this regard. This topic of "platform" versus "portal package" can be confusing, especially since Sitecore is often used as a platform for portals.

An analogy might help newbies understand how Sitecore differs from some of these other popular portal solutions. Let's use the example of a manufactured/mobile home versus a custom-built home.

Features of manufactured homes include:

- *Fast and cheap*: The most obvious point to make with mobile homes is they are fast to set up and are cheap. You literally go to the lot, pick one out with the features you want, and then they drive it to your lot and drop it off.

- *Easily configurable*: Mobile homes have many options and configurations to select from, and they're all optimized for people with little training to understand and use.

- *Rigid*: That configurability can turn to rigidity when your unique needs are not perfectly expressed in those options.

- *Customizable, to a point*: Yes, you can customize your mobile home, but doesn't that defeat the entire point of buying a mobile home? If you do customize it, you run into a rapid decline in benefit with ever-growing costs, as you push the home beyond its original intent.

- *Ugly*: You don't buy a mobile home to make a statement of elegance. You buy it for pure utilitarian purposes.

These seem like pretty good points and you can start to understand the tradeoffs that come with packaged portal solutions. You can get a *big* head start with them, and they all come with a nice "bag of tricks" to help you build sites quickly. However, this is never *YOUR* site; it's always built from a template and never quite captures your unique brand, perspective, or characteristics. From a development perspective, such sites are a pain. You're forced to play in a box, and customizing beyond the scope of that box is often painful and expensive, to the point where you begin to wish you had chosen a platform, not a packaged solution. With that segue in mind, let's look at the features of a home foundation (software platform):

Features of a foundation:

- *Access to core utilities (e.g., water, sewage, power, and gas)*: If you buy a homestead lot (licensing), you get access to all kinds of goodies that help your life as a homebuilder. You can hook right up the water supply and power without having to worry about generating your own electricity. Sitecore provides a lot of rich "core" capabilities such as a personalization and rules engine, analytics, and content management, all without pigeon-holing you.

- *Solid foundation using industry-standard approaches (block, rebar, etc.)*: You know that *any* homebuilder can build on this foundation because it uses industry-standard home building techniques (ASP.NET, MVC, design patterns, test-driven-development, etc.). Block, rebar, standard dimensions, etc. enable anyone who swings a hammer to jump in and get to work without much specific training. Being a "Sitecore developer" is not far from being a typical ASP.NET MVC developer.

■ **Note**   While being a "Sitecore developer" is not far from being a typical ASP.NET MVC developer, Sitecore MVC doesn't fully follow the principles of ASP.NET MVC. There is a bit of a learning curve for even seasoned ASP. NET MVC developers when starting to develop a Sitecore MVC-based solution.

- *Ability to customize the foundation and blaze your own path (use solar panels instead of the electric grid)*: Maybe you hate the idea of using the city's sewage system and you want to build your own septic. Not a problem. Sitecore has a vast network of "pipelines" (pun intended) that you can tap into and change the way Sitecore works in a supported, standard fashion.

- *You get to build whatever you want on top of that foundation*: Sitecore makes no point to tell you what your house should look like. Bungalow or Rambler? Victorian or Craftsman? Single-page-application (SPA), ASP.NET MVC, or good ol' fashioned ASP Web Forms? Doesn't matter (although we'll make a point in this book to outline best practices) to Sitecore. You decide what you build, what it looks like, and how it works.

You can be a productive Sitecore developer in just a few months. However, it takes years to understand the nuances of SharePoint to make the same claim. That's the beauty of a "platform" versus a packaged "portal solution".

Another key differentiator of Sitecore is how it separates content from its presentation. Many portal solutions combine the two, to the point where it's commonplace for the content itself to be HTML. Sitecore, on the other hand, treats it as severely as the separation of church and state. In Figure 1-2, you'll notice an additional element not shown in Figure 1-1—Sitecore itself. Sitecore is an administrative user interface that sits in a folder of your web site, allowing content authors to administer content and marketers to do things marketers do, such as manage their campaigns, optimize pages, and so forth. Sitecore is *not* your site! Your site is your site! You build your ASP.NET web site to look and feel however it ought to look and feel, in whatever way best expresses your company's brand. Sitecore doesn't get in the way of that by forcing your presentation details to conform to Sitecore rules (like you so often find in portal solutions); Sitecore is totally separate from your site's presentation.

■ **Note**   While I may have been speaking in extremes to make a point in the previous paragraph, Sitecore does provide a WYSIWYG (what-you-see-is-what-you-get) editor called the Experience Editor. This editor makes it very easy for marketers to edit content without having to guess what it'll look like after they click Publish. However, the editor is smart enough to reflect your site's custom presentation details while still being totally separate from your actual site. More on the Experience Editor in Chapter 2.

Sitecore's Key Features and Capabilities

It's time to talk about what Sitecore can do, now that you have a general sense of what Sitecore is. Sitecore has published a helpful Solution Architecture diagram (Figure 1-3) that is a good tool to use to review Sitecore's architecture, features, and capabilities.

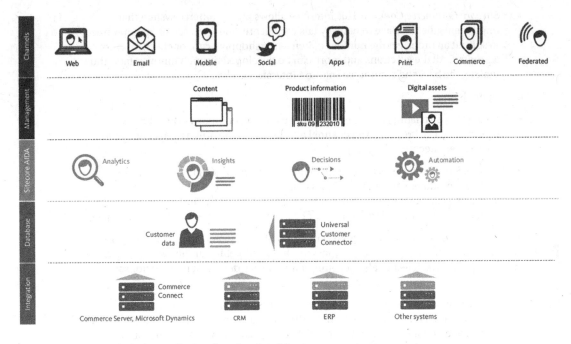

Figure 1-3. *Sitecore's de facto solution five-tiered architecture*

Sitecore's architecture is broken into five main service tiers: Channels, Management, Sitecore AIDA, Database, and the Integration Tier. The specific features and capabilities of Sitecore are spread throughout this architecture in various forms.

Channel Layer

Channels are the points of engagement from which customers enter as they interact with your brand. Sitecore provides a host of features and capabilities that maximize engagement across the following channels.

Key features and capabilities of the Channel layer include:

- *Email Experience Manager (EXM)*: With EXM, you can author e-mails, set personalization rules for those e-mails, and track e-mail click-throughs and other analytics.

- *Print Experience Manager (PXM)*: PXM allows you to dynamical generate print assets, such as brochures or manuals, on the fly. This is helpful because your brochures and digital properties can share the same content, for example, and you can even generate custom, personalized assets for customers on demand.

- *Federated Experience Manager (FXM)*: FXM allows you to share the same content and analytics across all your digital properties, regardless if they are on the Sitecore platform.

- *Social connections*: Provides integration into Facebook, Twitter, etc. for your digital properties.

- *Sitecore Commerce Connect*: This interface allows any commerce system that implements the interface to natively talk to Sitecore. Your web site or app may need to submit an order, get the number of items in a shopping cart, or check inventory of a product. All these actions and more can be developed through this interface, thus making the backend commerce solution interchangeable.

Those channels are:

- *Web*: The web channel is the core channel users will engage in from a browser experience. The browser/web channel also becomes the primary mechanism to administer Sitecore.

- *E-mail*: Sitecore engages the e-mail channel primarily through the Email Experience Manager module. This module allows marketers to create e-mail campaigns by leveraging customer profile data, preferences, or segments. The Email Experience Manager also allows for easy tracking of customer engagement within the campaign.

- *Mobile*: Sitecore accommodates a separation of content and presentation details. This makes it very easy for developers to create compelling mobile web experiences within Sitecore. Sitecore also accommodates device detection for situations where an adaptive experience is preferred.

- *Social*: Sitecore allows for easy integration with Social channels such as Facebook and Twitter. When you post content in Sitecore, you can configure it to automatically post to one or many pages in Facebook. You can also allow users to log into your site with their federated Facebook credentials. There is a ton of possibility for a marketer in this channel, from finding brand advocates, to capturing customer intelligence, to proactively seeking feedback and advice.

- *Commerce*: Sitecore has rich commerce capabilities to tap into your customer shopping behaviors across all your channels. Sitecore Commerce 8 is a new capability released in early 2015 that enables B2C and B2B ecommerce managed within Sitecore and a Microsoft Dynamics backend.

- *Print*: Print is another channel that customers interface with regularly, such as through brochures and print ads. Print Experience Manager, a feature of Sitecore, allows marketers to easily capture personalization data to create compelling, targeted print experiences for customers.

- *Apps*: Mobile apps have become a critical way customers interact with your brand, especially when considering ecommerce. One of the benefits of Sitecore is the ease of access to centralized content. Content for the web can be reused for content in an app. additionally, you can use Sitecore's Federated Experience Manager to tie in App engagement data into Sitecore to, again, create a single view of how your customer is experiencing your brand.

- Federated: Federated channels might be channels you don't own but still represent a view into your customer. Perhaps a partner web site captures valuable information about your target customers. Through the use of Federated Experience Manager, you can easily capture those very important, non-Sitecore managed experience's data and combine it with native representations of your customer to create a truer representation of your customer's engagement across all your channels (and even partners).

Management Layer

The Management layer of Sitecore is the core of the experience platform. This is where content administers manage content. It is also where they configure personalization rules, view engagement scores, and view reports. It is also what collects, evaluates, manages, and analyzes customer intelligence from patterns, behaviors, and decisions gathered across your channels. Additionally, from within Sitecore, you can manage all of your company's digital assets, in one place, used across all channels.

Key features and capabilities of the management layer include:

- *Unified content management*: Sitecore provides a one-stop-shop to manage all your content across all your digital properties and apps. Additionally, you get access to powerful content editing tools, such as the Experience Editor, to make content administration a snap.

- *The Sitecore Launchpad*: The Launchpad is your portal to all things Sitecore Administration; see "A Tour of the Sitecore Admin Interface" later in this chapter.

- *Viewing analytics and reports*: Sitecore captures every interaction a customer makes on your digital properties. You can view all these analytics and reports from the Launchpad.

- *Digital asset management*: Sitecore provides a media library capability to manage assets such as videos, imagery, and documents.

Sitecore AIDA Layer

Sitecore AIDA (Analytics, Insights, Decisions, and Automation) encompasses all the sexy features and capabilities over which marketers salivate. Therein lies the power to do advanced content testing, such as A/B or multivariate testing. You can also configure customer engagement goals, triggers, and reports to show progress and campaign outcome attainment. At its core, AIDA provides a rich suite of reporting and analytic capabilities so your marketing team can discover new insights and customer behavior patterns.

Key features and capabilities of the management layer include:

- *Experience profiles*: Profiles in Sitecore become the 360-degree view of a customer. Every event, goal, outcome, and interaction is tracked in the customer's profile. This provides rich data from which to personalize the experience later.

- *Personalization*: Every interaction in Sitecore can be personalized to fit each customer's unique needs, wants, pain points, buying patterns, etc. Sitecore provides two main ways to personalize content: rules-based personalization (e.g., if A, then B), and behavioral personalization, where Sitecore takes into consideration all the interactions in the current session or across multiple sessions to determine which content would best suit that customer (e.g., machine learning of sorts).

- *Experience optimization*: "Test everything" is Sitecore's motto. You can run tests that compare one page to another or compare multiple versions of a given page to find the combination that creates the most engagement from users. This is often called multivariate, or "A/B," testing.

- *Engagement plans*: Otherwise called "experience automation," engagement plans allow you to build a "customer journey". These plans enable Sitecore to facilitate that journey without outside intervention from a marketer (sending e-mails, etc.), therefore advancing a customer further down the buying cycle.

Sitecore Database Layer

The Database layer is the heart of Sitecore. Data is the lifeblood of your experience marketing solutions. It is otherwise impossible to deliver a highly relevant, personalized, channel optimized customer experience. Sitecore's xDB architecture leverages MongoDB for massive data capture and retention capabilities. This allows high volume, high velocity, unstructured data to be captured and become actionable in real time.

Key features and capabilities of the database layer include:

- *xDB (MongoDB):* Mongo is a NoSQL database that is highly denormalized, which enables massive scaling of flexible, unstructured data. Out-of-the-box, *tons* of data about a user is captured, but you can easily extend the xDB schema to track all kinds of custom properties and events, against which you can report or personalize.

- *Scalability:* Sitecore is built on the need to scale to support millions of visits a day. You can scale the web site to run on as many Content Delivery (CD) servers as you need (more in the next section on infrastructure), and you can scale the database servers as well with SQL availability groups and the like.

- *High availability (HA):* Like scalability, Sitecore supports HA scenarios. SQL availability groups, load balanced CD servers, geographically-distributed delivery clusters, and cloud-based deployments can provide the 99.95% uptime you're looking for.

Figure 1-4 shows more elements you didn't see in Figures 1-1 and 1-2, namely MongoDB and the corresponding xDB processing server. As was previously mentioned, Sitecore logs all interactions for a current user's browsing session to SessionState. Once the session ends (when Session.Abandon is called manually or when the timeout value configured on SessionState in web.config is exceeded), data from SessionState is flushed to the collections database in MongoDB. A separate server, namely the xDB processing server, crawls through all the new data in MongoDB, aggregates that data, and writes it into a reporting database for analytics purposes.

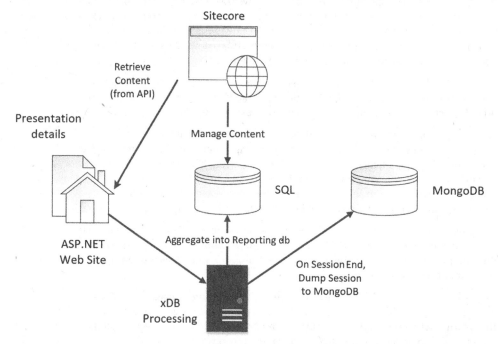

Figure 1-4. *MongoDB adds a few extra pieces to the puzzle, namely a MongoDB database and an xDB processing server*

Integration Layer

The Integration layer provides connectivity into backend systems such as your CRM or ERP systems. Tying these systems together forms the basis of a single view of your customer, as well as provides the data you need for more complex personalization rules (such as past purchases).

Key features and capabilities of the integration layer include:

- *CRM connectors*: Sitecore has connectors for Microsoft Dynamics CRM as well as for Salesforce to support two-way contact synchronization and submit actions for Web Forms (such as creating a lead in CRM).

- *Sitecore Commerce Connect*: This is an interface that allows any commerce system that implements the interface to natively talk to Sitecore. Your web site or app may need to submit an order, get the number of items in a shopping cart, or check the inventory of a product: All these actions and more can be developed through this interface, thus making the backend commerce solution interchangeable.

- *SharePoint connectors*: Sitecore has a connector to SharePoint to help publish content in SharePoint to Sitecore after it's approved.

- *Social connections*: Provides integration into Facebook, Twitter, etc. for your digital properties.

Infrastructure and Services Architecture Options

The goal of this section is to give developers a high-level understanding of Sitecore's infrastructure services and deployment options. Many developers are also asked to set up these configurations, but it's really a systems administrator job. You have to wear multiple hats, which is a common ask of many Sitecore professionals.

There are innumerable options when considering a deployment and each company should go through an exercise to determine which architecture best meets their needs; however, there are a few core concepts that apply to everyone or are common points to extend your unique needs. First we'll discuss the six types of servers/roles that Sitecore requires, and then we'll discuss three common deployment options worth considering.

- Content *management server*: This server is where authors and marketers go to edit content and view the Launchpad. It is common to put this server out of content-delivery rotation (even behind a firewall) to ensure that external users cannot access the Sitecore administrative interface.

- Content *delivery server*: This server serves up approved and published content to your customers.

- SQL Server *database server*: You need one or more SQL servers for the web, master, core, and reporting databases.

- MongoDB *database server*: Every interaction is dumped into a MongoDB database to be reported on later. Given the high velocity of data, MongoDB is used for performance and scalability needs.

- xDB *processing server*: This server pulls data out of the MongoDB database and stores it in a relational database optimized for reporting.

- Indexing/*search servers*: You may need one or more search and indexing servers depending on your chosen platform (Lucene, SOLR, Coveo, etc.) and architecture.

■ **Note**   There are many other infrastructure considerations, such as cloud versus on-premises, physical versus virtual, IaaS versus PaaS, capacity needs, networking and security, etc., that you should consider as well, but they are far beyond the scope of this book.

Basic Deployment

Figure 1-5 shows a common deployment for a small-to-medium-sized Sitecore installation. It features two content delivery servers and a SQL cluster to ensure high availability of the web site, one content management server for authors which doubles as the xDB processor, and a MongoDB server for the database.

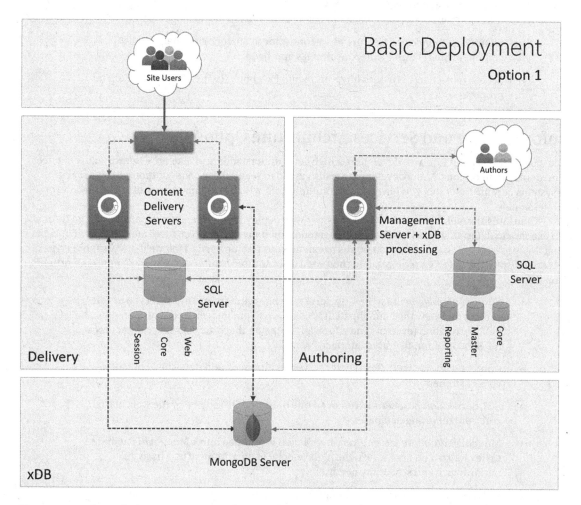

Figure 1-5. *A basic deployment minimizes licensing costs but doesn't sacrifice high availability for the more critical services*

Pros:

- Minimal licensing needs but still achieves high availability for web traffic (assumes relatively low traffic volumes)

- Isolated content authoring experience, security best practice

Cons:

- No high availability for MongoDB (could take the site down if the log piles up)

- No high availability for xDB processing (analytics would be delayed during an outage, possibly impacting the customer experience, such as personalization, testing, etc., if it's working off old data)

- No high availability for content management (you can't perform web site updates, view reports, etc. while the CM server is down)

- The CM server will need to be a pretty big box to ensure that marketers can do their job

---

■ **Note** SQL won't need a cluster if you're using a PaaS cloud model; otherwise, a cluster and/or mirror or SQL availability group is strongly recommended.

Highly Available Deployment

This option (Figure 1-6) extends the previous option by adding capacity for high-availability for the backend systems. Frontend services such as content delivery and SQL Server are table stakes; hardly anyone would be willing to risk the site going down, but there may be more room to discuss tolerance for some of the backend MongoDB and xDB processing to go down. If you don't want to risk it at all, spinning up a MongoDB replica set and a pair of xDB processing servers will create the confidence you're looking for (again, not taking capacity into account; you may need more).

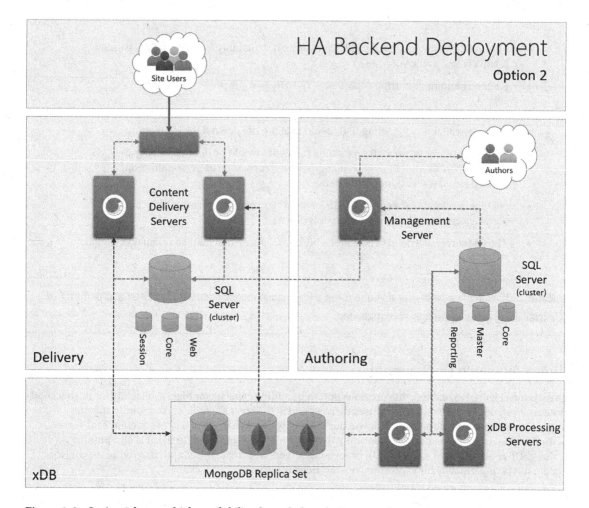

Figure 1-6. *Option 2 features high availability through the solution, save the management server*

Pros:

- Isolated content authoring experience, security best practice

- High availability for MongoDB

- High availability for xDB processing

- No concern that xDB processing will negatively impact a marketer's need to update content, etc.

Cons:

- Spending more on Sitecore licensing for the separate xDB processing servers and server costs to support a MongoDB replica set

- No high availability for content management

Cloud-Based xDB Deployment

This third option (Figure 1-7) is similar to the previous two but with the exception that you're using Sitecore's xDB cloud service. The main benefit is you've outsourced all xDB/MongoDB processing to Sitecore's cloud. This can be significant for companies who don't want to learn/support MongoDB, which is a rather new technology. The content delivery and content management servers are configured just as with the previous deployment options, but they point to Sitecore's cloud rather than your instances of MongoDB or xDB processing.

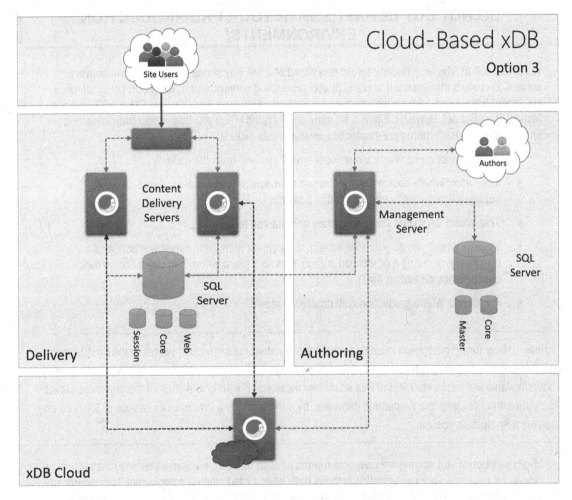

Figure 1-7. *This option removes the worry about xDB and MongoDB all together by outsourcing to Sitecore's cloud*

Pros:

- Same as previous
- You never have to worry about MongoDB or xDB; it just works!

Cons:

- xDB cloud annual licensing costs are significant, especially for B2C deployments

---

DO NOT CUT CORNERS WITH YOUR PRE-PRODUCTION ENVIRONMENTS!

We all know that Sitecore infrastructure is composed of a few key server roles, 1) content delivery servers, 2) content management servers, 3) xDB processing servers, and 4) MongoDB servers/replica set. Probably the most common architecture for production involves two CDs, one CM, 1 xDB, and one MongoDB replica set. However, it gets a bit more complicated when you think about pre-production environment needs. Common pre-production environments include:

- *Local development*: Where a developer writes and unit tests the code.

- *Integration*: Where source code is merged for developers to smoke test and on which automated acceptance and integration tests run.

- *Test*: Where QA will do their exploratory and manual testing.

- *Staging*: Where you do your load testing, deployment tests, and sometimes acts as a warm failover during a production outage. Acts as a place where end users can do their user acceptance testing (UAT).

- *Production*: Where production web databases reside.

■ **Note** Many times, customers mischaracterize the "content management" server in the Production environment as a "staging" environment, because you're previewing content that is not live. That is an understandable misinterpretation, but it is ultimately incorrect. If you have a content management server that's publishing content *to* a Production database, by definition it is a Production instance of Sitecore and requires a Production license.

Ideally production and staging are complete mirrors of each other. This ensures your load testing results are accurate, your configuration settings have been tested, and your deployment procedures are vetted before being attempted in production itself. Staging, in this case, would simply be a full copy of production; stage would be totally separate/isolated from production.

Many times, Test and Staging are combined, which is just fine; Test is still treated as a separate environment from production.

The bottom line: Don't cut corners with your pre-production environments!

A Tour of the Sitecore Admin Interface

The goal of this section is to give you a high-level sense of how to maneuver within the Sitecore Admin screens. For starters, every Sitecore site is administered from beneath the /sitecore path in the site's root, such as http://mysite/sitecore. When you first navigate to this path, you'll land on the Sitecore Launchpad, after you log in (Figure 1-8). You can navigate to all of the Sitecore administrative user interfaces from this Launchpad view.

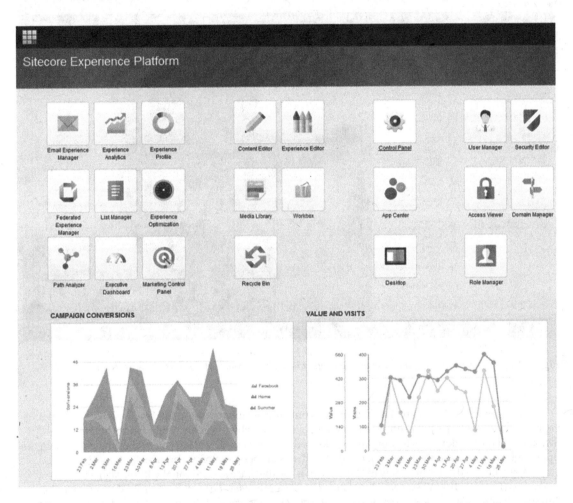

Figure 1-8. *The Sitecore 8 Launchpad offers an alternative to the windowed experience of the desktop view, featuring a couple of high-level analytic reports*

Alternatively, some prefer the more traditional desktop view (Figure 1-9). If you click the Sitecore icon on the lower-left, you'll see a launch panel appear, similar to what you'd expect from a Windows 7 or earlier operating system. Each of the screens loads in a "window" within the browser, similar to a Windows desktop experience. Alternatively, some prefer the Sitecore Launchpad (Figure 1-8) for their default view.

Figure 1-9. *This is the view of the Sitecore desktop, a launching point into Sitecore's settings and administration*

The benefit of the Launchpad is that you can configure default reports to load on the page for a quick view into how your site is performing, and it is also a bit more tablet-friendly. What's more helpful is the avoidance of the windows; each component is loaded as a full screen, leaving you to click the grid icon in the upper right to get back to the Launchpad. In the end, it is just a matter of preference.

A key point on the desktop view to take note of is the database selector on the lower-right side of the screen (Figure 1-10). When you administer content or other settings, you want to be doing that in the "master" database. When you're ready to publish your changes, you publish to the "web" database. Sitecore settings are stored in the "core" database.

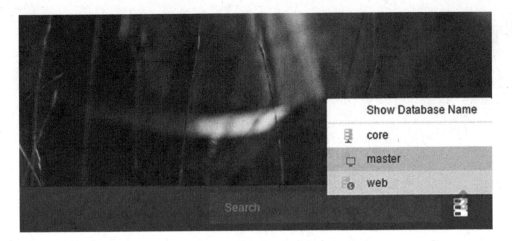

Figure 1-10. *From time to time, you may need to switch between the master and web databases*

By default, the Launchpad and content editors are pointing to the master database, which is where all content administration should take place. However, there are times where your master database and your web databases may be out of sync, such as before a large site update. In these cases, you may want to toggle the database to the web to confirm how things are set up in Production. Note, however, that you should avoid editing content in the web database or that content will likely be overwritten during the next publish.

■ **Note** You never want to make changes in the web database. The web database should be for published content only. Changes made to the web database run the risk of being overwritten when the master database changes are published.

Another stand-alone administrative tool that is extremely helpful is the Sitecore Instance Manager (SIM), as seen in Figure 1-11. SIM is available for download in the Sitecore Marketplace (found at http://bit.ly/1LIf5iZ), a place where community members can share freely downloadable modules for Sitecore. SIM is a small little GUI that helps you quickly track and administer your instances, and is especially helpful for developers who may have many instances of Sitecore on their development workstations. Some of the key features of instance manager are:

- Import and export entire Sitecore instances
- Quick links into IIS (resetting application pools, hot link into the inetpub folder, etc.)
- Quick links into the instance's Launchpad items
- Quick links to key configuration files
- Key administrative functions (back up, export/import, publish, etc.)
- Download and easily install modules/add-ins

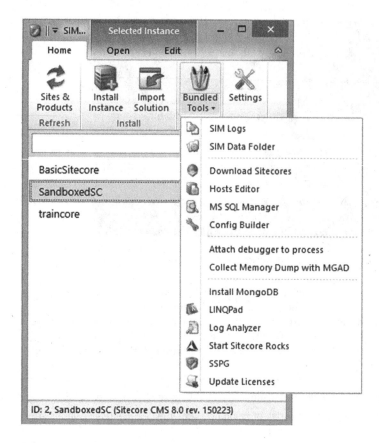

Figure 1-11. *The Sitecore Instance Manager is a great tool for administrators to keep track of their Sitecore instances, providing quick links into configurations, along with many other great efficiencies*

■ **Tip** There are many fabulous modules in the marketplace. Check them out at `https://marketplace.sitecore.net/`.

What's New in Sitecore 8?

There were many new enhancements made in Sitecore 8 that make it stand out from previous versions (as shown in Table 1-1). The most innovative feature that is widely acknowledged is the new Federated Experience Manager discussed earlier. These capabilities are really a game changer for marketers; namely, the ability to bring the power of Sitecore to all their properties, regardless of the platform.

Table 1-1. *Key Differences Between the Versions of Sitecore*

Feature	Sitecore 6+	Sitecore 7+	Sitecore 8
Marketing and engagement automation	X	X	X
Measurable value and efficiency data	X	X	X
Real-time personalization	X	X	X
Dashboards and reporting	X	X	X
Classified origin visits	X	X	X
Content experience platform	X	X	X
Device simulator	X	X	X
Page preview service	X	X	X
Native MVC support	X	X	X
Page Editor and Rich Text Editor	X	X	X
Supports SQL Server DB mirroring	X	X	X
Lucene.NET search engine	X	X	X
Executive Insight dashboard	X	X	X
Buckets		X	X
Content tagging/faceting		X	X
Search screens		X	X
Analytics collection database		X	X
Scalable analytics data architecture		X	X
Contact entities		X	X
Tracking across devices/visits		X	X
Content tagging using personas		X	X
Launchpad applications			X
Experience Explorer			X
Versioned layouts			X
Federated Experience Manager			X
List Manager and segmentation			X
Path Analyzer			X
Simple and advanced testing			X
Campaign creator			X
Personalization based on previous browsing sessions			X

Other notable enhancements for 8 include native integration with the Experience Explorer, a very popular feature for marketers who want to "explore" the experience of various personas to see if they are getting the expected experience. Marketers also get a nice set of tools with 8, including more robust segmentation capabilities and the native ability in the core platform to target content using a profile/persona. A key feature from an analytics perspective is the Path Analyzer report, showing entry points and highlighting the most valuable paths in your site.

The Sitecore Hierarchy

So, how is Sitecore structured? What do you actually build when you build a Sitecore site? Let's dive in a bit deeper and consider Sitecore's hierarchy of items.

Your first step as a Sitecore developer is to understand the treeview you see in the content editor. Figure 1-12 shows the default view of the content editor when you first open it, featuring the treeview off to the left.

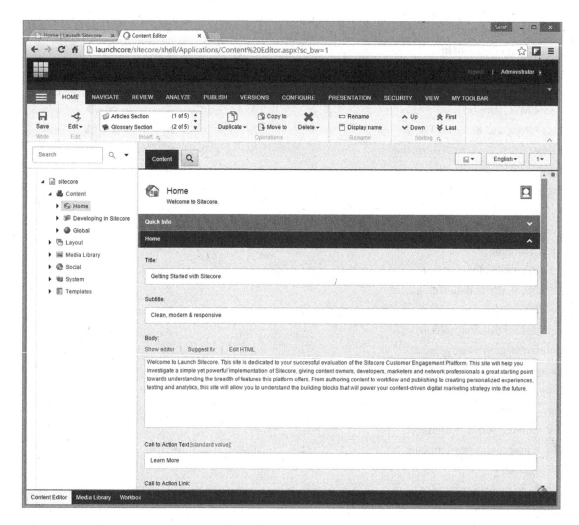

Figure 1-12. *This is the default view of the content editor, featuring a tree of items on the left, and an item's details on the right, with the ribbon across the top*

■ **Note**   See the next section, "Setting Up Your Development Environment" for steps on how to install Sitecore. Thereafter, just click Content Editor to see this view. The following screen shots are built from the Launch Sitecore starter pack available at `http://launchsitecore.net`. The examples in this book start from a fresh install, not from Launch Sitecore, so it is not necessary to install that starter pack (although it's helpful in its own right).

The three most important nodes in the tree to familiarize yourself with are Templates, Content, and Layouts. There are others, and they will be covered later. For now, it is important not to move beyond this section until you fully understand the concepts of these three nodes, as all else depends on them.

■ **Note**   Most marketers will only see Content and Media Library in the tree when they log in. The other areas, such as Templates, Layouts and Settings, are typically managed exclusively by developers and administrators. If you don't see these nodes in your treeview, ask your administrator to give you `Developer` access rights. See the *Practical Sitecore 8 Configuration and Strategy* book for more information around security access rights, as they aren't covered in this book.

"Everything in Sitecore is an item" is probably the most popular saying in the Sitecore world. Technically speaking, every "item" in the treeview inherits from the base template "Item" (eventually, you can have multiple sub-templates). Knowing that everything in Sitecore is an item is important because it shows you know that templates in Sitecore have an established parentage that ends at the "Item" root item. That, and you might look the fool when all your friends keep saying "everything in Sitecore is an item" and you don't know what they mean.

Templates

Templates are defined in the "Templates" node in the treeview. Templates, also commonly referred to as "data templates," are the foundation of the content in your Sitecore deployment. Every piece of content in Sitecore needs a data template to define what it is. For example, you might want a Carousel featured on your home page that rotates featured news stories. The first step to set this up is to create a new data template for this component/functionality. You may choose to name your data template "Carousel Item" and give it a few fields you would expect to see in a carousel, such as Title, Caption, an Image.

■ **Note**   Many people are often confused by the term "template" because they expect a visual representation, which, in Sitecore, is more akin to a "layout". Templates are just definitions of metadata around some type of object. I often say, "Templates are like class definitions. Content is just an instance of that class."

Figure 1-13 shows where, within the Templates node, the data template is defined (more on location best practices later). Note also in Figure 1-13 the data template's fields defining the template. Again, the data template does *not* store any data. It is simply a template you use when you create content.

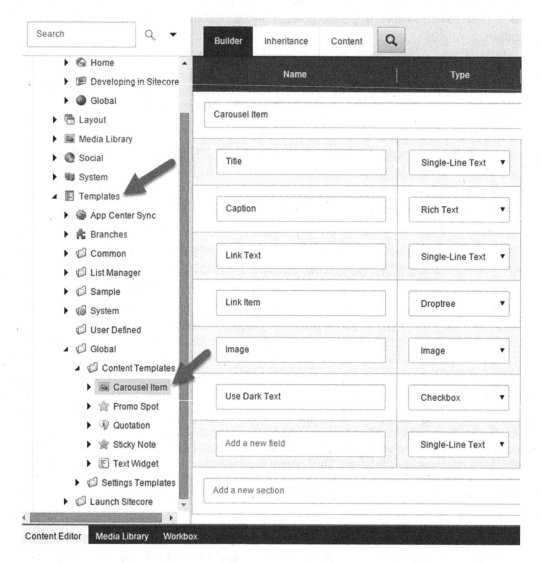

Figure 1-13. *Data templates define what metadata and settings get applied to content items*

■ **Note**   See Chapter 3 for more details on creating and managing data templates. Proper data template structure is one of the most foundational elements of a good Sitecore deployment.

Content

Content is administered below the "Content" node in the treeview. Sitecore end users and marketers will commonly spend the majority of their administration time below this node in the treeview. Administrators commonly restrict them via security settings to just this node, in addition to the Media Library node, where they can upload imagery, video, and other digital assets.

Content in the Content node is just an instance of a data template. When you create a new content item, you must select which data template you will use as the basis for that content. Figure 1-14 shows a user inserting a new carousel item to be used on the home page's image rotator. In this case, the administrator created an item called "Carousel Items" and limited that item's children to only allow items using the Carousel Item data template to be created below that node (more on the Saved Search and Insert from template options in Chapter 3).

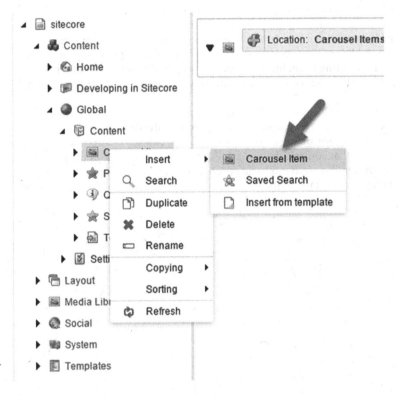

Figure 1-14. *You can insert child items below nodes in the treeview. In this case, we're inserting a carousel item below the Carousel folder*

Layouts and Components

Layouts are the third leg in our journey. We have content created from a template, but what does it actually look like when it's rendered on a page? What actually renders that content on the page?

Layouts tell Sitecore *where* to render the component, and components tell Sitecore *how* the content should be rendered. A layout contains one or more content placeholders into which marketers can add/remove components. A component has a controller (web control if you're using Web Forms; see the sidebar entitled "What Is a Component?") that renders the component on the page.

Should the title of the Carousel item be Heading 1 and red or Heading 3 and black? Should the image be to the left of the title, or as a background? This is the responsibility of the component's controller and view, and for better or worse, this is where you will rely on a developer. For better, because you and your development team will appreciate the near infinite control to meet the needs of your requirements, but for worse because as a marketer, your control is limited to how much control the developers build into the system to empower you to make these formatting changes (more on this later).

However, marketers can control where on the page components are dropped by adding components to placeholders. Placeholders can be configured to only allow certain components to help enforce a standard information architecture. Additionally, developers should be adding configuration properties onto components to make component settings editable by marketers. As a best practice, developers should consider making settings editable by marketers to make the solution as maintainable by as many people as possible.

As an example, notice the Presentation Layout Details dialog on the Home page (Figure 1-15). In this case a Carousel component was added to the components collection for the default device (mobile devices use the default in this case since there are no settings for mobile specifically). The default device is set to use a layout called Main that controls the positioning of the components on the page via placeholders. A developer builds, deploys, and maintains each layout, such as Main in this case, according to the marketer's specifications. But the marketer can choose where within Main the carousel should be rendered.

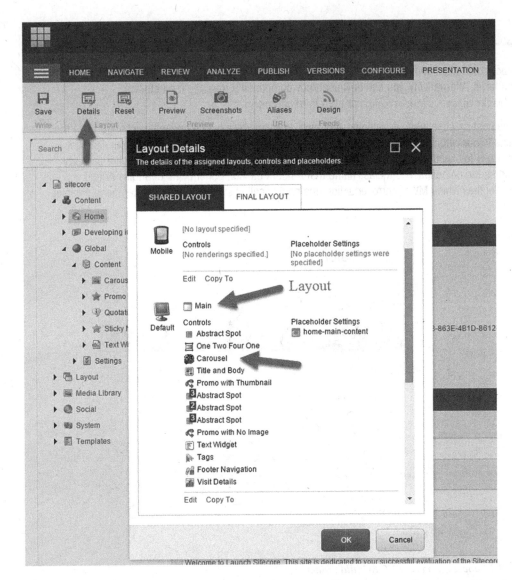

Figure 1-15. *An item's Presentation Layout Details, PLD, is where you can configure the settings that Sitecore uses to render an item*

WHAT IS A COMPONENT?

A developer can build a component via Web Forms (legacy) or via MVC (Model-View-Controller) design patterns. Alternatively, you can download/buy components from the marketplace (http://marketplace.sitecore.net) or from third parties.

MVC is the best practice when developing your own, in which case the component is configured in the Renderings folder within the Layout node. The controller rendering has a property that specifies the controller used to execute and render the component. In Figure 1-16, you see the Controller property that specifies the namespace and class name that renders the component. The Controller Action property specifies which MVC controller action (method) is called specifically for this component (view).

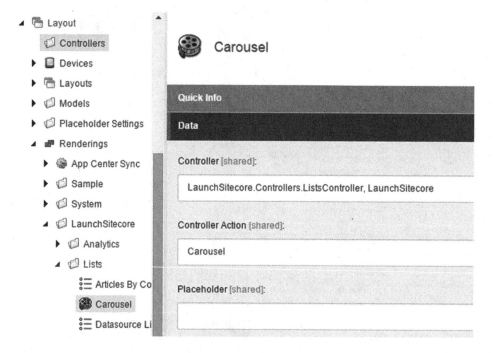

Figure 1-16. *Developers can use MVC to build renderings*

If you're an MVC veteran, Sitecore development is going to be a super easy transition for you. If you have a lot of ASP.NET Web Forms experience, but have never worked with MVC before, your journey will be a bit longer. In Chapter 2, we discuss how to build MVC components. Worst case, you can develop in Web Forms if that is most comfortable to you, but since it's legacy it isn't covered in this book. Chapter 4 is dedicated to helping you ramp up to MVC (although entire books have been written on that subject) if you're new to it. Even veterans will find Chapter 4 helpful, because Sitecore has a bit of its own unique MVC flavor they should familiarize themselves with as well.

For now, just remember that MVC components live in the Layout>Renderings node in the treeview and generate the HTML needed to render the content instance based on a data template. Marketers can add components can be added to pages in the page's Layout placeholders. We'll get into MVC later!

Setting Up Your Development Environment

Oh man, you are sooooo excited to see some Sitecore code, I can just tell! Well, hold your horses; we can't start the race just yet. You first need to set up your developer workstation with all the foundational tools and technology before you can get started. This section walks you through all the needed dependencies and the steps to set up each. After that, we'll get to that famed "Hello World" example you're chomping at the bit to see, I promise!

Tools Every Sitecore Developer Needs

What do you need to run on your dev PC before you can start writing Sitecore code? Table 1-2 has a list of all the core tools you need to set up as a Sitecore developer. There are many, many more tools that will be discussed throughout this book, such as Glass.Mapper, Simple Injector, etc., but this list forms the "core" of what every Sitecore Developer needs regardless of approach and design of their Sitecore solutions. The rest of the tools discussed later in this book are more about "best practice" approaches and are saved for later so we're not prematurely introducing advanced topics before you understand the basics.

Table 1-2. *Core Sitecore Development Tools*

Tool Name	Description
SQL Server 2008r2+	SQL Server is needed to run Sitecore's databases. You'll need a copy of SQL running on your dev PC. We will be using SQL 2014 for the purposes of this book.
Visual Studio 2012+	Visual Studio (2015+ preferred) is needed to develop custom Sitecore solutions, components, layouts, and the like.
Internet Information Services (IIS)	You need IIS installed on your dev PC to host Sitecore sites. IIS Express will not work because Sitecore runs outside of a Visual Studio "F5" build. IIS needs to run as a service so a full installation is necessary.
Sitecore 8.X+	You'll need one or more instances of Sitecore installed on your dev PC.
Sitecore Instance Manager (SIM)	SIM is a great little tool that provides tons of short cuts, backup/restore functionality, etc. to help you manage your Sitecore instances.
MongoDB	MongoDB is necessary to run Sitecore 8.0. Sitecore 8.1 introduced the Experience Management Edition that made MongoDB optional, but for the purposes of this book, we will be using Sitecore 8.1 in Experience Platform mode, requiring MongoDB.

Setting Up SQL Server

Sitecore needs SQL Server for its content and reporting databases. You'll need to install SQL on your development PC before you can install Sitecore. Our preference is to use a full copy of SQL 2014. With a full copy of SQL Server 2014, you won't have to worry about database size limits and other limitations with SQL Express. Use the following steps as a reference for how to install your copy of SQL Server (similar for most editions):

1. When you insert or mount the installation media, launch setup.exe. You will be greeted with the SQL Server Installation Center.

2. In the menu on the left, click Installation, then click the first option on the right—New SQL Server Stand-Alone Installation or Add Features to an Existing Installation—as you can see in Figure 1-17.

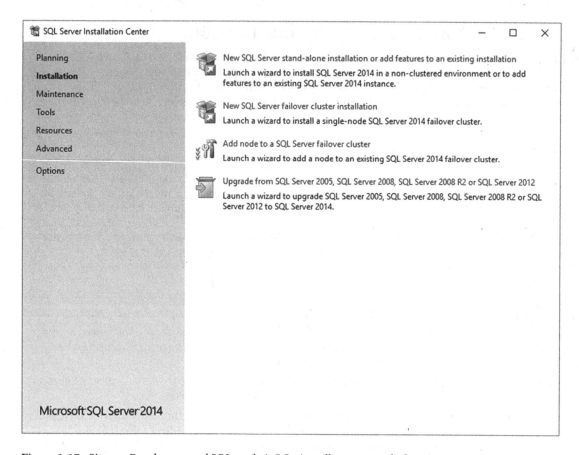

Figure 1-17. *Sitecore Developers need SQL on their PCs; install a new stand-alone instance*

3. After clicking that option, the SQL Server 2014 Setup will launch and run through the Global Rules and Install Setup Files steps. Once this is complete, you should get a result of the rules it ran, determining if setup can continue. Since this is your local environment, you may get a warning about the Windows firewall, if you have it enabled. In most cases, this can be safely ignored. However, any reported failures must be corrected before setup can continue.

4. When you are ready and click Next, you will be prompted with the option to install a new instance of SQL Server or add features to an existing installation. In this case, we are going to perform a new installation of SQL Server 2014.

5. Clicking Next presents you with the opportunity to enter your product key or specify a free edition. Make the appropriate selection, click Next, accept the license terms, and then click Next one more time.

6. It will ask you to specify the role of this installation. Select SQL Server Feature Installation and click Next.

7. Now, you may individually specify the features you want to install as well as specify a location for the installation. For these purposes, select Data Engine Services, Management Tools ➤ Basic, Management Tools ➤ Complete and SQL Client Connectivity SDK (as shown in Figure 1-18), then click Next.

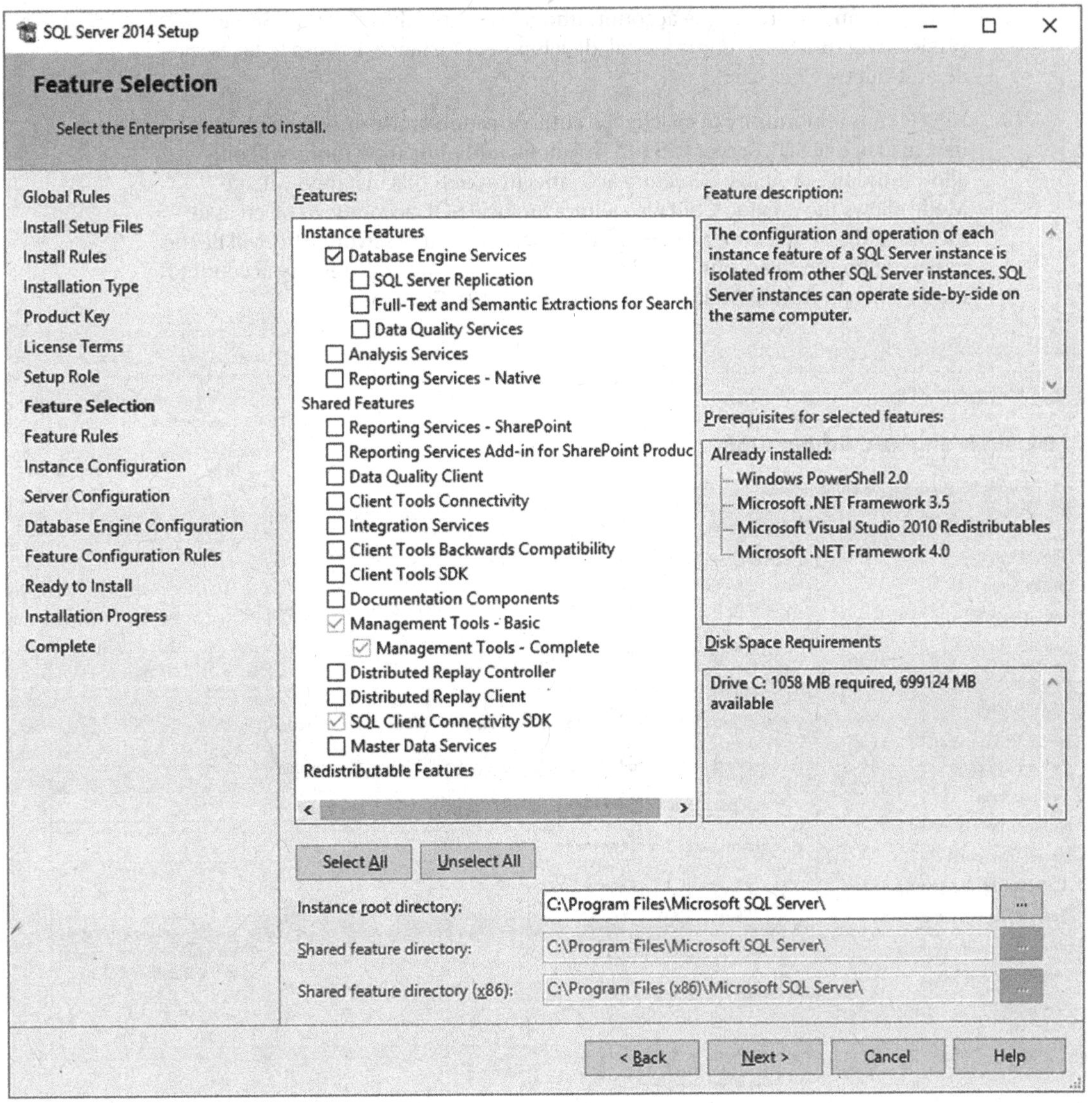

Figure 1-18. *Sitecore developers need the database engine, management tools, and the SQL SDK*

8. Now specify the instance configuration for SQL Server. In this case, we are installing a new Named Instance called *Sitecore*. You may also choose to install a Default Instance as well, if you don't have SQL Server installed already. Click Next.

■ **Note** A default instance can be used if one is already set up on your laptop. Just keep in mind your connection strings may deviate slightly from the ones presented throughout the book.

9. Next, you can specify service accounts under which the different SQL Server services will run. Since this is a local, development instance, I chose to leave the default values. Click Next.

10. Next is your opportunity to specify the authentication mode under which this new instance of SQL Server will run. Windows authentication mode will only allow Windows or Active Directory accounts to access this instance. Mixed Mode allows the previous, but also allows for local SQL accounts to be created, including the sa account. Select Mixed Mode, specify a password (this will be the password for the sa account), and add a Windows or Active Directory account to the SQL Server Administrators list (see Figure 1-19). Click Next.

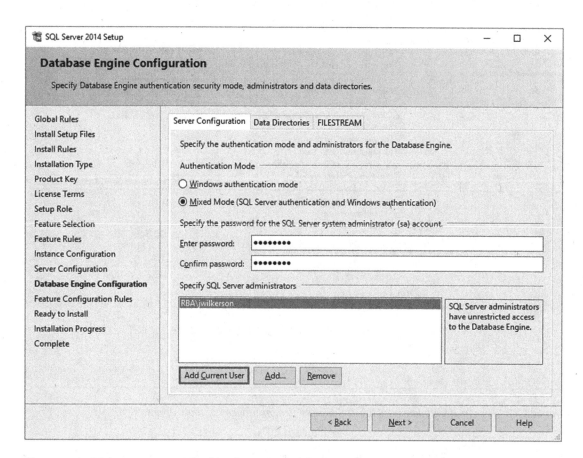

Figure 1-19. *Make sure you use Mixed Mode so you don't have to put domain credentials in your Sitecore connection strings*

11. Finally, you're presented with a summary of all the options you selected and the configuration you've specified, and you're ready to Install. Click Install.

After the install is complete, click Close and move on to install Sitecore, as presented in the next section.

Installing Sitecore

With SQL ready to go, it's time to actually install Sitecore! There are three main ways to install Sitecore: 1) with the downloadable EXE, 2) with Sitecore Instance Manager (SIM), and 3) you can download a ZIP of the web root and set it up manually (this is not recommended). Option 1 is the easiest and fastest approach, but you have less control. SIM is great because you get more control over the installation, but you also get a set of tools you can use to manage your instance after installation.

However, before you run off and install Sitecore, you need to install IIS first. Use the following steps to add the necessary roles onto your Windows 8/10 PC, which will be IIS installed in the process:

1. Click Start or the Windows icon on your keyboard and type **Control Panel**. Click Turn Windows Features On or Off.

2. In the Turn Windows Features On or Off dialog, select the options under Internet Information Services, as shown in Figure 1-20.

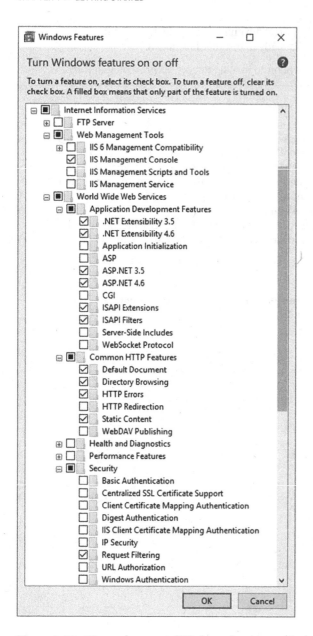

Figure 1-20. *Sitecore has several IIS dependencies, not the least of which is ASP.NET 3 and 4*

3. Click OK and then click Close after the installation is complete.

Installing Sitecore with an EXE

By far the easiest and fastest way to get Sitecore on your development PC is to simply download the EXE and run it. The wizard will prompt you to specify your SQL installation and ask for a name for your instance/site. Beyond that, it's pretty opaque what the EXE does. Many prefer the Sitecore Instance Manager (SIM; see the next section) because you have more control over database names, etc., but this option remains the easiest. Use the following steps to install Sitecore with the downloadable EXE:

1. Download the latest version of Sitecore from dev.sitecore.net/downloads. The following steps are up to date for installing Sitecore 8.1 update-2 (rev.160302).

2. Launch the Sitecore 8.1 rev. 160302.exe. Click Next from the Welcome screen, accept the licensing agreement, and click Next again.

3. As an Installation Type, select Complete and click Next.

4. Give your new Sitecore instance a name then click Next. I chose sitecoredev.

5. Click the Browse button to locate your license file, then click Next.

■ **Note** Your Sitecore Account Executive will provide you with your license file. It is an XML file named license.xml.

---

6. The next prompt allows you to specify the details of your database connection. Specify the instance name of the SQL Server you just created, then specify the sa username and password, as shown in Figure 1-21. These credentials are used to create the databases.

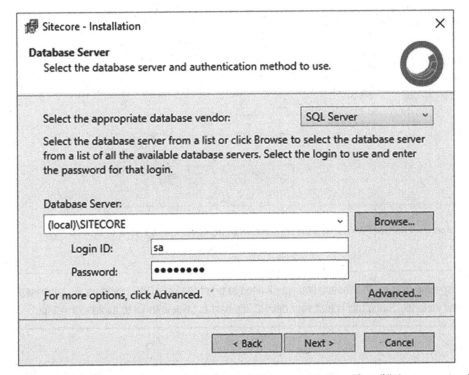

Figure 1-21. *Specify a path to your local Sitecore SQL instance. Just use "(local)" if you are using the default instance*

■ **Note** If you're using your default instance, just use "(local)" for the database server. If you're having trouble connecting and you're setting this up for the first time, check two things: 1) ensure your instance is set to run in mixed mode authentication (SQL and Windows) in Instance Properties, Security page, and 2) ensure the sa account is enabled (Account Properties, Status page, Enabled).

7. If you click the Advanced button, you can customize the names of the SQL database files that are created as well as specify a username and password to be used in the connection string of the instance being installed. I created a SQL login called sc-user (Figure 1-22) that will be used in the connection strings to accommodate a least privileged best practice. Once you have specified these details, click OK then Next.

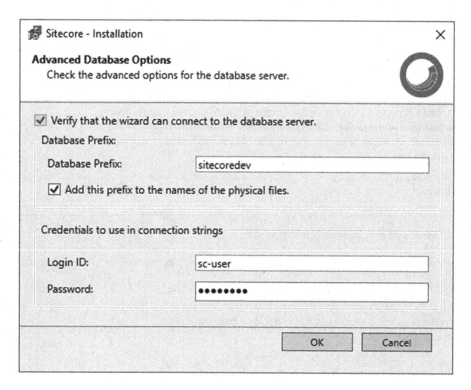

Figure 1-22. *You can specify a user to be used in your connection strings that doesn't need to be a sa SQL account*

■ **Note** If you use a specific user for this installation, you'll need to grant the user DBO rights on all databases associated with the new instance. Since this is just your dev PC, it's best to stick with sa to avoid extra steps.

8. Next, you can specify the location where you want the new instance to be installed. The installation process will create the web site and point it to this location. This is referred to as your *web root*. Now click the Advanced button. This dialog gives you the opportunity to specify the locations of the *Data* folder, which is the folder where the databases are held, as well as separate Data and Log file directories, if you want to separate them. You might do this if you have a separate D drive on your laptop. I left these as the default values. Click OK, then Next.

9. Now specify the name of the web site in IIS. I chose SitecoreDev. If you click the Advanced button, you can also specify the name of the App Pool that is created and the port number under which the site will run. Port 80 is the default and it works for most cases since the install will create a Hosts entry for local DNS purposes. Click OK, then Next.

10. The next dialog just summarizes the choices you've made. Click Install. Click Finish when complete. Optionally, click the check box to Launch Sitecore when the wizard closes; this will open a browser to your new Sitecore installation.

■ **Note** The nice thing about installing Sitecore from the EXE is that you can remove it from the Add or Remove Programs list.

Installing Sitecore with Sitecore Instance Manager

As discussed earlier, Sitecore's Instance Manager can do a lot of things. One of those things, most obviously, is manage your Sitecore instances. An "instance" of Sitecore is defined as a single copy of the /sitecore folder, the Sitecore DLLs (in the /bin) folder, and a single application pool in IIS.

■ **Note** A single instance of Sitecore is made of up three things: a single copy of the /sitecore folder, a single copy of the Sitecore DLLs (in the /bin folder), and a single application pool in IIS.

When you installed Sitecore with the EXE, it installed one instance/site onto your dev PC. You'll do the same with SIM next. Use the following steps to create a new instance of Sitecore, but this time using SIM:

1. First, go to http://dl.sitecore.net/updater/sim/ to download the Sitecore Instance Manager ClickOnce installer. Click Install and Launch. This will download the SIM.Tool.Application file to your computer. Once the download is complete, locate that file on your computer and run it.

2. Once the download completes, the installation process will begin and allow you to configure a few default settings. Click Next on the Welcome Message and License Agreement screens.

3. The next step in the wizard asks you to specify your Instances Root folder, also known as the web root. This is where SIM will install the default Sitecore web site. Specify the location where you want SIM to install the default Sitecore instance and click Next. In most cases the default, c:\inetpub\wwwroot, works fine.

4. Next, you can specify the location where the ZIP archive of Sitecore resides, downloaded from dev.sitecore.net, as well as the license file that will be copied into the Data directory. Once these locations have been set, click Next.

5. Next specify the connection string to your local SQL Server. Ensure that this account has permission to create and delete databases, such as your sa account. If you're not quite sure how to format this string, you can click the ".." button next to the text box to open a dialog where you can specify these values independently (Figure 1-23).

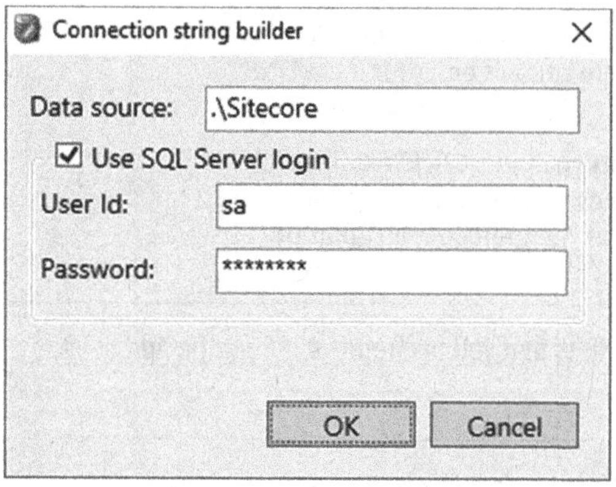

Figure 1-23. Type your connection settings to your SQL instance

6. Next, the installer will determine if the NETWORK SERVICE account has full access to the web root folder, specified earlier. If you click Next and the NETWORK SERVICE account does not have the necessary permissions, you will see an error message. Click OK then click the Grant button to grant the appropriate permissions.

■ **Note** If you get an error when you click Grant, ensure that your SQL Server service for your instance is running as "Network Service". If not, change it.

7. Click OK after the permissions are set. Then click Next.

■ **Note** If you click the *Grant* button but still get the permissions error message, ensure that the account specified in the Connection String dialog in Step 6 has permission to create and delete databases.

8. After clicking Finish When the Install Is Complete, SIM will launch. When SIM first launches, it scans your local repository for additional Sitecore ZIP archives, then displays a list of currently installed Sitecore Instances in your web root. Before you can install Sitecore with SIM, you need to download Sitecore with SIM. Click Bundled Tools and then click Download Sitecore 8.x.

9. Click Next a few times until you can select the version of Sitecore you want to install. You then will need to enter your login credentials to SDN. Once you've completed these steps, the download will commence.

10. There are a number of other settings you can adjust in the Settings dialogs; however, for now, just click Install Instance (Figure 1-24).

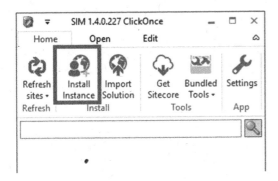

Figure 1-24. *Once SIM is installed, click Install Instance to install Sitecore*

11. In the Installing a New Instance dialog, you can specify a few values for the instance being installed. You can control the default format of these values from Settings ➤ Advanced Settings, but for this instance, configure them as shown in Figure 1-25. Then click Next.

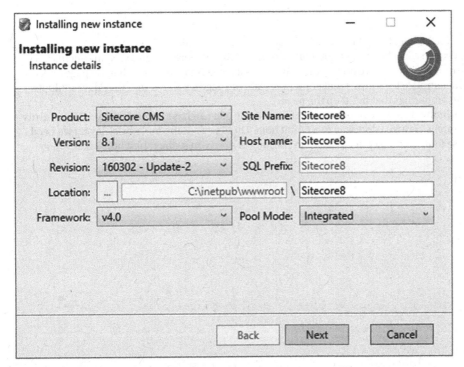

Figure 1-25. *SIM provides an easy configuration to get exactly what you want out of your install, such as specific Sitecore versions and SQL prefixes for the database*

12. Click Next on the next four screens, accepting the default selections, until you get to the Review screen. Then click Install.

13. Once Sitecore installation completes, you'll see a Completed dialog with a few post-installation options. Click Finish.

14. The Sitecore instance that was just installed is shown in the list of installed instances (Figure 1-26).

Figure 1-26. *After your instance is installed, it should show up in SIM, ready for administration*

Summary

You've just learned what Sitecore is, including its key features and capabilities, as well as some common infrastructure deployment scenarios. The chapter also discussed the Sitecore hierarchy. Components are added to placeholders. Placeholders are on layouts. A page has a layout that controls what the page looks like. A page has a data template to control what content or data the page can have, or it may have multiple datasources bound to renderings that build up the page.

This hierarchy is probably the most foundational knowledge you can have about Sitecore. Well, it turns out "the Sitecore hierarchy" is just a doorway to a rabbit hole. There's still some more brick laying we need to do to build on these foundational concepts. Join in the fun; let's see where the rabbit hole takes you in Chapter 2!

CHAPTER 2

■ ■ ■

Building Your First Component

Finally! It's time to bust out Visual Studio and start building something. I can hardly wait. Where does our Sitecore development adventure start? A Hello World example of course! This Hello World example is sure to be the most exciting Hello World example you've ever encountered, right?

In this chapter we'll build two components: a view rendering and a controller rendering. The view rendering will serve as our "Hello World" minimalist walkthrough. From there we'll discover a more "best practice" way to develop components with controller renderings.

By the end of this chapter you'll have a basic understanding of how to develop in Sitecore. It's a whirlwind tour no doubt, but it's just the first leg in a much larger journey, but at the end of which you'll know all you need to know to develop Sitecore solutions that meet all the best practices and standards. Let's begin!

Building a View Rendering

For this Hello World example we're going to build a Sitecore component (that render's "Hello World" of course!), create a placeholder to put the component into, and then actually edit a Sitecore page, add our Hello World content, and then drop the component into that placeholder. Thereafter, we'll publish our site and be amazed, because at that point, you can call yourself – finally – a Sitecore developer!

Let's begin!

Working with Layouts and Placeholders

Before we build our Hello World component, we need a place to put our component after it's built. Components are dropped into placeholders. Placeholders are added onto layouts. A page within Sitecore is assigned one layout to control what the page looks like. We need to get some of this plumbing set up first.

After the Sitecore installation you're given a Sitecore site with one layout and one page titled "Sitecore Experience Platform." Unfortunately, that layout is basically empty – it just has some hard coded text on it. Worse yet, it's a web forms layout! We don't want to use that page/layout as a result.

Let's build a new MVC layout and add a placeholder into it. Also, let's create a new page data template to store our "Hello World" text, because you *never* should hardcode content in Sitecore (what's the point of a CMS otherwise?) In the next section we can build our component that we drop into that placeholder. That component will render our content, namely "Hello World".

Use the following steps to guide you through the process of creating a new project in Visual Studio, creating the layout, creating the page template, and creating a new placeholder. Let's start by opening Visual Studio and creating a new, blank solution.

© Phil Wicklund and Jason Wilkerson 2016
P. Wicklund and J. Wilkerson, *Professional Sitecore 8 Development*, DOI 10.1007/978-1-4842-2292-8_2

1. Click File ➤ New ➤ Project. In the New Project dialog, in the left pane, select Installed ➤Templates ➤ Other Project Types ➤ Visual Studio Solutions. With that selected, in the middle, select Blank Solution and give your solution a name and specify its location. These selections can be seen in Figure 2-1. Click OK when complete.

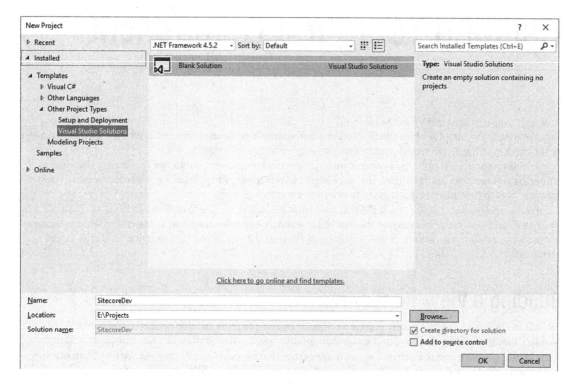

Figure 2-1. *Create a new blank solution within Visual Studio*

■ **Note** The folder created for our solution, in this instance E:\Projects\SitecoreDev, is referred to as our *dev root*. It is a best practice with Sitecore development to keep the *web root* (the location to which IIS points and from which the site actually runs) and the *dev root* separate.

Once the empty solution has been created, let's add a web project to it.

2. In Solution Explorer, right-click on the solution and select Add ➤ New Project. In the Add New Project dialog, select ASP.NET Web Application and give it a name. I chose to call it SitecoreDev.Web (see Figure 2-2). Click OK.

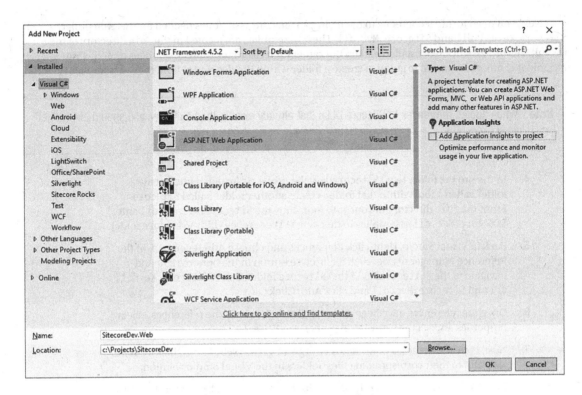

Figure 2-2. Add a new ASP.NET web application project to your solution

3. This will open the New ASP.NET Project dialog. Select the Empty ASP.NET 4.5.2 Template and then check the MVC box down below. Click OK. This will result in an empty ASP.NET MVC web site (see Figure 2-3).

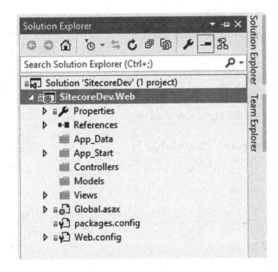

Figure 2-3. What a fresh web application project looks like

Next, you need to add a reference to the main two Sitecore assemblies needed for this web project – Sitecore.Kernel.dll and Sitecore.Mvc.dll. These assemblies are located in the /bin directory of the default Sitecore instance we installed earlier. But rather than reference those assemblies directly from the /bin folder of our *web root*, we're going to create a folder within the *dev root* to hold these assemblies.

■ **Note** When adding references to Sitecore DLLs that already exist in the bin folder, you should always set the Copy Local property to False.

---

4. In the project folder (e.g., SitecoreDev) the project is installed into, create a folder called libs. Within that folder, create another folder called Sitecore. From the /bin directory of your web root, copy the Sitecore.Kernel.dll and Sitecore.Mvc.dll assemblies to this new \SitecoreDev\libs\Sitecore folder.

5. Back in Visual Studio, right-click References and choose Add Reference. In the Reference Manager dialog, click the Browse button in the bottom right and navigate to the \SitecoreDev\libs\Sitecore folder. Select Sitecore.Kernel.dll and Sitecore.Mvc.dll and click Add. Click OK.

6. Once the references have been added, right-click each of the references, select Properties and set the Copy Local property to False.

7. Next, copy the contents of the Web.config and Views\web.config files from the web root to their corresponding files/folders in the Visual Studio solution.

8. In the App_Start/RouteConfig.cs file, in the RegisterRoutes method, remove the default route. It should look like Listing 2-1.

■ **Note** Routes are an important MVC topic. Check out Chapter 4 for more information on what routes are and how they work with Sitecore.

Listing 2-1. Change the MVC Default Routes So They Don't Conflict with Sitecore

```
namespace SitecoreDev.Web
{
        public class RouteConfig
        {
                public static void RegisterRoutes(RouteCollection routes)
                {
                        routes.IgnoreRoute("{resource}.axd/{*pathInfo}");
                }
        }
}
```

9. Finally, open the Global.asax.cs file and change the base class of
    MvcApplication from System.Web.HttpApplication to Sitecore.Web.
    Application. It should look like Listing 2-2.

Listing 2-2. Update the Parent Class to a Sitecore.Web.Application

```
namespace SitecoreDev.Web
{
        public class MvcApplication : Sitecore.Web.Application
        {
                protected void Application_Start()
                {
                        AreaRegistration.RegisterAllAreas();
                        RouteConfig.RegisterRoutes(RouteTable.Routes);
                }
        }
}
```

Now that we have the basics of the solution ready to go, let's create our new layout. Navigate to the Sitecore console of your new site. To log in, the username is admin and the default password is the letter b. Once you're logged in, you will see the Sitecore 8 Launchpad. Click on Content Editor. It's the top button in the fourth column from the left.

▓ **Note** If you followed the instructions thus far, the URL should be http://sitecoredev/sitecore if you installed with the EXE or http://sitecore8/sitecore if you installed with SIM.

---

10. In the tree on the left side of the page, navigate to /sitecore/Layout/Layouts.
    Right-click on the Layouts Item and create a new Layout Folder (see Figure 2-4).
    Name that folder Sitecore8Dev.

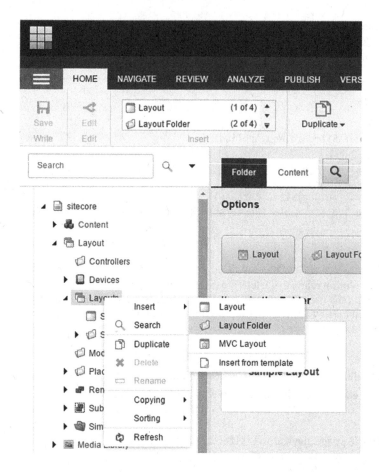

Figure 2-4. *We need to create a new layout into which we can place our new components; for organizational purposes, create a new folder where we can add our layouts within Sitecore*

■ **Note**   It is considered a best practice, for organizational purposes, to create folders underneath the default Sitecore Items, grouping Items that you create together by company. In our case, we'll create folders named Sitecore8Dev.

---

11. Right-click on your new Sitecore8Dev layout folder and choose Insert ➤ MVC Layout. Let's name this layout DefaultMVCLayout. Click Next. When asked for a location, select Sitecore8Dev and click Next.

12. Next, it will ask for the file location. The directory being displayed here is the directory of the web root. This is the directory to which our web site in IIS is pointing. Let's choose Website\Views\Shared. Click Create, then Close.

■ **Note**   If you look at the Data section of the new DefaultMVCLayout Item, in the Path field, you will see that it is pointing to /Views/Shared/DefaultMVCLayout.cshtml. When you clicked Create, it created this file in the web root.

---

13. Open Windows Explorer and navigate to the /Views/Shared folder in your web root. Open the DefaultMVCLayout.cshtml file and copy the contents.

Now, go back to Visual Studio and let's create that file in our SitecoreDev.Web project.

14. Start by creating a new folder called Shared under Views. Then right-click on the Shared folder and select Add ➤ View. In the Add View dialog, name your new view DefaultMVCLayout. Also, uncheck the Use a Layout Page checkbox (see Figure 2-5). Click Add.

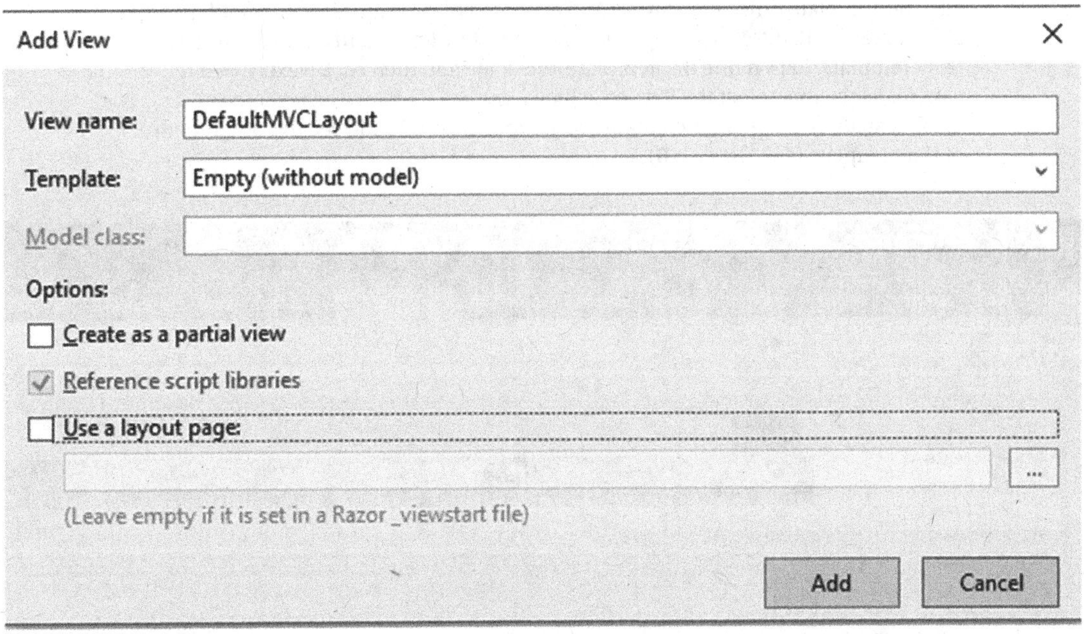

Figure 2-5. *A layout in Sitecore is akin to an MVC view*

15. Replace the contents of the new view that is added with the contents of the DefaultMVCLayout.cshtml file. It should look like Listing 2-3.

Listing 2-3. Enter the New Code for Your New Layout

```
@using Sitecore.Mvc
@* @using Sitecore.Mvc.Analytics.Extensions *@
@{
        Layout = null;
}
<!DOCTYPE html>
<html>
<head>
        <title>
          @Html.Sitecore().Field("title", new {DisableWebEdit=true }}
        </title>
</head>
```

```
<body>
        <h1>@Html.Sitecore().Field("title")</h1>
        <div>@Html.Sitecore().Placeholder("main")</div>
</body>
</html>
```

As a final step, let's go back to the Content Editor within Sitecore and create a new template that we'll use with our new page.

16.   In the left pane of the Content Editor, navigate to /sitecore/templates. Right-click on Templates and select Insert ➤ Template Folder. Name this new folder Sitecore8Dev. Right-click on the new Sitecore8Dev folder and choose Insert ➤ New Template. Let's name this template MVC Page and then click Next. When it asks for a location, select the Sitecore8Dev template folder we just created and click Next, then Close. After creating this template, you should see the Builder tab of that template (see Figure 2-6).

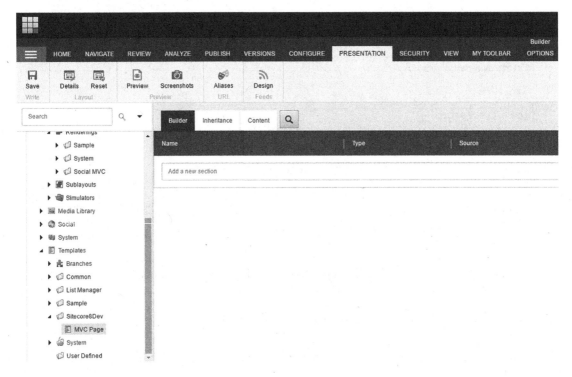

Figure 2-6. *When we create a new page in Sitecore, that page needs a template. The layout we previously created is assigned a template as well, so when a page is created it gets a template, which may have metadata and a layout to help describe what it is (metadata) and what it looks like (layout)*

■ **Note**   Templates will be covered in greater detail in Chapter 3, so if you're on this step and haven't a clue what's happening, just know that a fuller picture will come to mind in the next chapter.

17. Within that Builder tab, click on the textbox that states Add a New Section. Type in `Page Data`.

Anytime you create a new section, a new line will appear below, allowing you to create a new field.

18. Let's create two new fields: `Title` and `Additional Text`. Once you're done, your MVC Page Template should look like Figure 2-7.

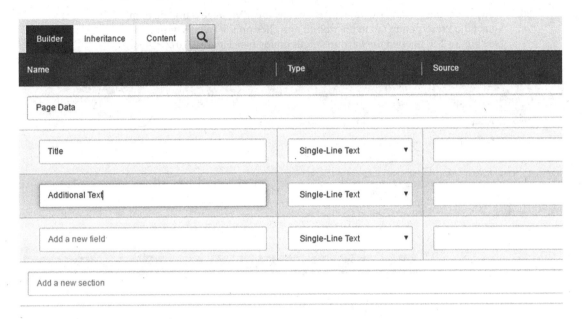

Figure 2-7. *You can add metadata to a template; components can access the current page's metadata and display it or do other things with it*

Now that we've created a new template for our MVC pages, let's configure a few standard values.

19. With the Builder tab selected on your MVC Page template, click the Options tab in the ribbon, then click on the Standard Values button (see Figure 2-8). This will create a Standard Values item for your new MVC Page Template.

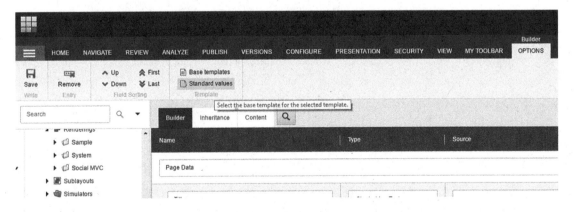

Figure 2-8. *Create standard values for the item to preset the layout to the template*

■ **Note**   Standard values might be better named "default values." When an item is created from a template, standard values set the defaults for the metadata and/or presentation details (such as the default layout assigned to the template). See Chapter 3 for more about standard values.

20.   Now, select the __Standard Values item below the MVC Page template item. Select the Presentation tab in the ribbon and click on the Details button (see Figure 2-9) to open the Layout Details dialog (see Figure 2-10).

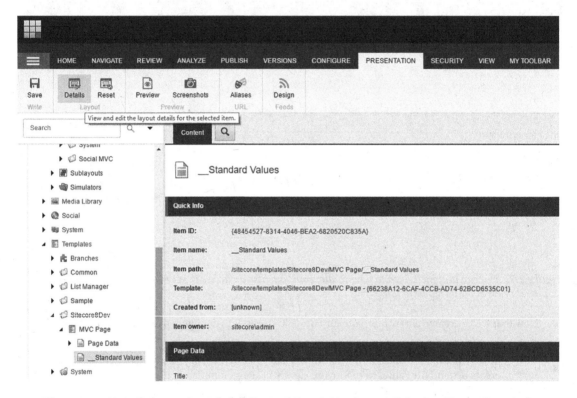

Figure 2-9. *Standard values are always below the item, denoted by the __Standard Values item name*

Figure 2-10. *A template's presentation details, on its standard values, is where you set defaults for layouts, and default components that should be on a page upon creation*

21. On the Shared Layout tab, to the right of the Default device profile, click on the Edit link. This will open the Device Editor dialog. On the Layout tab of the Device Editor dialog, click on the drop-down arrow to the right and select the DefaultMVCLayout layout (see Figure 2-11). Once you have selected your layout, click the OK button, then OK again on the Layout Details dialog. Save your changes.

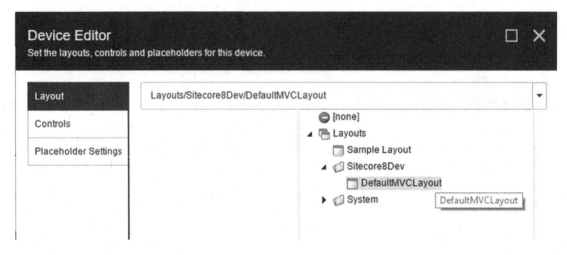

Figure 2-11. *Toggle the page to use the new layout*

The last step is to add a Placeholder item for the main placeholder in our `DefaultMVCLayout`.

22.   Navigate to `/sitecore/Layouts/Placeholder Settings`. Right-click on *Pl*aceholder Settings and select Insert ➤ Placeholder Settings Folder. Name it `Sitecore8Dev` and click OK. Right-click on the new `Sitecore8Dev` folder and select Insert ➤ Placeholder. Name it `main`, then click OK.

You should have something like Figure 2-12 when you're done.

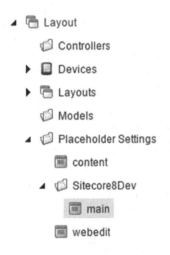

Figure 2-12. *Create a "main" placeholder we can add our components into*

> ■ **Note** The "main" placeholder corresponds to the `@Html.Sitecore.Placeholder("main")` code you saw in Listing 2-3. This is how Sitecore knows how to associate renderings with placeholders in MVC views so they are rendered in the right place within the placeholder in the MVC view.

Creating a Component

Okay, now that we have a place to put a component (a layout with a placeholder), let's build our first component! Again, this component is just going to be a very basic component that renders the text "Hello World". But since Sitecore is a content management system (CMS), we're *not* going to hard-code that content. We want it to be available for a marketer to update. Fortunately, in the last section we created a new page template to create a place for our content. The component we build now just needs to retrieve the content from the page and render it. Super easy! Use the following steps to build your first component!

1. Let's start by creating the view for our component in Visual Studio. In the SitecoreDev.Web project, right-click on the Views folder and select Add ➤ New Folder. Name this new folder `Components`.

2. Right-click on the new `Components` folder and select Add ➤ View. Name this view `AdditionalTextView` (see Figure 2-13), and then click Add.

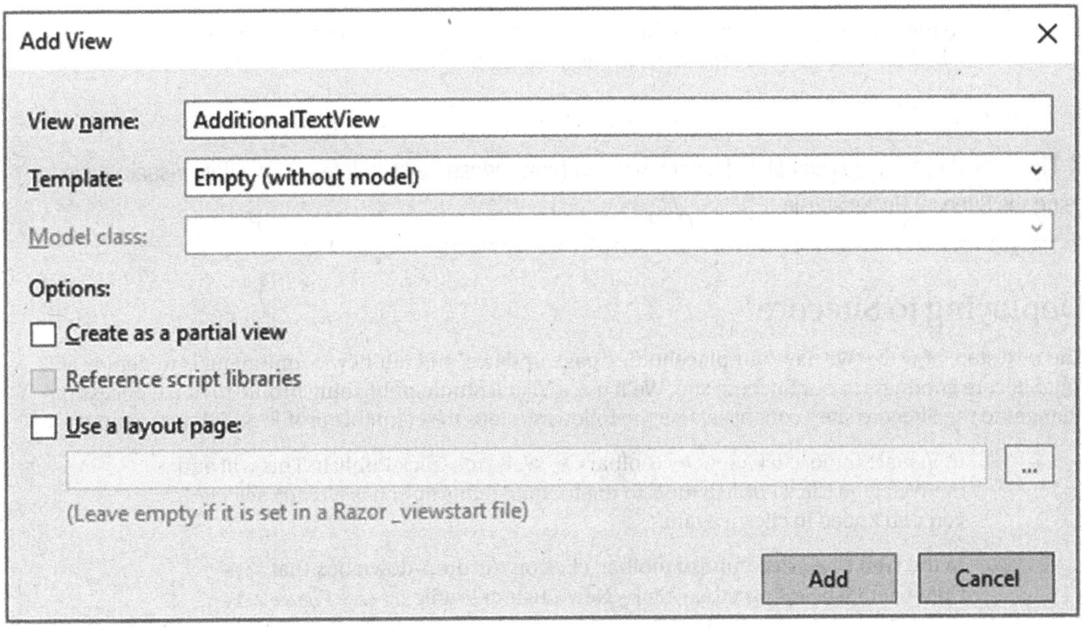

Figure 2-13. The view of a component needs a view; the view contains the components HTML/CSS needed to render the component

---

■ **Warning!**   Don't forget to uncheck the Use a Layout Page checkbox, if it's selected!

---

3. Replace the contents of the newly created view with the contents of Listing 2-4. A component view can be quite simple or complex; the view in Listing 2-4 simply renders the Additional Text field on the current page (the template was created earlier).

Listing 2-4. The Additional Text Field Rendered on the Current Page

```
<div>
        @Html.Sitecore().Field("Additional Text")
</div>
```

4. Save that file.

Now, let's create the View Rendering item in Sitecore and point it to our new file.

5. Open the Content Editor in Sitecore and navigate to /sitecore/layouts/ Renderings. Right-click on the Renderings item and select Insert ➤ Rendering Folder. Name this folder Sitecore8Dev.

6. Right-click on the new Sitecore8Dev rendering folder and select Insert ➤ View Rendering. Name this new item Additional Text, then click OK.

7. In the *Data* section, type the following into the Path field: /Views/Components/ AdditionalTextView.cshtml. Save your changes.

■ **Tip**   Most of the steps completed within Sitecore/browser can be completed from within Visual Studio using the Sitecore Rocks add-in.

Deploying to Sitecore

The next step, now that we have our placeholder, page updates, and our new component, is to deploy all that Sitecore goodness to our Sitecore site. We'll use a Visual Studio publishing profile to make necessary changes to the Sitecore site's codebase. Use the following steps to set up this profile and deploy your code:

1. In Visual Studio, click View ➤ Toolbars ➤ Web One Click Publish. This will add the Web One Click Publish tools to the toolbar. If this option is already selected, you don't need to click it again.

2. In the Web One Click Publish toolbar, click on the drop-down box that says Create Publish Settings, then click <New Custom Profile...> *(see Figure 2-14)*.

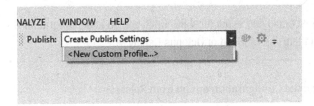

Figure 2-14. *Create a new publishing profile to push your code changes to Sitecore with just an F5 press*

3. This will open the Publish Web dialog. Let's name this new profile Local. Click OK.

4. For Publish Method, change the option from Web Deploy to File System. Then select the web root as your Target Location (see Figure 2-15).

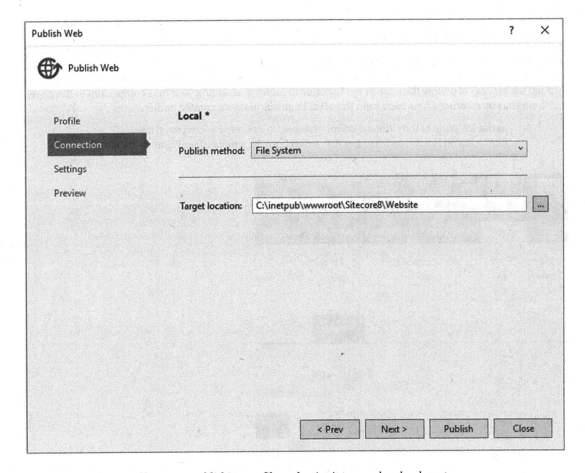

Figure 2-15. *Create a file system publishing profile and point it to your local web root*

■ **Note**   Web Deploy isn't needed yet since we're just deploying to our local PC. Once you go to an integration or test environment you should consider using a build tool like MSBuild or Octopus Deploy.

5. Click Next and, on the next step, change the Configuration option from Release to Debug. Then click Publish.

■ **Note**   When you go to test or production environments you may want a separate publishing profile with the configuration set to Release. Debug can be used for debugging aids (trace information) you wouldn't want on your production server, and minification of CSS/JS files can be disabled for easier script debugging, as well.

Adding a Component to a New Page

Okay, the last step, now that our code is deployed, is to edit the page and add your new component onto the page, followed by a "publish" so the entire world can see your changes! Use the following steps to guide you through the process of editing the page in the Experience Editor and adding your new component to the page.

Let's start by creating a new page from the MVC Page template we created earlier.

1. In the left pane of the Content Editor, navigate to /sitecore/content/Home. Right-click on Home and select Insert ➤ Insert from the template (see Figure 2-16).

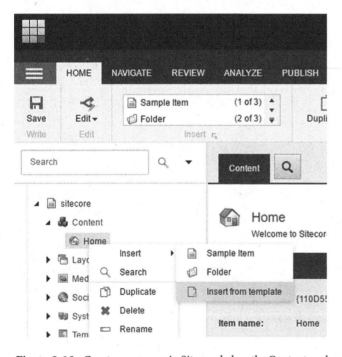

Figure 2-16. *Create new pages in Sitecore below the Content node and below the site you want the page within*

2. This will open the Insert from Template dialog. Select the Templates\Sitecore8Dev\ MVC Page template, name it MyPage and click Insert (see Figure 2-17).

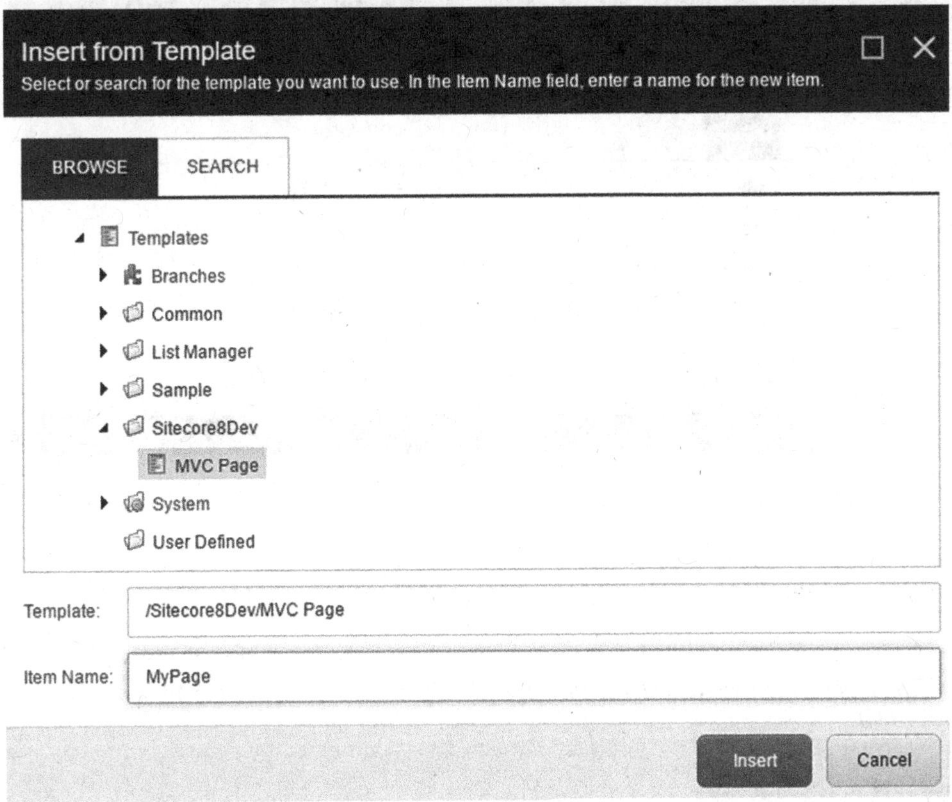

Insert from Template

Select or search for the template you want to use. In the Item Name field, enter a name for the new item.

BROWSE	SEARCH

▲ 🗐 Templates
  ▶ 🧩 Branches
  ▶ 🗁 Common
  ▶ 🗁 List Manager
  ▶ 🗁 Sample
  ▲ 🗁 Sitecore8Dev
    🗐 MVC Page
  ▶ 🗁 System
    🗁 User Defined

Template: /Sitecore8Dev/MVC Page

Item Name: MyPage

Insert   Cancel

Figure 2-17. When creating a page you must select a template; select the MVC page template we created earlier

3. In the Page Data section, fill in some text in the Title and Additional Text fields (see Figure 2-18).

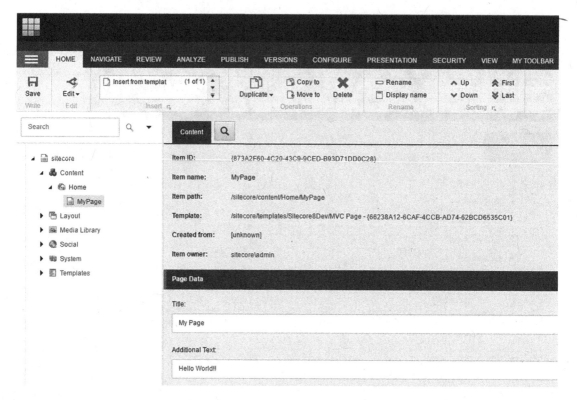

Figure 2-18. *After your page has been created, edit the page title and add some text into the Additional Text field (e.g., Hello World!!)*

4. Click Save.

5. Now that we've created our new page, let's publish it and see what we get! Select the Publish tab, click on the Publish button, and then click Publish Site (see Figure 2-19).

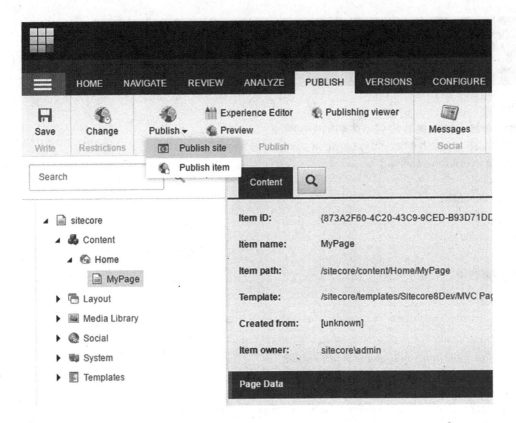

Figure 2-19. *Time to publish your page and check it out!*

6. In the Publish Site dialog, the default selections are fine for now, so click Publish (see Figure 2-20).

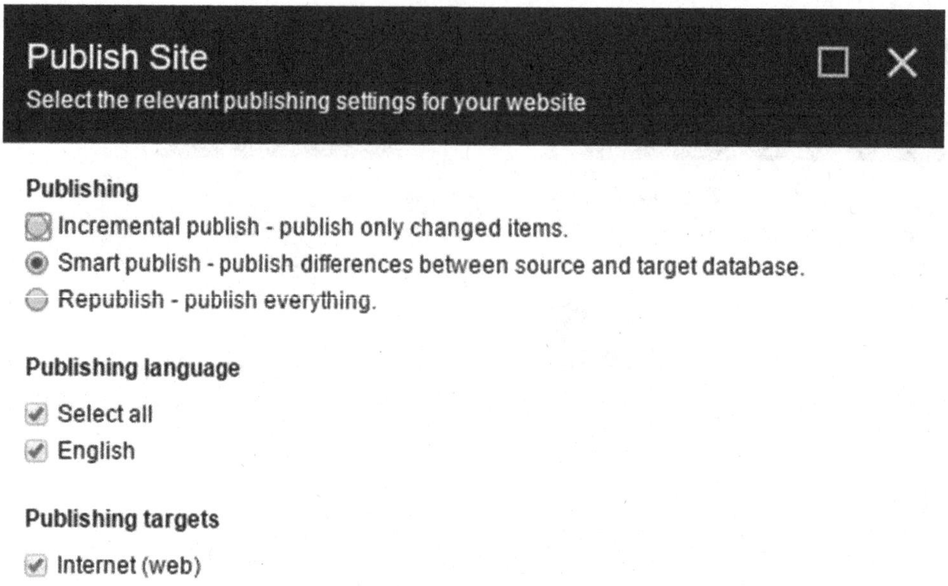

Publish Site
Select the relevant publishing settings for your website ☐ ✕

Publishing

◌ Incremental publish - publish only changed items.

◉ Smart publish - publish differences between source and target database.

◌ Republish - publish everything.

Publishing language

☑ Select all

☑ English

Publishing targets

☑ Internet (web)

Figure 2-20. *Most of the time you'll choose Smart Publish*

7. Once the publish is complete, open a new tab in your browser and navigate to http://sitecore8/mypage. You should see something like Figure 2-21.

◯ Content Editor ✕ | 🗋 My Page ✕

← → C | 🗋 sitecore8/mypage

My Page

Figure 2-21. *Yay, our new page! But no Hello World yet* ☹

■ **Note** Right now, the only thing being displayed is coming strictly from the markup of our DefaultMVCLayout. If you'll recall, the markup for that looked like what we showed in Listing 2-3 earlier. Currently, it's only displaying the content from the Title field because the Additional Text field is empty. Next, we'll add our new Additional Text View Rendering to the main placeholder to display that text.

---

8. Switch back to the Content Editor. In the left pane, select MyPage, click the Publish tab, then click Experience Editor (see Figure 2-22). Once Experience Editor loads, you should see something similar to Figure 2-23.

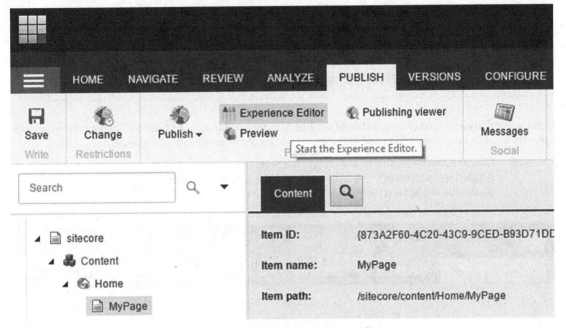

Figure 2-22. *Let's add our component to the page via the Experience Editor*

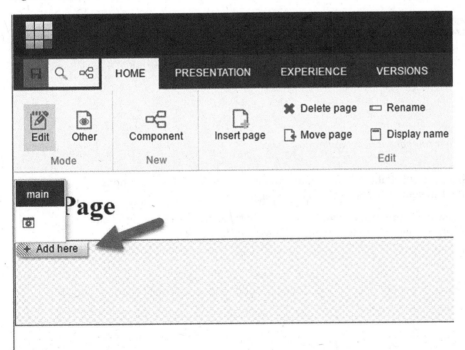

Figure 2-23. *To add a component, click the placeholder and then click Add here. Select the component and then click Add*

■ **Tip** The Experience Editor is the easiest way to edit page content in Sitecore. Content authors will use it all the time so it's important to optimize the Experience Editor to prevent those users from needing to learn the more complex Content Editor. See Chapter 6 for more information on optimizing the Experience Editor.

■ **Note** The checkered area in Figure 2-23 is your "main" placeholder.

If you select that checkered area, you should see a button appear that says Add Here. Clicking this button will open the Select a Rendering dialog and allow you to add components to your placeholders.

9. Click the Add Here button, and then in the Select a Rendering dialog, select Renderings\Sitecore8Dev\Additional Text. Click Select. Now, you should see your Hello World!! text (see Figure 2-24).

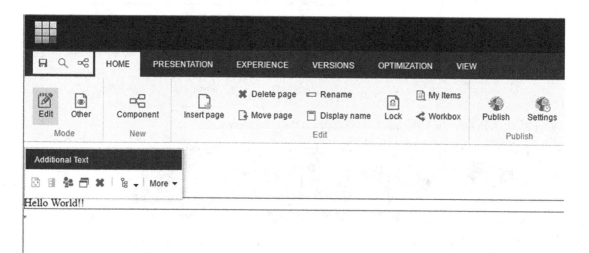

Figure 2-24. *There's our component in action! Almost done...*

10. Click Save. Click the Publish button in the ribbon, leaving the default selections in the Publish Item dialog, then click Publish again.

11. Open a new tab in your browser and navigate to http://sitecore8/mypage. You should see both lines of text fully rendered now (see Figure 2-25).

My Page

Hello World!!

Figure 2-25. *Your first Hello World!! Sitecore component*

Building a Controller Rendering

In the previous section, you built a "Hello World" component. It just so happens that it was a specific type of component called a "view rendering". There's another type of rendering called a "controller rendering" that is more commonly used because it has unique benefits over a view rendering. View renderings are very simplistic and the natural place to start, but now let's take a step further toward the best practice by exploring this other type a bit more, namely controller renderings.

Controller Renderings versus View Renderings

View renderings and controller renderings are both ASP.NET MVC concepts. Both have a .cshtml file that contains the markup inside the project and deployed to the site. However, a controller rendering also has a C# code file that goes along with it. Now, there's an abyss of MVC background information that we could get into here. Most of that is saved for Chapter 4; we don't want to water this introductory chapter down too much. Suffice it to say, a view rendering's corresponding class is auto-generated for you, whereas you have to build the controller rendering's class by hand.

■ **Note** What about ASP Web Forms? Legacy "web forms," the predecessor to MVC, is such a bad practice that we're just going to skip over them in their entirety. If your Sitecore 6/7 site uses web forms, we recommend throwing that code base away and starting over with MVC in Sitecore 8. You might be able to keep some of the front-end markup, but all the post-back logic needs to be refactored into the more modern MVC pattern, if you're serious about adopting best practices.

Having an auto-generated class is convenient; the MVC pipeline looks at your markup, identifies the data it needs, generates a class to go get that data, and shoves it into your view rendering at runtime. All you have to do is point the view rendering to the .cshtml file path in the site's web root, and MVC does the rest!

This is great, but what if you have custom business logic that needs to change the nature of the data being shoved into the view? What if you have business logic that determines what view should be used altogether? In that case you don't want to type the path to the .cshtml file; rather you want to type the *class* name that determines the view, along with the appropriate data that view needs. That class is called a "controller". The controller has one primary job—build a data model and send it to the appropriate view to render that data.

With a controller rendering you don't need to put the path to the .cshtml file. Instead, you put the path to the C# controller namespace. This is a better option because the controller may want to swap in and out different views depending on the business logic. That, and it's rare you would want the auto-generated class used by a view rendering. Binding to your own model is a best practice, because you want the ability to *test* your model. Custom controller/model data binding will be explored to a greater depth in Chapter 4.

Creating a Controller Rendering

It's time to build a controller rendering now that you know a bit as to why controller renderings are commonplace. Whereas the previous view rendering was a generic "Hello World" example, this example is going to be a real-world example, with a few extra tidbits we glossed over before. In this example, we're going to build a "Hero Image" component, much as you commonly find on many home pages. The requirements for this component are that it should display a hero image and use up the entire width of the page. What is more, the component will rotate between all of the images associated with the component.

This example will rely more heavily on some additional data template structures, and will also show a few more advanced front-end concepts. Data templates will be covered in a much greater depth in Chapter 3, and Chapter 6 is dedicated to front-end development patterns, but it can't hurt to give you a taste of them now.

Use the following steps to build the site's hero image rotator for the home page:

1. Let's start by creating the data template for our Hero Slider component. In the Content Editor, navigate to /sitecore/Templates/Sitecore8Dev and insert a new Template Folder called Components.

2. Right-click on that new Components folder and select Insert ➤ New Template. Name it Hero Slider. Leave the Base Template set to the default, Standard Template. Click Next.

■ **Note** Data Templates are covered in more detail in Chapter 3. Consider this a teaser. Basically, every content item in Sitecore is created from a template, so we need to create a new template for our hero image content that our hero image rotator component will render.

---

3. Click Next when asked for a location. It should already have your new Components folder selected. Click Close.

4. On the Builder tab, let's create a new section called Hero Slider Content. Then, create a new field called Hero Images. For the Type, select Treelist. Optionally, in the Source field, you can insert /sitecore/media library. When you're done, it should look something like Figure 2-26.

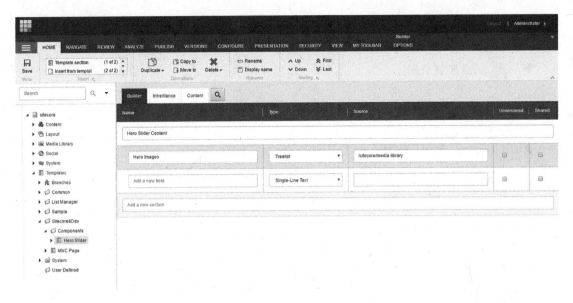

Figure 2-26. *Create a new data template with some fields for the use of our Hero Image content*

■ **Note** The Source field can be used to narrow down the treelist picker. Without it, content editors will have to find their images in the entire content tree. With it, their search starts in the Media Library, exactly where you'd expect images to be. Check out Chapter 3 for more details on creating templates.

---

5. Next, also under the `Sitecore8Dev` template folder, let's create another template folder called `Folder Templates`. Inside that new template folder, let's create a new template (Insert ➤ New Template) and name it `Components`. However, rather than leaving Base Template as Standard Template, as we've done before, change it to `Templates/Common/Folder`. Click Next, Next, and then Close. When you're done, you should have something like Figure 2-27.

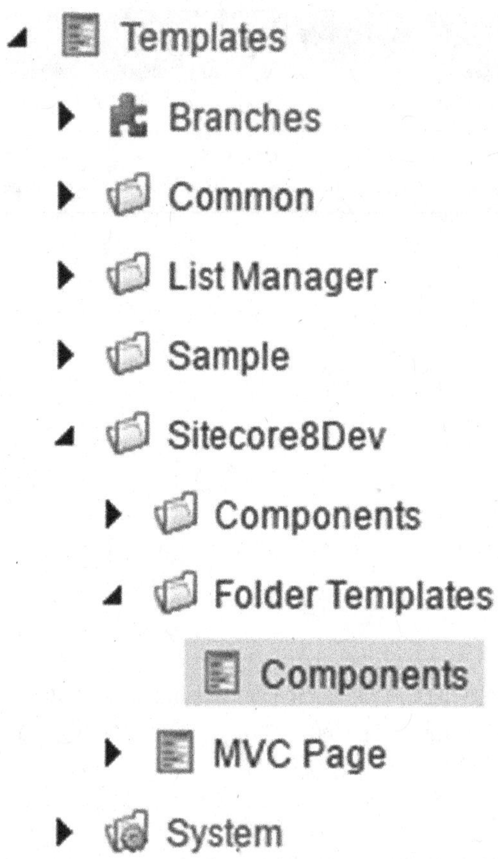

◢ ▤ Templates

   ▶ ♣ Branches

   ▶ 🗂 Common

   ▶ 🗂 List Manager

   ▶ 🗂 Sample

   ◢ 🗂 Sitecore8Dev

      ▶ 🗂 Components

      ◢ 🗂 Folder Templates

         ▤ Components

      ▶ ▤ MVC Page

   ▶ 🗂 System

Figure 2-27. *Creating a folder template is helpful when mange pages have subfolders of a consistent pattern, such as in this case a folder called Components to house component data items*

6. Before we're done with the Components template, let's change two more things. First, with the Components template selected, click on the Configure tab, then the Icon button.

7. At the bottom of this popover menu, click on More Icons (see Figure 2-28). This will launch the Change Icon dialog (see Figure 2-29).

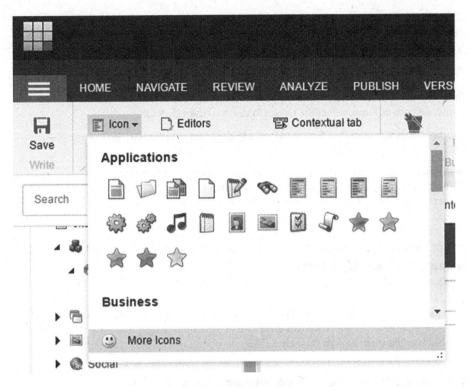

Figure 2-28. *Click More Icons to see a full list of helpful icons*

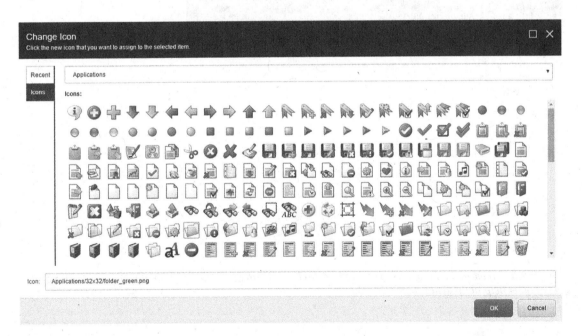

Figure 2-29. *Setting custom icons for data templates makes it easier for content authors to navigate items in the Content Editor*

■ **Tip** Picking custom icons can really help content authors when navigating the content editor; it helps make connections for visual learners.

8. Select the Icon tab on the left, then in the Applications group of icons, in the seventh row, seventh column, select the Green folder, and then click OK.

Finally, for the Components template (we'll refer to it as a folder from here on out), let's create a __ Standard Values item.

9. With the Builder tab selected, click on the Options tab and click the Standard Values button. This will create the __Standard Values item for the Components folder. Select the Configure tab again, then click on the Tree Node Style button.

■ **Note** Standard values allow for having default values when new items are created. Check out Chapter 3 for more details on other ways you can use standard values.

10. This will launch the Tree Node Style dialog. This dialog takes standard CSS and applies it to the style of items based on this template in the Content Tree. Type in the CSS, as seen in Figure 2-30, and then click OK.

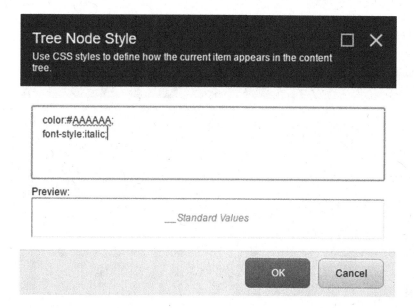

Figure 2-30. If we add a bit of CSS to our folder template we can distinguish it from other folders in Sitecore, yet another helpful tip to aid content authors

Because this folder is going to be used for a specific purpose throughout the site, this option provides an opportunity, other than with icons, to distinguish it from other items in the content tree (see Figure 2-31).

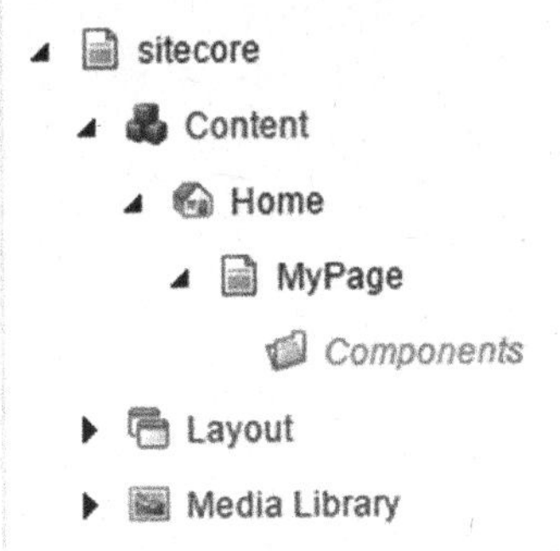

```
▲ 🗋 sitecore
    ▲ 🍇 Content
        ▲ 🏠 Home
            ▲ 🗋 MyPage
                   📁 Components
    ▶ 🗔 Layout
    ▶ 🖼 Media Library
```

Figure 2-31. *The result of our custom folder template and CSS*

11. Next, navigate to /sitecore/content/home/mypage. Right-click on this item and select Insert ➤ Insert from template. Select our new Components folder under Templates/Sitecore8Dev/FolderTemplates, name it Components, then click Insert. Your content tree should look like Figure 2-31.

▓ **Note** These Components folders will be used to store content items for components on their parent pages.

---

12. Next, let's create an instance of the Hero Slider template we created in Steps 2, 3, and 4. Right-click on the Components folder under MyPage and select Insert ➤ Insert from template. In the Insert from Template dialog, select /Sitecore8Dev/Components/Hero Slider and name it Hero Slider Content (see Figure 2-32). Click Insert.

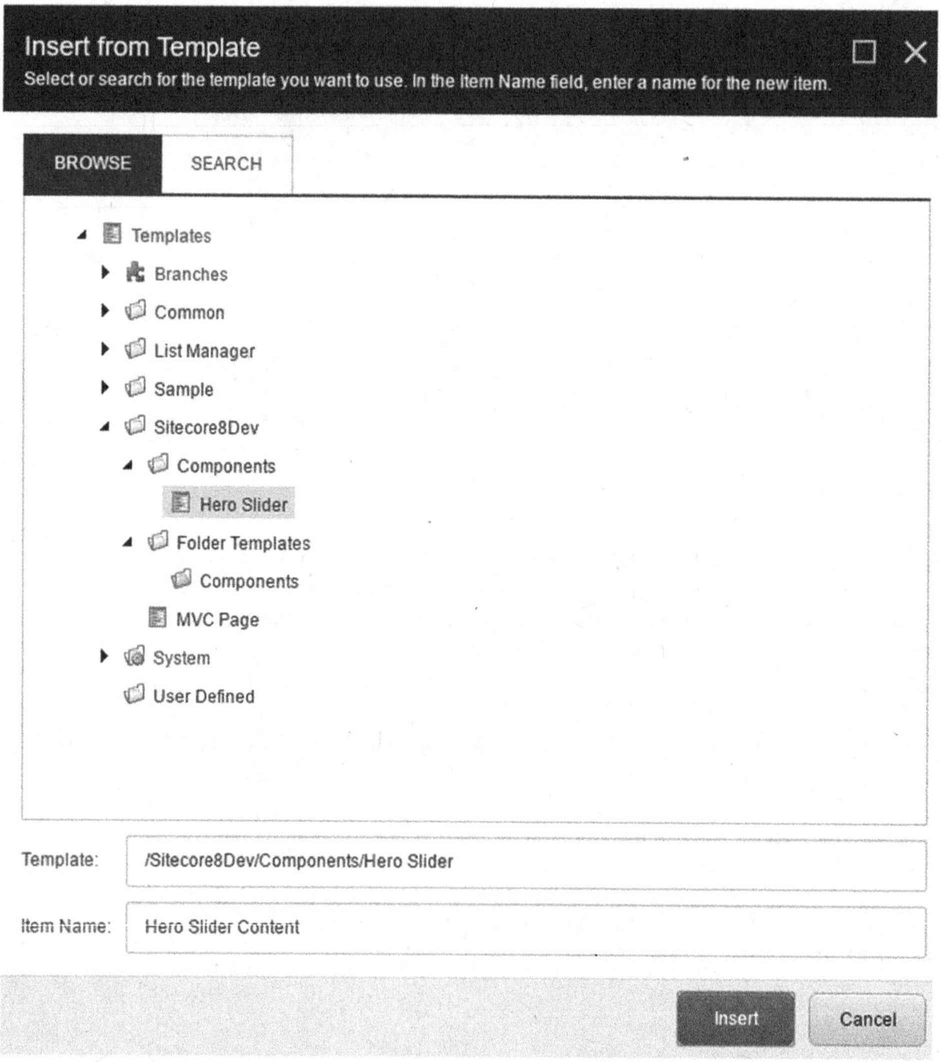

Insert from Template

Select or search for the template you want to use. In the Item Name field, enter a name for the new item.

BROWSE   SEARCH

▲ ▣ Templates
  ▶ 🔩 Branches
  ▶ 🗀 Common
  ▶ 🗀 List Manager
  ▶ 🗀 Sample
  ▲ 🗀 Sitecore8Dev
    ▲ 🗀 Components
        ▣ Hero Slider
    ▲ 🗀 Folder Templates
        🗀 Components
      ▣ MVC Page
  ▶ 🗀 System
      🗀 User Defined

Template: /Sitecore8Dev/Components/Hero Slider

Item Name: Hero Slider Content

Insert   Cancel

Figure 2-32. *Create a new content item from the Hero data template created earlier*

■ **Tip** Only admins will see the Insert from Template option. Developers should set up Insert Options to create specific items in the Insert menu that a marketer or content author would be allowed to create below a given node. This makes it easier for them and helps enforce a consistent information architecture. See Chapter 3 for more information about this.

Now, we need to insert a few images into the Media Library for use with our Hero Slider Content content item.

13. Navigate to /sitecore/Media Library. Right-click on Media Library and select Insert ➤ Media Folder. Name it Sitecore8Dev. Inside this folder, create another Media Folder named Hero Images. When it's complete, it should look like Figure 2-33.

▲ 🖼 Media Library

  ▶ 📁 Default Website

  ▶ 📁 Experience Explorer

  📁 Files

  ▶ 📁 Images

  ▲ 📁 Sitecore8Dev

    📁 Hero Images

  ▶ 📁 System

▶ 🌐 Social

Figure 2-33. *All media should go in the Media Library below a sensible folder structure*

14. With the Hero Images media folder selected, click on the Upload Files button. Select the four images from the %dev root%\files\chapter 1\images folder at the root of the GitHub repository and click Open. This will start the upload process.

■ **Note** If you haven't yet downloaded the source code for this book, you can find it at http://github.com/sitecoredevbook. Alternatively, upload other wallpaper-like images into this folder.

---

15. Navigate back to /sitecore/content/Home/MyPage/Components/Hero Slider Content. In the Hero Images Treelist, navigate to Media Library\Sitecore8Dev\Hero Images. Select each of the four images on the left and click the right-arrow button to move them to the Selected box on the right (see Figure 2-34). Click Save.

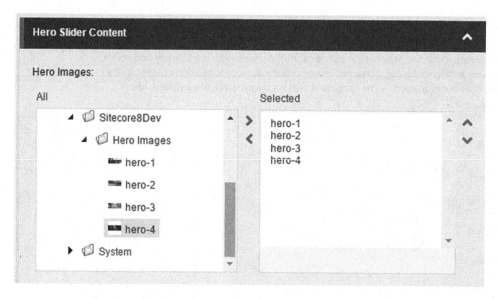

Figure 2-34. *Add a few images to our hero image slider content item*

Now that we have our templates and content created, let's go back to Visual Studio and write the code for the controller rendering.

16. First, let's install bootstrap from NuGet. In the `SitecoreDev.Web` project, right-click on References and select Manage NuGet Packages. Click on the Browse tab and search for `Bootstrap`.

17. As of the writing of this book, the latest version is v3.3.6. Click the Install button on the right.

18. After installing Bootstrap, open `/Views/Shared/DefaultMVCLayout.cshtml` and add references within the `<Head>` tag to the necessary JavaScript and CSS resources, as shown:

```
<script type="text/javascript" src="~/Scripts/jquery-1.9.1.js"></script>
<script type="text/javascript" src="~/Scripts/bootstrap.js"></script>
<link rel="stylesheet" href="~/Content/bootstrap.css" />
```

19. Next, right-click on the `Controllers` folder and select Add ➤ Controller. This will open the Add Scaffold dialog. Select MVC 5 Controller – Empty.

20. Click Add. Name your new controller `ComponentsController` and click Add again.

21. Add the following `using` statements:

```
using Sitecore;
using Sitecore.Data.Items;
using Sitecore.Mvc.Controllers;
using Sitecore.Mvc.Presentation;
```

22. Change the base class of ComponentsController from Controller to SitecoreController and then delete the generated index method.

23. Add a new controller method named HeroSlider into the ComponentsController class, using the code shown in Listing 2-5.

Listing 2-5. Add a HeroSlider View Result to Load the View When a Hero Image Component Is Requested

```
public ViewResult HeroSlider()
{
        Item contentItem = null;
        var database = Context.Database;
        if (database != null)
        {
                if(!String.IsNullOrEmpty(
                        RenderingContext.Current.Rendering.DataSource))
                {
                        contentItem = database.GetItem(new Sitecore.Data.ID(
                                RenderingContext.Current.Rendering.DataSource));
                }
        }
        return View(contentItem);
}
```

Before we move back into the steps, let's explore the code in Listing 2-5 a bit. The basic goal of the code is to pass the Hero Image's content item to the view for rendering purposes. The content item is where we set the images we wanted for the rotator. To make this happen, we need to retrieve that item out of the Sitecore database and pass it to the view. The variable database stores a reference to the Sitecore database, either the web database if viewing a published page, or the master database if previewing an unpublished page. If that database variable is not null, we next retrieve the hero image content item associated with the hero image component we'll add to the page in later steps. We can get that item by looking at the rendering context, specifically the current (hero image) rendering/component's DataSource property. This DataSource is the ID of the content item associated with the component. This ID is passed into the database's GetItem method to retrieve the item, which is then passed into the view.

Next, let's create the view for our HeroSlider component.

24. Navigate to the /Views/Components folder. Right-click on Components and select Add ➤ View. In the Add View dialog, name your new view HeroSlider. Be sure to uncheck the Use a Layout Page checkbox if it's selected and click Add.

25. In your new view, replace the contents with the code in Listing 2-6.

Listing 2-6. Our View Code Iterates Through Each Image in the Content Item and Renders its <img> Tag

```
@model Sitecore.Data.Items.Item
@using Sitecore.Data.Fields
@using Sitecore.Data.Items
@using Sitecore.Resources.Media

@if (Model != null)
{
<div id="myCarousel" class="carousel slide" data-ride="carousel">
        <ol class="carousel-indicators">
```

```
                <li data-target="#myCarousel" data-slide-to="0"
        class="active"></li>
                <li data-target="#myCarousel" data-slide-to="1"></li>
                <li data-target="#myCarousel" data-slide-to="2"></li>
                <li data-target="#myCarousel" data-slide-to="3"></li>
        </ol>
        <div class=carousel-inner" role="listbox">
        @{
                IEnumerable<Item> heroImages = null;
                var heroImagesField = new MultilistField(
                        Model.Fields["Hero Images"]);
                if (heroImagesField != null)
                {
                        heroImages = heroImagesField.GetItems();
                }
                if (heroImages != null)
                {
                        int i = 1;
                        foreach (var image in heroImages)
                        {
                                var mediaItem = (MediaItem) image;
                                <div class="item @(i == 1 ? "active" : "")">
                                    <img src="@MediaManager.GetMediaUrl(mediaItem)"
                                        style="width:1920px;" />
                                </div>
                                i++;
                        }
                }
        }
        </div>
</div>
}
```

Let's take a look at this code. Regarding the CSS/presentation, check out the source in the GitHub site. Rather, let's focus on the code as it relates to Sitecore. The first thing you'll notice is the view is assigned a model of type `Sitecore.Data.Items.Item`. This now strongly types the references to "Model" later to a Sitecore item object (e.g., `Model.Fields`). The rest of the code gets the images out of the "Hero Images" field and iterates through each image and renders the `<img>` tags for each. `MediaManager` is used to dynamically grab the URL out of the image's own Item object.

26. Now, let's publish! In the Visual Studio menu, select Build ➤ Publish SitecoreDev.Web and publish your changes to the web root.

27. Once the Publish has succeeded, let's go back to the Content Editor in Sitecore.

28. Navigate to /sitecore/Layout/Renderings/Sitecore8Dev. Right-click on Sitecore8Dev and select Insert ➤ Rendering Folder. Name it Components. Now, right-click on Components and select Insert ➤ Controller Rendering. Name your new rendering Hero Slider. Insert the values found in Table 2-1 and then be sure to click Save. Once you're done, it should look like Figure 2-35.

Table 2-1. *Fields for Our New Rendering*

Field	Value
Controller	`Components`
Controller Action	`HeroSlider`
Datasource Location	`./Components`
Datasource Template	`/sitecore/templates/Sitecore8Dev/Components/Hero Slider`

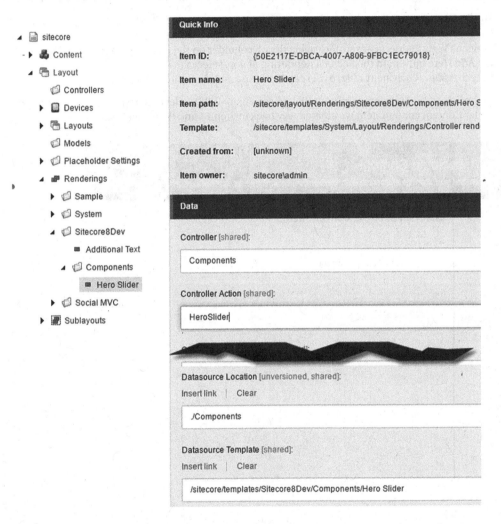

Figure 2-35. *Our controller rendering references the controller and the action (method) that returns the correct view*

You can tell here that our controller rendering is different than the view rendering created in the previous exercise. Instead of specifying the path to the view in the rendering item, we specify the controller name and the method/action within that controller which responds to the request. Now that we have coded our controller rendering and configured it in Sitecore, all that is left is to add it to our page!

■ **Note**   If you're still a bit fuzzy on how controllers work, have no fear! Chapter 4 goes much deeper into MVC fundamentals and it will become clear by then.

---

29. Still in the Content Editor, navigate to /sitecore/content/Home/MyPage. On the Publish tab, click the Experience Editor button. Like we did with our previous View Rendering example, select the placeholder on the page and click the Add Here button. In the Select a Rendering dialog, select the /Rendering/ Sitecore8Dev/Components/Hero Slider rendering and then click Select.

30. In the Select the Associated Content dialog (see Figure 2-36), select the Hero Slider Content content item we created way back in Step 14 and then click OK.

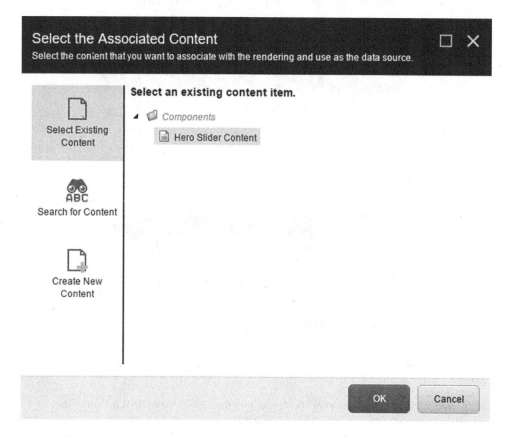

Figure 2-36. *When you add a component to a page, usually the next step is to associate the component to a content data item so it can render some content*

Voila! It should look something like Figure 2-37 when you're done! Be sure to save your changes.

Figure 2-37. *Your first controller rendering Sitecore component!*

Summary

Well there it is! You can now consider yourself a Sitecore developer! Not a very good one yet, but by the end of this book you will be. From here we'll begin introducing more concepts and best practices that build on these introductory concepts discussed in these first two chapters.

We built two components in this chapter. First, the famed "Hello World" example, this time featuring a generic view rendering to get things up and running quickly. However, we learned that controller renderings are a better practice when business logic is needed, so we built one of those as well and introduced the site that we'll use in all future chapters in the book.

CHAPTER 3

■■■

Data Templates and Content

It sure was fun creating a couple components in Chapter 2 and getting a feel for what Sitecore development is all about! I bet you feel you're ready to dive into the deep end and see more code! Not so fast, first we need to do some more brick laying and understand some more core Sitecore solution architecture concepts first, most notably data templates and standard values. From there we can introduce a few more content management fundamentals, and with all that under your belt, Chapter 4, the deep end, will make a ton more sense!

■ **Note** Content management fundamentals are covered in much more detail in *Practical Sitecore 8 Configuration and Strategy*. You'll get a taste in this chapter, enough to get you quite a long way. However, check out this book's sister book for more details.

Data templates are the foundation of your Sitecore deployment. They specify the data fields and many other settings that can be applied to content upon creation. For example, you might want to feature a "Promotion" of a given "Product". Both of these items represent content that a marketer will create, test, and perhaps personalize based on the user and their preferences. Before they can get started, however, a developer needs to configure the data templates that represent these content items, and thereafter a developer must create the components to render the promotions.

Standard values extend the data templates discussion by introducing how to set default settings and values when items are created. Additionally, you can set default layouts and other presentation details as well. This sounds trivial, but standard values are a core Sitecore development concept and should be studied in detail.

Data Template Fields

We know data templates are a collection of fields. However, it's a bit more complex than that. A data template can have sections. Fields can have types and sources. Fields can also be versioned. Let's understand these settings and options before we start building the data templates needed for our example site (Figure 3-1, for example).

© Phil Wicklund and Jason Wilkerson 2016

P. Wicklund and J. Wilkerson, *Professional Sitecore 8 Development*, DOI 10.1007/978-1-4842-2292-8_3

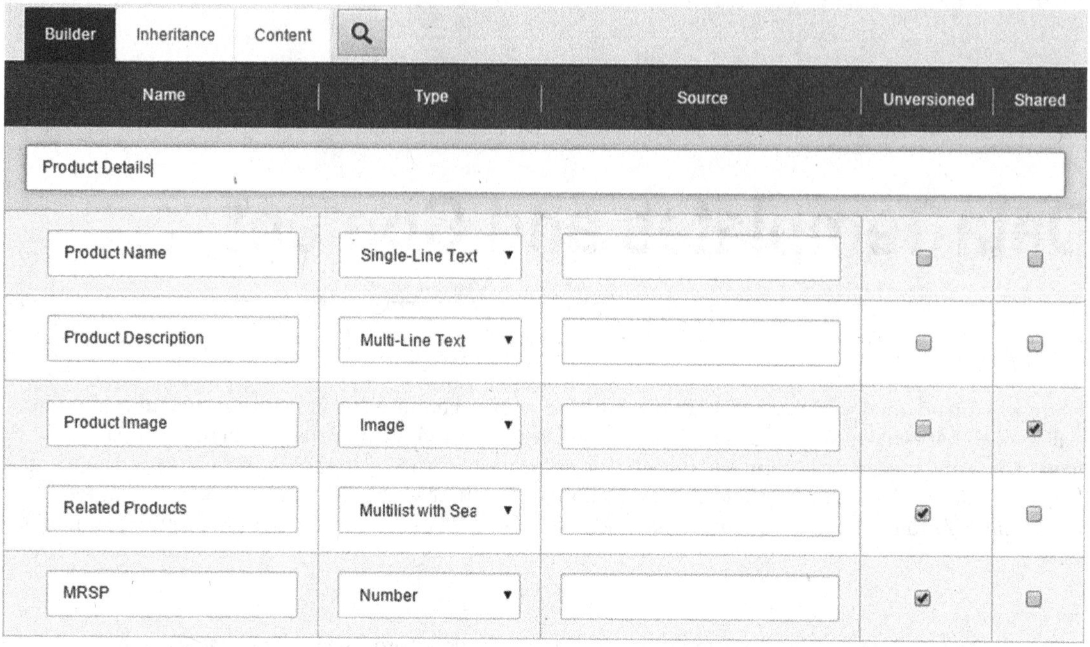

Name	Type	Source	Unversioned	Shared
Product Details				
Product Name	Single-Line Text ▼		☐	☐
Product Description	Multi-Line Text ▼		☐	☐
Product Image	Image ▼		☐	☑
Related Products	Multilist with Sea ▼		☑	☐
MRSP	Number ▼		☑	☐

Figure 3-1. *Fields have five common properties, including their name, type, source, and versioning requirements, either unversioned and/or shared*

Field Sections

Field sections are a great way to organize your fields by categories. From a Content Editor's perspective, the field sections will appear as an expandable/collapsible accordion. Figure 3-2 demonstrates this, where home, menu item and site root (among others) are that item's field sections.

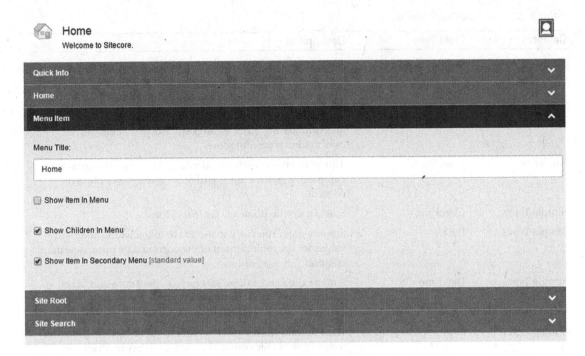

Figure 3-2. *Field sections allow you to categorize your fields. This makes content administration easier when you have a lot of fields*

Field Types

There are *many* field types to choose from! A field type establishes the format in which the data will be stored. For example, a Number column requires a number value, whereas a single-line text column can take any set of characters, letters, numbers or otherwise. Table 3-1 shows the various field types and an explanation of what they are and how they work.

Table 3-1. Field Type Descriptions

Category	Field Type	Description
Analytics	Profile Card Value	Allows the marketer to select a profile/persona that can be associated to the piece of content. You will almost never need to use this field because it's already in the standard template.
Analytics	Profile Cards	Similar to Profile Card Value, but more robust, accommodating other settings such as user segment, information type, and score.
Analytics	Tracking	This is an important field, allowing marketers to associate campaigns, goals, events, and other settings to a piece of content.
Simple Types	Checkbox	Stores a simple Boolean, Yes/No value.
Simple Types	Date	Stores a date. You can use the $date token within standard values for the replacement of the current date upon new item creation.
Simple Types	Datetime	Stores a date and a time. You can use the $date and $time tokens within standard values for the replacement of the current date upon new item creation.
Simple Types	File	The File field allows users to "attach" files to the content. The user can select files out of the Media Library to attach, or upload new ones.
Simple Types	Image	Similar to File but specific for images. Images rendered with FieldRenderer can have a MaxWidth applied. When applied, Sitecore will cache a resized image according to that width, thus speeding up download times. This offers a significant advantage over the File field when working with images.
Simple Types	Integer	Stores a whole number, without any decimal places.
Simple Types	Multi-Line Text	Allows for multiple lines of text.
Simple Types	Number	Takes any number, with or without decimal places.
Simple Types	Password	Offers the user a textbox but blurs the text so onlookers cannot see the value.
Simple Types	Rich Text	Similar to multi-line text, except that it offers a rich text editor to aid content editing. The text is stored as XHTML rather than straight text.
Simple Types	Single-Line Text	Straight text line with no rich text and no carriage returns.
Simple Types	Word Document	Allows for a Word document to be attached to the item, with links for Edit and Download. Inline editing of the document is only supported on IE.
Social	Accounts Multilist	Internal; you probably won't use this.
Social	Campaign Tree	Internal; you probably won't use this.
Social	Countable Edit	Internal; you probably won't use this.

(continued)

Table 3-1. (*continued*)

Category	Field Type	Description
List Types	Checklist	Allows for the user to check multiple checkboxes. The data source can be set to an item in the tree, and items below that parent item will appear as selectable options.
List Types	Droplist	Similar to Checklist except it renders a drop-down instead of selectable checkboxes. The disadvantage is you can only select one option in this case. Note: only the item name is stored, not an actual link to the item in the database. Therefore, use this sparingly if at all to avoid broken links. As an alternative use Droplink whenever possible.
List Types	Grouped Droplink	Similar to Droplist except that the grandparent is set to the data source. In this case, the child items are the "groups" in the drop-down and their children then become the options. Note: Droplink stores the ID of the item selected and is a better option than Droplist.
List Types	Grouped Droplist	Similar to Grouped Droplink except only the value is stored. Use sparingly if at all.
List Types	Multilist	Shows the left/right selector to select multiple items with left/right arrows. Also allows sorting on the selected items, perhaps making it preferable to Checklist.
List Types	Multilist with Search	Similar to Multilist but with the addition of a search box to allow users the ability to search for items instead of trying to find them in a list. This is helpful for large lists.
List Types	Name Lookup Value List	Similar to Name Value List in that this field lets you store key/value pairs, but it also lets you set a data source from where to allow the user to pick the key/values from.
List Types	Name Value List	This field type helps you store a collection of key/value pairs.
List Types	Treelist	Similar to the Multilist but rendered via a treeview versus a flat list. There are also many configurations you can set to include/exclude what shows up in the treeview.
List Types	TreelistEx	Similar to the Treelist but the tree is collapsed on load, making load time faster as items are fetched only when the user expands that item.
Link Types	Droplink	One of the best, most commonly used types for storing drop-down values as it links directly to the item in the database and thus the solution is safer from broken links.
Link Types	Droptree	Similar to Droplink but renders a treeview instead of a normal drop-down.
Link Types	General Link	Standard linking ability, commonly used for linking to external sites or if the user needs to add link settings, such as targeting a new window or calling JavaScript upon click.
Link Types	General Link with Search	Similar to General Link except it also provides the user a search box to search for items.

(*continued*)

Table 3-1. (*continued*)

Category	Field Type	Description
Link Types	Version Link	Clones use this field to track an items ID, language, and version number when cloning.
Developer Types	AccountSelector	Internal; you probably won't use this.
Developer Types	Icon	This field gives the user the ability to select an icon out of the icon library.
Developer Types	iFrame	Lets the user specify the path to another application.
Developer Types	Tristate	Lets the user select between Yes and No, but also Undefined.
Developer Types	Sitecore User	Lets the user select a user stored in the Sitecore database, such as a customer who has a login configured.
System Types	Attachment	Internal; you probably won't use this.
System Types	Custom	Internal; you probably won't use this.
System Types	Datasource	Internal; you probably won't use this.
System Types	File Drop Area	Internal; you probably won't use this.
System Types	Internal Link	Internal; you probably won't use this.
System Types	Layout	Internal; you probably won't use this.
System Types	Page Preview	Internal; you probably won't use this.
System Types	Query Builder	If you need a search query to be the data source of a control, you can use this field to help build that query versus having to type it in manually (which is error prone).
System Types	Query Datasource	Internal; you probably won't use this.
System Types	Rendering Datasource	Internal; you probably won't use this.
System Types	Rules	Internal; you probably won't use this.
System Types	Security	Internal; you probably won't use this.
System Types	Template Field Source	Internal; you probably won't use this.
System Types	Thumbnail	Internal; you probably won't use this. Instead set a MaxWidth on the ImageField.
Deprecated Types	N/A	Deprecated types are in Sitecore for the purposes of backward compatibility with previous versions of Sitecore only and should not be used for new data templates.

Custom Field Types

There's a good chance you didn't see the field type you need in the Table 3-1. Maybe you need a Google Map picker, or perhaps a carousel from which to select another item? Or, a color picker might come in handy instead of Googling, copying, and pasting a color's HEX value?

Creating custom field types is easy as well! The following steps are a basic example, walking you through the process of creating a custom field type. The example is a credit card textbox with the value of the numbers obscured when viewing page details or editing the page. Additionally, the value is encrypted in the database for safe storage. You could use this field type if you had a component that needed to query a secured web service and you needed to enter credentials, but you didn't want extra dependencies on web. config settings, for example.

In the SitecoreDev.Web project in Visual Studio, let's start by creating two new folders.

1. Right-click on the SitecoreDev.Web project name and select Add ➤ New Folder. Name this folder Custom. Within the Custom folder, add another folder called Fields.

2. Right-click on the new Fields folder and select Add ➤ Class. Name this class CreditCard. Insert the following using statements:

```
using System.Web.UI.HtmlControls;
using System.Text.RegularExpressions;
using Sitecore;
using Sitecore.Shell.Applications.ContentEditor;
using Sitecore.Web;
using Sitecore.Web.UI.Sheer;
```

Because this is a credit card field, we should mask the numbers in the field. To do this, we'll have our new CreditCard class inherit from Password.

3. Replace the default class with the code in Listing 3-1.

Listing 3-1. Create a New Class for Our Custom Field

```
public class CreditCard : Password
{
    private string _creditCardRegEx = @"^\d{4}([\-]?)\d{4}\1\d{4}\1\d{4}$";

    public CreditCard()
    {
        Class = "scContentControl";
    }

    public override void HandleMessage(Message message)
    {
        base.HandleMessage(message);

        if (message.Name == "creditcard:validate")
        {
            string currentvalue = WebUtil.GetFormValue(ID);
            string result = Regex.IsMatch(
                    currentvalue, _creditCardRegEx) ? "Valid" : "Invalid";
            SheerResponse.SetInnerHtml("validationResult_" + ID, result);
```

```
    }
  }

  protected override void OnPreRender(EventArgs e)
  {
    base.OnPreRender(e);
    ServerProperties["Value"] = ServerProperties["Value"];
  }

  protected override void Render(System.Web.UI.HtmlTextWriter output)
  {
    base.Render(output);

    HtmlGenericControl formatHtml = new HtmlGenericControl("div");
    formatHtml.Attributes.Add("style", "color:#888888;");
    formatHtml.InnerHtml = "xxxx-xxxx-xxxx-xxxx";
    formatHtml.RenderControl(output);

    HtmlGenericControl validationHtml = new HtmlGenericControl("div");
    validationHtml.Attributes.Add("ID", "validationResult_" + ID);
    validationHtml.Attributes.Add("style", "color:#888888;");
    validationHtml.InnerHtml = "";
    validationHtml.RenderControl(output);
  }

  protected override bool LoadPostData(string value)
  {
    value = StringUtil.GetString(new string[1] { value });

    if (!(Value != value))
      return false;

    Value = value;
    base.SetModified();
    return true;
  }
}
```

Our `CreditCard` class has two key override methods overridden from the `Password` class—the `Render` method, which controls the display pattern as seen when editing the item/page, and the `HandleMessage` method, which responds when invalid data is entered (doesn't match the credit card regex property). The `Render` method just renders whatever HTML or web controls you want to show up when editing the item/page. In our case, we need two controls, one for the textbox with obfuscated values (XXXX) and another to drop any validation messages.

Now that we have our custom `CreditCard` class implemented, let's patch in a config that creates a new control source prefix for our custom fields. We'll use this prefix when registering the control with Sitecore.

4. Within the App_Config\Include folder, right-click on the SitecoreDev folder and select Add ➤ Web Configuration File. Name this file SitecoreDev. CustomFields.config. Replace the contents of this new file with the code in Listing 3-2.

Listing 3-2. You Must Register Your Custom Fields in the Web.Config

```
<configuration xmlns:x="http://www.sitecore.net/xmlconfig/">
    <sitecore>
        <controlSources>
            <source mode="on"
                    namespace="SitecoreDev.Web.Custom.Fields"
                    assembly="SitecoreDev.Web" prefix="sitecoreDev" />
        </controlSources>
    </sitecore>
</configuration>
```

5. Now, publish your web project. Once the publish is complete, open your web browser and navigate to `http://sitecore8/sitecore`.

In order to add our new `CreditCard` field type to a data template, we need to register it in the core database.

6. From the Sitecore Launchpad, click on the Desktop button.

7. In the bottom-right corner of the desktop, click on the database icon and select Core.

8. Go back to the Launchpad and click on the Content Editor button. From within the Content Editor, navigate to `/sitecore/system/Field types/Simple Types`.

9. Right-click on the `Simple Types` folder and select Insert ➤ Insert from template. In the Insert from Template dialog, navigate to `/System/Templates` and select *Template field type*. Name this item `Credit Card` (see Figure 3-3) and then click Insert.

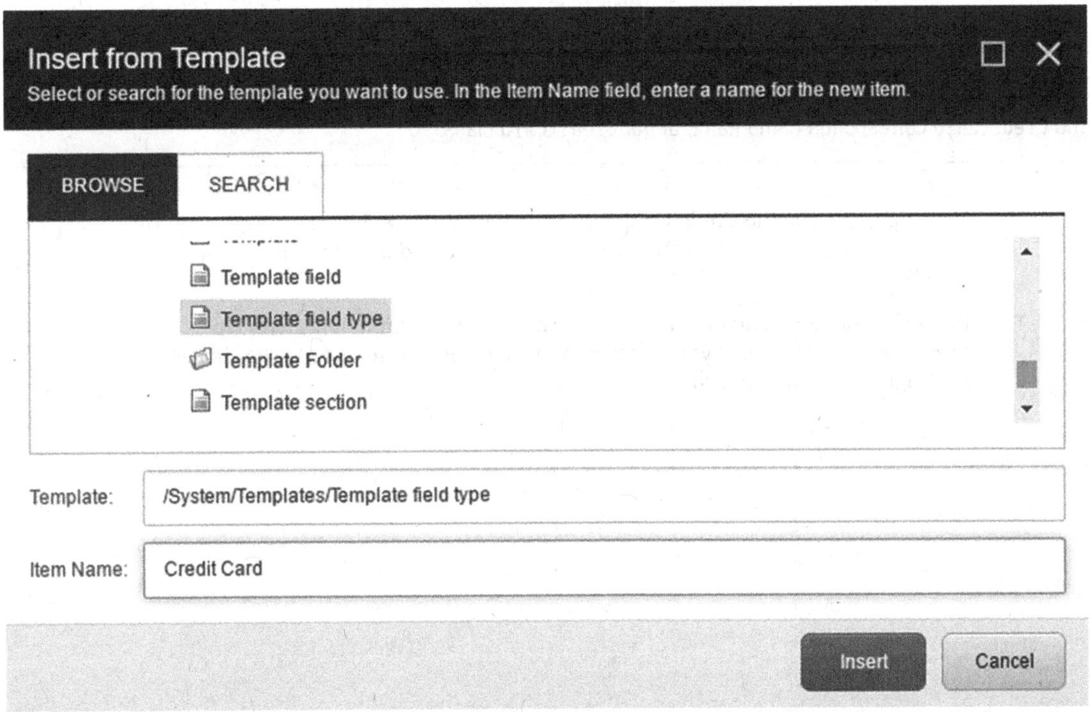

Figure 3-3. *Use a Template Field Type when Creating Custom Field Types*

10. In the Data section of our new Credit Card field, in the Control field, type sitecoreDev:CreditCard (see Figure 3-4) and then click Save.

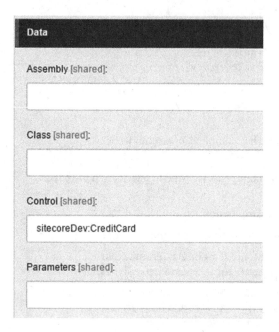

Figure 3-4. Use your prefix and class name to specify the class for your custom field type

---

■ **Note**   sitecoreDev corresponds to the prefix we defined in our SitecoreDev.CustomFields.config file and CreditCard corresponds to the name of our CreditCard class.

---

11. Next, right-click on the Credit Card item and select Insert ➤ Insert from template. Navigate to /templates/Common and select Folder. Name this item Menu.

12. Right-click on the Menu folder and select Insert ➤ Insert from template. This time, select /templates/System/Menus/Menu item and name this item Validate (see Figure **3-5**) and then click Insert.

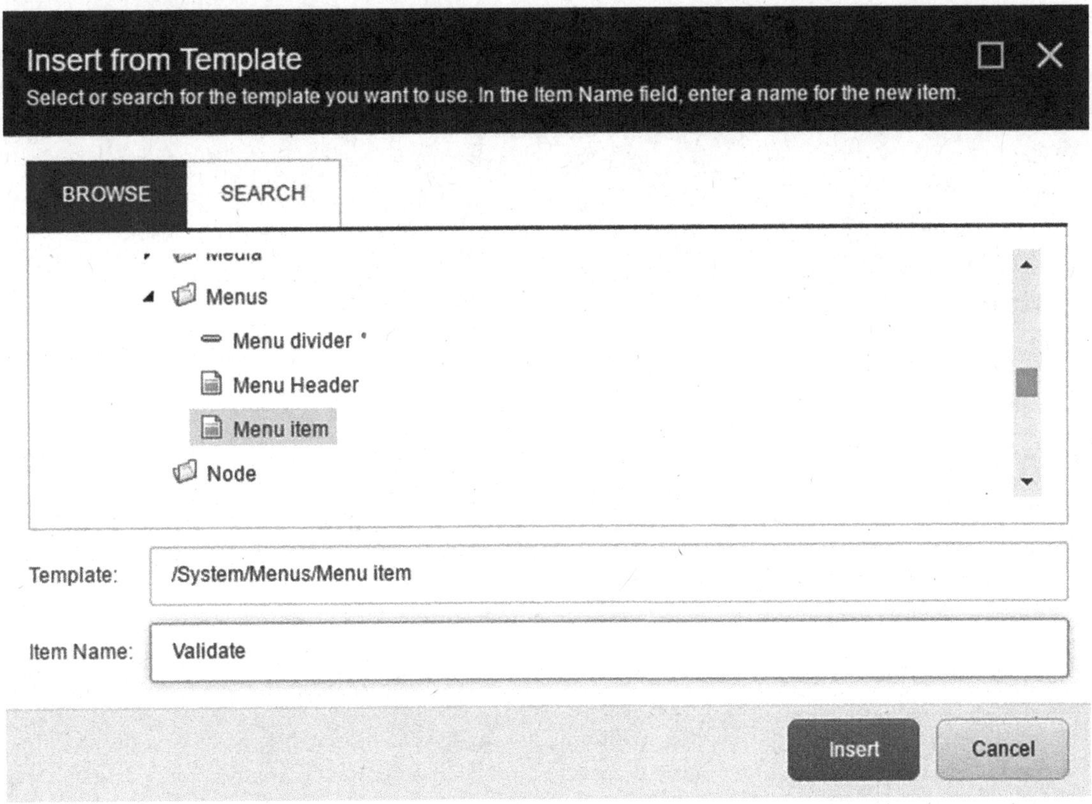

Figure 3-5. *Creating a menu item can help authors by providing extra functionality when within the Content Editor*

13. In the Data section of our new Validate item, fill in the following values (see Figure 3-6) and then click Save:

    Display Name: Validate

    Message: creditcard:validate

Data

Action [shared]:

[   ]

☐ **Checkbox** [shared]

Display name [unversioned]:

[Validate   ]

Hotkey [unversioned]:

[   ]

Icon [shared]:

Open icon | Clear

[   ]

ID [shared]:

[   ]

Message [shared]:

[creditcard:validate   ]

Figure 3-6. *The Validate menu item will fire the data validation for our Credit Card custom field type*

You have now created a custom field type called Credit Card! To test this, navigate back to the Desktop from the Launchpad and switch back to the master database. Open the Content Editor and navigate to /sitecore/Templates/Sitecore8Dev/MVC Page. Add a new field called Credit Card, then click on the dropdown in the Type column. Under Simple Types, you should see your Credit Card type (see Figure 3-7). Select that type and click Save.

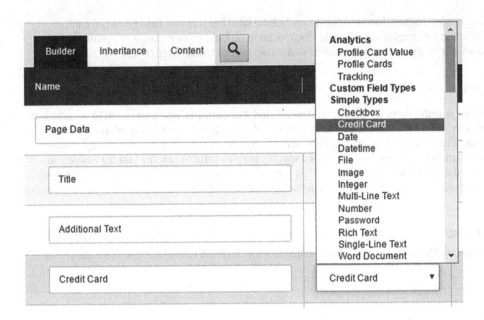

Figure 3-7. *Our custom Credit Card field type will show up next to the other out-of-the-box field types*

Now, navigate to /sitecore/Content/Home/MyPage. In the Page Data section, you should now see your new Credit Card field. Finally, type in a valid number in the specified format, such as 1111-1111-1111-1111 and click on the Validate button (see Figure 3-8). If it's valid, you should see the Valid message below the field.

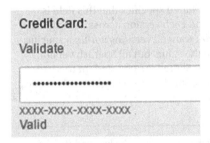

Figure 3-8. *Our custom field type in action!*

That was pretty painless, right? There are *many* very helpful (and free) custom field types you can download and install. Some examples are a Google Maps location picker, a color picker, and a multiple image selector. See the following blog post that summarizes all the cool stuff out there: `http://bit.ly/1DxntPv`.

Field Sources

Field sources help you specify where content should be located. For example, when you want to associate an image to a news article, you'd expect to be able to browse for images. However, what if you have hundreds or thousands of images? The source on a field helps you set a destination from where to select images (really any content, image as an example). Perhaps there is a specific folder within the Media Library where you want all images related to news articles to be stored. By putting that folder's path into the source field, you are limiting marketers to select just that folder's items and its descendants.

■ **Note** The field source format can vary. Sometimes a GUID is needed, sometimes an item path. Most of the times, a developer sets up the fields and you'll want to confirm the technical requirements/limitations of their configuration.

Field Versioning

An item in Sitecore can have multiple versions. These versions might be for languages, or perhaps you're running tests on your content with A/B or multivariate testing and want to test a few options before making a final decision. With some fields, you may want all versions sharing the same data. Other fields you might want each version to specify its own value. Language translation would be a good example of that, where each field shown to users must be translated. However, other fields used to control logic, such as numeric values or images, you might want shared.

There are two checkboxes on each field: Unversioned and Shared. Shared specifies that this field is likely numeric or an image, or possibly an internal field used for rules and each version across all languages should share the value when checked. You check unversioned when you want all versions *within* a specific language to share a value. In this case, all English versions would share the value, but all Spanish versions would have a different value. The default is that neither Unversioned nor Shared are checked. In this case, all values across all versions across all languages will have unique values. Say that five times! For all practical purposes, however, unversioned is rarely used.

■ **Note** You can check both Shared and Unversioned; the two are actually mutually exclusive, and the default would be Shared in this scenario. Using Unversioned or Shared also means that the field is not subject to workflow, an important consideration.

Field Validation

You can add field validators to enforce data integrity in your solution. For example, you may want to require all images to have an `alt` tag set to get the most out of your search engine optimization. It is simple to add the Image Has Alt Text field validator to each of your image fields. There are a few dozen validators such as this one that come out-of-the-box. You can also build custom validators for unique scenarios.

To add validators to a field, expand the data template's field section in the treeview that contains the field you want to modify. Select the field within the treeview. With the field selected you will notice a Validation Rules section below the Quick Info and Data sections. The Validation Rules section has four fields you can configure.

- *Quick Action Bar*: Used to add the Red/Yellow notifications in the gutter within the treeview (see Figure 3-9). These can help you spot validation errors even when you are not actively editing an item.

- *Validate button*: Used to add the validation feedback in the validation results popup when the Validation button is manually clicked in the ribbon (Review tab, Proofing section, Validation button).

- *Validation bar*: When on an item, you will notice little red icons to the right of the item showing how many fields are failing validation (see Figure 3-9, showing four fields failing validation).

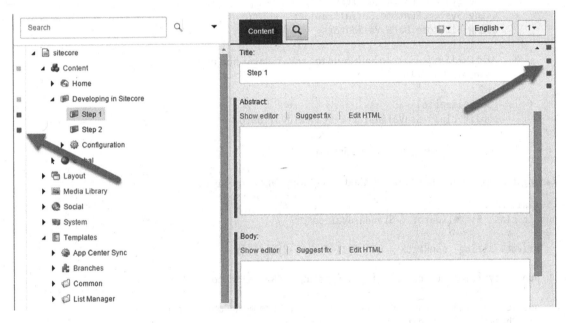

Figure 3-9. *Validators can help you enforce data integrity. There are several places where you are notified when an items fails its validation: In the gutter (left), in the validation bar (right), and in the validation popup when you try to save*

- *Workflow:* This section can be used to enforce validation rules before a workflow is allowed to progress from one state to another.

It is simple enough to add the validations in these sections. Simply find the validator you want to enforce and double-click it to move it to the right. Save the field item and the validator is now in effect for all item instances created from this template.

Custom Field Validators

Here again (just like field types), you may not see the validator you need in the list of out-of-the-box validators. Validating data before it's saved is super important. You don't want your Content Editors to save bad data, such as data you know will cause exceptions in your components. Building a custom validator may be necessary depending on what you're trying to do. Fortunately, it's rather easy!

Use the following steps to build a custom field validator to validate that the data entered matches the format of a social security number (not saying you should put social security numbers in Sitecore; it just serves as an easy-to-understand example!):

1. In the SitecoreDev.Web project in Visual Studio, add a new folder in the Custom folder called Validators. Right-click on this new folder and select Add ➤ Class. Name this class SsnValidator.

2. In this new class, add the following using statements:

   ```
   using System.Text.RegularExpressions;
   using System.Runtime.Serialization;
   using Sitecore.Data.Validators;
   ```

3. Add the [Serializable] attribute to SsnValidator and make it inherit from StandardValidator.

   ```
   [Serializable]
   public class SsnValidator : StandardValidator
   ```

4. Next, type Listing 3-3 into the SsnValidator class.

Listing 3-3. A Custom Class Can Be Called for Custom Validation Needs

```
[Serializable]
public class SsnValidator : StandardValidator
{
    private string _ssnRegEx = @"^\d{3}-?\d{2}-?\d{4}$";

    public override string Name { get { return "SSN Validator"; } }

    public SsnValidator(SerializationInfo info, StreamingContext context)
        : base(info, context)
    {
    }

    public SsnValidator()
    {
    }

    protected override ValidatorResult Evaluate()
    {
        string value = base.GetControlValidationValue();

        if (!string.IsNullOrEmpty(value) && Regex.IsMatch(value, _ssnRegEx))
            return ValidatorResult.Valid;
```

```
    base.Text = "SSN is not valid";

    return base.GetFailedResult(ValidatorResult.Error);
  }

protected override ValidatorResult GetMaxValidatorResult()
{
    return base.GetFailedResult(ValidatorResult.Error);
  }
}
```

The key point to make about Listing 3-3 is the Evaluate method. This method is called when an item is saved to ensure the data for the item meets validation expectations. In our case, we get the data value as a result of the GetControlValidationValue method call. We then take that value and match it against our SSN regular expression and return true or false, depending on the result.

5. Save this file and publish your web project. Once the publish is complete, open your browser and navigate to http://sitecore8/sitecore.

6. In the Content Editor, navigate to /sitecore/system/Settings/Validation Rules/Field Rules.

7. Right-click on the Field Rules folder and create a new folder (using the /templates/common/folder template) called Sitecore8Dev.

8. Right-click on this new Sitecore8Dev folder and select Insert ➤ Insert from template. Using the /templates/system/validation/validate rule template, name this item Social Security Number Rule and then click Insert (see Figure 3-10).

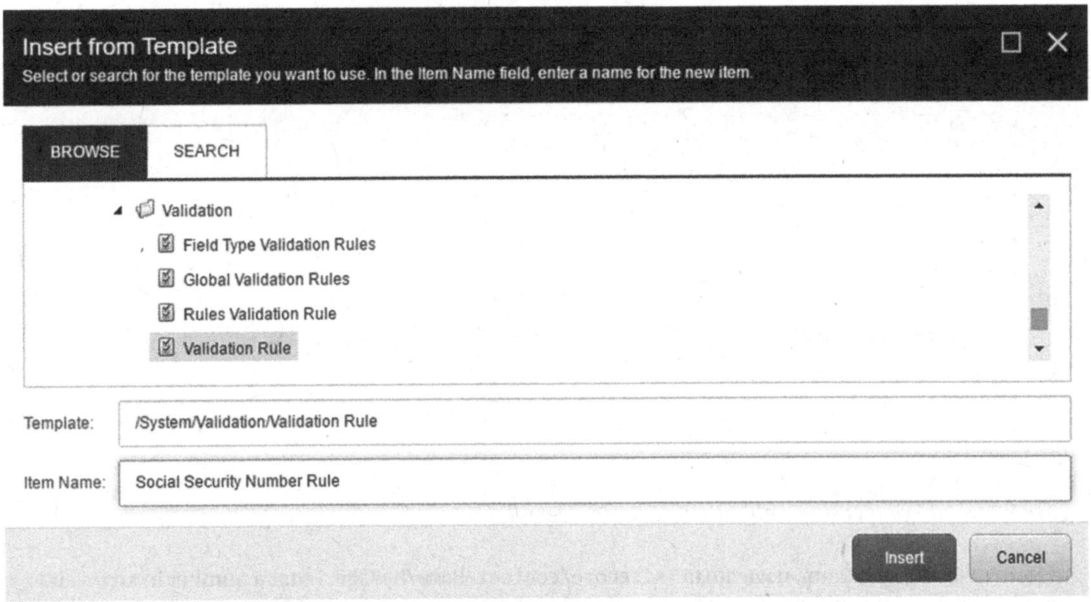

Figure 3-10. Create a new validation rule in the core database to be used in your templates.

9. On the Content tab, fill in the following values and then click Save:

   Title: Social Security Number Rule

   Description: The Social Security Number should match the format xxx-xx-xxxx

   Type: `SitecoreDev.Web.Custom.Validators.SsnValidator,SitecoreDev.Web`

10. Now that we've successfully created our new validation rule, let's add it to a field. Navigate to `/sitecore/Templates/Sitecore8Dev/MVC Page`.

11. Add a new field called `Social Security Number` and select Single-Line Text as the field type and then click Save.

12. Next, expand MVC Page ➤ Page Data. Select Social Security Number.

13. In the Validation Rules section, add the new `Field Rules\Sitecore8Dev\Social Security Number Rule` to the Quick Action Bar (see Figure 3-11), the Validate Button, the Validator Bar, and the Workflow fields. Then click Save.

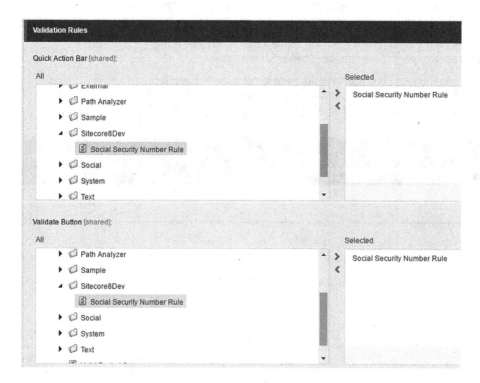

Figure 3-11. *Add your custom validator to your data templates*

Now, to test the validator, navigate to `/sitecore/content/Home/MyPage`. Enter a number in an invalid format and click Save. You'll see that the field now fails validation (see Figure 3-12)!

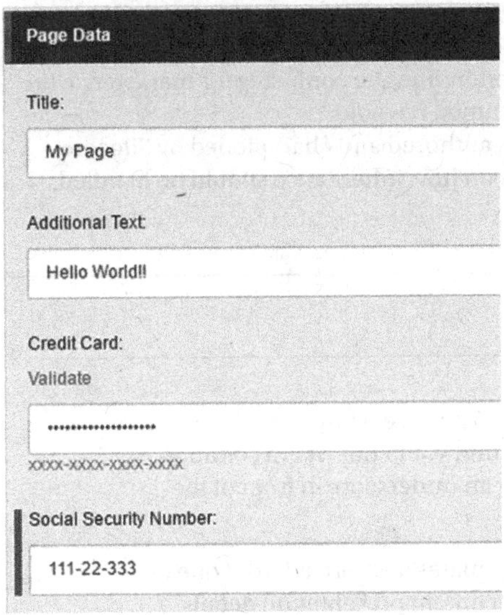

Page Data

Title:

My Page

Additional Text:

Hello World!!

Credit Card:

Validate

••••••••••••••••••

XXXX-XXXX-XXXX-XXXX

Social Security Number:

111-22-333

Figure 3-12. A custom validator will automatically check for data validation before the data can be saved

Data Template Inheritance

Data template inheritance is a great way to create a hierarchy of information and maximize reusability of templates. The unfortunate and common alternative is to have a proliferation of data templates—a data template for every page and every component—and as a result, no inheritance and no reusability. You are left with a mess.

It is a best practice to break your experience's information architectures down into reusable pieces and extend from there. This is similar to a developer trying to remove duplicate code; template inheritance is what enables this reusability, and in turn, significant cost savings for development time and maintainability as well.

■ **Tip** Make your inheritance broad, not deep. Breadth tends to beget reusability, whereas depth tends to beget hierarchy and rigidity. Three to four layers of hierarchy is about all you should allow yourself or you risk losing the benefits of reusable templates and components.

There are, however, some gotchas to consider. For example, you might have a base template that has a Title field, and then unknowingly you create a Title field in one of the child templates. In this case when the marketer goes to edit that content, they see two separate title fields and are left unsure which one to use. Developers, likewise, are confused as to how to programmatically retrieve what seems like duplicate data, when in reality the marketer could enter two separate values.

A data template can inherit more than one item. In this case, the combined fields from all the inherited templates will be consolidated in the Content Editor. Template inheritance can also be circular. For example, Template A can inherit from Templates B and C. Template C can inherit from Template A, too. In this case, again, all the fields are consolidated rather than showing duplicates. Circular templates wouldn't be a best practice for obvious reasons, but since it's possible, it's good to be aware.

It is also important to note that data templates can only inherit one set of presentation details. If a template inherits from two templates, and both have presentation details, only the first template's presentation details in the inheritance list will be used. This can oftentimes be confusing for marketers who are unsure as to why their content isn't displaying as they had assumed it would.

Helix, a set of Sitecore architecture principles and guidelines authored and championed by Sitecore architects, outlines five types of templates and recommendations on how inheritance should be handled. The five types are:

■ **Note** We'll be discussing Helix more in Chapters 4 and 5.

- *Interface templates*: These templates correspond to an interface within C#; a template used to map data in Sitecore into objects within your code. It is a common practice to denote Interface templates by prepending an underscore in front of the template name, e.g., _LinkMenuItem.

- *Page type templates*: A page within your site; these templates are derived from one or more interface templates for its data, but in addition, contain presentation details, such as a layout, for rendering purposes. These templates should never have any fields directly on the template nor be referenced by code; they are only for building pages.

- *Datasource templates*: These templates are referenced by components as their data source; they derive from interface templates but contain neither presentation details nor fields. Additionally, they are never referenced from code.

- *Settings templates*: These templates contain data used for site settings, business rules, dictionaries, and so forth.

- *Folder templates*: These templates are used for folders; mainly they enable reuse of a folder's set of insert options to maintain which items can be created in the folder.

■ **Note** The architecture does not have the concept of a single common base template across all templates, which is a practice that is commonly discouraged as it will often lead to bloated items with unnecessary fields. You can learn more about these template best practices at http://helix.sitecore.net/principles/templates/inheritance.html.

Figure 3-13 shows what this inheritance might look like, with data source templates and page type templates inheriting from interface templates, while leaving settings and folder templates off on their own. Check out the Helix documentation for more information on template best practices: http://helix.sitecore.net/principles/templates/index.html.

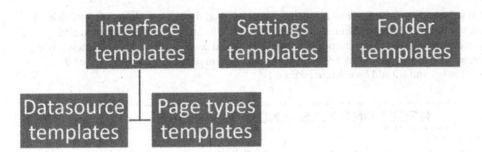

Figure 3-13. *Structure your data templates in five categories: interface templates, datasource templates, page templates, settings templates, and folder templates*

BRANCH TEMPLATES AND COMMAND TEMPLATES

Data templates are great, but what if I want one new item action in the Content Editor to create more than one item? This is accomplished with *branch templates*. Branch templates are handy, especially for large, complex page templates with many child dependencies. For example, one page item may have many items below it upon which the page's components are dependent. Without branch templates, you need to create the page, drop each component on the page, and create all the dependent items for each component. Creating one page can really slow down your content author and could lead to mistakes. As you can imagine, branch templates are very important for developers to understand. Branch templates are rather simple to configure. Basically, you create a branch template definition item that specifies which items ought to be created when an item is created off a branch.

Command templates take branch templates one step further. Instead of a definition item that has a predefined structure, a command template invokes code to tell Sitecore what to do when an item is created off the command template. Simply create a data template that extends the Command Template base data template. Then, specify the config ID of the class you want to run when an item is created using this command template.

Both branch templates and command templates have a number of steps you need to perform to create them and set them up. Check out the section later in this chapter called "Creating Data Templates" for a walkthrough.

Working with Standard Values

Standard values are an important concept in Sitecore. Some might argue that a better name for them would be "default values" because they are a way of assigning default values to items upon their creation. However, standard values do a lot more than that, so perhaps that's why they have a more generic definition.

Standard values can have the following types of defaults, among others:

- Default field values

- Insert options

- Presentation details

- Workflow

The rest of this section covers the first two types that can be applied to data templates. Presentation details is a much larger topic that will be covered in greater depth in Chapter 4, along with how to add presentation details onto standard values. Introducing that here would confuse you with all the new terms and nomenclature, so it's being saved for later. Workflows are covered in detail in *Practical Sitecore 8 Configuration and Strategy* and should be referenced there.

RESETTING TO STANDARD VALUES

There may be times when you want to revert an item's settings back to standard values of the template from which it was created. You can revert field values, presentation settings, and insert options back to the template's standard values. The following shows where in the ribbon you can find each of these buttons:

Field values: Versions tab ➤ Reset button in the Fields section

Presentation: Presentation tab ➤ Reset button in the Layout section

Insert options: Configure tab ➤ Rest button in the Insert Options section

After clicking these reset buttons, the content items values/settings will again reflect the standard values of their template.

Configuring Default Values

A new data template does not have the ability to assign standard values. You first need to add a standard values item onto the data template. One of the most confusing things about standard values is the data template item and the standard values item for that data template look identical. It is common to apply settings to the data template thinking you are applying standard values and you are not.

You can tell if you have a standard values item or not by looking below the data template. Notice in Figure 3-14 how the Product Promotion data template has a __Standard Values item below it. This child item is where you will assign your standard values.

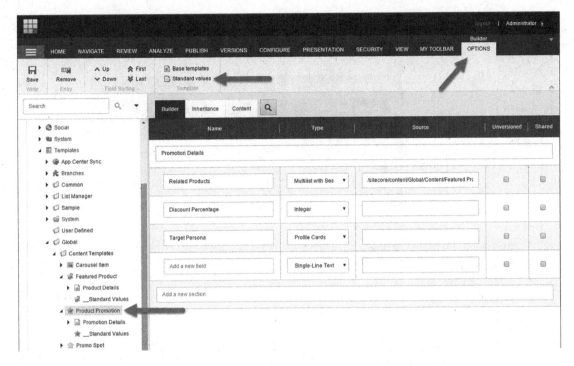

Figure 3-14. *You set up default values within a data template's __Standard Values item*

To create this standard values item, select the data template and then click the Builder Options tab. Click Standard Values below the Builder Options tab and you will notice the new standard values item appear.

A standard values item can be added to any of the five template types mentioned earlier; however, configuring Presentation Details should be reserved for Page Type Templates only. Additionally, Insert Options should never be set on Interface Templates.

You can start assigning default field values when you click the standard values item. Notice how Figure 3-15 shows the standard values item selected with the fields showing. You can set default values by entering data into those fields and thereafter saving the item. Then, when users create new items from that data template, those values will be present in the new item by default.

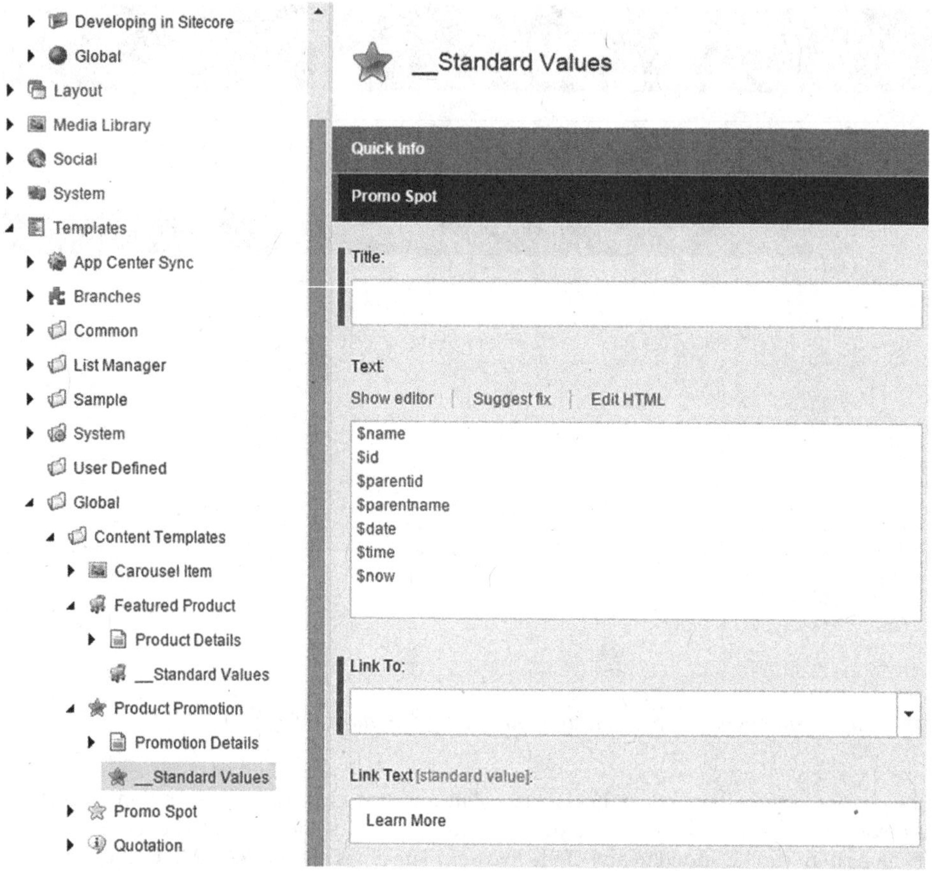

Figure 3-15. *Tokens allow your default field values to be somewhat dynamic, such as replacing $name with the name of the item*

■ **Note** Layout deltas are an important concept in template inheritance. When an item receives its values from its template's standard values, and those values are changed, the link back to the standard values is not broken. Rather, a "layout delta" is created to track just the delta from the standard values. If the standard values are updated later, all item field instances will be updated where there is no delta.

Notice also the $tokens in Figure 3-15. Tokens are replaced during item creation with dynamic values. For example, $name is replaced with the item name during creation. In Figure 3-16 you'll notice an item created with the name "Phil test" and the $name token was replaced as expected. The following are the supported tokens:

- $name: The name of the item
- $id: The ID of the item
- $parentid: The ID of the parent of the item
- $parentname: The name of the parent of the item

- $date: The system date (yyyyMMdd)
- $time: The system time (HHmmss)
- $now: The date and time (yyyyMMddTHHmmss)

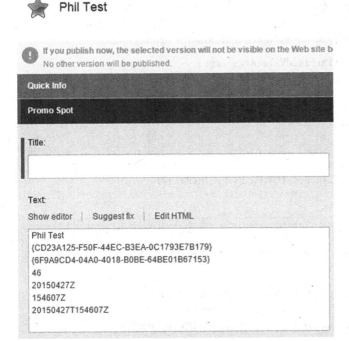

Phil Test

If you publish now, the selected version will not be visible on the Web site b
No other version will be published.

Quick Info

Promo Spot

Title:

Text:
Show editor | Suggest fix | Edit HTML

Phil Test
{CD23A125-F50F-44EC-B3EA-0C1793E7B179}
{6F9A9CD4-04A0-4018-B0BE-64BE01B67153}
46
20150427Z
154607Z
20150427T154607Z

Figure 3-16. Notice how each of the tokens was replaced with a dynamic value at creation time

CREATING CUSTOM STANDARD VALUE TOKENS

That's not a long list of out-of-the-box tokens! You may find yourself needing to create custom tokens from time to time. Perhaps you want to show the path to the parent item (think breadcrumbs). Use the following steps to create a custom token for this very purpose, as an example to follow for your unique needs:

1. In Visual Studio, in the SitecoreDev.Web project, create a folder called Tokens in our Custom folder.

2. Right-click on the new Tokens folder and select Add ➤ Class. Name this class ParentPathTokenProcessor.

3. Add the following using statement.

```
using Sitecore.Pipelines.ExpandInitialFieldValue;
```

4.   Make your new class inherit from ExpandInitialFieldValueProcessor.

```
public class ParentPathTokenProcessor : ExpandInitialFieldValueProcessor
```

5.   Next, override the Process method from ExpandInitialFieldValueProcessor and type what's shown in Listing 3-4.

Listing 3-4. Our Process Method Checks the Data for the Token and Does the Replacement

```
public override void Process(ExpandInitialFieldValueArgs args)
{
    var token = args.SourceField.Value;
    if (!String.IsNullOrEmpty(token) && token.Contains("$parentPath"))
    {
        if (args.TargetItem != null)
        {
            args.Result = args.Result.
                Replace("$parentPath", args.TargetItem.Paths.ParentPath);
        }
    }
}
```

Save and close this file. Now that we have our new token processor, we need to patch it into the config.

6.   In the App_Config\Include folder of the Web project, right-click on the SitecoreDev folder and select Add ➤ Web Configuration File. Name this file SitecoreDev.TokenReplacements.config. In this new config file, replace the contents with Listing 3-5.

Listing 3-5. Register Your Token Replacer in TokenReplacements.config

```xml
<?xml version="1.0"?>
<configuration xmlns:patch="http://www.sitecore.net/xmlconfig/">
    <sitecore>
        <pipelines>
            <expandInitialFieldValue>
                <processor type="SitecoreDev.Web.Custom.Tokens.ParentPathTokenProcessor,
SitecoreDev.Web" patch:after="processor[@type='type=Sitecore.Pipelines.
ExpandInitialFieldValue.ReplaceVariables, Sitecore.Kernel']"/>
            </expandInitialFieldValue>
        </pipelines>
    </sitecore>
</configuration>
```

Save and close this file. Finally, publish your web project. Once the publish is complete, you'll be able to use $parent*Path* as a new token replacement in __Standard Values!

Configuring Insert Options

Only administrators can add content or folders in the content tree, unless you specify insert options that allow non-admins the ability to create content specifically permitted within that folder. The Insert from Template option allows an admin to select from all data templates that exist, but that option is only available to admins. It is important, then, to specify insert options, since marketers can't create content if you don't. Additionally, you want to control what content goes where. Insert options become your way to enforce an information architecture and prevent the "wild, wild, west" where users are adding content in places they shouldn't or simply wouldn't make sense.

■ **Tip**   The rules engine is another way to set insert options, an advanced approach to control what's available to content authors.

It is very simple to set up Insert options on a data template's standard values. Simply click the __Standard Values item below the data template and click the Configure tab, then the Assign button in the Insert Options section. You can then use the selector to select which data templates should appear as insert options when users are creating new items.

When it's complete, the insert fly-out should look something like Figure 3-17 (note again that only admins will see the Insert from Template option).

Figure 3-17. *Insert options allow you to control your information architecture by limiting which types of items can be created where*

Templates and Configurations

Over the course of the next few chapters, now that we have the core terms and definitions under our belt, we'll be creating a series of data templates, branch templates, command templates, etc… for our example site. Let's get started with branch templates!

Creating Our Branch Templates

If you recall from earlier, branch templates help us create Sitecore items faster because most of the time, a given item or page will have many dependent child items that need to be in place for that page or item to function properly. One option is to create each dependency manually. That is prone to human error and takes a lot of time. With branch templates, you can specify a predefined hierarchy of dependencies that are created each time an item is created from the template. We'll create a branch template that will automatically add the Components folder below the page so we don't have to configure it manually like we did in Chapter 2.

> ■ **Note** Command templates are similar to branch templates, except that instead of a predefined hierarchy, we'll use code to create the dependencies. This is helpful for advanced settings where configurations won't suffice. Command templates are fairly advanced and are beyond the scope of this book.

Use the following steps to create this branch template:

Like we've done many other places already, let's start by creating a branch folder called `Sitecore8Dev` under `/sitecore/Templates/Branches`.

1. Right-click on Branches and select Insert ➤ Branch Folder. Name this folder `Sitecore8Dev`.

2. Right-click on the newly created `Sitecore8Dev` branch folder and select Insert ➤ New Branch. This will open the Create a New Branch dialog.

This is asking for the type of template from which you'd like to create a branch. In our case, we need to create a branch template for our MVC Page template.

3. Expand `Sitecore8Dev` and select MVC Page and then click Create.

Looking at the result of our new branch template, you can see the branch template item is called MVC Page, after the name of the template selected. You can also rename this branch template to be more descriptive. We will do that in a moment. But notice the item underneath MVC Page. Everything underneath MVC Page is the structure of what will be created when this particular branch template is used. Not only can you create an item/folder structure underneath the item, but you can also configure the presentation details of the root item, configure security, set insert options, etc. For now, we're just going to create one sub-item under $name and rename the branch template.

4. First, let's create a sub-item under $name. Right-click $name and select Insert ➤ Insert from template. In the Insert from Template dialog, select `/Sitecore8Dev/Folder Templates/Components`. Name this item `Components` and click Insert.

Finally, let's rename the MVC Page branch template to `Basic Empty Page`. Because we could conceivably have many variations of the MVC Page within our site, you should give them more appropriate names to help content authors.

5. Right-click on MVC Page and select Rename. Rename the item to `Basic Empty Page` and click OK. When you're done, it should look something like Figure 3-18.

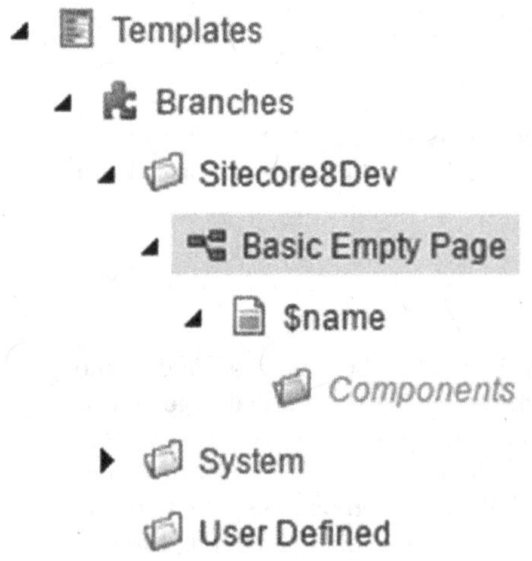

◢ ▤ Templates

   ◢ 🔩 Branches

      ◢ 🗀 Sitecore8Dev

         ◢ 🔩 Basic Empty Page

            ◢ 🗎 $name

               🗀 *Components*

      ▶ 🗀 System

      🗀 User Defined

Figure 3-18. Our branch template will create a Components folder below the new item

Now, anytime a user creates an item in the Content node from the Basic Empty Page branch template, a page will get created with a Components folder directly beneath it. This will help drive consistency.

Content Management Fundamentals

With your data templates established, you can finally begin entering some content! As you would expect, content is managed from the Content node within the Content Editor treeview. More commonly, marketers tend to favor editing content in the Experience Editor, because they see visually how the content will look real-time while editing the content. You got a sneak peak at the Experience Editor in Chapter 2. *Practical Sitecore 8 Configuration and Strategy* goes much deeper into content editing fundamentals, such as working with components in the Experience Editor, custom approval workflows, and many other important topics. However, in the following sections you'll find some of the key points to get you started.

Where Do You Manage Content?

You saw a bit of what it takes to manage content in Chapter 2, but there's lots more to learn. Without going into too much detail and repeating myself, suffice to say there's two main places you can go to administer content in Sitecore—the Content Editor and the Experience Editor. The Content Editor tends to be favored by highly-technical users, such as developers, because everything is in one place (data templates, content, layouts, etc.). The Experience Editor on the other hand is much easier to grasp by non-technical users, such as marketers, and is heavily favored by that audience. As a result, a developer needs to ensure both options are optimized and available for use. More on this in Chapter 11 when we get into front-end developer techniques and specifically how to develop for the Experience Editor.

By way of a more formal introduction, the Experience Editor within Sitecore allows users to administer content within a WYSIWYG editor (what-you-see-is-what-you-get). This can be very helpful, because in the content tree you are often left guessing what it will look like when you click Publish (or better yet Preview), leaving you to click Preview dozens of times before getting it right. With the Experience Editor you can see those changes immediately. See the Figure 3-19 for an example. In this case, the user is updating the hero image header text to "I know exactly where this will go" by simply selecting the text and typing the new message.

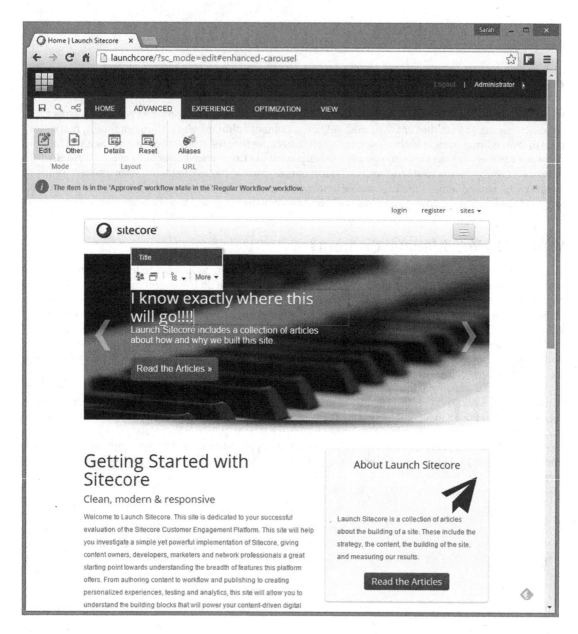

Figure 3-19. *To update the content on a page, users simply select the content placeholder that they want to update and start typing! Very easy*

Architecting Your Content Tree

There are three schools of thought on how to organize content stored the Content node within the Content Editor. The first, and probably the most common, is to store content with the page to which it's associated. For example, consider the following hierarchy:

- Site Definition
  - Home
    - Page A
      - Content folder
        - Single-use content item A
        - Single-use content item B
    - Page B
      - Content folder
        - Single-use content item A
        - Single-use content item B
    - Page C
  - Shared Site Content
    - Content group A (e.g. "Calls to Action")
    - Content group B (e.g. "Header and footer content")
- Global Content
  - Content
    - Multi-use content item A (e.g. "Button Text Options")
    - Multi-use content item B (e.g. "Alignment Options")
  - Global Site Options
    - Settings item A (e.g. "Theme Options")

The benefit of this approach is that all the content is stored together with its associated page. You know to look below the page for that page's content. If you delete the page you know that all the content with that page was also deleted; you don't need to go find orphaned content elsewhere to clean up. Similarly, security permissions for items below the page can inherit from the page making security easy. Otherwise you need to set security in multiple places. Additionally, components on the page benefit from having individual content items below the page; they can swap in and out different content for personalization purposes. If all the content fields were on the page itself this would not be possible. The disadvantages of this approach is a perceived "cluttered" hierarchy, and that you will have items below the Home node that are URL navigable (resulting in an error message if a user were to ever reach that path).

> ■ **Note**   While the next two options exist and are espoused by many reputable Sitecore MVPs and others in the community, we (Phil and Jason) tend to use option one most often.

An alternative approach is to move *all* content out of the Home node and centralize it within a Site Content folder. See the following hierarchy as an example:

- Site Definition
  - Home
    - Page A
    - Page B
      - Page C
  - Content
    - Content Type 1
    - Content Type 2
    - Content Type 3
  - Settings
    - Settings item A (e.g., Theme Options)

You can see the main benefit of this approach is that all items below the Site node (e.g., Home) are just page items. It keeps that aspect simple; everything that is URL navigable is expected to be navigable. Additionally, this approach advocates no page specific content; all content could be shared across multiple pages. However, now all the components on those pages must reference items stored elsewhere in the hierarchy. For non-technical folk this requires extra training to ensure it doesn't spin out of control. Security as well needs to be managed in multiple places and for complex requirements could get untenable. You also run the risk of orphaned items; when a page is deleted it is not intuitive to know what else might need to be deleted.

A third option, and the option that is unfortunately probably the most common, is to store all the data for a page on the page itself. In this case, the hierarchy is much simpler:

- Site Definition
  - Home
    - Page A
    - Page B
      - Page C

In the "Data Template Inheritance" section earlier in this chapter, this example was demonstrated by having a News Article page template contain all the fields necessary to render an article. The challenge with this approach is with content personalization. If you have a component on that page that needs to swap in/out content, you would want to have multiple content items from which to select. If the content is on the page itself, you only have one item. Now, for a News Article this likely isn't a big deal, since all users would probably see the same content. However, a Related News component on that page might need to be personalized. In that case you might start using mixed methods for storing content. The data is on the page for the article, but now you have child items for other page dependencies. We advocate going with the first approach all the time to remain consistent; every page should be built the same way.

Managing Rich Media

You will want to store all your rich media in the Media Library node within the treeview. The Media Library is your one stop show for all your digital assets, including images, documents, videos, and audio recordings. You will want to organize your items within folders named appropriately. After you create a folder, when you click on that folder you will see three options: Upload Files, Upload Files (Advanced), and New (Sub) Folder. You can upload one or many files by simply clicking the Upload Files button and selecting the files you want to upload.

SHOULD YOU STORE MEDIA IN THE DATABASE, FILE SYSTEM, OR A CDN?

By default, all media is stored in the SQL database. An alternative to storing your media as BLOBs in the SQL database is to store them on a network path with SQL simply serving as a pointer, similar in concept to remote BLOB storage.

Storing media in the database offers unique advantages and disadvantages. Some of the advantages to this approach are a simplified architecture (less steps to worry about during a disaster recovery), content publishing (no need to ensure files are copied to proper locations outside of Sitecore), and respect for publishing restrictions. The biggest disadvantage is the potential for very large databases that might make recoverability times longer during an outage if you needed to restore from a full backup.

Performance, in some cases, might benefit from getting the files out of the database. Specifically, large, infrequently used files such as videos, would benefit from being served from the file share. The ASP. NET BLOB cache can be used on your web front-end servers to cache large, frequently accessed files, thus mitigating performance concerns in those cases. However, if you have thousands of videos being accessed a lot, but each individually infrequently, that initial deserialization out of SQL can be a doozie. In these limited scenarios you have a strong case to move your media files out of SQL. A CDN is the best choice if performance is a concern. Offloading all assets to a separate provider can have a significant positive impact on your infrastructure. However, using a CDN can be more expensive, depending on many factors.

For 99% of the cases, leaving the media files in the database is the best practice. Fortunately, files can, on a case-by-case basis, be put in the database or the file share. This can be helpful for the edge cases; however, users will need a lot of training to understand when to select the Upload as Files checkbox. Or, you can force it one way or another.

Consider the following `web.config` settings to tweak this behavior:

`Media.DisableFileMedia`: By default, Sitecore permits the user to specify at upload time where the file should be placed, in the database or in the file share. This setting by default is false, thus permitting file share uploads. You can disable file share uploads by setting this to true, forcing all files into the database.

`Media.UploadAsFile`: By default, media files are uploaded into the database. This setting changes the default behavior to upload to the file system (The Upload as Files setting checked in Advanced Upload dialog). This setting is ignored if `DisableFileMedia` is set to true.

`Media.FileFolder`: Here you can specify the UNC of the path to which files will be uploaded.

Content Personalization

With content personalization, you can ensure that all your content on your site is timely and relevant for each individual user. Sitecore has two main ways it accommodates content personalization: rules-based personalization and behavioral/profile(persona)-based personalization.

With rules-based personalization, you can set rules (see Figure 3-20) on a component that controls that component's data source. For example, a user in Canada might need to see a different promotion than a user in the United States. Entire components can be swapped out for totally different components, as well. For example, we may have static promotion pieces for customers in the United States and Canada, where a simple data source swap is sufficient, but for our Latin America customers we have a video we want to show instead. In this case, you could set up a third rule to swap out the generic promotion all together for a video component. The bottom line is these rules-based personalization settings follow a conventional "if-then-else" paradigm familiar to developers.

Behavioral-based personalization is a bit more nuanced. Basically, Sitecore tracks every interaction a user takes on the site across all their sessions. Content can be tagged with Profile Cards that designate the type of user generally interested in that content. Over time, a user gets matched to pattern cards (more commonly called "personas" in the marketing world). You can then start personalizing content based on the pattern against which the user was matched. For example, you might have a persona called "Lenny" who is mostly interested in learning about your products, whereas a persona called "Ned" who is more interested in news and updates about your company. Your home page might look different for Lenny than it does for Ned in this case. There is a personalization rule, much like the case of United States/Canada discussed earlier, where you can specify the personalized content to be shown, based on the pattern card matched (as shown in Figure 3-20).

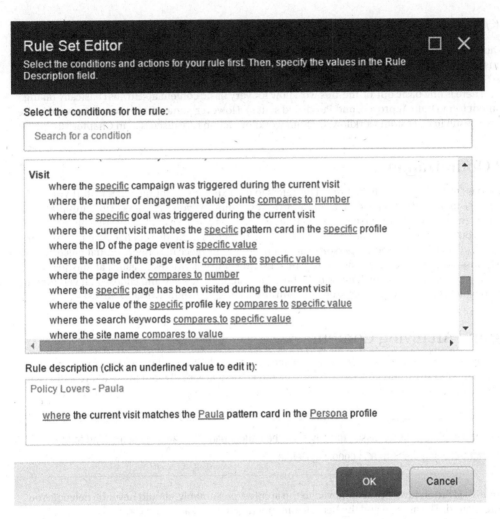

Figure 3-20. *The personalization rules editor lets you quickly apply rules to your content to change how it behaves based on your users' needs*

Content Versioning

Anytime you make a change to a piece of content, that change is tracked as a historical version. This is great for historical purposes, obviously, but it also has some other benefits. Versions can be helpful for testing (see which version of a page performs better). Also, versions can be used for publishing. Maybe your home page has a unique promotion going out for a Black Friday special. You might create a new version of the home page and set it to be the published version within a specific date range. That way, as 12:00am, your home page is updated without needing human intervention.

Content Approval and Publishing Workflows

Who gets to author X content? Who can approve X content? Who can publish X content? What notifications or integrations with external systems need to occur at any of these stages in a piece of content's lifecycle? Workflows in Sitecore are where you can configure all your business rules such as these around content management. There is one basic out-of-the-box workflow for very basic content approvals (basically taking a piece of content from Draft, Approved, and Published states). However, some of your content may be more or less sensitive, justifying a custom workflow. Custom workflow actions are discussed in Chapter 10.

Content Optimization

Sitecore's motto is "test everything all the time". This refers to the Experience Optimization features of Sitecore, otherwise more typically called "A/B" or multivariate testing. As you can guess, with multiple versions of pages each with unique personalization rules it can be easy to lose confidence that all the fiddling around you've been doing to your home page is actually helping. Did this change help my users or hurt their experience? Does the "Lenny" persona care more about this piece of content, or that piece? With Experience Optimization in Sitecore you don't have to guess. Sitecore will run tests against all the possible variations of the page and tell you which test did the best. You can then, if you want, choose that variation to be the new published version. Simply click Approve with Test in the publishing workflow to test your change!

Deleting and Archiving Content

When you delete a piece of content in Sitecore it's not actually deleted. This is why your Sitecore environment can tend to grow, and grow, and grow. Deleted content is actually sent to the Recycle Bin. This is similar to the Recycle Bin in a Windows PC. Stuff will accumulate there indefinitely until you clear it.

■ **Note**   The Recycle Bin can be accessed directly from the Launchpad. You can send something to the Recycle Bin by right-clicking the item and choosing Delete.

An alternative is the archive. Content moved to the archive, presumably, should never be deleted. You want it to hang around. The archive and the Recycle Bin function in the exact same way and differ by name only. But, a name is important and has different connotations.

Sitecore might not be the best place for an archive. Perhaps you have an enterprise archive you want to use for expired content, but you want the out-of-the-box Sitecore archive to route information to the enterprise archive automatically. A custom Sitecore pipeline is a great way to accomplish this (pipelines will be used throughout the steps in Chapters 4 and 5)!

■ **Note**   The Archive can be accessed from the Start menu (Launchpad ➤ Desktop ➤ Start menu icon in the lower left) ➤ All Applications ➤ Archive. You can send something to the Archive by clicking the item, and then in the Review ribbon tab, under the Schedule section, click the Archive drop-down and choose one of the Archive options.

Content Cloning

Content cloning is a handy tip every Sitecore developer should understand. Let's say you have two pieces of content that need to share most of their data, but differ in just one field, for example. One option is to create a copy of that item (by right-clicking and choosing Duplicate) and change that one field. However, now you're managing a lot of duplicate data for the fields that are not different. Developer instinct tells us this is bad, and it is! Fortunately, you can also clone items. A *clone* is superior to a *duplicate* because the clone refers back to the original for all field data that hasn't changed. If the clone source item's field updates, all the clones themselves will update as well where the data is still set to the original. Only the delta is changed.

■ **Note**   You can clone an item by clicking it and, from the Home tab in the ribbon, clicking the Duplicate drop-down and then clicking Clone.

Multilingual Content Translations

In a global world, you're most likely going to need your site to support multiple languages. Fortunately, Sitecore does an amazing job at multilingual and translations. Basically, you can configure languages you need your site to support. Each content item can have one or more of those languages added to it, and Sitecore will give you a nice side-by-side comparison (see Figure 3-21) for your translators to do the translation. That language version is saved and published like any other page version.

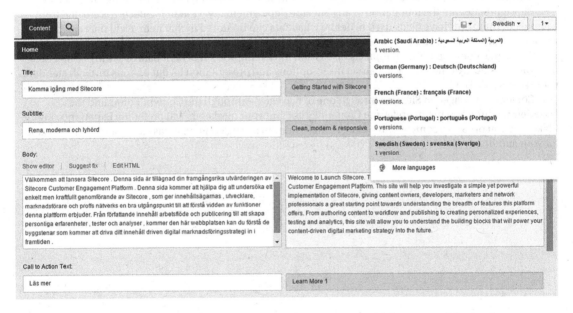

Figure 3-21. *Translation is made easy with a side-by-side comparison of the source and destination languages*

■ **Tip**   It's also worth checking out external translation vendors such as Clay Tablet or Translations.com if you want to route content for external translation. Their Sitecore connectors make for the easiest content translation imaginable. See more at `http://www.clay-tablet.com/products/cms-connectors/sitecore`.

A user can browse to that translation of that page in one of two ways: by putting `?sc_lang=sv-se` in the URL (in the case of Swedish), or by using a more typical convention of `http://www.site.com/sv-se`. The latter method is preferred for SEO purposes.

■ **Tip**   A good thing for your developers to consider is what the language fallback strategy should be. A developer can configure Sitecore to fall back to the default language if not all fields are translated (called a "partial language fallback"). Without this in place, you'll notice portions of your page are blank. By default, if the content hasn't been translated for that language, it won't show up.

Summary

Well, there you have it! We've put down some of the most foundational themes a Sitecore developer should know: data templates, standard values, and managing content. From here, you can start building on Chapter 2's development practices, because we now know how to structure items and templates within Sitecore.

Data templates are the foundation of any Sitecore deployment. Every item in Sitecore is created from a template. Templates have fields used to define what data can be stored in that item. Field data can be versioned and validated, and can store different types of data.

Standard values extend the templates discussion by helping you set default data or settings when new items are created. Additionally, you can set insert options and presentation layout options through standard value settings as well.

Content is managed in Sitecore through one of two ways—through the Content Editor and the Experience Editor. You might prefer the Content Editor, but your marketers will prefer the Experience Editor. Make sure you optimize content entry there to make administering content as easy and painless as possible for your authors.

CHAPTER 4

■ ■ ■

Back-End Dev Architectures

Up to this point you've written some code in Chapter 2 and a bit in Chapter 3, but you might not fully understand how the code works. In Chapter 2 we wanted to get a Sitecore component built as quickly as possible without over-complicating the steps or the explanation, but now in Chapter 4, it's time to take a peek under the hood, you could say, and explain the various patterns and foundational architectures upon which Sitecore is built.

This chapter is really a segue before diving deep into the patterns and best practices you'll find in Chapters 5 and 6. But before you skip ahead, there are really three things you need to level set on in this chapter. You need to:

- Understand MVC in more detail than what you saw in Chapter 2

- Understand modular architecture

- Refactor your Chapter 2 solution into a modular architecture

With those things in mind, you'll be better situated to understand the more complex patterns presented in the subsequent chapters, and you'll also have the shell of a Visual Studio solution rife for implementation of those best practices. Without more delay, let's begin with a proper introduction to ASP.NET MVC, the foundation of all things Sitecore!

The Model-View-Controller Design Pattern

Model-View-Controller (MVC) is the most foundational design pattern every Sitecore developer needs to understand. It's critical to understand ASP.NET MVC (Microsoft's implementation of MVC) if you are to become a great Sitecore developer. ASP.NET MVC will likely be new to many developers. Even Sitecore developers may have never worked with pure ASP.NET MVC before. I'd wager the vast majority of Sitecore sites built before Sitecore 8 were built not with ASP.NET MVC, but rather ASP.NET Web Forms. For those in that precarious situation, you'll find rebuilding your site using ASP.NET MVC will bring tons of value in productivity, testability, and maintainability of your site.

■ **Note** MVC is so important that immediately after reading this book you should read Apress' *Pro ASP.NET MVC 5* book by Adam Freeman. *Pro ASP.NET MVC 5* should be considered required reading for anyone serious about Sitecore development. Additionally, ASP.NET MVC is Microsoft's implementation of MVC. You can use the MVC pattern in other languages too, such as Java and JavaScript.

© Phil Wicklund and Jason Wilkerson 2016

P. Wicklund and J. Wilkerson, *Professional Sitecore 8 Development*, DOI 10.1007/978-1-4842-2292-8_4

If you're a .NET developer and have never done ASP.NET MVC before, you're probably quite familiar and comfortable with ASP.NET Web Forms development. Web Forms development is quite different than MVC. Every request is a page, such as Home.aspx, ProductDetails.aspx, Checkout.aspx, and so forth. This can be challenging because you may end up with a lot of duplicate front-end code where pages need similar presentations. ASP.NET Web Forms introduced the concept of master pages (akin to MVC layouts) from which a page could inherit, as well as user controls. These help, but what if you need nested layouts? Additionally, ASP.NET Web Forms has the following pitfalls that MVC doesn't:

- *View State weight*: ASP.NET web forms pages can become very large, which can hurt the performance of the site. This happens because web forms pass data between the client and the server within View State, and it is passed with every request, whether necessary or not. In contrast, view state is not needed at all in MVC.

- *Page lifecycle*: The ASP.NET web forms page lifecycle is complex; understanding the order of execution between a control's Render method and its CreateChildControls method, and a myriad of others, is hard to remember, which makes state difficult to manage and pages prone to error. By contrast, there is no "page lifecycle," per se, in ASP.NET MVC.

- *False sense of separation of concerns*: The idea of a page's "code-behind" file seems to express a degree of separation of concern. However, the markup and code-behind are tightly coupled, and quite often the patterns stop at the code-behind, resulting in massive code-behind files that end up becoming nightmarish to maintain. In contrast, MVC accommodates extreme cases of separations of concern (see next section on modular architectures, for example).

- *Limited control over HTML*: ASP.NET Web Forms rely a lot on ID attributes in markup and other mechanics that are not suggested, according to modern web standards. In contrast, ASP.NET MVC applications have no limitations of your markup.

- *Low testability*: It's nearly impossible to unit test a page's PreRender method because a unit test is challenged to simulate the page lifecycle. ASP.NET Web Forms gets the opposite of the benefits of test-driven development: lower productivity, more challenging to maintain, more bugs, longer bug resolution times, etc. In contrast, the value of MVC, for its testability alone, is enough to prove its superiority.

ASP.NET MVC may feel new to you if you've never used it before, but actually, the MVC design pattern dates back to 1978 and the Smalltalk project at Xerox. The Microsoft's implementation of the MVC design pattern is composed of three core components:

- *Model*: The model defines the data schema being interacted upon; models are defined as C# classes.

- *View*: The view renders that data; the view contains the HTML/CSS markup for presentation purposes.

- *Controller*: A controller responds to a request from a browser, for example, and determines what model and what view is appropriate for that request.

Notice how, as shown in Figure 4-1, ASP.NET MVC responds to a request.

■ **Note**   For more in-depth discussion on how the Sitecore MVC pipeline differs from traditional ASP.NET MVC, take a look at the two-part video series by Martina Welander at http://bit.ly/2ci7MSt & http://bit.ly/2c9R6iE.

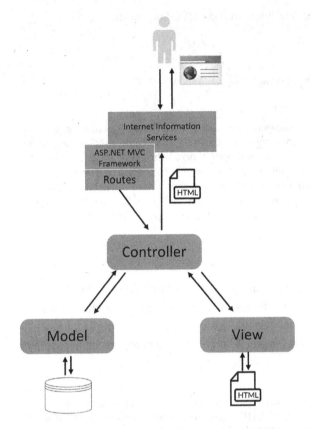

Figure 4-1. *ASP.NET MVC is composed of three main components: 1) the model which represents the data, 2) the view which knows how to display the data, and 3) the controller who knows what model and what view is needed given what the user is requesting*

You saw in Figure 4-1 how a request comes into the server (in our case, Sitecore) and how IIS takes the request and asks ASP.NET MVC how it should handle it. ASP.NET MVC takes that URL and compares it to a route table. Notice the following "out-of-the-box" URL route pattern:

`{controller}/{action}`

If you look at the following URL example, you begin to see pretty quickly how a route works:

`http://mysite.com/Products/HomeAndGarden`

In this example, `Products` would be the name of the controller class which is called by the ASP.NET MVC framework to handle the request. `HomeAndGarden` would be a controller action (a method in that class) which specifically will handle the request, by populating a model, loading that model into an appropriate view, and returning that view to the ASP.NET MVC framework to be returned to the browser. The code for this in the Route table would look similar to Listing 4-1.

Listing 4-1. Use the MapRoute Method to Register Your Route with the MVC Framework

```
Routes.MapRoute(
        name: "Default",
        url: "{controller}/{action}",
        defaults: new { controller = "Home", action="Index" }
        );
```

The default values help you specify what should happen if the user browses to the root of the site (http://mysite.com/) or the root of a controller (http://mysite.com/Products). In these cases, a default value has been provided for the controller, namely the Home controller. If no controller action method is specified, the Index action method should be used as a default. In the case of http://mysite.com/Products/ HomeAndGarden the HomeAndGarden controller action method will be used, rather than the default action.

Custom routes can be created as well by making changes to the RouteConfig.cs files in a traditional ASP.NET MVC project's App_Start folder. For example, maybe you wanted to support a URL that looks like this:

http://mysite.com/Product/123

■ **Note** Sitecore has overridden standard route registration procedures because Sitecore doesn't want you overriding their routes and potentially breaking things. Instead, you will register most of your routes during Sitecore's initialize pipeline. The code to register a custom route is the same as the route registration in a traditional ASP.NET MVC project. See Chapter 8 for an example of registering a route to be used by an AJAX request.

In this case, 123 isn't the name of the controller action (method) you want called, but rather the product ID you want pass to the controller's default action. In this case, you would register a route similar to {controller}/{id} in the RouteConfig.cs file, again using the MapRoute method, as can be seen in Listing 4-2.

Listing 4-2. This Route Sets Up a Default Controller and a Default Action Without Needing the Action To Be in the Route Itself

```
Routes.MapRoute(
        name: "Product",
        url: "Product/{id}",
        defaults: new { controller = "Product", action="GetProduct" }
        );
```

In this case we noted in the route that all requests to /Product will use the Product controller and the GetProduct controller action. That controller action method will have an id parameter and might look something like Listing 4-3.

Listing 4-3. The Product Controller Has a Method and a Name Which Match the Defaults in Listing 4-2

```
public class ProductController : Controller
{
        public ActionResult GetProduct(string id)
        {
                return View(ProductRepository.GetProduct(id));
        }
}
```

In this listing, the Product's controller's GetProduct action is being called by the ASP.NET MVC framework whenever a URL matches the /Product/{id} pattern in the route table. Beyond that, a ProductRepository class is called to get the model and that data is passed into the view for presentation. This is a very basic example of routes, and we could probably have a hundred or so more pages on them, but at the very least, this should give you a bit of background into how traditional ASP.NET MVC handles requests.

Now let's go back and look at the code from Chapter 2 again. Notice the ComponentsController in Listing 4-4 we wrote then. Hopefully the controller code makes a lot more sense now. You can see the HeroSlider() controller action is calling the Sitecore database, via the Sitecore API, to get the Item. It then returns that item to the view as the model.

Listing 4-4. Controller Code from Chapter 2

```
public class ComponentsController : SitecoreController
{
   public ViewResult HeroSlider()
   {
     Item contentItem = null;

     var database = Context.Database;
     if (database != null && !String.IsNullOrEmpty(
           RenderingContext.Current.Rendering.DataSource))
     {
        contentItem = database.GetItem(new Sitecore.Data.ID(
           RenderingContext.Current.Rendering.DataSource));
     }
     return View(contentItem);
   }
}
```

You'll see in Listing 4-4 how we have a View(contentItem) being returned in our action result. It's not specifying a specific view by name. This means the controller will return the default view for that request. How does MVC know what the default view to return? In this regard, ASP.NET MVC uses a pattern for locating controllers in views, relying on convention over configuration (see http://bit.ly/1SSpl7k). Notice the solution structure seen in Figure 4-2. The default view for the HeroSlider controller action is always going to have the same name as the controller action, and it will also be in a folder matching the name of the controller itself, such as Components in the Views folder (see Figure 4-2). Likewise, where does ASP.NET MVC know to find the controller itself? Controllers will always be in the Controllers namespace/folder below the solution.

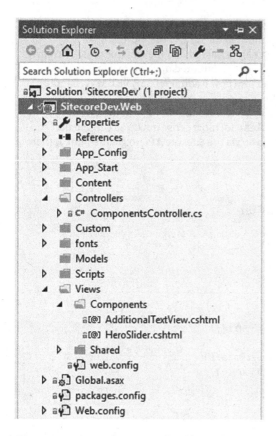

Figure 4-2. *Our web project after Chapter 3*

Alternatively, going back to the Product example, you could change the view to a custom view based on some logic, as shown in Listing 4-5.

Listing 4-5. You Can Control Whether the Controller Should Return a Default or Custom View

```
public ActionResult GetProduct(string id)
{
    if (DetailView)
    {
        return View("ProductDetails", ProductRepository.GetProduct(id));
    }
    else
    {
        return View(ProductRepository.GetProduct(id));
    }
}
```

Listing 4-5 shows an example of the controller returning a custom view named ProductDetails. For this to work, you will need a ProductDetails.cshtml file in the Views folder, below a folder with the same name of the controller (Products in this case). Similarly, a strongly typed data model is passed to that view for presentation as before.

So how do you create a view in ASP.NET MVC? Well, you already created one in Chapter 2, so this is a bit of a refresher, whence before we skipped over all the ASP.NET MVC plumbing specifics. Similar to before, you right-click on the View's controller folder (e.g., Views/Home node for the products example) and click Add, View. You'll get a similar popup to the one you see in Figure 4-3. You'll need to specify the view name, an optional template, and an optional data model the view can render.

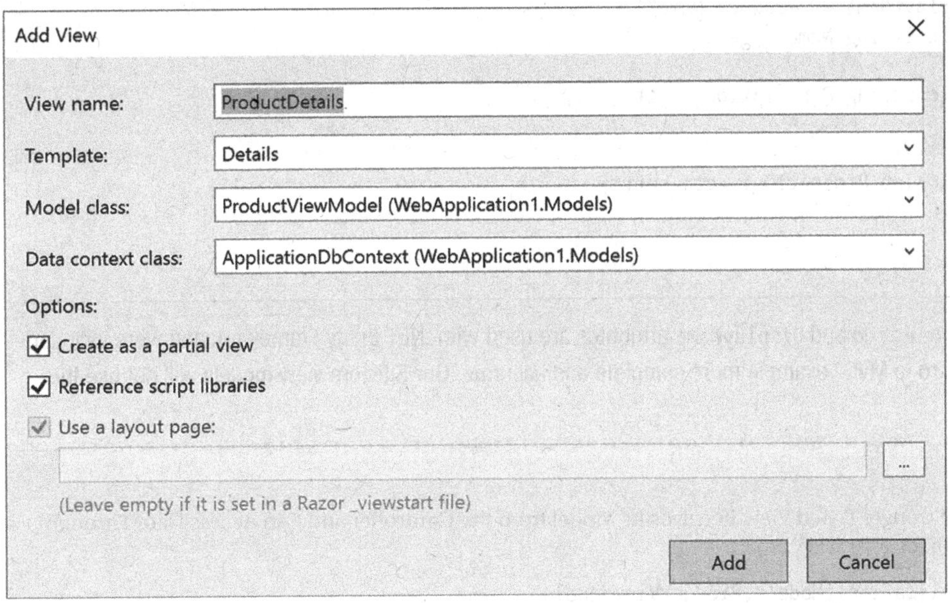

Figure 4-3. *Creating a new view is easy, just right-click Add ➤ View. Then, set any model or template preferences you need*

■ **Note**   Figure 4-3 shows a more standard ASP.NET example. Our Sitecore example from Chapter 2 didn't need a template, model class, data context, nor any checkboxes selected. This is because we are wiring that from scratch.

In the case of Figure 4-3, we're creating a new view titled Products to match our Products controller, and we're putting this view below the Products folder within the Views parent folder. We are also specifying a model for the view called ProductViewModel. This is a C# class file that defines the model, as can be seen in Listing 4-6. Lastly, we specified to create a partial view. Since components in Sitecore will be given a layout within Sitecore itself, all your views will be partial, except for the layouts themselves (more on this in Chapter 6 if you're confused). After you click Add, you'll notice a new cshtml file stubbed out, similar to Listing 4-7.

Listing 4-6. Views Can Be Strongly Typed to a Model to Provide IntelliSense and Compilation Errors

```
namespace WebApplication1.Models
{
    public class ProductViewModel
    {
        [Required]
        [Display(Name = "Product Name")]
        public string Name { get; set; }

        public string Description { get; set; }

        [Key]
        public int ProductID { get; set; }
    }
}
```

■ **Note** The Required and DisplayName attributes are used with .NET Entity Framework and were included to make the "intro to MVC" example more complete and accurate. Our Sitecore view models will not use this convention.

Listing 4-7. A Strongly Typed View Receives Its Model from the Controller and Can Access Data Through the "Model" Object

```
@model WebApplication1.Models.ProductViewModel
<div>
    <h4>Product Details</h4>
    <hr />
    <dl class="dl-horizontal">
        <dt>
            @Html.DisplayNameFor(model => model.Name)
        </dt>
        <dd>
            @Html.DisplayFor(model => model.Name)
        </dd>
        <dt>
            @Html.DisplayNameFor(model => model.Description)
        </dt>
        <dd>
            @Html.DisplayFor(model => model.Description)
        </dd>
    </dl>
</div>
<p>
    @Html.ActionLink("Edit", "Edit", new { id = Model.ProductID }) |
    @Html.ActionLink("Back to List", "Index")
</p>
```

You'll also notice in Listing 4-7 a couple `ActionLinks` in the view. These actions, or often referred to as "HTML helpers," are what can call back to the server. In the case of the Edit ActionLink, a link will be rendered on the page with a text value of `Edit"` and the `Edit` controller action method will be called when that link is clicked, passing the current product's ProductID into that controller action method. The `Back to List` ActionLink behaves similarly except no parameter is passed or expected, but in this instance the controller action method would be the default, `Index` action. This is how the code in the controller is wired up to the code in the view.

At this point, just like you did in Chapter 2, you need to register this view in Sitecore as a controller rendering. You'll see another example of these steps later in this chapter, but they'll be familiar to what you already did in Chapter 2. Chapter 6 takes the concept of renderings and HTML helpers to a whole new level, where we focus on front-end development.

■ **Note**   Sitecore has its own host of HTML helpers you'll read more about throughout the course of this book, but most notably in Chapter 6.

This was just a primer into ASP.NET MVC development. You may have noticed that in standard ASP. NET MVC we do a few things different than in Sitecore. However, you really should read an ASP.NET MVC 5 book if you're serious about becoming a Senior Sitecore developer, as many principles are common and MVC internals are not covered in this book.

But, you know enough now to launch deeper into Sitecore development specifically. As far as core ASP. NET MVC background information goes, we stop here. Everything else in this book is Sitecore development-specific as it relates to ASP.NET MVC, including Chapter 6's discussion of layouts.

Sitecore Modular Architecture

As we just discussed, MVC patterns are brilliant because they add a great deal of separation of concerns into our solution. It's miles ahead of legacy Web Forms solutions! However, it isn't quite a home run either. Over time you can end up with a proliferation of controllers, models, views, the result of which is a project, like the old days, is a highly coupled solution. This is often called "code rot" where the project starts out with a few good patterns and a ton of good intentions, but over time it drifts away into the abyss. Productivity goes down as the site grows and becomes more coupled. The ability to unit test becomes increasingly challenging as coupling increases, too. Maintaining a decoupled solution is incredibly important if you want to maintain high-levels of productivity and testability. MVC, it turns out, isn't a silver bullet.

The solution we are proposing in this book is to incorporate a modular architecture into your overarching Sitecore solution. This modular architecture still leverages ASP.NET MVC as its core; however, instead of one big web project with all the controllers and views in one place, we're going to break it apart into modules.

■ **Note**   This modular architecture is based off and inspired by a set of patterns and principles called "Helix" from Sitecore. Helix represents an amazing contribution to the Sitecore community, led by Thomas Eldblom. There is also an example implementation that follows the Helix design principles called "Habitat". Habitat is not a "starter pack," it is a reference implementation. We have chosen to use the phrase "Sitecore modular architecture" because that is really the foundation of Helix and Habitat. If you want to see an example of a Sitecore modular architecture, download Habitat (`https://github.com/sitecore/habitat`) or follow along in this book. Also, the official documentation for Helix can be found at `http://helix.sitecore.net`.

A Sitecore modular architecture helps sustain:

- *Simplicity*: Make it super easy to open the code an understand what features are in the solution and where you go to make changes.

- *Flexibility*: Make changes to features without having to worry about breaking other features.

- *Extensibility*: Easy to add new features without needing to learn the entire solution

Notice the architecture diagram in Figure 4-4. A modular architecture in Sitecore is broken into three core layers, the Project layer, the Feature layer, and the Foundation layer. The layers of this architecture helps control the direction of dependencies, described by the Stable Dependency Principle, which is a cornerstone of the Sitecore modular architecture.

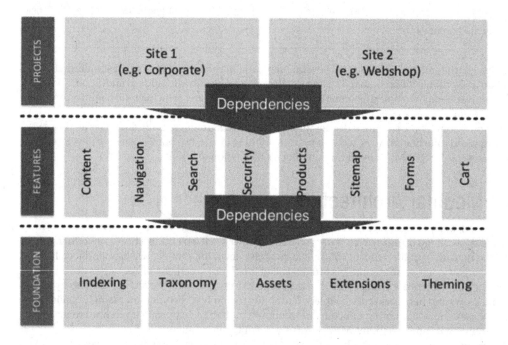

Figure 4-4. *A modular architecture implemented in Sitecore will be comprised of three core layers: 1) a Project layer that brings all lower level layers together, 2) a Feature layer for your business-related features, and 3) a Foundation layer for more wide-reaching or generic dependencies. (Image courtesy of Ruud van Falier. Used with permission.)*

- *Project Layer*: Ties all the features together into a common experience (a.k.a, the web site) and provides the context of the solution. This layer contains the page types, the layouts, and the graphical design or CSS.

- *Feature Layer*: Where all the functionality for the various business features can be found, along with any feature specific/unique layouts, placeholders, HTML markup/views, and JavaScript. All the features are broken into isolated modules. Following the Common Closure Principle, no module in the Feature layer has references to other modules in the Feature layer. Any module in the Feature layer should be able to be added, changed, or removed without affecting any other modules in the Feature layer.

- *Foundation Layer*: Forms the foundation of your solution. Following the Stable Dependency Principle, the modules in this layer are considered the most stable in your solution. A change to any of these modules would likely impact many other modules in your solution and would require considerable regression testing. These modules may include frameworks your solution depends upon, such as Bootstrap, common APIs such as connections to Sitecore, or other repositories which connect to external systems. Also, any functionality that must span Features should be located in the Foundation layer (more on this in Chapter 5). Unlike the Feature layer, modules within the Foundation layer can depend on other modules in the Foundation layer, as long as they follow the Acrylic Dependencies Principle and the Stable Abstractions Principle, meaning there are no circular dependencies and any dependencies are abstract.

■ **Note** Where's my "Web" or "UI" Layer? If you're used to typical "three-tier" architectures, with a web, business, and data layers, you might be asking this question. However, with Sitecore we're not always building web sites! It might be a web site, or a mobile app, or some other application needing common features and access to Sitecore data.

■ **Note** The patterns mentioned in the Sitecore modular architecture layers are described by Robert Martin (a.k.a. Uncle Bob) as (http://bit.ly/2bZ3Pla):

Stable Dependency Principle: "The dependencies between packages should be in the direction of the stability of the packages. A package should only depend on packages that are more stable than itself."

Common Closure Principle: "Classes that change together are packaged together."

Acrylic Dependency Principle: "The dependency graph of packages must have no cycles."

Stable Abstractions Principle: "The dependency graph of packages must have no cycles."

Everything in this proposed architecture is a module. No utilities. No helpers. You want to keep things decoupled as much as possible. What goes into a module? Code, configuration, templates, renderings, items—EVERYTHING. Everything should be version controlled and managed together.

If you make an update to the "Navigation" feature, you shouldn't have to fully regression test "News and Events". If you remove the "Accounting" feature, "Search" should not be impacted. Horizontal coupling should not exist in this architecture.

■ **Tip** What becomes a module? Classes that change together belong together, and when you start to see this happening, you've likely identified a module. If one change requires changes across multiple modules, this architecture has become pointless. If you start noticing your modules getting large, where changes in one part do not affect other parts, you may need to split the module up.

What about the code? How does this get structured in Visual Studio? If you take a look at Figure 4-5 you'll notice the benefit of simplicity right away. It only takes a few seconds to know where you ought to start digging, if for example, you need to make an update to the top navigation. If it isn't so obvious, one could guess code for the top navigation could be found within the "Navigation" module.

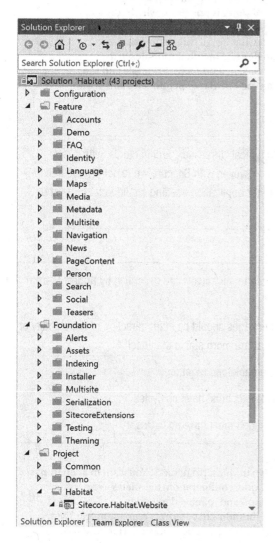

Figure 4-5. *Notice how easy it is to navigate a Habitat solution; all the features are grouped into their associated modules, isolated from external changes*

Likewise, you'll see a similar pattern within Sitecore itself in Figure 4-6. You'll notice that the Feature, Foundation, and Project folders in Sitecore map directly back to the solution. So, whether you're looking for the code or for the Sitecore items, the pattern is the same.

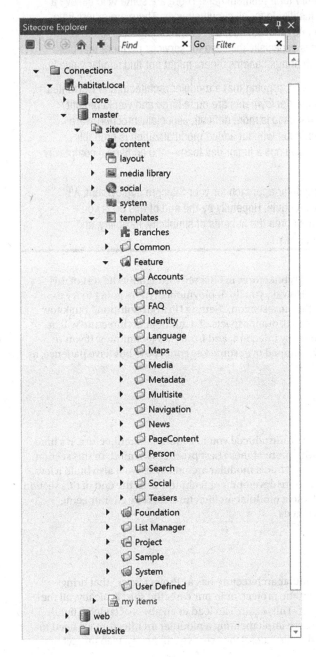

Figure 4-6. *A modular architecture takes a similar form within Sitecore itself; just as in Visual Studio, the structure is familiar within Sitecore Rocks*

WHEN SHOULDN'T YOU USE A MODULAR ARCHITECTURE?

Let's wade into unsettled and controversial territory for a moment here. There are some who believe a modular architecture is overly complex and not justifiable for all circumstances. There are others who say once you get the hang of it, it isn't so heavy and should be used in all circumstances. At the very least, they argue, consistency rules the day. This is especially the case for services partners that build many sites a year. Standardizing on one approach brings benefits others might not find similar value in.

We take the "it depends" approach to this discussion, arguing that a modular architecture is warranted for most Sitecore deployments, since most Sitecore deployments are quite large and would benefit from modularization. However, for smaller sites the case is more difficult, especially brochureware or microsites. A standard Sitecore MVC implementation without added modularization is probably appropriate in those cases, especially if the client/you has a junior dev team—the additional complexity of modularization might overwhelm them.

The rest of the book assumes you will follow a modular approach for your Sitecore deployment. All future steps/examples will be implemented into a module. Hopefully by the end of this book you'll be comfortably familiar with this approach and will agree the benefits of simplicity, flexibility, and extensibility outweigh the cons of perceived complexity.

A ton more can and will be said about modular architectures in Sitecore throughout the rest of this book. How do you create them? How do they work? How do you do deployments? We're going to try to introduce answers to these high level questions in this next section, "Setting Up Your Solution," but know that in subsequent chapters, especially Chapters 5 and 6, other aspects of a modular architecture will be covered in more detail, such as repositories, dependency injection, and front-end techniques. If you're familiar with Helix, for example, you may feel we've skipped over some key concepts—but have patience, as modularity in all its glory will be unfolded in due time.

Setting Up Your Solution

Now that you have a bit of MVC background, and we've introduced you to a modular architecture, it's time to expand upon the solution created in Chapter 2 with more of these best practices in mind. In this section we're going to refactor the solution created in Chapter 2 into a modular architecture. We'll also build a few more components along the way to showcase some more development techniques. At the end of this section you'll have a solid start to a Sitecore site refactored into a modular architecture, thereby guaranteeing simplicity, flexibility, and extensibility for all future needs.

Stubbing Out a Web Project

You may recall from earlier in this chapter that a modular architecture has a "Project layer" that brings together all the modules to work in unison to support the project, or in our case, the site. Typically, all the controllers and views are all in one single web project. This, again, can lead to an abyss of code all tightly coupled, making it challenging to maintain. Since we're implementing a modular architecture we need to move those controllers and views into their respective modules. However, we still need a web project that ties it all together.

Chapter 6 covers front-end development techniques in much greater detail. You may think we're skipping a lot of web goodness in this section, but have no fear—it is intentional. Front-end web development for Sitecore is a big topic. Some of the following steps might be a bit confusing, but trust we'll cover the theory in greater depth later (Chapter 6). For now, let's just focus on stubbing out a web project that will integrate our modules. We'll save the discussion on the "secret sauce" for later.

Use the following steps to set up a new web project in your solution created in Chapter 2. Let's start by creating a few Solution Folders in our Visual Studio solution for the layers of our overall solution: Project, Foundation, and Feature. We'll also create a Solution Folder for Configuration.

1. In Solution Explorer in Visual Studio, right-click on your SitecoreDev solution and select Add ➤ Solution Folder. Name this folder Project. Repeat this process, creating three new folders named Foundation, Feature, and Configuration. When you're done, it should look like Figure 4-7.

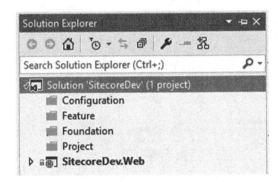

Figure 4-7. *Create our three architecture layer folders, including an extra folder for our configuration files*

2. In the Project folder, let's go one level deeper and create a solution folder named SitecoreDev. This corresponds to the name of our site.

3. Next, let's create a new ASP.NET Web Application in this new SitecoreDev folder. Right-click on SitecoreDev and select Add ➤ New Project. Name this new web site SitecoreDev.Website, configuring it similar to Figure 4-8.

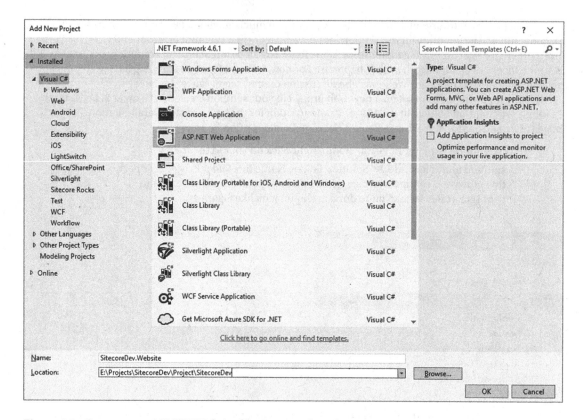

Figure 4-8. *Create a new ASP.NET Web Application to replace the one created in Chapter 2*

Ultimately, we'll end up deleting the project we created in Chapter 2 in favor of this structure, so we're going to name it a little differently. Notice, in the Location field, we're going to have our projects follow the same folder structure as our solution in Visual Studio.

4. On the next step, as we did in Chapter 2, select the empty ASP.NET 4.6.1 template and check the MVC checkbox under Add Folders and Core References For field (see Figure 4-9).

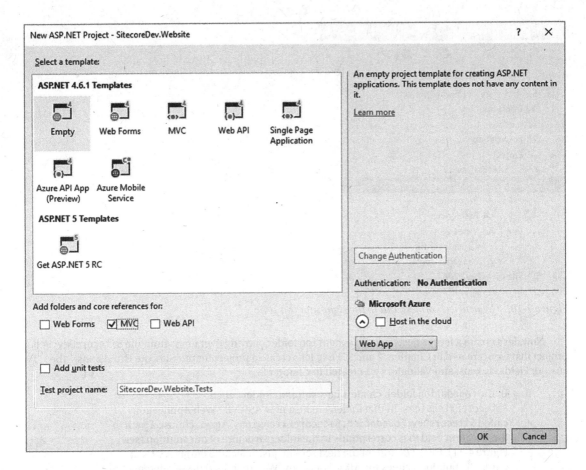

Figure 4-9. Create an empty MVC project

Next, let's delete a few items from this project.

5. Delete the App_Data, App_Start, Controllers, and Models folders as well as the Global.asax and Web.config files. Once you're done, it should look something Figure 4-10.

Figure 4-10. *The new web project, but in the right spot this time*

Now, let's create a few projects in our Foundation folder, moving over items from the SitecoreDev.Web project that were created in Chapters 2 and 3. First, let's create a project for our Sitecore Extensions—the custom Fields, Tokens, and Validators we created in Chapter 3.

6. In the Foundation folder, create a new solution folder called SitecoreExtensions. In that folder, create a new ASP.NET Web Application called SitecoreDev.Foundation.SitecoreExtensions. Again, choose a path in the Location field that corresponds to the folder structure of our solution (see Figure 4-11). Click OK and on the next screen, just select the empty ASP.NET template, but don't check the MVC checkbox. We don't need those references in this project.

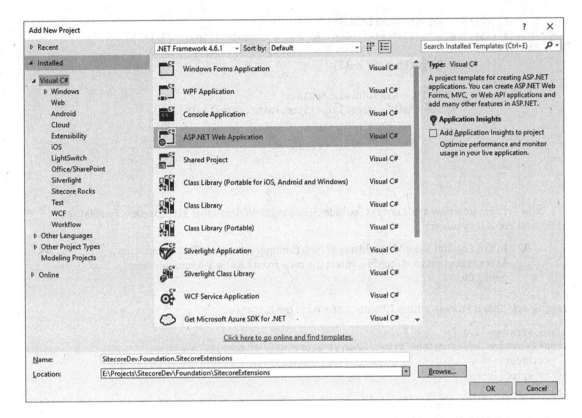

Figure 4-11. *Create a new project for the Sitecore extensions (e.g., the token processor created in Chapter 3)*

Once you click the OK button and the project is created, delete the `Web.config` file and add references to the `Sitecore.Kernel.dll` and `Sitecore.Mvc.dll` assemblies found in the `/libs/Sitecore` folder.

7. Next, in the new `SitecoreDev.Foundation.SitecoreExtensions` project, create a new folder called `Tokens`.

8. Inside this `Tokens` folder, create a new class called `ParentPathTokenProcessor`. We'll be taking the contents of the `SitecoreDev.Web.Custom.Tokens.ParentPathTokenProcessor` class and putting it here. The resulting code should look like Listing 4-8.

Listing 4-8. Move the Token Processor Code into the Right Spot

```
using System;
using Sitecore.Pipelines.ExpandInitialFieldValue;

namespace SitecoreDev.Foundation.SitecoreExtensions.Tokens
{
    public class ParentPathTokenProcessor : ExpandInitialFieldValueProcessor
    {
        public override void Process(ExpandInitialFieldValueArgs args)
        {
```

```
        var token = args.SourceField.Value;
        if (!String.IsNullOrEmpty(token) && token.Contains("$parentPath"))
        {
          if (args.TargetItem != null)
          {
            args.Result = args.Result.Replace(
              "$parentPath", args.TargetItem.Paths.ParentPath);
          }
        }
      }
    }
  }
}
```

Now, let's create a new App_Config\Include\Foundation folder in this SitecoreDev.Foundation. SitecoreExtensions project.

9. In this Foundation folder, add a new Web Configuration file called Foundation. SitecoreExtensions.config. Insert the code from Listing 4-9 into this new config file.

Listing 4-9. Token Processor from Chapter 3 Moved to the Right Spot

```
<?xml version="1.0"?>
<configuration xmlns:patch="http://www.sitecore.net/xmlconfig/">
  <sitecore>
    <pipelines>

      <!-- Token replacements -->
      <expandInitialFieldValue>
        <processor type="SitecoreDev.Foundation.SitecoreExtensions.
Tokens.ParentPathTokenProcessor, SitecoreDev.Foundation.SitecoreExtensions"
patch:after="processor[@type='type=Sitecore.Pipelines.ExpandInitialFieldValue.
ReplaceVariables, Sitecore.Kernel']"/>
      </expandInitialFieldValue>

    </pipelines>
  </sitecore>
</configuration>
```

This file will replace the SitecoreDev.Web\App_Config\Include\SitecoreDev\SitecoreDev. TokenReplacements.config file, where the bolded text (the path to the new ParentPathTokenProcessor class) being the only difference. Because the SsnValidator custom validator and CreditCard custom field were only examples and won't be used in our project going forward, we won't be reimplementing them. Once you're done, the new SitecoreDev.Foundation.SitecoreExtensions project should look like Figure 4-12.

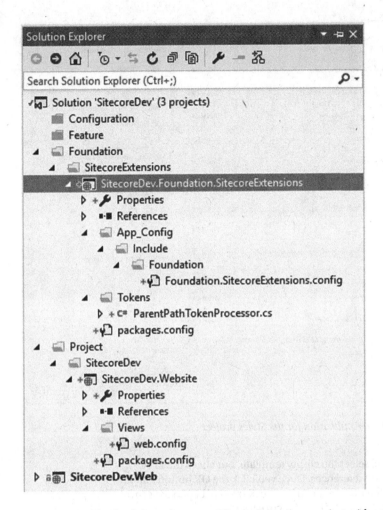

Figure 4-12. *The final view of our new SitecoreExtensions project with our token processor from Chapter 3*

Now that we've refactored our custom Sitecore items into a Foundation project, let's create another Foundation project for our front-end styles.

10. In the Foundation folder, create a new solution folder named Styles.

11. In the Foundation\Styles folder, create a new ASP.NET Web Application named SitecoreDev.Foundation.Styles. Remember to set the Location path appropriately (see Figure 4-13)!

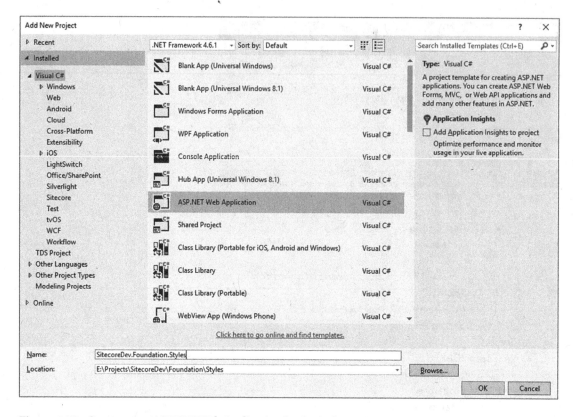

Figure 4-13. Create a new ASP.NET Web Application for the Styles project

12. This time, on the next step, select the empty template, but check the MVC checkbox to add folders and references. Once you click the OK button and the project is created, add references to the `Sitecore.Kernel.dll` and `Sitecore.Mvc.dll` assemblies found in the `/libs/Sitecore` folder.

13. Delete the `App_Data`, `App_Start`, and `Models` folders. Also delete the `Global.asax` and `Web.config` files.

■ **Tip** Because we deleted the `Web.config` file, using the Add ➤ View option could throw an error. It's just the scaffolding we're not using anyway. If you get this error, select Add ➤ MVC 5 View Page (Razor) and proceed as normal—it's faster anyway! (see Figure 4-14).

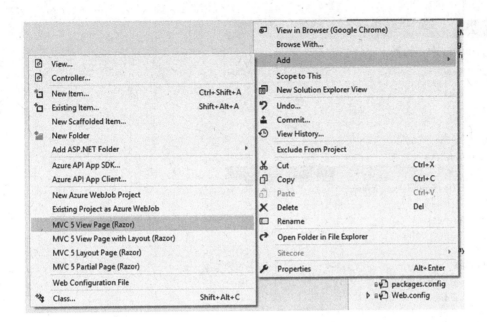

Figure 4-14. *Add ➤ View might not work. Try Add ➤ MVC 5 View Page (Razor) instead*

Finally, let's move the Layout file from the old project to our new Project layer.

14. In the Views folder of the SitecoreDev.Website project, add a folder called Shared. In this folder, create a new view named DefaultMVCLayout. Copy the contents of the SitecoreDev.Web\Views\Shared\DefaultMVCLayout.cshtml file and put them in this new file.

Once this is complete, these two projects in your solution should look like Figure 4-15.

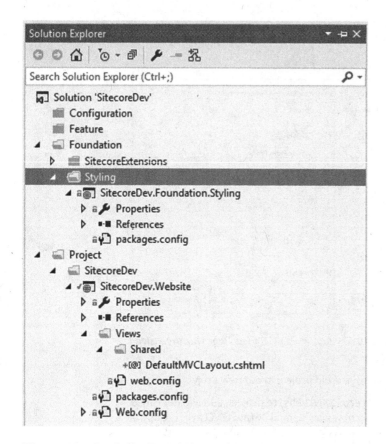

Figure 4-15. *Our Styling Foundation project*

Now that we've refactored our project, changed some namespaces and removed some example customizations, we need to do a little cleanup and refactoring on the Sitecore side.

15. Start by opening the Content Editor in Sitecore and navigating to /sitecore/ Templates/Sitecore8Dev. Expand MVC Page and Page Data. Delete the Credit Card and Social Security Number fields.

16. Next, navigate to /sitecore/system/Settings/Validation Rules/Field Rules/Sitecore8Dev. Delete this node and its children.

17. Finally, let's switch over to the Core database from the Desktop (select Launchpad ➤ Desktop, click the database icon in the bottom right of the screen) and open the Content Editor again. Navigate to /sitecore/system/Field types/Simple Types and delete the Credit Card field type.

The last items we need to clean up are the web root on the file system.

18. Open File Explorer and navigate to your web root. In the Website folder, open the App_Config\Include folder. Delete the SitecoreDev folder.

19. Now, go to the bin directory in the Website folder and delete the SitecoreDev.Web.* files.

20. Finally, in the Website\Views\Shared folder, delete DefaultMVCLayout.cshtml.

Don't worry, all will get republished, but from our new projects!

Now that we've cleaned up items we don't need any longer, let's add in a few more that we do need. In step 1 above, we created solution folders for Project, Feature, and Foundation. We're going to continue that structure throughout the Sitecore tree as well, creating Project, Feature, and Foundation folders in places like /templates, /layout/placeholder settings and /layout/renderings. Once we have these folders created, we'll move a few more items around.

21. Back in the Content Editor, navigate to /templates/Sitecore8Dev. Within Sitecore8Dev, create folders for Project, Feature, and Foundation.

22. Inside the new Project folder, create a new folder called Sitecore8. This corresponds to the name of our site.

23. Inside the new Sitecore8 folder, create two more folders: Content Types and Page Types.

24. Inside the new Feature folder, create a new folder called Metadata.

25. In the Metadata folder, create a new interface template called _Metadata, configured as shown in Figure 4-16.

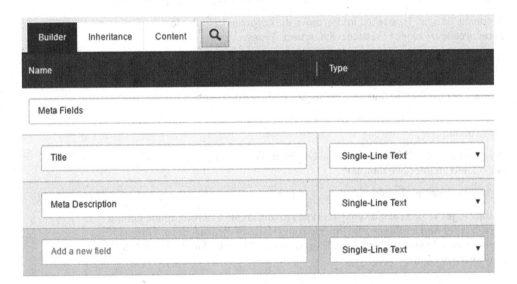

Figure 4-16. The template configuration of the new _Metadata template

26. From the root of the Sitecore8Dev folder, move the MVC Page template to the /Sitecore8Dev/Project/ Sitecore8/Page Types folder.

27. Select the MVC Page template. In the Data section of the Content tab, select the new /Sitecore8Dev/Feature/Metadata/_Metadata template as a base template, as shown in Figure 4-17.

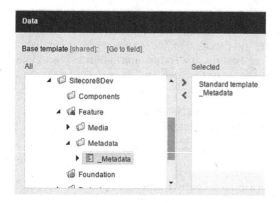

Figure 4-17. *Configure the MVC Page template to inherit from the _Metadata interface template*

28. Expand the MVC Page template and delete the Page Data node.

29. Select the __Standard Values item and, in the Title field, type in the $name token.

30. Inside the Folder Templates folder, move the Components folder to / Sitecore8Dev/Project/Sitecore8/Content Types.

31. Delete the Folder Templates folder.

32. Inside the Feature folder, create a new folder called Media. This corresponds to the name of the feature that we'll be adding in the next section.

33. In the Components folder, move the Hero Slider template to the new Feature/ Media folder.

34. Rename the Hero Slider template to be _Hero Slider. This will now be considered an interface template.

35. Delete the Components folder.

36. In the Project/Sitecore8/Content Types folder, create a new template named Hero Slider and configure it to inherit from /Feature/Media/_Hero Slider. This is now a datasource template. Your Sitecore8Dev template folder should now look like Figure 4-18.

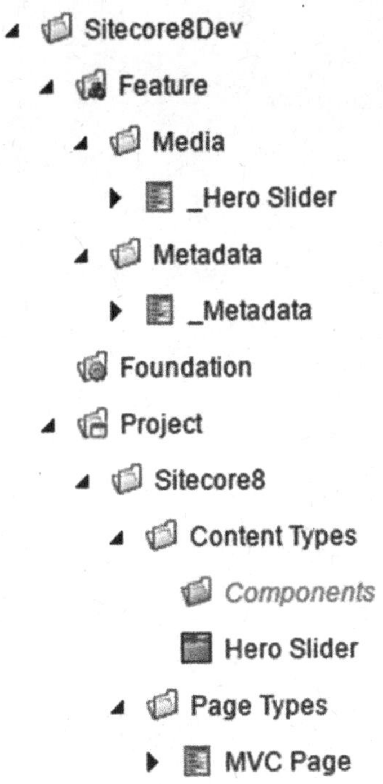

- ▲ 📁 Sitecore8Dev
  - ▲ 📁 Feature
    - ▲ 📁 Media
      - ▶ 📄 _Hero Slider
    - ▲ 📁 Metadata
      - ▶ 📄 _Metadata
    - 📁 Foundation
  - ▲ 📁 Project
    - ▲ 📁 Sitecore8
      - ▲ 📁 Content Types
        - 📁 *Components*
        - 📄 Hero Slider
      - ▲ 📁 Page Types
        - ▶ 📄 MVC Page

Figure 4-18. *After reconfiguring your /template node, it should resemble this structure*

■ **Note** In Figure 4-18, notice the icons used on the Project, Feature and Foundation folders. Changing these icons is optional, but is considered a good practice to remain consistent with the Habitat example implementation. Anywhere else we create these three folders, we will be using these icons to enforce the consistency.

---

37. In `/sitecore/content/Home/MyPage/Components`, select Hero Slider Content. On the Configure tab, click the Change button in the Template section of the ribbon. Change the template type from `/Sitecore8Dev/Feature/Media/_Hero Slider` to `/Sitecore8Dev/Project/Sitecore8/Content Types/Hero Slider`.

38. Next, in the `/layout/Placeholder Settings/Sitecore8Dev` folder, create the `Project`, `Feature`, and `Foundation` folders.

39. Now, in the `/layout/renderings/Sitecore8Dev` folder, create the `Project`, `Feature`, and `Foundation` folders.

40. Finally, create a new folder in the `Feature` folder called `Media` and move the `/Sitecore8Dev/Components/Hero Slider` controller rendering to it. You can now delete the `Components` folder and the `Additional Text` rendering. Your `/layout` node should now look like Figure 4-19.

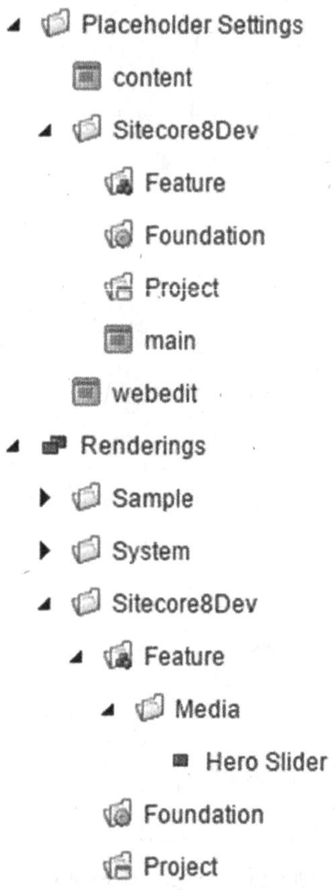

◢ 🗐 Placeholder Settings

   🖾 content

  ◢ 🗐 Sitecore8Dev

    🗐 Feature

    🗐 Foundation

    🗐 Project

    🖾 main

  🖾 webedit

◢ 🗐 Renderings

 ▶ 🗐 Sample

 ▶ 🗐 System

 ◢ 🗐 Sitecore8Dev

  ◢ 🗐 Feature

   ◢ 🗐 Media

    ■ Hero Slider

  🗐 Foundation

  🗐 Project

Figure 4-19. After reconfiguring your /layout section, it should resemble this structure

Creating Your First Module

Okay, we now have a web project stood up and all the applicable code moved over. Now it's time to move the rest of the stuff created in Chapter 2 into a new module. We'll be moving the HeroSlider component into a new module called Media that will store all our media related components, such as our hero slider, video components, and so forth. At the end of this section you'll have everything refactored into a modular architecture with Chapter 2's web project deleted, since its contents had been moved into the new design. Use the following steps to set up the Media module:

1. Like we did with the Foundation projects, let's create a new solution folder in the Feature folder named Media.

2. In this Media folder, create a new ASP.NET MVC Application named SitecoreDev.Feature.Media. Click OK and select the empty template and check the MVC checkbox to add folders and references.

3. Once you click the OK button and the project is created, add references to the Sitecore.Kernel.dll and Sitecore.Mvc.dll assemblies found in the /libs/ Sitecore folder.

4. Delete the App_Data, App_Start, and Models folders. Also delete the Global.asax file.

5. In the Controllers folder, add a new Controller named MediaController and copy the code from the HeroSlider controller action in the SitecoreDev.Web\Controllers\ComponentsController. It should end up looking like Listing 4-10.

Listing 4-10. HeroSlider Action Method Moved Into New Media Controller

```
using System;
using System.Web.Mvc;
using Sitecore;
using Sitecore.Data.Items;
using Sitecore.Mvc.Controllers;
using Sitecore.Mvc.Presentation;

namespace SitecoreDev.Feature.Media.Controllers
{
    public class MediaController : SitecoreController
    {
        public ViewResult HeroSlider()
        {
            Item contentItem = null;

            var database = Context.Database;
            if (database != null && !String.IsNullOrEmpty(RenderingContext.Current.Rendering.
            DataSource))
            {
                contentItem = database.GetItem(
                    new Sitecore.Data.ID(RenderingContext.Current.Rendering.DataSource));
            }

            return View(contentItem);
        }
    }
}
```

■ **Tip** As of the release of Sitecore 8.2, there is now an official Sitecore NuGet feed. Read more from Sitecore MVP, Jeremy Davis at http://bit.ly/2bRZFPV.

6. Finally, in the Views folder, right-click on the Media folder and create a new View named HeroSlider.

7. Copy the code from the HeroSlider view from SitecoreDev.Web\Views\Components (see Listing 4-11).

Listing 4-11. Our HeroSlider View from Chapter 2

```
@model Sitecore.Data.Items.Item
@using Sitecore.Data.Fields
@using Sitecore.Data.Items
@using Sitecore.Resources.Media

@if (Model != null)
{
    <div id="myCarousel" class="carousel slide" data-ride="carousel">
        <ol class="carousel-indicators">
            <li data-target="#myCarousel" data-slide-to="0" class="active"></li>
            <li data-target="#myCarousel" data-slide-to="1"></li>
            <li data-target="#myCarousel" data-slide-to="2"></li>
            <li data-target="#myCarousel" data-slide-to="3"></li>
        </ol>

        <div class="carousel-inner" role="listbox">
            @{
                IEnumerable<Item> heroImages = null;
                var heroImagesField = new MultilistField(
                    Model.Fields["Hero Images"]);
                if (heroImagesField != null)
                {
                    heroImages = heroImagesField.GetItems();
                }

                if (heroImages != null)
                {
                    int i = 1;
                    foreach (var image in heroImages)
                    {
                        var mediaItem = (MediaItem)image;
                        <div class="item @(i == 1 ? "active" : "")">
                            <img src="@MediaManager.GetMediaUrl(mediaItem)"
                                style="width:1920px;" alt="@mediaItem.Alt" />
                        </div>
                        i++;
                    }
                }
            }
        </div>
    </div>
}
```

8. Finally, now that we've moved everything over from the `SitecoreDev.Web` project, right-click on that project and remove it from the solution.

Now, your solution should look a little something like Figure 4-20!

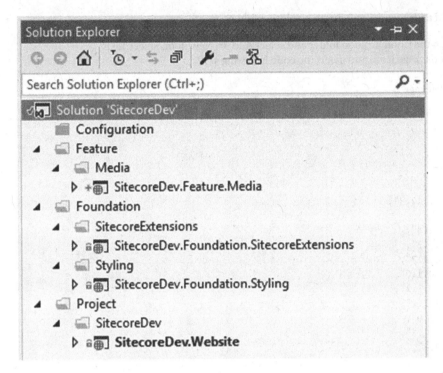

Figure 4-20. *The site refactored into a modular architecture*

Deploying Your Code

In Chapter 2 we published our code via Web Deploy to the local file system. In those days, publishing your code was simple. One button! However, in a modular architecture the simplicity of a deployment is no longer something we have going for ourselves. The issue is we no longer have one single web project; we have many! Many in the sense that our controllers and view are all over the place; we need to combine them. Instead, we need to turn to Gulp to save the day.

Gulp is a task running service built on top of Node.js. Both are required to support our modular architecture, and both have strong open source community support and are widely used. If you're unfamiliar with Gulp, have no fear that this is a hack garage code solution from a random dude. Gulp is growing as a serious contender, even in the continuous integration space.

Gulp tasks are written in JavaScript. You can really do anything imaginable with these tasks. You can move files around in a solution, consolidate files into one big file, move files to other servers, and so on and so forth. These are all examples of Gulp tasks we're going to write throughout the course of this book. First, to get our views into the right spot in the site, second to consolidate/minify our CSS and JavaScript files, and even to publish our files to our sites, server, and beyond. Some of these topics won't be covered until Chapter 6 (such as CSS magnification). For now, be content with your first introduction to Gulp and the basics of a Gulp deployment.

Use the following steps to set up your Gulp deployment. We need to start by downloading and installing Node.js, if you don't have it installed already.

1. Navigate to https://nodejs.org and download the latest version of Node.js. We'll be working with Node.js v4.4.3. Once you've downloaded the installer, run it and accept all the default settings, then click Install.

Next, we need to add a file to our Configuration solution folder.

2. Right-click on the Configuration folder and select Add ➤ New Item. Select Text File, name it package.json, and insert the code in Listing 4-12.

Listing 4-12. Our Gulp Package

```
{
  "name": "sitecoredev",
  "version": "0.0.1",
  "description": "",
  "main": "gulpfile.js",
  "dependencies": {
    "browser-sync": "^2.12.3",
    "gulp": "^3.9.1",
    "gulp-clean": "^0.2.4",
    "gulp-debug": "^2.1.2",
    "gulp-cssmin": "^0.1.7",
    "gulp-foreach": "^0.1.0",
    "gulp-msbuild": "^0.3.2",
    "gulp-rename": "^1.2.2",
    "gulp-newer": "^1.1.0",
    "gulp-rimraf": "^0.1.1",
    "gulp-sass": "^1.3.3",
    "gulp-watch": "^4.3.5",
    "run-sequence": "^1.1.5"
  },
  "devDependencies": {},
  "author": ""
}
```

Next, let's add a config file to set some project configuration entries.

3. Right-click on the Configuration solution folder and select Add ➤ New Item. Select JavaScript File, name it gulp-config.js, and type the code from Listing 4-13.

Listing 4-13. Our Gulp Configuration File Specifies Where to Put Our Stuff When We Publish, Among Other Configuration Values

```
module.exports = function () {
  var config = {
    webRoot: "C:\\inetpub\\wwwroot\\Sitecore8\\Website",
    devRoot: "E:\\Projects\\SitecoreDev",
    solutionName: "SitecoreDev",
    buildConfiguration: "Debug"
  }
  return config;Sitecore modular architecturecode via Web Deploy
}
```

■ **Note** If these values differ from yours, enter the appropriate values for your environment.

Finally, let's add one last file.

4.   Right-click on the Configuration solution folder and select Add ➤ New Item.
     Select JavaScript file and name it gulpfile.js. Type the code found in Listing 4-14.

Listing 4-14. Gulp Tasks for Our Publishing Needs

```javascript
var gulp = require("gulp");
var msbuild = require("gulp-msbuild");
var debug = require("gulp-debug");
var foreach = require("gulp-foreach");
var gulpConfig = require("./gulp-config.js")();
module.exports.config = gulpConfig;

gulp.task("Publish-Site", function () {
    return gulp.src("./{Feature,Foundation,Project}/**/**/*.csproj")
        .pipe(foreach(function (stream, file) {
            return stream
                .pipe(debug({ title: "Publishing " }))
                .pipe(msbuild({
                    targets: ["Build"],
                    gulpConfiguration: gulpConfig.buildConfiguration,
                    properties: {
                        publishUrl: gulpConfig.webRoot,
                        DeployDefaultTarget: "WebPublish",
                        WebPublishMethod: "FileSystem",
                        DeployOnBuild: "true",
                        DeleteExistingFiles: "false",
                        _FindDependencies: "false"
                    }
                }));
        }));
});
```

5.   Save the file.

6.   Now, in the Visual Studio menu, click on View ➤ Other Windows ➤ Task
     Runner Explorer (see Figure 4-21).

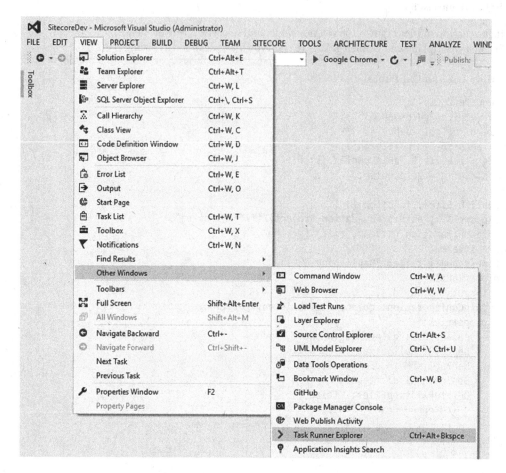

Figure 4-21. *The Task Runner Explorer is where you publish your projects with Gulp*

This will open the Task Runner Explorer. You should see a window that shows all of the tasks from the `gulpfile.js` file (see Figure 4-22). In order to execute one of these tasks, simply double-click on the task name.

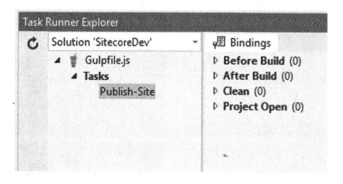

Figure 4-22. *Our Gulp jobs can be run from the Task Runner with a simple double-click to publish our files*

7. Finally, publish your site by double-clicking the item in the list, Publish-Site.

■ **Tip** The Habitat example project has several other Gulp jobs worth checking out. One is called "Publish-All-Views" if you want to update your front-end code without recompiling (saves Sitecore reload times), another to publish just the configuration files, and three to publish each layer respectively if you only want to recompile/republish particular layers. Additionally, it would be easy enough to add your own Gulp jobs for each feature to enable extremely granular deployments.

Summary

At this point in the book you've been exposed to many of the most foundational techniques a Sitecore developer needs to understand. You have a fair bit of ASP.NET MVC experience by now and how MVC and Sitecore work together. This is important because MVC is really the backbone of every Sitecore site.

Additionally, you now understand the benefits of a Sitecore modular architecture. Implementing a modular architecture ensures your solution was developed with simplicity, flexibility, and extensibility in mind. The last third of this chapter focused on refactoring your code from Chapter 1 into this modular design.

From here, with this foundation poured, it's time to really pour some gas on the design and refactor some things to align to some tried-and-true Sitecore development best practices. If best practices don't interest you, feel free to skip Chapter 5!

CHAPTER 5

■ ■ ■

Improving the Design with Patterns

In Chapter 4, we covered the Model-View-Controller design pattern. We learned about the importance of separation of concerns, keeping code simple, focusing on only doing one thing and doing that thing well. We even went so far as to delve into the concept of a modular architecture to accommodate extreme isolation between solution's various features and capabilities. You're probably thinking, how in the world can we have another chapter dedicated to separation of concerns following an entire chapter dedicated to separation of concerns? Is it really that big of a deal?

Short answer: Yes!

Sitecore solutions get BIIIIIIIIGGGGGGG over time. This isn't your ma' and pa's WordPress site here, folks. This is "Enterprise" application development, and as such, we need to take extreme care that we set up our solution in such a way as to maximize its flexibility, extensibility, maintainability, testability, and even its simplicity.

If you don't read this chapter, we can guarantee you that your Sitecore solution, sooner or later, will turn into a rat's nest of highly coupled, fear invoking, spaghetti code. So, before we dive into front-end development techniques we need to dig a bit deeper into the back-end architecture. The last chapter poured a foundation. Now it's time to build on that foundation with additional best practices, design patterns, and other techniques any enterprise application developer would be expected to graft into his or her solutions.

These best practices include using reusable repositories to ensure the same Sitecore API code isn't duplicated all over your solution. Additionally, we need to remove business logic out of our controllers, or our controllers will become *massive*, unwieldy, and will break the single-responsibility principle, the most important of the SOLID principles (`http://bit.ly/1Da1b16`).

Furthermore, after a while you'll find it hard to remove duplicate code out of even your repositories. What's the best way to remove duplicate code, you might ask? Generics! A bit of refactoring will help a ton when generics are incorporated.

With all this in place, you can finally move on and write your front-end code (Chapter 6), knowing you have all the necessary plumbing in place to start building your house.

Refactoring: Incorporating the Repository Pattern

The first place to start, if we're to clean up our code, is to take a closer look at the controller. If you recall Chapter 4 you might recognize Figure 5-1. The controller is clearly the center of the universe in an MVC (Sitecore for that matter) solution. The risk is high that your controllers will become, over time, very complex and difficult to maintain. Additionally, the code that builds the model off an external database (Sitecore in our case) is rife for reuse. It would be a shame to have duplicate Sitecore code in all your controllers. Shouldn't that code be abstracted out into a reusable library, allowing other controllers to benefit from it as well? Yes!

© Phil Wicklund and Jason Wilkerson 2016

P. Wicklund and J. Wilkerson, *Professional Sitecore 8 Development*, DOI 10.1007/978-1-4842-2292-8_5

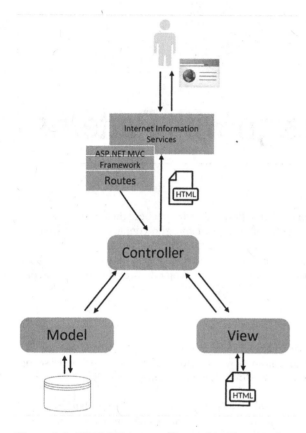

Figure 5-1. *The MVC pattern discussed in Chapter 3 has one pitfall: the controller can get very large and complex over time*

In fact, the pattern we're really talking about here is called a *repository* pattern. The repository pattern abstracts the data access layer from the business or domain layer. There's no business logic in a repository, just simple data access. Still, the data access code can oftentimes be lengthy and complex, so an abstraction is an obvious solution.

■ **Note** Although it's true that the repository pattern abstracts the data access layer from the business or domain layer, it's rather a simplistic definition. For more background on repositories, check out http://bit.ly/2cGg851.

Take a look at Figure 5-2. We've updated the solution architecture to incorporate a couple repositories that abstract away data access, as necessary for those source systems. In particular, our solution of a blog post in Sitecore finds its data in two source systems: 1) Sitecore, for the blog post itself, and 2) an external SQL database that houses the blog's comments. A repository was created to accommodate CRUD operations for each. All controllers can now access that data through the repository, removing the back-end dependency through abstraction. Additionally, that repository code can be unit tested apart from and independent of a web request, another primary benefit.

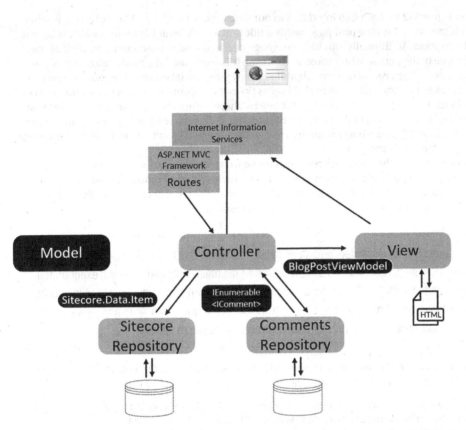

Figure 5-2. *A repository can help improve the controller design by providing centralization/reusability of data access code*

The biggest benefit of this repository implementation is the simplification it brings to the controller. Now the controller only has to worry about getting the data and sending that data to the view, versus knowledge of the source system and its intricacies. Note however, that some added abstraction was added to the design around how that data is passed back and forth. Instead of concrete model classes, we've refactored the model to use interfaces exclusively (except in the case of the view model, where we'll use a concrete class since the controller needs to instantiate it).

■ **Tip** The cleanest code is highly decoupled from its dependencies. All dependencies should be injected into the constructor, whenever possible, or through properties. Also, return types between application layers should be interfaces. Figure 5-2's implementation of interfaces is a huge step toward clean code.

We've also identified the need for two models: 1) a model representing the underlying data source, e.g. IArticle, and 2) a model that represents the needs of the view. You shouldn't assume the model returned from the repository/data source matches the needs of the view. Most of the time your data model could contain many more properties and other undesirables (such as method signatures) that your view doesn't need or care about. This rule is the "I" in SOLID principles; dependent clients shouldn't depend on properties or methods they don't use. So, to be good coding citizens, we recommend having two models: a model representing the data and a ViewModel representing only the data the view needs, as well as other UI state-type properties.

For example, in Figure 5-2 we have two interfaces in our data model, one for an IArticle and another for a IEnumerable<IComment>. Our blog post page needs a title and a body, which is found in IArticle, but it doesn't need a description. Additionally, our blog post page needs to render the comments, such as the comment text and name of the person who posted it. However, it doesn't need the moderation status you might find in an IComment object. As such, we've identified a new view model class that meets the exact needs of the view. We called it BlogPostViewModel. BlogPostViewModel contains properties for the parts of an IArticle it needs, as well as the parts of IComment it needs. There are also Boolean state properties that can be used as conditional statements in the view like HasComments. This is a read-only property that returns the result of Comments.Count() > 0. That way, in the view, we only need to check the value of HasComments rather than inserting Comments.Count() > 0.

In the case of the controller, the controller responds to the web request as usual. However, it first gets the article from the Sitecore repository, and then matches that article with the comments associated with it in the comments database. After it has both data models back from the repositories, it populates the BlogPostViewModel and sends that view model to the view for display.

■ **Note** This might sound like an extra step, adding all these interfaces. This might be especially daunting if you haven't used interfaces often. However, the benefits of future maintainability can't be over-exaggerated. For example, if you decided to switch to Disqus for commenting and WordPress for your blog content, because of these abstractions you wouldn't have to change a single line of code in your controllers and views. Simply update the repositories, and since they return their data as an interface, you're done!

It's easy to draw a picture, but harder to write the code. As such, let's refactor our Hero Slider example created in Chapter 3 to use this repository pattern. Use the following steps to guide you.

1. In Visual Studio, let's start by creating a folder in our SitecoreDev.Feature. Media project called Repositories. In this new folder, create a new interface called IMediaRepository. In IMediaRepository, let's add a new method signature called GetItem that takes a string as a parameter. It should return an object of type Item. It should look like Listing 5-1.

Listing 5-1. Create an Interface for Our Repository

```
using System;
using System.Collections.Generic;
using System.Linq;
using System.Web;
using Sitecore.Data.Items;

namespace SitecoreDev.Feature.Media.Repositories
{
    public interface IMediaRepository
    {
        Item GetItem(string contentGuid);
    }
}
```

2. Next, in the same Repositories folder, create a new class called SitecoreMediaRepository. This new class should implement IMediaRepository and look like Listing 5-2.

Listing 5-2. Our New Repository!

```
using System;
using System.Collections.Generic;
using System.Linq;
using System.Web;
using Sitecore;
using Sitecore.Data;
using Sitecore.Data.Items;

namespace SitecoreDev.Feature.Media.Repositories
{
    public class SitecoreMediaRepository : IMediaRepository
    {
        private Database _database;

        public SitecoreMediaRepository()
        {
            _database = Context.Database;
        }

        public Item GetItem(string contentGuid)
        {
            return _database.GetItem(new ID(contentGuid));
        }
    }
}
```

3. Before we modify our MediaController to use this new repository, we should create the ViewModel that the view will need. This is what the MediaController will construct and pass to the view, based on the data returned from the repository. Start by adding a new folder to SitecoreDev. Feature.Media called ViewModels. In this new folder, create a new class called HeroSliderImageViewModel. It should look like Listing 5-3.

Listing 5-3. A New View Model for Our Media

```
using System;
using System.Collections.Generic;
using System.Linq;
using System.Web;

namespace SitecoreDev.Feature.Media.ViewModels
{
    public class HeroSliderImageViewModel
    {
        public string MediaUrl { get; set; }
        public string AltText { get; set; }
        public bool IsActive { get; set; }
    }
}
```

    4.   Also in the ViewModels folder, let's create a new file called HeroSliderViewModel. It should contain the code from Listing 5-4.

Listing 5-4. A New View Model

```
using System;
using System.Collections.Generic;
using System.Linq;
using System.Web;

namespace SitecoreDev.Feature.Media.ViewModels
{
    public class HeroSliderViewModel
    {
        public List<HeroSliderImageViewModel> HeroImages { get; set; } =
            new List<HeroSliderImageViewModel>();
        public int ImageCount => HeroImages.Count;
        public bool HasImages => ImageCount > 0;
    }
}
```

    5.   Now that we've created our view models, let's refactor our MediaController to take advantage of our new repository! Modify the MediaController as shown in Listing 5-5.

Listing 5-5. Updates to Our Controller

```
using System;
using System.Web.Mvc;
using Sitecore.Data.Fields;
using Sitecore.Data.Items;
using Sitecore.Mvc.Presentation;
using Sitecore.Resources.Media;
using SitecoreDev.Feature.Media.Repositories;
using SitecoreDev.Feature.Media.ViewModels;

namespace SitecoreDev.Feature.Media.Controllers
{
    public class MediaController : Controller
    {
        private readonly IMediaRepository _repository;

        public MediaController()
        {
            _repository = new SitecoreMediaRepository();
        }

        public ViewResult HeroSlider()
        {
            var viewModel = new HeroSliderViewModel();
```

```
    if (!String.IsNullOrEmpty(
        RenderingContext.Current.Rendering.DataSource))
    {
        var contentItem = _repository.GetItem(
            RenderingContext.Current.Rendering.DataSource);
        if (contentItem != null)
        {
            var heroImagesField = new MultilistField(
                contentItem.Fields["Hero Images"]);
            if (heroImagesField != null)
            {
                var items = heroImagesField.GetItems();
                var itemCounter = 0;
                foreach(var item in items)
                {
                    var mediaItem = (MediaItem)item;
                    viewModel.HeroImages.Add(new HeroSliderImageViewModel()
                    {
                        MediaUrl = MediaManager.GetMediaUrl(mediaItem),
                        AltText = mediaItem.Alt,
                        IsActive = itemCounter == 0
                    });
                    itemCounter++;
                }
            }
        }
    }

    return View(viewModel);
    }
  }
}
```

In Listing 5-5, we added a read-only member that gets set in the constructor. The type is IMediaRepository because that is our new dependency. In the constructor, we are instantiating an instance of SitecoreMediaRepository because it fits the criteria for what our controller needs. In a future example, we will refactor our constructor to have this dependency injected through inversion of control. But for now, we just instantiate SitecoreMediaRepository.

6. The final step is to refactor the view for our HeroSlider. Because we have introduced the new view model, our view will be much simpler! It should now look like Listing 5-6.

Listing 5-6. Updates to Our View

```
@model SitecoreDev.Feature.Media.ViewModels.HeroSliderViewModel

@if (Model.HasImages)
{
    <div id="myCarousel" class="carousel slide" data-ride="carousel">
        <ol class="carousel-indicators">
            @for (int i = 0; i < Model.ImageCount; i++)
            {
                <li data-target="#myCarousel" data-slide-to="@i"
                    class="@(Model.HeroImages[i].IsActive ? "active" : "")"></li>
            }
        </ol>

        <div class="carousel-inner" role="listbox">
            @foreach (var image in Model.HeroImages)
            {
                <div class="item @(image.IsActive ? "active" : "")">
                    <img src="@image.MediaUrl" style="width:1920px;"
                        alt="@image.AltText" />
                </div>
            }
        </div>
    </div>
}
```

Well that's it! Our slider should behave just as it did before, but the code is much cleaner!

Refactoring: Incorporating a Service Layer Pattern

A key point about a repository is that its only job is to access data. There should be no business logic in your repositories. But where then does that business logic go? In Figure 5-2 the only place for business logic to go is in the controller itself. However, that extends the controller beyond its mandate to *just* assemble data fit for a View. Now, it needs to *also* perform business logic on that data *before* it's ready for the view. Clearly we're again breaking the single responsibility principle of SOLID and we're running the risk of our controller code getting too lengthy and complex.

What is the alternative? We must move the business logic into a "Service Layer," which is situated conveniently between our controllers and the underlying repositories. Any data manipulation is the responsibility of the service layer. You can see this architecture in action in Figure 5-3.

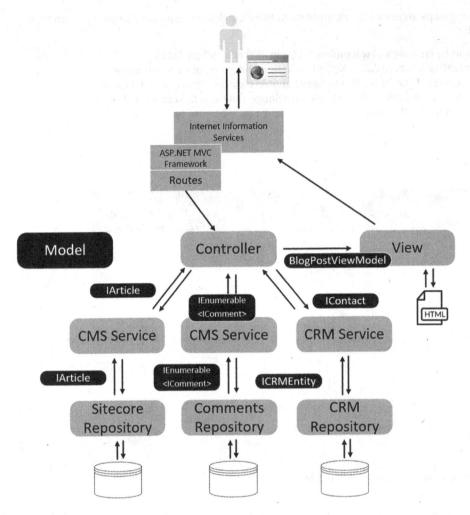

Figure 5-3. *With a domain layer we can move all our business logic out of our controllers to delegate any data manipulation, if necessary*

Figure 5-3 highlights a few other benefits of the design. For example, business logic can be moved into the service for the repository. Similarly, we have a CRM service used to handle all our business logic related to our CRM integration. This service object knows when a controller is looking for a IContact, what it really wants is an "entity" from CRM. The translation of an entity into a contact is totally abstracted away from the controller.

In the end, however, an IArticle might *still* be bigger than what the view is actually rendering. As such, our controller still maps the data model to the view model, leaving the view with just what it needs and no more. Additionally, our controller now is relegated to having one single responsibility—mapping the right data to the right view. That's easy to maintain!

Use the following steps to create a new feature module for articles, using the service layer pattern that was just described:

1. Let's start by creating a new template folder in /sitecore/Templates/
   Sitecore8Dev/Feature called Articles. In that folder, create a new interface
   template named _Article. This template should have a section called Article
   Template. In that section, there should be a Single-Line Text field called Title and
   a Rich Text field called Body.

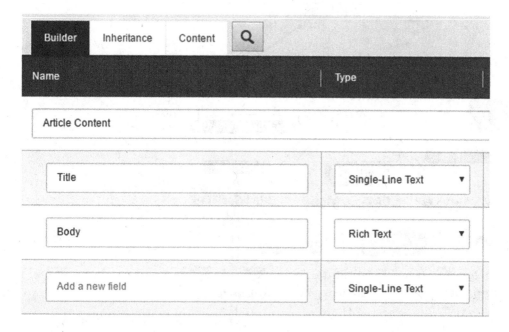

Figure 5-4. *Building a basic template for our article*

2. Next, create a new template in /sitecore/templates/Sitecore8Dev/Project/
   Sitecore8/Content Types folder named Article. This is a datasource template.
   Using the Content tab, in the Data section, select /Templates/Sitecore8Dev/
   Feature/Articles/_Article as a base template.

3. Now, in Visual Studio, in the Feature solution folder, create another solution
   folder called Articles. In this folder, we'll create another empty ASP.NET MVC
   web project called SitecoreDev.Feature.Articles.

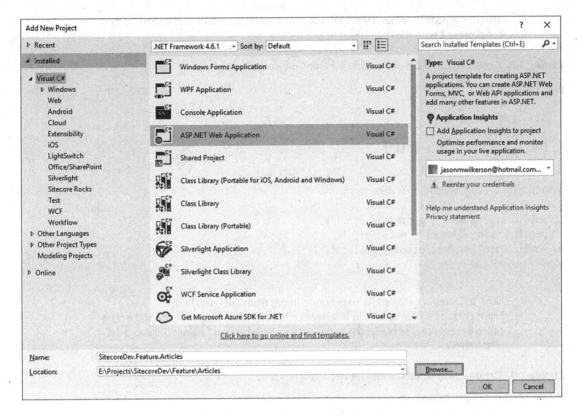

Figure 5-5. *Stub out a new project for the Articles module*

4. Once the folder has been created, delete the `App_Data` and `App_Start` folders as well as the `Global.asax` and `Web.config` files. Then create a folder called `Repositories`, another called `ViewModels` and another called `Services`.

5. Add references to the `Sitecore.Kernel.dll` and `Sitecore.Mvc.dll` assemblies found in the `libs\Sitecore` folder.

6. Next, in the `Models` folder, create a new interface named `IArticle` and a new class named `Article` with the definitions listed in Listing 5-7.

Listing 5-7. Create a New Interface Named IArticle

```csharp
public interface IArticle
{
    string Id { get; }
    string Title { get; }
    string Body { get; }
}

public class Article : IArticle
{
    public string Id { get; set; }
    public string Title { get; set; }
    public string Body { get; set; }
}
```

7. Also in the Models folder, create an interface named IComment and a class named BlogComment with the definitions in Listing 5-8.

Listing 5-8. Create an Interface and a Class for Our Comments

```
public interface IComment
{
    string Name { get; }
    string Comment { get; }
    DateTime DatePosted { get; }
}


public class BlogComment : IComment
{
    public string Name { get; set; }
    public string Comment { get; set; }
    public DateTime DatePosted { get; set; }
}
```

8. Now, let's create a repository to get our content from Sitecore. In the Repositories folder, create an interface called IArticlesRepository and a class called SitecoreArticlesRepository with the definitions in Listings 5-9 and 5-10, respectively.

Listing 5-9. Create a New Interface for Our Repository

```
using Sitecore.Data.Items;

namespace SitecoreDev.Feature.Articles.Repositories
{
    public interface IArticlesRepository
    {
        Item GetArticleContent(string contentGuid);
    }
}
```

Listing 5-10. Create a Class that Implements Our Repository Interface

```
using Sitecore;
using Sitecore.Data;
using Sitecore.Data.Items;

namespace SitecoreDev.Feature.Articles.Repositories
{
    public class SitecoreArticlesRepository : IArticlesRepository
    {
        private Database _database;

        public SitecoreArticlesRepository()
        {
            _database = Context.Database;
        }
```

```
    public Item GetArticleContent(string contentGuid)
    {
        Assert.ArgumentNotNullOrEmpty(contentGuid, "contentGuid");
        return _database.GetItem(ID.Parse(contentGuid));
    }
  }
}
```

This article repository simply has one method to get article content from Sitecore using a supplied item ID. The Sitecore Item with that ID is returned.

9. Also in the Repositories folder, let's create a repository to get comments for our blog post. Create an interface named ICommentRepository and a class named FakeBlogCommentRepository with the definitions in Listings 5-11 and 5-12, respectively. (Because we haven't set up a separate SQL database for comments, we're just going to fake it.)

Listing 5-11. Create Another Interface and Class for Our Comments Repository

```
using System.Collections.Generic;
using SitecoreDev.Feature.Articles.Models;

namespace SitecoreDev.Feature.Articles.Repositories
{
    public interface ICommentRepository
    {
        IEnumerable<IComment> GetComments(string blogId);
    }
}
```

Listing 5-12. Create Another Interface and Class for Our Comments Repository

```
using System;
using System.Collections.Generic;
using SitecoreDev.Feature.Articles.Models;

namespace SitecoreDev.Feature.Articles.Repositories
{
    public class FakeBlogCommentRepository : ICommentRepository
    {
        public IEnumerable<IComment> GetComments(string blogId)
        {
            var comments = new List<IComment>();
            comments.Add(new BlogComment() {
                Name = "Jack",
                Comment = "This post was really helpful!",
                DatePosted = DateTime.Parse("05/12/2016") });

            comments.Add(new BlogComment() {
                Name = "Jane",
                Comment = "You're a really smart guy! Keep up the good work!",
                DatePosted = DateTime.Parse("03/16/2016") });
```

```
            return comments;
        }
    }
}
```

Similarly to the Article repository, this Comments repository returns the comments associated with a particular blog post. Since comments would typically be stored in an external database and not in sitecore, and since we didn't want to overly complicate the example, we simply hard-coded in some comments to demonstrate the concept. Now that we have created our repositories, let's create the service that will hold any business logic for getting content from the Sitecore repository and potentially manipulating that data.

10. In the Services folder, create an interface named IContentService and a class named SitecoreContentService with the definitions listed in Listings 5-13 and 5-14, respectively.

Listing 5-13. Create an Interface for Our New Content Service

```
using SitecoreDev.Feature.Articles.Models;

namespace SitecoreDev.Feature.Articles.Services
{
    public interface IContentService
    {
        IArticle GetArticleContent(string contentGuid);
    }
}
```

Listing 5-14. Create a Class for Our New Content Service

```
using SitecoreDev.Feature.Articles.Models;
using SitecoreDev.Feature.Articles.Repositories;

namespace SitecoreDev.Feature.Articles.Services
{
    public class SitecoreContentService : IContentService
    {
        private readonly IArticlesRepository _repository;

        public SitecoreContentService()
        {
            _repository = new SitecoreArticlesRepository();
        }

        public IArticle GetArticleContent(string contentGuid)
        {
            Article article = null;

            var item = _repository.GetArticleContent(contentGuid);
            if (item != null)
```

```
            {
                article = new Article();
                article.Id = item.ID.ToString();
                article.Title = item.Fields["Title"]?.Value;
                article.Body = item.Fields["Body"]?.Value;
            }

            return article;
        }
    }
}
```

This article service gets the article item from the repository and then pulls the item data out of that item and into a custom data model class of type IArticle. This interface is return to the controller and is eventually displayed in the view.

Next, let's create our service for getting comments.

11. In the Services folder, create an interface named ICommentService and a class named BlogCommentService with the definitions in Listings 5-15 and 5-16, respectively.

Listing 5-15. Create an Interface for Our New Comments Service

```
using System.Collections.Generic;
using SitecoreDev.Feature.Articles.Models;

namespace SitecoreDev.Feature.Articles.Services
{
    public interface ICommentService
    {
        IEnumerable<IComment> GetComments(string blogId);
    }
}
```

Listing 5-16. Create a Class for Our New Comments Service

```
using System.Collections.Generic;
using System.Linq;
using SitecoreDev.Feature.Articles.Models;
using SitecoreDev.Feature.Articles.Repositories;

namespace SitecoreDev.Feature.Articles.Services
{
    public class BlogCommentService : ICommentService
    {
        private readonly ICommentRepository _repository;

        public BlogCommentService()
        {
            _repository = new FakeBlogCommentRepository();
        }
```

165

```
    public IEnumerable<IComment> GetComments(string blogId)
    {
        return _repository.GetComments(blogId).OrderBy(c => c.DatePosted);
    }
  }
}
```

This service is very simple. It just gets the comments for a blog post out of the repository. Only business logic should be in a service, no data access. However, in this simple example there is no business logic; it's just a pass-through.

12. The last step, before creating our controller, is the view model. In the ViewModels folder, create a class called BlogPostViewModel with the definition in Listing 5-17.

Listing 5-17. Create a New View for Our Presentation

```
public class BlogCommentViewModel
{
    public string Name { get; set; }
    public string Comment { get; set; }
    public DateTime DatePosted { get; set; }
}

public class BlogPostViewModel
{
    public string Title { get; set; }
    public bool HasTitle => !String.IsNullOrEmpty(Title);
    public string Body { get; set; }
    public List<BlogCommentViewModel> Comments { get; set; } =
        new List<BlogCommentViewModel>();
    public bool HasComments => Comments.Count > 0;
}
```

13. Now, to our controller... In the Controllers folder, add a new controller named ArticlesController with the definition in Listing 5-18.

Listing 5-18. Create a New Controller that Calls the Two Services

```
using System;
using System.Web.Mvc;
using Sitecore.Mvc.Presentation;
using SitecoreDev.Feature.Articles.Services;
using SitecoreDev.Feature.Articles.ViewModels;

namespace SitecoreDev.Feature.Articles.Controllers
{
    public class ArticlesController : Controller
    {
        private readonly IContentService _contentService;
        private readonly ICommentService _commentService;
```

```
public ArticlesController()
{
    _contentService = new SitecoreContentService();
    _commentService = new BlogCommentService();
}

public ViewResult BlogPost()
{
    var viewModel = new BlogPostViewModel();

    if (!String.IsNullOrEmpty(
        RenderingContext.Current.Rendering.DataSource))
    {
        var blogContent = _contentService.GetArticleContent(
            RenderingContext.Current.Rendering.DataSource);
        if (blogContent != null)
        {
            viewModel.Title = blogContent.Title;
            viewModel.Body = blogContent.Body;

            var comments = _commentService.GetComments(blogContent.Id);
            if (comments != null)
            {
                foreach(var comment in comments)
                {
                    viewModel.Comments.Add(new BlogCommentViewModel()
                    {
                        Name = comment.Name,
                        Comment = comment.Comment,
                        DatePosted = comment.DatePosted
                    });
                }
            }
        }
    }

    return View(viewModel);
}
}
}
```

14. Finally, let's create the view for our blog post! In the Views folder, create a new folder called Articles, then create a new MVC 5 view page (Razor) named BlogPost. Replace the contents with the markup in Listing 5-19.

Listing 5-19. Create a New View for Our Post!

```
@model SitecoreDev.Feature.Articles.ViewModels.BlogPostViewModel

<div>

    @if (Model.HasTitle)
    {
        <h3>@Model.Title</h3>
    }

    <p>@Model.Body</p>

    <h4>Comments</h4>
    @if (Model.HasComments)
    {
        foreach(var comment in Model.Comments)
        {
            <div>
                <div>@comment.Name</div>
                <div>@comment.DatePosted</div>
                <div>@comment.Comment</div>
            </div>
                <br />
        }
    }
    else
    {
        <div>No Comments</div>
    }

</div>
```

15. Now that we have all our code completed, we will build the solution, and then in the Visual Studio Task Runner, execute the Publish-Site Gulp task to publish our changes. Once publish has completed, navigate to `http://sitecore8/sitecore`.

16. In the Content Editor, navigate to `/sitecore/Layout/Renderings/Sitecore8Dev/Feature`. Add a new rendering folder named `Articles` to correspond to our new `Articles` module. In this new `Articles` rendering folder, create a new controller rendering named `Blog Post`. Add the values:

```
Controller: SitecoreDev.Feature.Articles.Controllers.ArticlesController, SitecoreDev.
            Feature.Articles
Controller Action: Blog Post
Datasource Location: ./Components
Datasource Template: /sitecore/templates/Sitecore8Dev/Project/Sitecore8/Content Types/Article
```

17. Finally, let's add a new page for our blog post! Navigate to `/sitecore/content/Home`. Right-click on Home and select Insert ➤ Insert from template. In the Insert from Template dialog, select `/Branches/Sitecore8Dev/Basic Empty Page`. Name this new page `MyBlogPost` and click Insert.

18. In the Components folder under the new `MyBlogPost` page, right-click and select Insert ➤ Insert from template. Select `/Sitecore8Dev/Project/Sitecore8/Content Types/Article`, name it `My Blog Entry`, and then click Insert.

19. Add some content to the Title and Body fields.

20. Now, with the `MyBlogPost` page selected, click on the Publish tab and the Experience Editor button to open Experience Editor. Once Experience Editor has loaded, select the main placeholder and click the Add Here button. In the Select a Rendering dialog, select `/Renderings/Sitecore8Dev/Feature/Articles/Blog Post` and click Select.

21. In the Selected Associated Content dialog, select My Blog Entry. Click OK. You should see your new blog post rendered with comments!

Refactoring: Incorporating Object-Relational Mapping

At this point our architecture is developing nicely. We have achieved an "n-tier" status with our application, with web, service, repository and data tiers. We can almost declare victory, having achieved a great deal of separation of concerns. However, as far as Sitecore is concerned, we still have opportunities to get closer to "clean code."

What code smells am I referring to? Ask yourself, "Where do I still see a lot of risk for code duplication?" The answer that is probably jumping out at you is the repository layer. You can end up with *lots* of Sitecore API code in your repositories. You can also end up with *lots* of code mapping the results of those API calls into our model that's being passed back to the service layer. You can't say all the code is duplicate code; each repository method has unique code and a unique purpose. But you can say all the repository/service patterns have lots of similar code in them, and they all carry the same flow: 1) query Sitecore, 2) get back results, 3) create new concrete model classes, and 4) map the results into those model classes. If they all follow the same behavior, isn't there a way to simplify the code?

```
Answer, you guessed it: Yes!
```

Enter Object-Relational Mapping (ORM). ORM tools abound, but they basically do one thing: retrieve data then map two different incompatible objects to each other. An ORM can be the bridge between Sitecore and your solution. Without ORM you're writing a ton of mapping code. With ORM, you're writing hardly any code at all!

■ **Note** April Fools! Why'd we have your write all that API code if you now know a way to completely get rid of it? Well, it's not bad to know a bit about the Sitecore API. Secondly, now you *really* understand why an ORM can be very helpful. It's like how I felt when I first bought a pneumatic nailer; I would've never known how much I hate hammers until I tried an air nailer for the first time. Learning the long way is just as important as learning how to leverage tools to optimize your code.

There are a few tools that are specific for Sitecore—Glass.Mapper, Synthesis, and Fortis—but they have differences. As `Glass.Mapper` (`http://bit.ly/2d7tjRd`) is the most popular tool in the community, we'll be using it throughout the rest of the book. Imagine all the repository code you wrote and now check out Listing 5-20.

■ **Note** As mentioned earlier, `Glass.Mapper`, Synthesis, and Fortis are all tools that end in the same result, but get there in different ways. These differences are important to understand and are explained quite well by Kam Figy at `http://bit.ly/2cGgysd`.

"Glass is more of a traditional ORM tool, similar to say nHibernate for SQL. If you're looking to map your Sitecore templates onto pure POCO (Plain Ol' C# Object) classes that use primitive values (e.g. strings), then Glass may be your jam. Glass' claim to fame is that is does not internally wrap the Sitecore Item class, and actually does map directly to C# object properties. In other words, its model objects have zero ties to Sitecore once mapped.

Fortis works fairly similarly to Glass at a conceptual level, but unlike Glass (and like Synthesis), it is a wrapper. In other words, Fortis' objects are essentially facades over the Sitecore Item class and are internally tied to Sitecore's objects. This can result in improved performance over a mapper in some cases, although Glass has been pretty well optimized.

Synthesis integrates the code generator with the mapping framework (separate tools/processes when done through Glass.Mapper or Fortis), which allows the model and framework code to be more harmonious. For example, Synthesis objects are always template type safe (you cannot map an item onto the wrong template class), cast compatible (if template B inherits template A, then you can cast any instance of B to an A using C# casting), and represent template inheritance with an interface hierarchy. Synthesis objects may be natively used as Content Search query models (even as interfaces). This integration also makes Synthesis ridiculously fast and reflection-free, because the mappings are all done with pregenerated code."

Listing 5-20. Using Glass.Mapper Significantly Reduces the Code in Repositories

```
public interface IArticle
{
    public Guid Id;
    public string Title;
    public DateTime Date;
    public string Body;
}

public void GetCurrentArticle(ISitecoreContext sitecoreContext)
{
    var article = sitecoreContext.GetCurrentItem<IArticle>();
    var title = article.Title;
}
```

The type of our model, IArticle, now simply gets passed into Glass.Mappers' SitecoreContext. GetCurrentItem method as a generic type. The result of which is an instance of our IArticle returned as an interface back to the calling service layer object. Now *that* is maintainable code!

When you use an ORM, you are essentially mapping properties from one data source to the properties of a different model. If all the property names between the data source and the target model are identical, most ORMs on the market will handle that mapping without any additional configuration. Glass.Mapper is no different. However, if property names are different (e.g., "CustomerNumber" vs "Customer Number") or the structure of the data is different altogether, you must provide a means to resolve that discrepancy.

With Glass.Mapper, there are two methods of providing this mapping: attribute mapping and fluent configuration. Both are completely valid methods, so ultimately it comes down to preference. For instance, you could something similar to Listing 5-21..

Listing 5-21. An Example Glass Model Interface

```
[SitecoreType(AutoMap = true)]
public interface IArticle
{
    [SitecoreId]
    Guid Id { get; }
    [SitecoreField(FieldName = "Title")]
    string Title { get; }
    [SitecoreField(FieldName = "Body")]
    string Body { get; }
    [SitecoreField(FieldName = "Author Name")]
    string AuthorName { get; }
}
```

This works just fine, but because it is performing more than one function (it's defining the model as well as providing configuration information for mapping back to a data source), it's violating SOLID design principles. The answer to this (and it just happens to be my preference as well!) is to use fluent configuration.

Let's take the previous model and strip out the attributes, as seen in Listing 5-22.

Listing 5-22. A Trimmed Down Model Is a Better Approach

```
public interface IArticle
{
    string Id { get; }
    string Title { get; }
    string Body { get; }
    string AuthorName { get; }
}
```

Now, if we wanted to configure the property mapping with fluent configuration, it might look something like Listing 5-23.

Listing 5-23. A Fluent Configuration Example

```
public class IArticleMap : SitecoreGlassMap<IArticle>
{
    public override void Configure()
    {
        Map(config =>
        {
            config.AutoMap();
            config.Id(f => f.Id);
            config.Field(f => f.Title).FieldName("Title");
            config.Field(f => f.Body).FieldName("Body");
            config.Field(f => f.AuthorName).FieldName("Author Name");
        });
    }
}
```

171

This configuration would then get added to Glass.Mapper's configuration factory.

■ **Note**   With AutoMap enabled, configuring individual properties where property names and template field names match isn't necessary. However, to maintain readability, consistency, and maintainability for future developers, it is a good practice to follow.

Now let's refactor or blog post example to incorporate ORM! Follow these steps to refactor our code:

1. Start by adding a reference to Glass.Mapper.Sc to the SitecoreDev.Feature.
   Articles project from NuGet. As of the writing of this book, the latest version
   is v4.0.11.63. This will add a few files and folders to your project as well as the
   references. It will add two configuration files with patches in them, but most
   importantly, it will add the GlassMapperScCustom.cs class to the App_Start
   folder. It is in this file that we will eventually add our fluent configuration to
   Glass.Mapper's config factory.

2. Now, open the IArticle interface in the Models folder and change the type of the
   ID field from string to Guid. You'll need to make this same change in the Article
   implementation class.

3. Next, let's add a new folder under Models called Configuration. In this folder,
   add a class named IArticleMap with the definition in Listing 5-24.

Listing 5-24. Our IArticle Mapper

```
using Glass.Mapper.Sc.Maps;

namespace SitecoreDev.Feature.Articles.Models.Configuration
{
    public class IArticleMap : SitecoreGlassMap<IArticle>
    {
        public override void Configure()
        {
            Map(config =>
            {
                config.AutoMap();
                config.Id(f => f.Id);
                config.Field(f => f.Title).FieldName("Title");
                config.Field(f => f.Body).FieldName("Body");
            });
        }
    }
}
```

4. Now, open the GlassMapperScCustom class in the App_Start folder. Modify the
   AddMaps method and add this line:

```
mapsConfigFactory.Add(() => new IArticleMap());
```

Adding this IArticleMap class to the configuration factory of Glass.Mapper is what ties our IArticle interface together with the configuration provided in IArticleMap. Without this step, Glass.Mapper wouldn't know how to map an IArticle object.

5. In the IArticlesRepository interface in the Repositories folder, change the return type from Item to IArticle, as shown in Listing 5-25.

Listing 5-25. Update the Return Type

```
public interface IArticlesRepository
{
    IArticle GetArticleContent(string contentGuid);
}
```

6. In the SitecoreArticlesRepository class, modify the class to match Listing 5-26.

Listing 5-26. Update Our Repository

```
using System;
using Sitecore.Diagnostics;
using Glass.Mapper.Sc;
using SitecoreDev.Feature.Articles.Models;

namespace SitecoreDev.Feature.Articles.Repositories
{
    public class SitecoreArticlesRepository : IArticlesRepository
    {
        private readonly ISitecoreContext _sitecoreContext;

        public SitecoreArticlesRepository()
        {
            _sitecoreContext = new SitecoreContext();
        }

        public IArticle GetArticleContent(string contentGuid)
        {
            Assert.ArgumentNotNullOrEmpty(contentGuid, "contentGuid");
            return _sitecoreContext.GetItem<IArticle>(Guid.Parse(contentGuid));
        }
    }
}
```

7. Next, in the SitecoreContentService class in the Services folder, update the GetArticleContent method to match Listing 5-27, removing the mapping code from Item to IArticle.

Listing 5-27. Update the GetArticleContent Method

```
public IArticle GetArticleContent(string contentGuid)
{
    return _repository.GetArticleContent(contentGuid);
}
```

8. Finally, in the `BlogPost` controller action of the `ArticlesController` controller, change the call to `_commentService.GetComments` to match the following line:

```
var comments = _commentService.GetComments(blogContent.Id.ToString());
```

Now, build your solution then, from the Visual Studio Task Runner, execute the Publish-Site Gulp task. Once the publish is complete, navigate to `http://sitecore8/myblogpost` and all should still be working, but this time with no mapping code!

Refactoring: Incorporating Generics

You just got done refactoring all the repositories to leverage an ORM. ORM can help you reduce and remove a lot of similar code. Significant improvement! However, what if we said you could reduce it again by the same order of magnitude? Would you believe us? Well, that's just what we're going to attempt in this section.

You may have already guessed it by looking at the title of this section, but that repository code is a great candidate for improvement via the use of generics. Why? Because all the Sitecore repositories now do basically the same thing. Glass retrieves the item from Sitecore and the repository returns an object of the type specified. That's it! What's the difference between all the repositories? The only difference is the type itself.

A repository that uses a generic type would allow us to consolidate all of the Sitecore repositories down to one single generic repository that handles almost all our Sitecore needs. That's the power of generics; extreme reductions in very similar code.

Look at Listing 5-28 for a method signature as an example of a generic method.

Listing 5-28. A Generic Repository, with the Help of Glass.Mapper, Can Help Reduce Your Repository Code to a Few Lines

```
public T GetContent<T>()
{
    var item = sitecoreContext.GetCurrentItem<T>();
    return item;
}
```

You'll notice the method's return type is T. This is the identifier for an unknown return type. Additionally, notice the <T> after the method name. This means that at compile time the caller of the method must pass a type to declare the type at runtime. For example, the following code might be found in a service layer method calling a generic repository:

```
IArticle article = _contentRepository.GetContent<IArticle>(contentGuid);
```

In this method call we're calling into a common repository and declaring the type. This type is passed to the method at runtime as an `IArticle`. That type is then passed into the generic equivalent of `Glass.Mapper`'s `GetItem` method. Glass, too, is smart enough to interpret the generic type requested and map to the right object as necessary.

Since `Glass` provides great support for generics, it now seems obvious what we need to do. We need to define a base Sitecore repository in a new Foundation module that will be available to the entire solution. Figure 5-6 depicts the updated design of our solution.

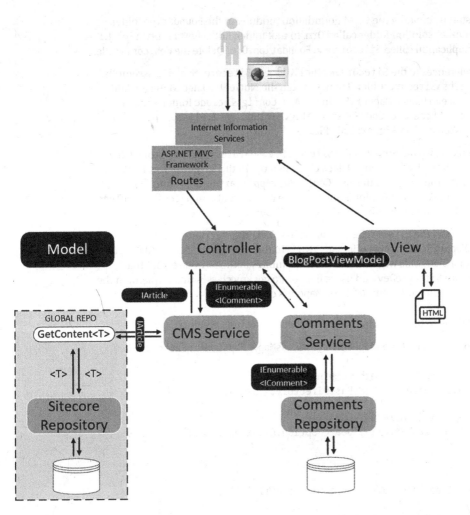

Figure 5-6. *All of our Sitecore repository needs can be accommodated in one global repository via the use of generics*

Use the following steps as a guide to refactor accordingly. In this example, we are going to introduce three new Foundation modules:

- *ORM*: This is where we will configure Glass to load all of our model configuration classes through reflection.

- *Repository*: Here, we will define our base repository implementation using Glass. Mapper. All repository implementations will inherit from this implementation.

- *Model*: Because our base repository class will be a Foundation module, we need to provide a few base interfaces that will be available to the entire solution.

1. Let's start by creating the ORM Foundation module. In the Foundation folder, add another solution folder called Orm. In that folder, add a new empty ASP.NET Web Application called SitecoreDev.Foundation.Orm. Delete the Web.config file.

2. Add references to the Sitecore.Kernel.dll and Sitecore.Mvc.dll assemblies in the libs\Sitecore folder. Then, through the NuGet Package Manager, add a reference to Glass.Mapper.Sc. In the App_Config\Include folder, remove the Glass.Mapper.Sc.CodeFirst.config.exclude and z.Glass.Mapper. Sc.ViewRender.config.exclude files.

3. If you recall, we did Step 2 in the SitecoreDev.Feature.Articles project. Since we're centralizing that control, let's clean that up. In the SitecoreDev.Feature. Articles project, delete the App_Config and App_Start folders completely. Then, open Windows Explorer and navigate to %webroot%\App_Config\Include. Delete the four files that begin with Glass.Mapper.

4. Next, back in the SitecoreDev.Foundation.Orm project, open the GlassMapperScCustom class in App_Start. In the AddMaps method, add the code in Listing 5-29. This will search all the assemblies in the /bin directory that begin with SitecoreDev and use reflection to get any classes that implement the IGlassMap and add them to Glass.Mapper's config map.

Listing 5-29. Add Code to the AddMaps Method to Search the bin Directory

```
public static void AddMaps(IConfigFactory<IGlassMap> mapsConfigFactory)
{
    string binPath = System.IO.Path.Combine(
    System.AppDomain.CurrentDomain.BaseDirectory, "bin");

    foreach (string dll in Directory.GetFiles(
        binPath, "SitecoreDev*.dll", SearchOption.AllDirectories))
    {
        try
        {
            Assembly loadedAssembly = Assembly.LoadFile(dll);

            Type glassmapType = typeof(IGlassMap);
            var maps = loadedAssembly.GetTypes().Where(x =>
                glassmapType.IsAssignableFrom(x));

            if (maps != null)
            {
                foreach (var map in maps)
                    mapsConfigFactory.Add(() =>
                        Activator.CreateInstance(map) as IGlassMap);
            }
        }
        catch (FileLoadException loadEx)
        { } // The Assembly has already been loaded.
        catch (BadImageFormatException imgEx)
        { } // If exception is thrown, the file is not an assembly.
    }
}
```

In Listing 5-29, we're using reflection, executed in the Initialize pipeline, to scan the assemblies in our bin directory to find any class that implement IGlassMap and automatically add them to the configuration factory of Glass.Mapper. This will save us from having to register each configuration class individually, saving time and eliminating developer forgetfulness.

5.   If you build your solution and publish the site through the Publish-Site Gulp task at this point, everything should still work!

6.   Next, let's create our new model Foundation module. In the Foundation folder, create a new solution folder named Model. In that folder, create a new class library named SitecoreDev.Foundation.Model. Delete Class1.cs.

7.   Let's start by creating a new, empty interface named ICmsEntity:

```
public interface ICmsEntity
{
}
```

For now, this is all we're going to create in this project. This interface will be included on a model object that represents a Sitecore item. Non-sitecore models (e.g., IComment) will not implement this interface. I will explain its purpose shortly.

■ **Note**   Earlier in the chapter, when we created our Repository layer, Service layer, and Models for the Articles feature, we created all of them in the SitecoreDev.Feature.Articles project. While this approach is fine for the purposes of the examples in this book, in an actual production project, you would be well served by providing some sort of automated enforcement of the separation of concerns we have worked so hard to achieve. This can be accomplished in two ways. You could separate your layers into separate projects. You would have a SitecoreDev.Feature.Articles project, a SitecoreDev.Feature.Articles.Model project, a SitecoreDev.Feature.Articles.Service project, and a SitecoreDev.Feature.Articles.Repository project. Another method to enforce separation of concerns would be through custom rule definitions in FxCop.

Having this separation, either through separate projects or through FxCop rules, will ensure that more junior members of your team don't accidently derail the dependency flow as they learn and get more comfortable with these principles.

---

8.   In the IArticle interface in the SitecoreDev.Feature.Articles project, have IArticle implement ICmsEntity. This will require adding a reference to the SitecoreDev.Foundation.Model project. It should now look like Listing 5-30.

Listing 5-30. Update IArticle to Implement ICmsEntity

```
public interface IArticle : ICmsEntity
{
    Guid Id { get; }
    string Title { get; }
    string Body { get; }
}
```

9. Next, let's create our repository Foundation module. In the Foundation folder, create a new solution folder named Repository. In this folder, create a new Empty ASP.NET Web Application named SitecoreDev.Foundation.Repository. Delete Web.config and add a reference to the SitecoreDev.Foundation.Model project. Also add references to the Sitecore.Kernel.dll and Sitecore.Mvc. dll assemblies in the libs\Sitecore folder. Then, through the NuGet Package Manager, add a reference to Glass.Mapper.Sc. Delete the App_Config and the App_Start folders.

10. Add a new folder in this project called Content. In this new folder, add a new interface named IContentRepository with the definition from Listing 5-31.

Listing 5-31. Add a New Interface Named IContentRepository

```
using SitecoreDev.Foundation.Model;

namespace SitecoreDev.Foundation.Repository.Content
{
    public interface IContentRepository
    {
        T GetContentItem<T>(string contentGuid) where T : class, ICmsEntity;
    }
}
```

Here is where we introduce the use of ICmsEntity. When you are using generics, T can be any type. It can be a value type (i.e. int, char, bool, etc...) or a reference type (i.e. class, object, string, etc...). However, when we use generics, we generally know, at a minimum, what should be allowed for that type or what shouldn't. So with the where T : class, ICmsEntity statement, we're providing a constraint on that generic T. We're saying that, at a minimum, whatever is passed in for T should be a reference type that implements ICmsEntity. This is known as "constraining generics." Because we modified IArticle to implement ICmsEntity in Step 8 above, that means we can now specify IArticle as the generic for the GetContentItem method. We cannot, however, use IComment, since it doesn't implement ICmsEntity.

11. Moving along, now that we've defined our interface, let's create its implementation. In the Content folder, add a new class named SitecoreContentRepository with the definition listed in Listing 5-32.

Listing 5-32. Create an Implementation for the IContentRepository

```
using System;
using Glass.Mapper.Sc;
using Sitecore.Diagnostics;
using SitecoreDev.Foundation.Model;

namespace SitecoreDev.Foundation.Repository.Content
{
    public abstract class SitecoreContentRepository : IContentRepository
    {
        private readonly ISitecoreContext _sitecoreContext;
```

```
public SitecoreContentRepository()
{
    _sitecoreContext = new SitecoreContext();
}

public virtual T GetContentItem<T>(string contentGuid) where T : class,
    ICmsEntity
{
    Assert.ArgumentNotNullOrEmpty(contentGuid, "contentGuid");

    return _sitecoreContext.GetItem<T>(Guid.Parse(contentGuid));
}
}
}
```

12. Now, back up in the SitecoreDev.Feature.Articles project, add a reference to the SitecoreDev.Foundation.Repository project. Then, in SitecoreContentService in the Services folder, change the reference to IArticlesRepository to IContentRepository and SitecoreArticlesRepository to SitecoreContentRepository. You'll also have to change the GetArticleContent method call to return _repository.GetContentItem<IArticle>(contentGuid). When you're done, it should look like Listing 5-33.

Listing 5-33. Update the GetArticleContent Method to Call into the Repo

```
using SitecoreDev.Feature.Articles.Models;
using SitecoreDev.Foundation.Repository.Content;

namespace SitecoreDev.Feature.Articles.Services
{
    public class SitecoreContentService : IContentService
    {
        private readonly IContentRepository _repository;

        public SitecoreContentService()
        {
            _repository = new SitecoreContentRepository();
        }

        public IArticle GetArticleContent(string contentGuid)
        {
            return _repository.GetContentItem<IArticle>(contentGuid);
        }
    }
}
```

At this point, you can delete the IArticlesRepository and SitecoreArticlesRepository files in the Repositories folder.

Finally, build your solution and publish the site with the Publish-Site Gulp task. Once the publish has completed, navigate to http://sitecore8/myblogpost and everything should still be in working order, *and* you just removed a bunch of duplicate code in the process!

Refactoring: Incorporating Inversion of Control

Another "clean code" best practice we must take into consideration is all the instantiation of objects we're doing. If you're a clean code purist, you'll know that objects should never instantiate other objects. Objects creating objects is the path to the dark side, Yoda once said. Martin Fowler's has a wonderful article describing inversion of control that can be viewed at `http://bit.ly/2d4kQuU`.

■ **Note** Okay, Yoda didn't have much to say about software engineering, but we still feel object proliferation is the path to the equivalent of the dark side as far as software engineering is concerned. Or, at the very least, the path to tightly coupled code.

Why is it bad to instantiate objects, you might ask? The basic reason is that it leads to tightly coupled code. When a class creates another class, by definition that class is now dependent on the class is created. If that "child class" changes later for some reason, those changes may create the need for refactoring in the "parent class". If you do this all the time in all your classes now one change may break stuff all over the place. You're left with fragile code that breaks easily.

■ **Note** Unit testing is another *big* reason you don't want your code instantiating objects! If your constructors take parameters or you have your dependencies exposed as properties, it is much easier to unit test than if there exist hard-coded dependencies. Chapter 7 is solely about unit testing Sitecore.

In an ideal world, classes *never* create other classes. Rather, a class takes its dependencies as interfaces within its constructor (aka, constructor injection). Class dependencies can also be overridden by exposing them as properties (aka, property injection). In either case, loose coupling is achieved by abstraction, through the use of interfaces. If this sounds like a nirvana fairy-tale, you probably have not yet been introduced to inversion of control (IoC) or dependency injection (DI).

With DI, your classes can declare their dependencies. Then, in your DI container configuration, you specify all of your dependency interfaces and what implementation of those interfaces should be returned when requested. You are "inverting control" of object creation from your classes to the DI container.

For example, in our `ArticlesController`, we have a dependency on a service that returns our content. That dependency is `IContentService`. Right now, we're simply instantiating a new `SitecoreContentService` in the constructor, but that is creating a tight coupling between our `ArticlesController` and the `SitecoreContentService`. However, through dependency injection, we can configure our container to return an instance of `SitecoreContentService` whenever `IContentService` is requested. Now, all we need to do is specify `IContentService` as a parameter of the `ArticlesController` constructor and the ASP.NET MVC `DependencyResolver` will resolve that dependency, through our DI container, as `SitecoreContentService`. This is just one example of loosely coupled code.

There are a number of dependency injection frameworks on the market—Unity, Castle Windsor, Ninject, and SimpleIoC, just to name a few—but they all have their own features and limitations. Some are really fast but have fewer features, such as lifetime management and constructor factories, while others are very mature and fully featured but are slower. In the Sitecore community, SimpleInjector (`http://bit.ly/2d3eQEF`) is one of the most popular DI Frameworks used.

There was a performance benchmark test done by Nat Mann back in 2015 (`http://bit.ly/2dkC3Qa` and `http://bit.ly/2cKaGA8`), testing various IoC containers against Sitecore implementations. SimpleInjector was a clear winner over others, so it's the one we'll use in this book.

■ **Note** In Sitecore 8.2, dependency injection changed within Sitecore. Version 8.2 now leverages the Microsoft Dependency Injection framework introduced in .NET core. A more detailed explanation of the DI changes in 8.2 is laid out by Kam Figy at `http://bit.ly/2cUlPiC`.

Check out the following steps, contributed by Kevin Brechbühl in a public fork of the Habitat project on `github.com`, where we'll refactor our blog post example to use dependency injection:

1. Start by adding a new solution folder called IoC to the Foundation folder. In that folder, add a new ASP.NET web application called SitecoreDev.Foundation.Ioc, checking the MVC box for including the folders and core references for MVC. You can delete all of the files and folders in the project, except for packages.config.

2. Add a reference to the Sitecore.Kernel.dll from the libs/Sitecore folder, then, through the NuGet Package Manager, add references to SimpleInjector and SimpleInjector.Integration.Web.Mvc.

3. Now, let's add a few folders. Add two new root folders—App_Config and Pipelines. Inside the App_Config folder, create a folder called Include. Inside that folder, create one called Foundation. Then, in the Pipelines folder, create a folder called InitializeContainer. When you're done, it should look like Figure 5-7.

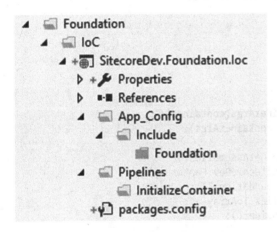

Figure 5-7. *Folder structure for our new modules*

4. In the Pipelines\InitializeContainer folder, add a new class named InitializeContainerArgs with the definition in Listing 5-34.

Listing 5-34. Add a New Pipeline Class to Pass Our Args to Our Container

```
using SimpleInjector;
using Sitecore.Pipelines;

namespace SitecoreDev.Foundation.Ioc.Pipelines. InitializeContainer
{
    public class InitializeDependencyInjectionArgs : PipelineArgs
    {
        public Container Container { get; set; }
```

```
        public InitializeDependencyInjectionArgs(Container container)
        {
            this.Container = container;
        }
    }
}
```

5. Also in the Pipelines\Initialize folder, create another new class named
    InitializeContainer with the definition in Listing 5-35.

Listing 5-35. Add a New Pipeline Class to Initialize Our Container

```
using System;
using System.Linq;
using System.Web.Mvc;
using SimpleInjector;
using SimpleInjector.Integration.Web.Mvc;
using Sitecore.Diagnostics;
using Sitecore.Pipelines;

namespace SitecoreDev.Foundation.Ioc.Pipelines. InitializeContainer
{
    public class InitializeContainer
    {
        public void Process(PipelineArgs args)
        {
            var container = new Container();

            var containerArgs = new InitializeContainerArgs(container);
            CorePipeline.Run("initializeContainer", containerArgs);

            var assemblies = AppDomain.CurrentDomain.GetAssemblies()
                .Where(a => a.FullName.StartsWith("SitecoreDev.Feature.") ||
                a.FullName.StartsWith("SitecoreDev.Foundation."));
            container.RegisterMvcControllers(assemblies.ToArray());
            container.RegisterMvcIntegratedFilterProvider();

            DependencyResolver.SetResolver(
                new SimpleInjectorDependencyResolver(container));
        }
    }
}
```

6. In the App_Config\Include\Foundation folder, add a new web configuration file
    named Foundation.Ioc.config with the configuration from Listing 5-36.

Listing 5-36. Add a New Config to Store Our IoC Settings

```xml
<configuration xmlns:patch="http://www.sitecore.net/xmlconfig/">
    <sitecore>
        <pipelines>
            <initialize>
                <processor type="SitecoreDev.Foundation.Ioc.Pipelines.InitializeContainer.
InitializeContainer, SitecoreDev.Foundation.Ioc"
                            patch:before="processor[@type='Sitecore.Mvc.Pipelines.Loader.
InitializeControllerFactory, Sitecore.Mvc']" />
            </initialize>

            <initializeContainer>
            </initializeContainer>
        </pipelines>
    </sitecore>
</configuration>
```

7. Now that we have our initial configuration and creation of the IoC Container done and patched in to Sitecore's initialize pipeline, let's register the dependencies in our Articles feature! In the SitecoreDev.Feature.Articles project, add a reference to SimpleInjector through the NuGet Package Manager. You'll also need to add a reference to the SitecoreDev.Foundation.Ioc project.

■ **Note** Implementation of dependency injection can be a very hotly debated topic in many circles. There are ultimately many ways to achieve our end goal, with this being one. Another approach, following the Composition Root pattern, is described by Richard Seal at http://bit.ly/2d3eHRp.

---

8. Create a new folder called Pipelines and, in that folder, add a folder called InitializeContainer.

9. In the InitializeContainer folder, create a new class named RegisterDependencies with the definition in Listing 5-37.

Listing 5-37. Add a Class to Register the Dependencies

```csharp
using SitecoreDev.Foundation.Ioc.Pipelines.InitializeContainer;
using SitecoreDev.Feature.Articles.Repositories;
using SitecoreDev.Feature.Articles.Services;

namespace SitecoreDev.Feature.Articles.Pipelines.InitializeContainer
{
    public class RegisterDependencies
    {
        public void Process(InitializeContainerArgs args)
        {
            args.Container.Register<ICommentRepository,
                FakeBlogCommentRepository>();
```

```
        args.Container.Register<ICommentService, BlogCommentService>();
        args.Container.Register<IContentService, SitecoreContentService>();
      }
    }
}
```

10. Create a folder called App_Config. Inside that folder, create another called Include. Inside the Include folder, create one last folder called Feature.

11. In the new App_Config\Include\Feature folder, add a new web configuration file named Feature.Articles.config with the configuration from Listing 5-38.

Listing 5-38. Add the Pipeline Config File

```xml
<configuration xmlns:patch="http://www.sitecore.net/xmlconfig/" xmlns:set="http://www.
sitecore.net/xmlconfig/set/">
  <sitecore>
    <pipelines>
      <initializeContainer>
        <processor type="SitecoreDev.Feature.Articles.Pipelines.InitializeContainer.
                        RegisterDependencies, SitecoreDev.Feature.Articles" />
      </initializeContainer>
    </pipelines>
  </sitecore>
</configuration>
```

Now that we've registered our dependencies in the IoC container and patched in our registration code into the initializeContainer pipeline, let's go refactor our services and controller to have the dependencies injected into the constructors rather than instantiating them ourselves.

12. In the constructor of the Services\BlogCommentService class, remove the instantiation of the FakeBlogCommentRepository and replace the constructor with the code in Listing 5-39.

Listing 5-39. Refactor the Comment Service to Take an Interface

```
public BlogCommentService(ICommentRepository repository)
{
    _repository = repository;
}
```

13. In the SitecoreContentService class, replace the constructor with the code from Listing 5-40.

Listing 5-40. Refactor the Content Service to Take an Interface

```
public SitecoreContentService(IContentRepository repository)
{
    _repository = repository;
}
```

14. Are you seeing a pattern yet? ☺

15. Finally, in the ArticlesController in the Controllers folder, replace the constructor with the code from Listing 5-41.

Listing 5-41. Refactor the Controller to Take a Couple Interfaces for Our Services Defined in the IoC Configuration

```
public ArticlesController(IContentService contentService, ICommentService commentService)
{
    _contentService = contentService;
    _commentService = commentService;
}
```

Now that we've set up our Articles feature project to have dependencies injected, we have one final step. In the SitecoreDev.Foundation.Repository project, we need to register our IContentRepository.

16. In that project, add a reference to SimpleInjector through the NuGet Package Manager. You'll also need to add a reference to the SitecoreDev.Foundation.Ioc project.

17. Now, create a new folder called Pipelines and in that folder add a folder called InitializeContainer.

18. In the InitializeContainer folder, create a new class named RegisterDependencies with the definition in Listing 5-42.

Listing 5-42. Specify the Implementation of IContentRepository

```
using SitecoreDev.Foundation.Ioc.Pipelines.InitializeContainer;
using SitecoreDev.Foundation.Repository.Content;

namespace SitecoreDev.Foundation.Repository.Pipelines.InitializeContainer
{
    public class RegisterDependencies
    {
        public void Process(InitializeContainerArgs args)
        {
            args.Container.Register<IContentRepository,
                SitecoreContentRepository>();
        }
    }
}
```

19. Create a folder called App_Config. Inside that folder, create another called Include. Inside the Include folder, create one last folder called Foundation.

20. In the new App_Config\Include\Foundation folder, add a new web configuration file named Foundation.Repository.config with the configuration from Listing 5-43.

Listing 5-43. Add Our Custom Pipeline into the Sitecore Pipeline

```
<configuration xmlns:patch="http://www.sitecore.net/xmlconfig/" xmlns:set="http://www.
sitecore.net/xmlconfig/set/">
  <sitecore>
    <pipelines>
      <initializeContainer>
        <processor type="SitecoreDev.Foundation.Repository.Pipelines.InitializeContainer.
RegisterDependencies, SitecoreDev.Foundation.Repository" />
      </initializeContainer>
    </pipelines>
  </sitecore>
</configuration>
```

That's it! Build your solution, then publish your site using the Publish-Site Gulp task from the Visual Studio Task Runner. Navigating to `http://sitecore8/myblogpost` should return your blog post content.

Summary

Well, that was a whirlwind of refactoring! It probably felt like some weird combination of Robert Martin's seminal book, *Agile Principles, Patterns, and Practices in C#* and Martin Fowler's classic, *Refactoring*. At this point you might be wondering, man—we just threw away a lot of code, why didn't we just jump to the point and start with all this in mind with our original project back in Chapter 1? Well, the answer is two-fold.

First, the *why* is more important than the *how*. If we'd have started with an N-tier modular architecture back in Chapter 2 you'd have been overwhelmed or frustrated by what would have seemed like an overcomplicated design. You would have put the book down, never to pick it up again. However, now you know the value of repositories, service layers, and abstraction through generics. They all serve to help us reduce code *and* complexities, even if the architecture, at first blush, appears complex. You now know why the complexity reduces complexity later.

Secondly, concepts such as object relational mapping and dependency injection are rather advanced topics, even for senior Sitecore developers at times. There again, they help us reduce duplicate code and tight coupling from our solutions, making them easier to extend, maintain, and reuse in future situations. However, they fit within a much larger architecture, which begs a lot of explanation.

At this point, you really are starting to know what it means to be a Sitecore developer. This isn't a toy platform, clearly. This is serious, enterprise application development; it's not for the faint of heart. However, we're not even halfway done yet. We've only just begun our journey down the Sitecore rabbit hole!

CHAPTER 6

■■■

Front-End Dev Techniques

A Sitecore site without a front-end isn't much to look at (pun intended). As you can imagine, therefore, front-end development techniques are just as critical to Sitecore success as back-end techniques. We've just spent five chapters focusing on back-end, but in this chapter, we turn our focus to the front-end.

Specifically, we need to level set on core front-end principles with Sitecore, such as the building blocks of layouts and placeholders. We breezed over them a few times in previous chapters, but in this chapter we'll take a deeper look.

With that foundation set, it's easy enough to round out this conversation of front-end development techniques by discussing front-end coding practices, such as Razor syntax in ASP.NET MVC, CSS, JavaScript, and AngularJS. These topics are deep topics, warranting books in and of themselves, with only quick primers given here. However, hopefully these introductions will expose Sitecore newbies to these broader concepts that are still very much critical to their success and advancement as a senior Sitecore developer.

Let's begin!

Presentation and Applying Layouts

Everything below the Home node within the Content tree is URL accessible. It is important to note, therefore, that everything below the Home node needs a layout assigned that will tell Sitecore how that piece of content (such as a page) should be rendered when a user navigates to it. A layout has placeholders where users can add/remove/configure components. Components render content. Figure 6-1 shows this hierarchy.

© Phil Wicklund and Jason Wilkerson 2016
P. Wicklund and J. Wilkerson, *Professional Sitecore 8 Development*, DOI 10.1007/978-1-4842-2292-8_6

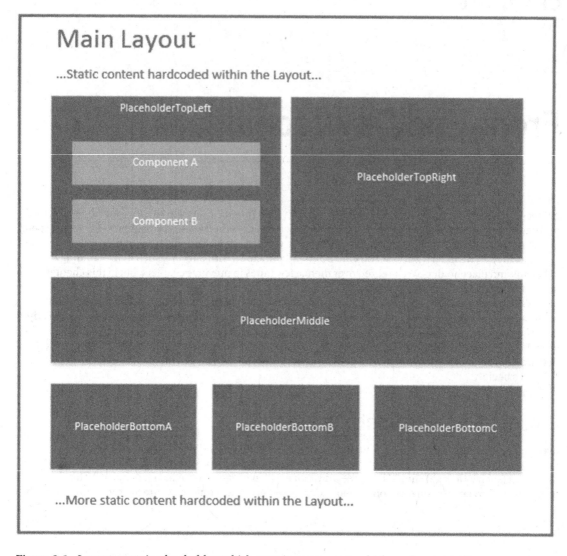

Figure 6-1. *Layouts contain placeholders which contain components which render content items*

Notice how this layout example has some hard-coded content at the top and bottom. A layout is basically an HTML file with HTML markup within it and placeholders for marketers to administer components. You may opt to hard-code in basic things, such as the company logo or the footer. However, it is a best practice to build as much as possible as components within placeholders to give marketers as much freedom as possible to control the presentation of the site.

Below the static content there are several placeholders. A developer can put as many placeholders on the page as they want or you ask them to. They can orient those placeholders in any configuration you may want, such as one column, two column, or whatever. An empty placeholder will collapse when rendered, so there's no need to worry about having more than necessary. However, some prefer the simplicity of many layouts with different configurations to, say, one single layout with endless possibilities. A marketer may understand what "Layout with 2 Columns" versus, say a layout named "Main" with 15 columns/row combinations.

Notice also in Figure 6-2 how each placeholder has a unique key. End users and marketers will not need to know this key if they are administering the page through the Experience Editor. However, they will need to know the key if they add components/renderings to the page through the Content Editor. So, it helps to have placeholder key names that make sense. Notice in Figure 6-2 from the Helix example site Habitat, a slew of placeholder orientations, each with a common sense name.

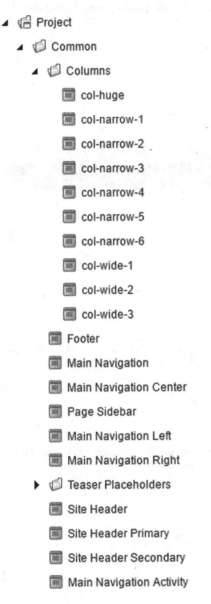

Figure 6-2. Your placeholder design is very important. You want to empower marketers with flexibility to meet changing presentation demands

You can create new placeholders by simply right-clicking the folder below Layout -> Placeholder Settings and choosing the new Placeholder Insert option. However, it will require a developer to add that placeholder either onto a layout or within a component (see the sidebar entitled, "Use Nested Placeholders") before a user or marketer can add components into it on a page. Additionally, you can configure Allowed Controls on a placeholder from the Content Editor, as shown in Figure 6-3. As a reminder, the Allowed Controls setting controls which components are permitted to be added to a placeholder. You can use this to enforce an information architecture on your site, such as keeping wide controls out of the right rail or keeping tall controls out of the footer.

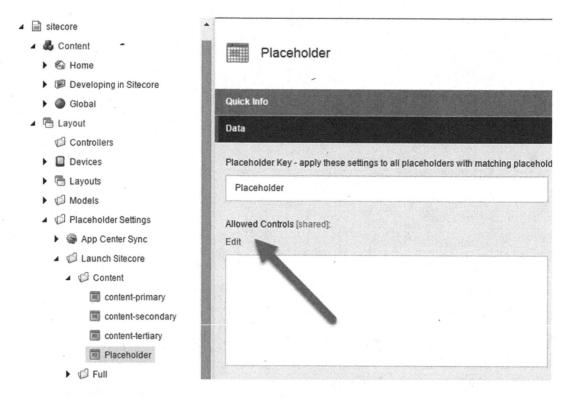

Figure 6-3. *Placeholder allowed controls lets you configure which components are permitted to be added into which placeholders. This is yet another way to enforce your information architecture*

USE NESTED PLACEHOLDERS TO ENABLE ULTIMATE LAYOUT FLEXIBILITY

Imagine a moment that Component A, as seen in Figure 6-3, has placeholders within it. Can a component render placeholders? Yes! Let your imagination run wild for a minute… this enables infinite flexibility for marketers!

Instead of creating 12 layouts, each with different patterns for placeholder orientation, you can create one single layout with one single placeholder: A "main" layout with a "Main" placeholder.

Sounds limiting? Not if you have components that render placeholders. Perhaps you had three components called "Two Column," "Single Column," and "Three Column." You could simply add these three components into the "Main" placeholder within the layout. Then, within those components you have child placeholders that you could add your child components to.

This pattern gives unlimited freedom to marketers to design a page however they want. They can add as many "placeholder components" as they like, without needing to go back to a developer to ask for yet another one-off layout design to meet the needs of a specific use case.

While this seems like dream land, it does come with a cost. The cost is that the marketer will only be able to design these pages in the Experience Editor. The reason is the placeholder keys need to be unique and therefore dynamic (usually accomplished by using GUIDs). Imagine you have two of the same components on the page, each rendering the same placeholders. Since a layout cannot have more than one of the same placeholder key, the code needs to create a dynamic key. A marketer won't know what this value is and therefore cannot administer the layout in the Content Editor. This is likely not a problem since most users will opt for the Experience Editor anyway.

Setting up dynamic placeholders is very easy. Check out the section entitled "Configuring Dynamic Placeholders" in Chapter 11 for instructions.

Layouts, like placeholders, can also be created in the Content Editor. Again, however, you will need a developers help before they can be used. You can create layouts below the Layout -> Layouts folder by right-clicking and adding the new layout (preferably below a custom folder). Notice the Path property, as seen in Figure 6-4. This needs to be set to the relative path of a HTML file on the server, in the inetpub\ wwwroot\[site] folder specifically. A developer can create and publish this HTML file, with placeholders, etc., coded therein.

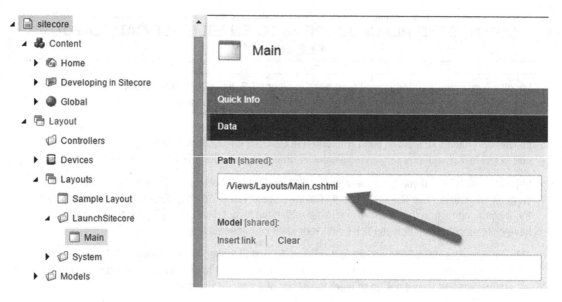

Figure 6-4. *A layout in Sitecore is a pointer to a file on the file system that controls where placeholders are rendered*

The Experience Editor can be used to add/remove/configure components on a page. However, that page first needs a layout or you won't even be able to browse to it to launch the Experience Editor in the first place. Notice in Figure 6-5 how the Glossary page, for example, was assigned to use the Main layout to control its rendering behavior. You can check which layout a page is assigned by clicking the content item (page), and then selecting Details from the Presentation tab's Layout section. The Layout Details settings box is often called the PLD (pronounced plid, which stands for Presentation-Layout-Details). Within the PLD you can also notice which controls are added onto the page, as well as what placeholders are on the layout. You can click on a control to change its placeholder. You can also click the placeholder to update its settings, such as the placeholder ID.

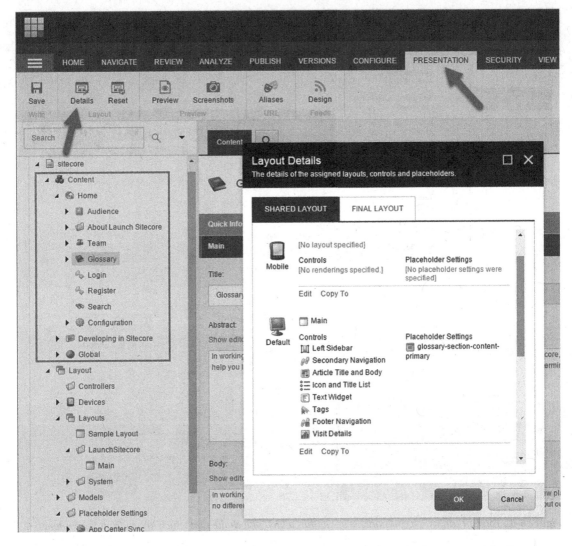

Figure 6-5. *You can still manage a page's settings from the content tree if you don't want to use the Experience Explorer*

You can similarly add/remove/configure components within this setting popup (see Figure 6-5) much like you can in the Experience Editor. By clicking Edit below the Device, such as the default device, you can select which components you want on that page, as well as assign a layout to that device. Notice the Layout, Controls, and Placeholder Settings tabs in the Edit popup (Figure 6-6). The Layout tab shows a drop-down from which you can select the layout for the device. The options are selected from the items below the Layout ➤ Layouts path in the content tree.

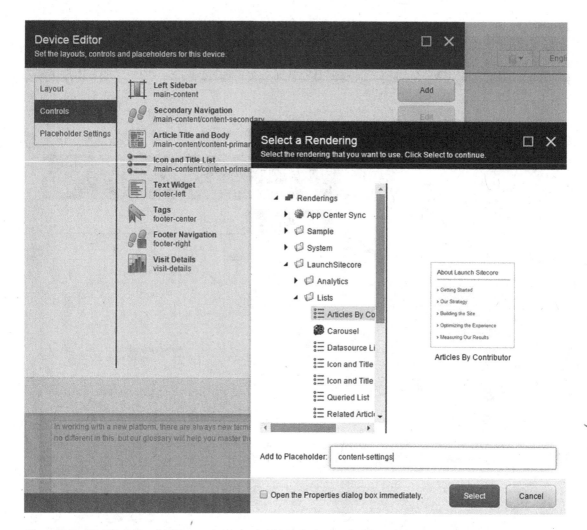

Figure 6-6. *You can edit which components are within which placeholder on which layout from the content tree*

Figure 6-6 shows the Controls tab, allowing you to select which controls you want on the layout and into which placeholders they will be placed. Here is where you need to know the placeholder key, whereas in the Experience Editor knowing the key is unnecessary. When you click a component, you can edit its settings, much the same as you would in the Experience Editor.

The Placeholder Settings tab shows all the placeholders assigned to the layout. You can add/remove and configure placeholders. By clicking Edit on the placeholder you are essentially loading the same settings menu that would appear if you selected it from the content tree. This is just a shortcut, but it is also how you can override global placeholder settings in a particular item or its standard values.

One thing you may have noticed in Figure 6-5 was the two tabs at the top of the PLD settings popup: Shared Layout and Final Layout. This is when we start to segue back into the standard values conversation. On any given item that has layout details specified, Sitecore only stores the delta between the settings from __Standard Values of the template and the layout details of the item itself. The Shared Layout tab shows the settings from __Standard Values of that page's template. The Final Layout shows you the combination of the Shared Layout configuration and any changes that were made to that specific item. Different versions of an item can have different Final Layout details as well. For example, the China-Mandarin version might have different components than the US-English version. The Final Layout tab shows that version's unique configuration, apart from the default configuration. If you need a refresher on versioning, refer back to the section on Data Templates -> Field Versioning. The concept of field versioning likewise applies to the PLD.

APPLYING PRESENTATION DETAILS TO STANDARD VALUES

Now that we have some much needed terms and nomenclature under our belt, we need to continue our discussion from Chapter 2. Specifically, let's discuss how you can apply presentation details onto standard values so that new pages come preloaded with layouts, placeholders, components, etc.

You configure the PLD on a data template's standard values much in the same way as it's configured on a content item. Simply click the data template and expand it to show the __Standard Values item. With the standard values selected, click Details from the Presentation tab's Layout section (again, the PLD). From there, you can configure all the aforementioned settings, and the new items will take these settings as their defaults. Once again, as with standard values, if the standard values are updated later all instances will receive those updates. It's a great way to get reusability out of your PLD settings.

Razor, CSS, JavaScript, and Gulp

We've talked so far about some basic concepts, such as placeholders and layouts. However, now it's time to start taking a look at some front-end coding concepts. You'll find the discussion on Razor to be quite pragmatic for a Sitecore developer. Beyond that we'll discuss other front-end topics more on the periphery of a Sitecore developer, including CSS, JavaScript, and Gulp, that, while not Sitecore specific, are still usually skills common to Sitecore developers, and thus are given introductory coverage within this section as a launching point into other books that go deeper into those subjects.

Programming Razor and Forms

Razor and ASP.NET MVC are two peas in a pod. Razor is the default view engine for ASP.NET MVC and is used for rendering HTML. You have already seen Razor in action within this book, whether you knew it or not. In our Hero Slider we used `@Html.Sitecore().Field` within the view to get a value out of the field within the current page's item. Earlier in this chapter we used `@Html.Sitecore().Placeholder` to register where our placeholders will be positioned within the view. Essentially there are many such examples of Razor helping us get complex markup on the page with just a single line of code.

You can even write your own "Html Helpers." Writing custom helpers is great when you want to process some complex logic in C# (rather than load the view with C#) or if you have the desire to achieve markup/ HTML code reuse across many views but that code is too small to work well in a partial view (partials are another way to achieve code reuse in ASP.NET MVC). Table 6-1 shows a list of common HTML Helper methods used in Sitecore.

Table 6-1. *Note Some Common HTML Helper Methods Used in Sitecore*

Helper	Description
@Html.Sitecore().CurrentItem	Retrieves the data source item associated with the view the helper is in. Example: @{ *var item = @Html.Sitecore().CurrentItem* *var title = item.Field("Title")* *}* *<h1>@{ title }</h1>*
@Html.Sitecore().Field	Retrieves a field within the data source item associated with the view the helper is in. Example: *<h1>@Html.Sitecore().Field("Title")</h1>*
@MediaManager. GetMediaUrl(mediaItem)	The MediaManager helper is useful for formatting Images. Calling this will result in an <img> tag being added to the DOM. You can see an example of MediaManager in use in Chapter 2, Listing 2-6.
@Html.Sitecore().Placeholder	Tells Sitecore where within the view you want a placeholder. Example: *@Html.Sitecore().Placeholder("main")*
@Html.BeginForm	Use this ASP.NET MVC helper to register a form and submit button within a controller rendering. @Html.BeginFormRoute is also available, and when paired with @Html.Sitecore.FormHandler("Controller", "Action"), you can post to a specific controller/action, versus all forms on the page, as is the case with BeginForm. See Listings 6-1 and 6-2 for an example.
@Html.LabelFor() and @Html.EditorFor()	LabelFor and EditorFor are used in ASP.NET MVC forms to render a friendly display name for a field and an appropriate input type for that field for the form. See Listing 6-2 for an example.
@Html.ValidationMessageFor()	Used within ASP.NET MVC forms to render a validation message if the data fails to validate. See Listing 6-2 for an example.
@Html.ActionLink	In ASP.NET MVC these helpers link the view back to the controller for processing. Example: *@Html.ActionLink("Edit Product", EditProduct,* *Product, new { id = ProductViewModel.Id })* Where EditProduct is the action name, PRODUCT is the controller name, and id is the required parameter for that action.

> ■ **Note** ActionLink will technically work but it has two limitations—Edit Product text is not CMS-able, and ActionLink isn't Experience Editor friendly; you would need to edit the link in the Content Editor. Check out the following Glass Razor extensions as a better practice.

(continued)

Table 6-1. (*continued*)

Helper	Description

Glass HTML Helpers

The following helpers are available because we're using Glass, as was set up in Chapter 5. Since we're using Glass we don't need to get a data item out of Sitecore and therefore won't be using the @Html.Sitecore HTML Helpers when rendering our view model. Given that, we need Glass to add in some extra markup to make the data editable via the Experience Editor.

Helper	Description
@Editable	Editable enables the model to be editable from within the Experience Editor. Your goal should be that all data is editable in this fashion, to make it easy for Content Editors to edit their content. Note the following example: *@Editable(ProductViewModel, x => x.Title)* *Or* *@Editable(x => x.Title)* *Where the model is inferred.* ■ **Tip** CMS data can be made editable from within the Controller as well. The benefit is your view markup will be simpler; you can just use @Model.Title instead of wrapping everything in @Editable. Later in this section we'll walk through an example of this option.
@RenderLink	RenderLink should be favored over ActionLink because the link text and URL can be CMS editable, specifically within the Experience Editor. Example: *@RenderLink(x => x.Link, isEditable: true)* In this case, Link needs to be of type Glass.Mapper.Sc.Fields. Link, and the URL for the link is simply the route path, such as / product/editproduct/{id}.
@RenderImage	RenderImage should be favored over building an <img> tag or rendering an image via MediaManager because, when using Glass, your controller shouldn't need to get the context Sitecore data item. Example: *@RenderImage(x=>x.Image, isEditable: true)* Or, to fix an image size: *@RenderImage(x=>x.Image, new {W = 120, Width = 100, Height = 50}, true)*
@BeginRenderLink	Sometimes you want greater control over what a link is wrapping, such as placing a link around an image but still enabling both to be editable with the Experience Editor. Example: *@using (BeginRenderLink(* *x => x.GeneralLink, isEditable: true))* *{* *@RenderImage(x => x.Image)* *}*

Listing 6-1. Example Standard MVC Action Methods to Handle a Form Post

```
[HttpGet]
public ActionResult EditProduct(int id) {
    var p = _repository.GetProduct(id);
    return View(p);
}


[HttpPost]
public ActionResult EditProduct(Product viewModel)
{
    if (!ModelState.IsValid)
    {
        return View(viewModel);
    }

    _repository.SaveProduct(viewModel.Id);

    return View("Saved Successfully");
}
```

■ **Warning**   The code in Listing 6-1 works only if there is only one form on the page. If there is more than one form, BeginForm will post to all forms when any submit is clicked. To get around this, you need some defensive code to ensure the post-back to the ActionResult method is coming from the correct form. This can be done through the use of storing the controller and action within hidden fields within each form. Then, you have an action attribute that checks if the value in those hidden fields match expected values. This process can be found at http://bit.ly/26PjOne.

Listing 6-2. Example Standard MVC View to Handle a Form Post

```
@model ProductViewModel

@using (Html.BeginForm())
{
    @Html.LabelFor(x => x.ProductName)
    @Html.ValidationMessageFor(x => x.ProductName)
    @Html.EditorFor(x => x.ProductName)

    @Html.LabelFor(x => x.ProductDescription)
    @Html.ValidationMessageFor(x => x.ProductName)
    @Html.EditorFor(x => x.ProductDescription)

    @Html.ValidationSummary("errorMessage")
    <input type="submit" />
}
```

■ **Note** LabelFor uses the [DisplayName("Friendly Name")] model attribute for the display name and ValidationMessage uses the [Required(ErrorMessage = "message")] attribute for its error value. These can be hard-coded or CMS-able with a query to settings item data within Sitecore.

Using Glass.Mapper to Make Content Editable

With some basic Razor-syntax under our belt, we now turn our attention to optimizing the Experience Editor to enable all data to be CMS-able. You already saw some of this in Chapter 2 when we built our Hero Slider, but back then we weren't using Glass or the Editable field. We just stuck with Sitecore's MediaManager HTML Helper, but that helper requires a Sitecore item to be within the view. Because a Sitecore item is extremely difficult to mock for unit testing, this is considered a poor practice. Let's go back to our Hero Slider example we created in Chapter 2 and refactor that code to use Glass, as well as some of the Glass HTML Helper methods, to optimize the view for Experience Editor.

As mentioned earlier, there are two methods for using Glass.Mapper to render Experience Editor-friendly content—using Html Helper classes in your views and calling these methods from your controller. In the following steps, I'll demonstrate both.

Using Html Helpers

In order to use methods like @Editable, @RenderImage, and @RenderLink, your view must inherit Glass. Mapper.Sc.Web.Mvc.GlassView<T>. These methods are only available from the GlassView<T> class. The only constraint on the generic type T is that it must be a class. We can still use our HeroSliderViewModel class, however, in order for the Html Helpers to function properly, they must have access to the model that is mapped in Glass.Mapper—in this case SitecoreDev.Feature.Media.Models.IHeroSlider.

■ **Note** If your view doesn't inherit from GlassView<T>, you can access these methods using @Html. Glass().Editable, @Html.Glass().RenderImage, etc...

1. Let's start by editing HeroSliderViewModel in in the Models folder of the SitecoreDev.Feature.Media project. Add the following property in that class.

   ```
   public IHeroSlider HeroSliderItem { get; set; }
   ```

2. Then, in the HeroSlider controller action in Controllers\MediaController, add the assignment in the following code to the end of the if (!String. IsNullOrEmpty(RenderingContext.Current.Rendering.DataSource)) code block.

   ```
   viewModel.HeroSliderItem = contentItem;
   ```

3. Now, in the HeroSlider.cshtml view, rather than specifying the HeroSliderViewModel with the @model directive, use this @inherits directive:

   ```
   @inherits Glass.Mapper.Sc.Web.Mvc.GlassView
       <SitecoreDev.Feature.Media.ViewModels.HeroSliderViewModel>
   ```

4. Finally, replace the code inside the if (Model.IsInExperienceEditorMode) code block with Listing 6-3.

Listing 6-3. Using a @RenderImage Helper to Enable Editable Images

```
<div>
    @foreach (var image in Model.HeroSliderItem.Slides)
    {
        <div class="item imageContainer">
            @RenderImage(image, i => i.Image, isEditable:true)
        </div>
    }
</div>

<div style="clear:both;">
    <!-- This button calls the webedit:new command to add a new
        Item to the content tree -->
    <a href="#" class="btn btn-default"
        onclick="javascript:Sitecore.PageModes.PageEditor.postRequest(
            'webedit:new(id=@(Model.ParentGuid))')">
        Add new image
    </a>
</div>
```

Notice that we left the Add New Image button from our previous exercise, but removed the Edit Image button. When we make our content editable through the Experience Editor in this manner, that Edit Image button becomes unnecessary.

Also notice that when we loop through our slides, we're accessing the Slides property from the IHeroSlider model interface. This is necessary, since the @RenderImage method needs access to the Glass. Mapper-mapped object.

Using this approach is good when you simply want to return data from your Controller in any format—JSON, XML, etc.—and let your view decide how it needs to render it and whether it needs to support Experience Editor.

Calling These Methods from the Controller

This approach is a more appropriate choice when you want your views to be very simple and very dumb. This approach is my personal preference (and is the method we'll use from here on out), but make the decision that best fits the needs of your implementation.

1. Start by undoing the changes from the previous section—using the @ RenderImage method, inheriting from GlassView<T>, and the changes to the HeroSliderViewModel and the MediaController.

2. Next, in the HeroSliderImageViewModel class, replace the Id, MediaUrl, and AltText properties with the property in this code:

   public HtmlString Image { get; set; }

3. Moving back to the MediaController, let's inject another dependency into our constructor, shown in Listing 6-4.

Listing 6-4. Inject the Glass Dependency into the Constructor

```
private readonly IGlassHtml _glassHtml;

public MediaController(IContextWrapper contextWrapper, IMediaContentService
mediaContentService, IGlassHtml glassHtml)
{
    _contextWrapper = contextWrapper;
    _mediaContentService = mediaContentService;
    _glassHtml = glassHtml;
}
```

Now, in the HeroSlider controller action, you'll notice, where we're adding a new HeroSliderImageViewModel to the HeroImages collection of the viewModel, there's an error. There should be—we removed the properties!

4. Modify that section of code as shown in Listing 6-5.

Listing 6-5. Update the Image in the Collection to Get its Data from Glass

```
viewModel.HeroImages.Add(new HeroSliderImageViewModel()
{
    Image = new HtmlString(_glassHtml.Editable<IHeroSliderSlide>(
        slide, i => i.Image))
});
```

5. Finally, back in the HeroSlider.cshtml file, you'll need to modify two places. In the if (Model.IsInExperienceEditorMode) code block, modify the contents of the <div> element inside the foreach loop with that from Listing 6-6.

Listing 6-6. Update the foreach Within the IsInExperienceEditor Block

```
@foreach (var image in Model.HeroImages)
{
    <div class="item imageContainer">
        @image.Image
    </div>
}
```

6. Then, in the else block, modify that foreach loop as shown in Listing 6-7.

Listing 6-7. Update the else Block

```
@foreach (var image in Model.HeroImages)
{
    <div class="item @(image.IsActive ? "active" : "")">
        @image.Image
    </div>
}
```

7. Lastly, build your solution and publish your changes using the Publish-Site Gulp task.

Getting CSS and JS on a Page

JavaScript and CSS need to get added to your layouts in order to style and animate your site. CSS is most commonly added into the <head> tag within the layout, and you typically put as much of the JavaScript as possible at the bottom of the page to ensure it runs after the page loads. It's easy enough to add your styles or scripts directly within the HTML, but what if you have many style sheets, many JavaScript references, and many layouts? The result: a lot of references to manage and potentially duplicate code! Since we're not fans of difficult things, it's worth investigating other options. A default ASP.NET MVC site includes an option for bundling and minification through the WebGrease NuGet package:

```
@Styles.Render("~/content/css")
@Scripts.Render("~/content/js")
```

■ **Note** A new ASP.NET MVC site comes preloaded with a bunch of CSS and JS, such as Bootstrap for building responsive CSS, unless you chose the empty template, as we have in the steps thus far.

Instead of having 12 <style> tags within the <head> of each layout, you can simply have one line of code registering your minified bundle in one fell swoop. Similarly, you can use the Render helper to render all your JavaScript dependencies at the bottom of your page. You'll notice that in an out-of-the-box ASP.NET MVC project you have a BundlesConfig.cs file within your App_Start folder. Within that file you'll notice a lot of lines similar to the following:

```
bundles.Add(new StyleBundle("~/content/css").Include("~/content/site.css"));
```

This line of code takes the site.css file located in the Content folder within your project and adds it to a bundle called content/css. All CSS files registered in that bundle will be rendered onto the page when you use the @Styles.Render("~/content/css") helper. The same is done with JavaScript files.

CSS and JS Minification with Gulp

As Microsoft continues its move to .NET Core, a transition is being made from runtime bundling and minification, with tools like WebGrease, to deploy-time bundling and minification using task runners like Gulp or Grunt. Since we introduced Gulp to you in Chapter 4 for deployment reasons, we'll extend that discussion by writing some gulp tasks to do our minification. Use the following steps to configure Gulp to do your bundling and minification:

1. Before we create our Gulp tasks, let's rearrange a couple of things in our solution. In the SitecoreDev.Website project, create a new folder named Content. In this folder, create a new style sheet named sitecoredev.website.css.

2. In the new sitecoredev.website.css file, insert the CSS shown in Listing 6-8.

Listing 6-8. Additional CSS for our Hero Slider

```
.imageContainer {
  float: left;
  min-height: 100px;
  width: 500px;
  background-color: #808080;
```

```
  margin: 10px;
  position: relative;
  }
  .imageContainer img {
    height: 200px;
    width: 500px;
  }

.carousel-inner img {
  height: 768px;
  width: 1920px;
}
```

■ **Note** Following the Helix principles, all styling for any feature modules should live within the Project layer, since feature modules can be included in any site.

---

3. Next, from the Package Manager Console, type the command in the following code. This will install the two new Gulp dependencies we don't already have.

```
npm install gulp-concat gulp-uglify --save-dev
```

4. Now, at the root of the solution in the Configuration folder, open the gulpfile.js file. Add the two new references found in the following code to the top of the file:

```
var cssmin = require("gulp-cssmin");
var rename = require("gulp-rename");
var concat = require("gulp-concat");
var uglify = require("gulp-uglify");
```

5. Next, at the bottom of this file, add the code from Listing 6-9.

Listing 6-9. Additional Gulp Tasks to Minify the CSS and JS and to Watch for CSS or JS Changes

```
var minifyCss = function (destination) {
  gulp.src("./{Feature,Foundation,Project}/**/**/Content/*.css")
    .pipe(concat('sitecoredev.website.min.css'))
    .pipe(cssmin())
    .pipe(gulp.dest(destination));
};
var minifyJs = function (destination) {
  gulp.src("./{Feature,Foundation,Project}/**/**/Scripts/*.js")
    .pipe(concat('sitecoredev.website.min.js'))
    .pipe(uglify())
    .pipe(gulp.dest(destination));
};
gulp.task("minify-css", function () {
  minifyCss();
});
```

```
gulp.task("minify-js", function () {
  minifyJs
});

gulp.task("css-watcher", function () {
  var root = "./";
  var roots = [root + "**/Content", "!" + root + "/**/obj/**/Content"];
  var files = "/**/*.css";
  var destination = gulpConfig.webRoot + "\\Content";
  gulp.src(roots, { base: root }).pipe(
    foreach(function (stream, rootFolder) {
      gulp.watch(rootFolder.path + files, function (event) {
        if (event.type === "changed") {
          console.log("publish this file " + event.path);
          minifyCss(destination);
        }
        console.log("published " + event.path);
      });
      return stream;
    })
  );
});
gulp.task("js-watcher", function () {
  var root = "./";
  var roots = [root + "**/Scripts", "!" + root + "/**/obj/**/Scripts"];
  var files = "/**/*.js";
  var destination = gulpConfig.webRoot + "\\Scripts";
  gulp.src(roots, { base: root }).pipe(
    foreach(function (stream, rootFolder) {
      gulp.watch(rootFolder.path + files, function (event) {
        if (event.type === "changed") {
          console.log("publish this file " + event.path);
          minifyJs(destination);
        }
        console.log("published " + event.path);
      });
      return stream;
    })
  );
});
```

What we've added here are four new Gulp tasks. Two are manually run and two are watchers that run whenever a file changes.

- *minify-css:* This task is manually run and outputs a single, minified file of all CSS from any Content folder in any of the Foundation, Feature, or Project folders. It calls a common minifyCss method.

- *minify-js:* This task does the same as the minify-css task, only for any JavaScript files in any Scripts folder in any of the Foundation, Feature, or Project folders. It calls a common minifyJs method.

- *css-watcher:* This task runs `minifyCss` whenever any CSS file from any `Content` folder changes and is saved.

- *js-watcher:* This task runs `minifyJs` whenever any JavaScript file from any `Scripts` folder changes and is saved.

6. The last item we need to modify is the `DefaultMVCLayout.cshtml` file in the `Views\Shared` folder of the `SitecoreDev.Website` project. Open this file and change the link reference to `~/Content/sitecoredev.website.min.css`.

7. Add a new script reference shown in the following code:

```
<script type="text/javascript" src="~/Scripts/sitecoredev.website.min.js"></script>
```

8. If you were to add all of the `bootstrap.css`/`.js` files and the jQuery script files to the solution as well, these files would also get concatenated and minified into a single file, leaving only one reference needed for a JavaScript and a CSS file.

9. Last, but not least, open the Task Runner Explorer in Visual Studio. Run the `css-watcher` and the `js-watcher` tasks. This will start those watcher tasks so that they run anytime their respective files change. You can also bind these two tasks to the Project Open event so that they start up as soon as you open the project. Simply right-click on the task and select Bindings->Project Open. Your bindings should now look like Figure 6-7!

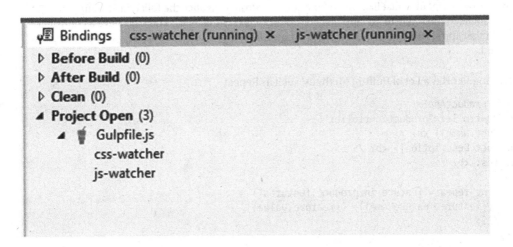

Figure 6-7. Our Gulp watchers are running! No more need to manually deploy CSS/JS when developing

AngularJS

AngularJS really has nothing to do with Sitecore, per se. However, most Sitecore sites are data-intensive sites and there is no better way to do client-side data manipulation than with AngularJS. Additionally, Angular is a fantastic choice when wanting to make client-side requests to back-end REST services or even our ASP.NET MVC controllers! As you can imagine, therefore, a brief primer into AngularJS is necessary, considering this chapter is all about front-end development techniques Sitecore developers ought to know.

Check out the Hello World example found in Listing 6-10. You'll see in that example the h1 tag has been assigned a controller to process data for that scope. The HelloWorldController is defined as a JavaScript function that is called on page load, and that function sets the scope's helloText variable to "Hello World".

Listing 6-10. A Simple "Hello World!" Angular Example

```
<h1 ng-controller="HelloWorldController">{{helloText}}</h1>

<script src="angular.min.js"></script>

<script type="text/javascript">
   function HelloWorldController($scope) {
      $scope.helloText = "Hello World";
   }
</script>
```

Typically, you would never define your Angular code on the page. You usually will have your controllers each as separate JavaScript files, just like we do for our C# controllers. Notice the following example where we've associated the scope to an "app" called ProductApp (Listing 6-11). Then, we have a controller associated with that app (Listing 6-12), which can then be referenced in any view below a scope where that app is registered.

Listing 6-11. Angular Has a Lot of Built-In Methods, such as Repeat

```
<div ng-app="productApp">
   <div ng-controller="productController">
      {{product.Name}} <br />
      {{product.Description}} <br />
      Features: <br />
      <ul>
         <li ng-repeat="feature in product.features">
            {{feature.featureName}}: {{feature.value}}
         </li>
      </ul>
   </div>
</div>
```

■ **Note**   Notice how Angular is awesome at data manipulations. Repeat is just one example of the many actions that come bundled with Angular.

Listing 6-12. Typically your Angular Controllers Are Defined in Separate JavaScript Files

```javascript
'use strict';
productApp.controller('productController',
    function productController($scope) {
        $scope.product = {
            name: 'Graphite Hammer',
            description: 'Super cool hammer!',
            features: [
                {
                    featureName: 'Frame Type',
                    value: 'Graphite'
                }
                {
                    featureName: 'Handle Type',
                    value: 'Rubber'
                }
            ]
        }
    }
}
```

One of the best uses of Angular for Sitecore sites is when you need to build a site that needs a lot of Ajax post-backs. We saw in the previous section that there are a lot of nuances to using ASP.NET MVC and Razor for form posts (defense against posting multiple forms at once), and Angular provides a cleaner, more modern client-side experience, bypassing the need for a post-back altogether. Additionally, you'll notice the concept of a "factory" in Listing 6-13. Factories in Angular are like classes in C#. They help you reduce code duplication by defining discrete modules of functionality that can be called within any scope registered to the "app."

For example, Listing 6-13 has a factory with a getProduct method. Code to get products can easily be reused across many other places and is a great example for a factory. Additionally, we don't want to post back when we get product data and instead use a client-side HTTP request back into our ASP.NET MVC Product controller. This callback can return HTML just like any other request, where Angular perhaps updates the content of a <div> or something. However, JSON is an ideal result set because it's so easy for Angular to manipulate. In this case we've added a new C# controller action (Listing 6-14) that returns the product view model as a JSON result, differentiated by the json as a parameter signifying to the action method that raw data should be returned instead of the view.

Listing 6-13. Your Angular Code Can Call Your C# Controllers Too!

```javascript
productApp.factory('productData', function ($http, $productId) {
    return {
        getProduct: function (successcb) {
            $http({method: 'GET', url: '/product/$productId/json'}).
                success(function (data, status, headers, config) {
                successcb(data);
            }).
            error(function (data, status, headers, config) {
                console.log(status);
            });
        }
    };
});
```

Back in our productController (Listing 6-14) we now are calling this factory method to get our product, versus having it hard-coded as it was in Listing 6-12. Listing 6-15 shows how the action method on the back-end might look (in C#).

Listing 6-14. An Updated Controller Calling Into Our Factory, Which Then Calls Our C# Controller

```
'use strict';
productApp.controller('productController',
    function ProductController($scope) {
        productData.getProduct(function(product) {
            $scope.product = product;
        });
    }
}
```

Listing 6-15. A Quick Example Showing a C# Controller Returning a JSON Result Rather Than Your Typical View Result

```
public JsonResult GetProductJson(string id)
{
    return Json(ProductRepository.GetProduct(id));
}
```

■ **Note**   You'll need a custom route registered to get /product/123/json to work, such as:

```
Routes.MapRoute(
        name: "Product",
        url: "Product/{id}/json",
        defaults: new { controller = "Product", action="GetProductJson" }
        );
```

All this was a super quick primer to Angular, but it's easy to see the power and potential for most Sitecore sites, especially those sites with a lot of data or those requiring few, if any, hard post-backs, such as those striving to be Single-Page-Applications (SPAs). In those cases, Angular becomes a core skill Sitecore developers will need to make progress on. Angular2 is currently in beta and brings with it tons more features, benefits, and capabilities worth watching for.

Summary

Well that was a whirlwind tour of front-end development techniques, of which all Sitecore developers should have at least a cursory understanding. We started by discussing presentation details, the purpose of layouts, and how placeholders fit. These core front-end concepts prepared us to launch into a discussion on core front-end coding principles. Razor is commonly used in ASP.NET MVC sites; however, it comes with some must-understand nuances. Registering CSS and JavaScript on a page is table stakes for a front-end Sitecore developer, but we went a bit deeper by covering the steps to minimize and consolidate all your CSS and JavaScript to help the performance of your site. We finished the chapter with a quick primer into AngularJS, a must-learn JavaScript framework for those seeking to build data-driven, Single-Page-Applications (SPAs).

CHAPTER 7

■ ■ ■

Unit Testing Sitecore

Unit testing is non-negotiable as far we we're concerned. In fact, we argue it's absolutely critical if you care about having a quality Sitecore deployment. Why? Confidence.

Unit testing, if you're not familiar, isolates independent pieces of your solution to ensure they are working properly. If you have continuous integration enabled, each time you commit code, all of the unit tests in your solution will run, providing immediate feedback regarding the impact of your change. This feedback is essential to reducing bug density and increasing developer productivity.

If you already have quite a bit of unit testing experience, you'll understand the importance of the architecture and patterns laid out in Chapters 4 and 5, and how they enable the concepts outlined in this chapter. Success with unit testing is incredibly dependent upon the design of the solution. Chapters 4 and 5 make unit testing your solution a piece of cake. A modular, n-tiered architecture, abiding by the SOLID principles, in particular the Single-Responsibility principle, make unit testing easy.

■ **Tip**   This is why test-driven development (test-first development) has been proven to enable higher development productivity than test-last development (writing the tests after the code is complete), because when you test first you are more intentional to ensure the design is agile, extensible, and testable. With test-last development, it's easy to paint yourself into a design corner and skip the tests because it would require too much rework. Write your test *first*!

For those of you already quite familiar with unit testing, you probably can just jump right in and start writing tests! The only thing in this chapter that might be uniquely helpful is the last section on Sitecore FakeDb. That section helps you understand how to test your Sitecore object model code in isolation when it has a dependency on a database. Sitecore FakeDb is your answer; it replaces the database connection, at the data provider level, so that you can fake that dependency and be confident your code is tested in isolation from other, external variables.

For those of you who are new to unit testing, the first section will walk you through a bit of an introduction. We'll talk more about the purpose of unit testing, how it works, and how to get started. An example set of steps will walk you through creating some tests within the book's sample project so you have an example to follow. The next section after that will cover AutoFixture, an old favorite of most unit testing veterans. You'll learn how AutoFixture can enable you to write tests faster and easier.

Let's begin!

© Phil Wicklund and Jason Wilkerson 2016
P. Wicklund and J. Wilkerson, *Professional Sitecore 8 Development*, DOI 10.1007/978-1-4842-2292-8_7

Getting Started Unit Testing

We're not going to assume you have any experience unit testing. This section will help you understand what unit test frameworks are available, how to write a basic test, and thereafter, how to go into the book's example solution and add some basic tests around a controller, a service, and a repository.

Your first big decision, before you can get started unit testing is to pick your unit testing framework. There are many popular frameworks out there. A few of the most popular for Sitecore developers include MSTest, NUnit, and xUnit.net. There are pros and cons of each which we won't attempt to exhaust here in this chapter. However, one of the pros of MSTest is the lack of configuration/installation needed to get started, beyond simply having Visual Studio installed. As a result all the test examples found in this chapter will use MSTest, for the sake of simplicity and to avoid unnecessary tangents.

Your unit testing journey begins by creating a new Unit Test Project in your solution. You'll find the Unit Test Project template below the Test project category, as shown in Figure 7-1.

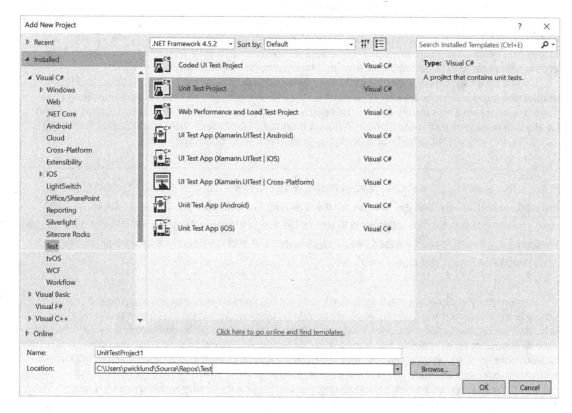

Figure 7-1. *To get started, create a new Unit Test Project to hold your tests*

When you first create the test project it will generate a single empty test called `UnitTest1` (see Listing 7-1). You can actually run this test without doing anything to it and it will pass. Simply open the Test Explorer and click Run All if you want to give it a try.

Listing 7-1. An Empty Test Created When You Create a New Test Project

```
using System;
using Microsoft.VisualStudio.TestTools.UnitTesting;

namespace POC.Tests
{
    [TestClass]
    public class UnitTest1
    {
        [TestMethod]
        public void TestMethod1()
        {
        }
    }
}
```

You will want to consider what needs to happen in a test before you start writing it. A common test paradigm is to organize the code in your test along the "arrange, act, and assert" methodology:

- *Arrange*: This is where you set up your dependencies before you do any testing; you will create the thing you want to test and load any data needed to support the test.

- *Act*: This is where you actually exercise the method you want to test.

- *Assert*: This is where you check results of the test; you confirm, for example, that the method call you made in "act" did something correctly to the object you set up in "arrange."

Additionally, before you write your tests it's good to remember some key principles of what makes a good test. A few of these principles to keep in mind are:

- *Atomic*: You should only be testing one piece of functionality; one class might have dozens of tests to ensure all dimensions of the class work, otherwise when the test fails you'll have no clue why it failed and you'll need to debug the test each time to understand what could be wrong with the class.

- *Deterministic*: Tests should pass or fail; they should never be inconclusive.

- *Repeatable*: Tests should consistently pass or consistently fail; you need to remove all outside influences (atomic) that might make a test pass or fail based on external variables.

- *Order independent:* Again, no outside factors should cause a test to fail, such as order of operations of other tests.

- *Fast*: Tests should be fast; large projects will likely have thousands of tests running with every commit.

- *Easy to set up:* If you need to do a lot of coding to get a test to run there's probably a better way to do things. This is where you need to start thinking about some sort of "test harness" or test base class to provide efficiencies for all other tests requiring similar configurations.

Okay, with some best practices understood, let's create a simple test for the newbies to get a sense for how this works! Before we begin, we need to consider what actually will be tested. To provide a simple example, consider the `Calculator` class in Listing 7-2.

Listing 7-2. A Simple Class We Can Test

```
public class Calculator
{
    public int Subtract(int from, int num)
    {
        return from - num;
    }
}
```

Clearly this is an overly simplistic example, but it helps demonstrate the concept. What we want to do is test the business logic within the Subtract method, to ensure that logic is behaving as expected. A simple example of subtracting a number from another number is business logic (albeit simplistic) that might change over time; a test will provide immediate feedback if that logic is broken. Consider the test in Listing 7-3.

Listing 7-3. A simple Test that Validates the Calculator Subtract Method

```
[TestMethod]
public void TestMethod1()
{
    // Arrange
    Calculator sut = new Calculator();
    var from = 4;
    var number = 3;

    // Act
    var result = sut.Subtract(from, num);

    // Assert
    Assert.AreEqual(result, 1);
}
```

■ **Tip** It's common to use a variable named sut, which stands for "system under test," as a convention to make it clear what is being tested. Using comments to demark //Arrange, //Act, and //Assert is also another convention commonly used by developers to make clear which lines of code belong to which organizational block.

In this test, you can see how we structured the code along the Arrange, Act, and Assert paradigm. This is a good practice, especially for larger tests where it can get harder to know what's going on. In the arrange phase, we instantiate the object that is being tested. Another common practice is to use the sut variable name, which stands for "system under test." This makes it obvious what object this test is testing. Beyond creating the SUT in "arrange," we may also need to provide other dependencies, such as loading the object with dummy data. Instantiating the SUT and loading up dummy data are the two core things that happen in arrange.

In the Act phase we actually perform the test. For this simple example we called the Subtract method against our two numbers. This method call is stored in the result variable.

Lastly, in the Assert phase we check to ensure the result from our test is what we expected. In this simple case, 4 minus 3 should be 1. The Assert.AreEqual method compares two objects to make sure they are equal, which in this case they obviously are. Other Assert options include IsNull, IsNotNull, IsTrue, and IsFalse.

Click the Run All link in Test Explorer (see Figure 7-2) to run your test. It will show a green checkbox if it passed, and a red X if it failed. If it failed, you can debug the test. Simply set a breakpoint, right-click the test, and choose Debug Selected Tests. You'll then be able to step through the test and see why it failed.

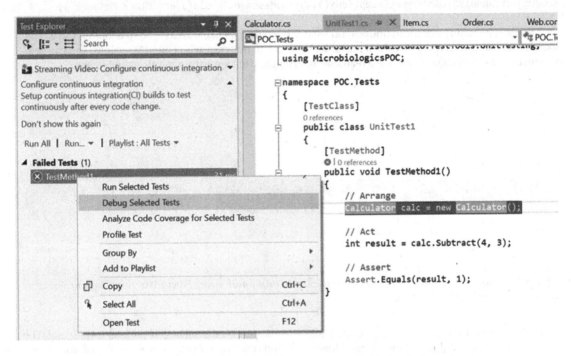

Figure 7-2. *You can run your tests by clicking Run All, and you can also debug tests*

With a simple test under your belt we can now move forward and start building tests into the book's example project. There are three main things we need to test in our N-tiered architecture: our repositories, our services, and our controllers. But before we do that, let's discuss a few tools we can use to make writing our unit tests easier, namely fluent assertions, AutoFixture, and Moq.

■ **Note** Always test from bottom up. Not a rule, but not a bad practice either. In this section we're skipping the tests for our repositories, because we need FakeDb to help with that (discussed later in the chapter). So, we're already breaking our own rule ☺.

Making Tests Easier to Read with FluentAssertions

`Assert.AreEqual(x, y)` isn't necessarily the easiest thing to read and understand. Enter FluentAssertions. FluentAssertions is a NuGet package (see Figure 7-3) that will help you write test assertions in what looks like plain English, compared to `Assert` statements. For example:

```
result.Should().Be(1);
```

That line of code is the equivalent to `Assert.AreEqual(result, 1)`. It uses common English words to describe what the expected results ought to be. This is a very simple example, but with more complex tests, FluentAssertions really start to show their value. Consider the following example:

```
someObject.Should().BeOfType<Exception>().Which.Message.Should().Be("Other Message");
```

It would be mind boggling to understand what this would look like with `Assert` statements. You would likely need multiple `Asserts` to make it readable. However, in this case, with FluentAssertions, you can see how in one line of code we can make a readable assertion in what appears to mimic plain English.

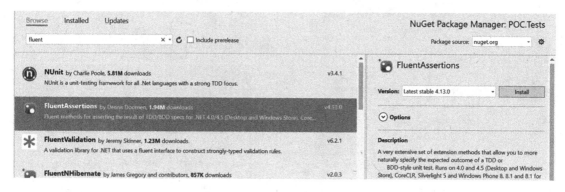

Figure 7-3. *FluentAssertions come in a NuGet package; simply add "using FluentAssertions" to your test classes to start using them!*

While it's not necessarily a best practice, FluentAssertions is becoming hugely popular testing tool. The rest of the examples in this chapter will use FluentAssertions and will provide more examples of what they look like and how they work.

Creating Dummy Data, the Easy Way, with AutoFixture

The `Calculator` test we created in the previous section sure was neat, but it was also a very simple example. Consider Listing 7-4.

Listing 7-4. It's Common to Hard-Code a Bunch of Data to Test Against

```
// Arrange
Calculator sut = new Calculator();
var from = 4;
var number = 3;
```

Most tests will need some sort of dummy data to test against, such as this. However, "real world" tests will likely require a lot more code to set up good data. Do you really need to hard-code that much data just to set up a test? No! Enter AutoFixture.

AutoFixture is a neat little utility that will generate data for you! All you need to do is tell AutoFixture the type of data you want generated and it will return an instantiated object with random dummy data. As is obvious already, this can save you a ton of code, time, and frustration!

■ **Note** AutoFixture comes in a NuGet package for easy installation into your Sitecore solutions.

The key class within AutoFixture is Fixture. The Fixture class provides the Create() method, which generates the anonymous data. It supports chars, strings, numbers, guids, datetimes, and custom objects. Listings 7-4 through 7-11 provide some examples of basic AutoFixture techniques.

We are really just scratching the surface here, but hopefully it helps you understand the power and ease of AutoFixture. Hereafter, we'll dig into some step-by-step procedures to refactor our test from the previous section, where we needed to manually hard-code in a ton of setup data to test against. This section's example will show you how AutoFixture can make your life a lot easier and remove a lot of that code.

Listing 7-5. Create a New Autogenerated String

```
var fixture = new Fixture();
var autoGeneratedText = fixture.Create<string>();
```

Listing 7-6. Create a New String with a Prefix of "Phil"

```
var fixture = new Fixture();
var generatedTextWithPrefix = fixture.Create("Phil");
```

Listing 7-7. Create an IEnumerable of Strings

```
var strings = fixture.CreateMany<string>();
```

Listing 7-8. Create a New Random Positive Integer

```
var fixture = new Fixture();
int autoGeneratedNumber = fixture.Create<int>();
```

Listing 7-9. Create a New Complex Object with All the Properties of that Object Filled Out

```
var fixture = new Fixture();
var autoGeneratedClass =
    fixture.Create<ComplexParent>();
```

Listing 7-10. Use a Custom Algorithm Instead of the Default. "Phil" Will Be the Generated String Each Time

```
var fixture = new Fixture();
fixture.Register<string>(() => "Phil");
string result = fixture.Create<string>();
```

Listing 7-11. Manually Set a Property of Some Custom Class

```
var fixture = new Fixture();
var mc = fixture.Build<CustomClass>()
    .With(x => x.SomeProp, "Phil")
    .Create();
```

Listing 7-12. Remove a Property (Property Will Be Left Null)

```
var fixture = new Fixture();
var employee = fixture.Build<Employee>()
    .Without(e => e.Manager)
    .Create();
```

Isolating Tests with Moq

You now know how to write a basic test and how to generate a bunch of dummy data with AutoFixture to test against. However, so far we've only been discussing easy methods to test against. The Subtract method in the Calculator class is about as simplistic as it gets. What do you do, however, if the Subtract method had something more complex within it? Consider Listing 7-13.

■ **Note**   NSubstitute is a good alternative to Moq that is also very popular among Sitecore developers.

Listing 7-13. The Subtract Method Has a Bunch of External Calls

```
public class Calculator
{
    private readonly IExternalProcessor _externalProcessor;
    public Calculator(IExternalProcessor processor)
    {
        _externalProcessor = processor;
    }

    public int Subtract(int from, int num)
    {
        var resultOfExternalCall = _externalProcessor.ProcessSomething(from);
        return resultOfExternalCall - num;
    }
}
```

You can see pretty quickly that our Subtract method is not so innocent anymore. Instead of just subtracting num from from, we first need to run the from variable through some external business logic. However, that business logic is not what we want to test. The test we're writing now is only supposed to test the logic within the Subtract method. How in the world are we supposed to isolate the Subtract method from its dependencies? Enter Moq. Moq allows you to tell the test framework what to do when different things happen, such as bypass the ProcessInBackendSystem method call. Consider the test in Listing 7-14.

Listing 7-14. A Test Using Moq to Replace the ProcessSomething Call

```
[TestMethod]
public void TestCalculator()
{
    // Arrange
    var processResult = 5;
```

```
var external = new Mock<IExternalProcessor>();
external
    .Setup(x => x.ProcessSomething(It.IsAny<int>()))
    .Returns(processResult)
    .Verifiable();

Calculator sut = new Calculator(external.Object);
var from = 4;
var number = 3;

// Act
var result = sut.Subtract(from, num);

// Assert
external.Verify();
result.Should().Be(2);
}
```

This test looks a bit scarier, but it isn't after you get the hang of this. Basically, our goal is to tell Moq what we want to happen when the ProcessSomething method is called. In this case, we want Moq to return 5. This is handled by the Setup method call, when we say when any integer is passed into ProcessSomething return the processResult variable. We then create our new Calculator object, passing our dependency of the IExternalProcessor and use the same values for from and num. We then call the Subtract method, and the result of subtracting 4 from 3 is 2!

You'll see Moq used throughout the rest of this chapter, since it is a must have tool for writing good unit tests. Similar to AutoFixture, Moq is installed with a NuGet package. Simply add using Moq; to your test class and start mocking up objects/methods!

■ **Note**   Notice also the .Verify() method call in the Assert phase. If you put .Verifiable() on your mocked object, Moq will ensure the method is actually called! Sometimes you can put a lot of work into a test and not even know if the methods you've set up are even called. Verify() is another assert that will cause the test to fail if a method you expected to get called didn't.

AUTOFIXTURE VERSUS MOQ?

AutoFixture uses reflection to create "well-behaved" instances of public types. It auto-generates instances of other types if necessary to fill in arguments for a constructor, and also assigns values to public writable properties. In essence, it simply uses the requested type's public API to instantiate and populate it. It doesn't do anything that you, as a developer, couldn't do manually—it just does it for you automatically.

In contrast, most Dynamic Mock libraries derive from known types to override the behavior of virtual members. Their purpose is to perform Behavior Verification of the System Under Test (SUT).

You can combine AutoFixture with Moq to turn it into an automocking container. This topic, while important to understand, is getting well beyond the scope of this chapter. You can learn more at http://bit.ly/2b5wS4q.

Unit Testing a Service

How about a more serious example? Let's write some service layer tests for a service we created earlier in the book.

1. Let's start by creating a new project. In the Feature\Media folder, add a new unit test project called SitecoreDev.Feature.Media.Tests. Delete UnitTest1.cs.

2. Create a new folder called Services.

3. Create a new class named GetHeroSliderContentTests with the basic definition shown in Listing 7-15.

Listing 7-15. Create a Test for Getting Hero Slider Slides

```
using Microsoft.VisualStudio.TestTools.UnitTesting;

namespace SitecoreDev.Feature.Media.Tests.Services
{
  [TestClass]
  public class GetHeroSliderContentTests
  {

  }
}
```

4. Next, using the NuGet Package Manager, add references to the following NuGet packages:

    - FluentAssertions

    - Moq

    - Glass.Mapper.Sc

    - AutoFixture

    - AutoFixture.AutoMoq

    - Microsoft.AspNet.Mvc.

5. You'll also need to add references to SitecoreDev.Feature.Media, SitecoreDev. Foundation.Model, and SitecoreDev.Foundation.Repository from the solution and to Sitecore.Kernel.dll and Sitecore.Mvc.dll.

6. After adding Glass.Mapper.Sc, you can safely delete the App_Config and App_ Start folders.

▪ **Note** In the latest version of Glass.Mapper.Sc, Mike and Nat have created a Glass.Mapper.Sc.Core NuGet package that does not add the App_Config or App_Start folders. This is beneficial for adding Glass. Mapper to class libraries.

---

7. Now, in order to create the objects our mock repository is going to return, we need to create implementations of IHeroSliderSlide and IHeroSlider. Create these implementations using Listings 7-16 and 7-17, respectively.

Listing 7-16. Create an Implementation of HeroSliderSlide So We Can Mock It

```
using Glass.Mapper.Sc.Fields;
using SitecoreDev.Foundation.Model;

namespace SitecoreDev.Feature.Media.Models
{
  public class HeroSliderSlide : CmsEntity, IHeroSliderSlide
  {
    public Image Image { get; set; }
  }
}
```

Listing 7-17. Create an Implementation of HeroSlider So We Can Mock It

```
using System.Collections.Generic;
using SitecoreDev.Foundation.Model;

namespace SitecoreDev.Feature.Media.Models
{
  public class HeroSlider : CmsEntity, IHeroSlider
  {
    public IEnumerable<IHeroSliderSlide> Slides { get; set; }
  }
}
```

You might notice a new base class that doesn't exist—CmsEntity. So that we don't have to implement Id on every object individually, create a new class named CmsEntity in the SitecoreDev.Foundation.Model project with the definition shown in Listing 7-18.

Listing 7-18. A New Object that's a Base for Our Mocked Objects

```
namespace SitecoreDev.Foundation.Model
{
  public class CmsEntity : ICmsEntity
  {
    public Guid Id { get; set; }
  }
}
```

8. Now, back in the SitecoreDev.Feature.Media.Tests project, in Services\GetHeroSliderContentTests, add the test method shown in Listing 7-19.

Listing 7-19. Complete the GetHeroSliderContentSuccessful Test

```
[TestMethod]
public void GetHeroSliderContentSuccessful()
{
  //Arrange
  var fixture = new Fixture();

  var heroSlide = fixture
    .Build<HeroSlider>()
    .Without(x => x.Slides)
    .Create();
  var children = fixture
    .CreateMany<HeroSliderSlide>()
    .ToList();

  var repository = new Mock<IContentRepository>();
  repository
    .Setup(x => x.GetContentItem<IHeroSlider>(It.IsAny<string>()))
    .Returns(heroSlide)
    .Verifiable();
  repository
    .Setup(x => x.GetChildren<IHeroSliderSlide>(It.IsAny<string>()))
    .Returns(children)
    .Verifiable();

  var service = new SitecoreMediaContentService(repository.Object);

  //Act
  var result = service.GetHeroSliderContent("123");

  //Assert
  repository.Verify();
  result.Should().NotBeNull();
  result.Slides.Should().NotBeNullOrEmpty();
  result.Slides.Count().Should().Be(children.Count());
  var slides = result.Slides.ToList();
  foreach (var slide in slides)
    slide.Image.Should().NotBeNull();
}
```

The test first uses AutoFixture to generate some test data (a hero slide). The CreateMany method generates an IEnumerable<type> collection of objects, because we need more than one. Next, the code uses Moq to mock up our content repository. Otherwise our unit test would be testing the repository, in addition to the service. This is a no-no, otherwise it could be considered an integration test. Moq helps us isolate the test to just the particular method under test by specifying a return type when the GetContentItem method is called in the repository. In this case, the "heroSlide" dummy data is returned (similar for GetChildren). Next the service itself is called, and then, in Assert, we test to ensure the result produced by that service call is what we expected.

If you run this test, it should run perfectly and pass. That was a good test for testing the happy-path scenario. But what happens if contentGuid is null or empty? It'd be a great idea to test that scenario as well.

9. So, create another test called GetHeroSliderContentEmptyContentGuid with the definition shown in Listing 7-20.

Listing 7-20. Create a New Test to Determine What Happens When the Content Is Null

```
[TestMethod]
public void GetHeroSliderContentEmptyContentGuid()
{
  //Arrange
  var contentGuidNullException = new ArgumentNullException("contentGuid");
  var parentGuidNullException = new ArgumentNullException("parentGuid");

  var repository = new Mock<IContentRepository>();
  repository
    .Setup(x => x.GetContentItem<IHeroSlider>(String.Empty))
    .Throws(contentGuidNullException);
  repository
    .Setup(x => x.GetChildren<IHeroSliderSlide>(String.Empty))
    .Throws(parentGuidNullException);

  var service = new SitecoreMediaContentService(repository.Object);

  //Act
  var result = service.GetHeroSliderContent(String.Empty);

  //Assert
  result.Should().BeNull();
}
```

If you run this test, it will fail. If an empty string is passed into either of those repository methods, an exception will be thrown. However, we didn't handle that scenario in our earlier example. Our failing test is a clue that we need to improve the design of the system.

10. So, in the GetHeroSliderContent method in SitecoreMediaContentService, update it to match the code shown in Listing 7-21.

Listing 7-21. Add a Null/Empty Check

```
public IHeroSlider GetHeroSliderContent(string contentGuid)
{
  if (string.IsNullOrEmpty(contentGuid))
    return null;

  var heroSlider = _repository.GetContentItem<IHeroSlider>(contentGuid);
  heroSlider.Slides = _repository.GetChildren<IHeroSliderSlide>(contentGuid);
  return heroSlider;
}
```

■ **Note** How you handle these types of error scenarios really depends on your requirements. Should you return null or should you return some sort of status message instead? That's for you to decide.

Now, if you go back and run the GetHeroSliderContentEmptyContentGuid test, it should pass. This is a great example of unit testing helping to improve our design.

Refactoring to Include a Service Test Harness

If you find yourself doing the same //Arrange over and over and over and over in each test, this is probably a good clue that you should start doing something differently. We don't want a lot of duplicate, hard-to-read, and hard-to-maintain tests, either! Creating a "test harness" is a great practice when you find yourself in this situation. A test harness is basically an encapsulation of functionality that can be shared among similar tests. Use the following steps as an example of how you might create a test harness for your service layer tests:

1. First, using the NuGet Package Manager, add a reference to SimpleInjector.

2. Next, create a new interface called ITestHarness with the definition from Listing 7-22. This is an empty interface that will mainly be used for constraining a generic in the next step.

Listing 7-22. ITestHarness.

```
public interface ITestHarness
{
}
```

3. Also in the root of the project, create a class called TestBase with the definition shown in Listing 7-23.

Listing 7-23. TestBase Base Class Used in Our Test Harness

```
using Microsoft.VisualStudio.TestTools.UnitTesting;

namespace SitecoreDev.Feature.Media.Tests
{
  public abstract class TestBase<T> where T : ITestHarness, new()
  {
    protected T _testHarness;

    [TestInitialize]
    public void Setup()
    {
      _testHarness = new T();
    }
  }
}
```

4. Finally, create another class named TestHarnessBase with the definition shown in Listing 7-24.

Listing 7-24. Test Harness Implementation

```
using Ploeh.AutoFixture;
using SimpleInjector;

namespace SitecoreDev.Feature.Media.Tests
{
  public abstract class TestHarnessBase : ITestHarness
  {
```

```
    protected Container _container = new Container();

    protected IFixture _fixture;
    public IFixture Fixture { get { return _fixture; } }
  }
}
```

TestBase is the class that the test class inherits. This is where the [TestInitialize] method is that instantiates the test harness. This ensures that each test runs in a completely isolated environment.

5. Now, in the Services folder, add a new class named ServiceTestHarness with the definition shown in Listing 7-25.

Listing 7-25. Create a Test Harness Used for Our Services

```
using Moq;
using Ploeh.AutoFixture;
using SimpleInjector;
using SitecoreDev.Feature.Media.Services;
using SitecoreDev.Foundation.Repository.Content;

namespace SitecoreDev.Feature.Media.Tests.Services
{
  public class ServiceTestHarness : TestHarnessBase
  {
    private Mock<IContentRepository> _contentRepository;
    public Mock<IContentRepository> ContentRepository
    {
      get
      {
        if (_contentRepository == null)
          _contentRepository =
            Mock.Get(_container.GetInstance<IContentRepository>());
        return _contentRepository;
      }
    }

    private IMediaContentService _contentService;
    public IMediaContentService ContentService
    {
      get
      {
        if (_contentService == null)
          _contentService = _container.GetInstance<IMediaContentService>();
        return _contentService;
      }
    }
```

```
  public ServiceTestHarness()
  {
    InitializeContainer();
    _fixture = new Fixture();
  }

  protected void InitializeContainer()
  {
    _container.Register<IContentRepository>(() =>
      new Mock<IContentRepository>().Object, Lifestyle.Singleton);
    _container.Register<IMediaContentService,
      SitecoreMediaContentService>(Lifestyle.Transient);
  }
 }
}
```

Listing 7-25 is the implementation of our Services test harness, and you can already start to see the value of having one. This class creates an instance of our ContentRepository and ContentService that can be used for all Services tests. The real value is shown in the ContentRepository variable, since all that Mocking code can be reused. Again, we don't want our services tests testing our repositories. This centralized repository mocking code ensures isolation for all services tests. Next we need to update our tests to use the harness:

6.   In GetHeroSliderContentTests, have your test class inherit from TestBase as shown in this code line:

```
public class GetHeroSliderContentTests : TestBase<ServiceTestHarness>
```

7.   Next, modify the GetHeroSliderContentSuccessful method shown in Listing 7-26.

Listing 7-26. Update Tests to Use the Test Harness

```
[TestMethod]
public void GetHeroSliderContentSuccessful()
{
  //Arrange
  var heroSlide = _testHarness.Fixture
    .Build<HeroSlider>()
    .Without(x => x.Slides)
    .Create();
  var children = _testHarness.Fixture
    .CreateMany<HeroSliderSlide>()
    .ToList();

  _testHarness.ContentRepository
    .Setup(x => x.GetContentItem<IHeroSlider>(It.IsAny<string>()))
    .Returns(heroSlide)
    .Verifiable();
  _testHarness.ContentRepository
    .Setup(x => x.GetChildren<IHeroSliderSlide>(It.IsAny<string>()))
    .Returns(children)
    .Verifiable();
```

```
//Act
var result = _testHarness.ContentService.GetHeroSliderContent("123");

//Assert
_testHarness.ContentRepository.Verify();
result.Should().NotBeNull();
result.Slides.Should().NotBeNullOrEmpty();
result.Slides.Count().Should().Be(children.Count());
var slides = result.Slides.ToList();
foreach (var slide in slides)
  slide.Image.Should().NotBeNull();
}
```

8. Modify the GetHeroSliderContentEmptyContentGuid test as shown in Listing 7-27.

Listing 7-27. Update Tests to Use the Test Harness

```
[TestMethod]
public void GetHeroSliderContentEmptyContentGuid()
{
  //Arrange
  var contentGuidNullException = new ArgumentNullException("contentGuid");
  var parentGuidNullException = new ArgumentNullException("parentGuid");

  _testHarness.ContentRepository
    .Setup(x => x.GetContentItem<IHeroSlider>(String.Empty))
    .Throws(contentGuidNullException);
  _testHarness.ContentRepository
    .Setup(x => x.GetChildren<IHeroSliderSlide>(String.Empty))
    .Throws(parentGuidNullException);

  //Act
  var result = _testHarness.ContentService.GetHeroSliderContent(String.Empty);

  //Assert
  result.Should().BeNull();
}
```

If you run your tests, all should still be good and passing!

Unit Testing a Controller

Controllers should be really dumb. All they should do is take a model from a service and map it into a model the view needs, a ViewModel. However, there may be some logic in that mapping and, as a result, unit testing your controllers is necessary. Even if you don't have any logic, you still should unit test your controllers. For three main reasons: in the future you may have logic that needs to be tested, that logic may screw up what the view expects, and writing controller tests are super easy; it should only take a few minutes. A fourth, and arguably the most important, reason for testing your controllers, is testing all of the error paths, in addition to happy-path. What happens if you pass an empty string in to your service layer? Your controller should gracefully handle that scenario. What happens if your service layer throws an exception? Your controller should handle that gracefully. These are the most important reasons for any of the unit testing we do. Check out the following steps for a walkthrough on how to create a quick test for one of the controllers we created earlier in the book:

1. In `SitecoreDev.Feature.Media.Tests`, add a new folder called `Controllers`.

2. Add a class called `HeroSliderTests` with the basic definition shown in Listing 7-28.

Listing 7-28. Stub Out a Test Class for Our Controller

```
using Microsoft.VisualStudio.TestTools.UnitTesting;

namespace SitecoreDev.Feature.Media.Tests.Controllers
{
  [TestClass]
  public class HeroSliderTests
  {

  }
}
```

3. Let's start by adding a happy-path test called `HeroSliderSuccessful` with the definition shown in Listing 7-29.

Listing 7-29. Add a Happy-Path Test that Compares the Result of the Controller Action to a Mocked Up View

```
[TestMethod]
public void HeroSliderSuccessful()
{
  //Arrange
  var fixture = new Fixture();

  var content = fixture.Build<HeroSlider>()
    .With(x => x.Slides, fixture.CreateMany<HeroSliderSlide>().ToList())
    .Create();

  var contentService = new Mock<IMediaContentService>();
  contentService.Setup(x => x.GetHeroSliderContent(It.IsAny<string>()))
    .Returns(content)
    .Verifiable();

  var contextWrapper = new Mock<IContextWrapper>();
  contextWrapper.Setup(x => x.GetParameterValue(It.IsAny<string>()))
    .Returns("500")
    .Verifiable();
  contextWrapper.SetupGet(x => x.IsExperienceEditor)
    .Returns(true)
    .Verifiable();
```

```
var glassHtml = new Mock<IGlassHtml>();
glassHtml.Setup(x => x.Editable(
    It.IsAny<IHeroSliderSlide>(),
    It.IsAny<Expression<Func<IHeroSliderSlide, object>>>(),
    It.IsAny<object>()))
  .Returns("test")
  .Verifiable();

var controller = new MediaController(
  contextWrapper.Object, contentService.Object, glassHtml.Object);

//Act
var result = controller.HeroSlider();

//Assert
result.Should().NotBeNull();
result.Model.Should().BeOfType<HeroSliderViewModel>();
var viewModel = result.Model as HeroSliderViewModel;
viewModel.Should().NotBeNull();
}
```

This test first uses AutoFixture to generate a HeroSlide. We then mock up our MediaContentService to tell it to return our HeroSlide content when the GetHeroSliderContent method is called. Next we need to mock up the ContextWrapper, as well as Glass, two additional dependencies of our controller. GetParameterValue and the IsExperienceEditor method calls will fail if we don't set up a junk return value. We then call the HeroSlider action and assert our results.

If you run this test, it will fail. It's because, even though we've abstracted away any hard dependencies, one was forgotten. We have a call to RenderingContext.Current.Rendering.DataSource. Let's add the DataSource property to IContextWrapper.

4. In SitecoreDev.Foundation.Repository\ Context\IContextWrapper, add the property shown in the following code line:

```
string Datasource { get; }
```

5. In SitecoreContextWrapper, add the implementation of that property as shown in this code line:

```
public string Datasource => RenderingContext.Current.Rendering.DataSource;
```

6. Now, back in SitecoreDev.Feature.Media, in Controllers\MediaController, modify the code as shown in Listing 7-30. We are updating the controller to pull the data source out of the context wrapper instead of RenderingContext. Current, which would fail because there's no Sitecore context.

Listing 7-30. Update the Controller

```
//Instead of
if (!String.IsNullOrEmpty(RenderingContext.Current.Rendering.DataSource))
{
  var contentItem = _mediaContentService.GetHeroSliderContent(
    RenderingContext.Current.Rendering.DataSource);

//Use
if (!String.IsNullOrEmpty(_contextWrapper.Datasource))
{
  var contentItem = _mediaContentService.GetHeroSliderContent(
    _contextWrapper.Datasource);
```

7. In your HeroSliderTests class, let's add one more SetupGet, shown in Listing 7-31.

Listing 7-31. Update the Test to Set Up this Data Source

```
contextWrapper.SetupGet(x => x.Datasource)
  .Returns(Guid.NewGuid().ToString())
  .Verifiable();
```

8. Now, if you run your test, it should pass! However, we're not really done with our assertions in this test. Add the code from Listing 7-32 to the bottom of this test and run it.

Listing 7-32. Add Some More Assertions to Really Ensure Our Test Passes

```
viewModel.HasImages.Should().BeTrue();
viewModel.ImageCount.Should().Be(content.Slides.Count());
viewModel.SlideInterval.Should().Be(500);
viewModel.IsSliderIntervalSet.Should().BeTrue();
viewModel.IsInExperienceEditorMode.Should().BeTrue();
viewModel.ParentGuid.Should().Be(content.Id.ToString());
```

9. Next, write a test that tests an empty Datasource property from IContextWrapper, as shown in Listing 7-33.

Listing 7-33. Write a New Test to Test a Non-Happy-Path (Data Source Is Null)

```
[TestMethod]
public void HeroSliderEmptyDatasource()
{
  //Arrange
  var fixture = new Fixture();

  var contentService = new Mock<IMediaContentService>();

  var contextWrapper = new Mock<IContextWrapper>();
  contextWrapper.Setup(x => x.GetParameterValue(It.IsAny<string>()))
    .Returns("500")
    .Verifiable();
```

```
contextWrapper.SetupGet(x => x.IsExperienceEditor)
  .Returns(true)
  .Verifiable();
contextWrapper.SetupGet(x => x.Datasource)
  .Returns(String.Empty)
  .Verifiable();

var glassHtml = new Mock<IGlassHtml>();

var controller = new MediaController(contextWrapper.Object,
  contentService.Object, glassHtml.Object);

//Act
var result = controller.HeroSlider();

//Assert
result.Should().NotBeNull();
result.Model.Should().BeOfType<HeroSliderViewModel>();
var viewModel = result.Model as HeroSliderViewModel;
viewModel.Should().NotBeNull();
viewModel.HasImages.Should().BeFalse();
viewModel.ImageCount.Should().Be(0);
viewModel.SlideInterval.Should().Be(500);
viewModel.IsSliderIntervalSet.Should().BeTrue();
viewModel.IsInExperienceEditorMode.Should().BeTrue();
viewModel.ParentGuid.Should().BeNullOrEmpty();
}
```

If you run this test, it should pass. You should also be starting to see a pattern to how and why we test our code. Don't just test happy-path scenarios, test all of the error scenarios as well. This will help you improve the quality and design of your code as well as provide you with an enormous amount of confidence should someone need to refactor code in the future.

Refactoring to Include a Controller Test Harness

Earlier we refactored our Service tests to use a base class test harness. This was helpful because we ran the risk of needing tons of duplicate code to set up each test. You probably guessed it, but we run the same risk with our controller tests. Use the following steps as a guide to similarly set up a test harness for your controllers:

1. In the `Controllers` folder of `SitecoreDev.Feature.Media`, create a new class named `ControllerTestHarness` with the definition shown in Listing 7-34. We are creating a new test harness using the same base class we created earlier in the chapter. This class follows the same pattern as the `ServiceTestHarness` class.

Listing 7-34. Create a New Test Harness.

```
using Moq;
using Ploeh.AutoFixture;
using SimpleInjector;
using SitecoreDev.Feature.Media.Controllers;
using SitecoreDev.Feature.Media.Services;
using SitecoreDev.Foundation.Repository.Context;
```

```
namespace SitecoreDev.Feature.Media.Tests.Controllers
{
  public class ControllerTestHarness : TestHarnessBase
  {
    private Mock<IContextWrapper> _mockContextWrapper;
    public Mock<IContextWrapper> ContextWrapper
    {
      get
      {
        if (_mockContextWrapper == null)
          _mockContextWrapper = Mock.Get(
            _container.GetInstance<IContextWrapper>());
        return _mockContextWrapper;
      }
    }

    private Mock<IMediaContentService> _mockContentService;
    public Mock<IMediaContentService> ContentService
    {
      get
      {
        if (_mockContentService == null)
          _mockContentService = Mock.Get(
            _container.GetInstance<IMediaContentService>());
        return _mockContentService;
      }
    }

    private Mock<IGlassHtml> _mockGlassHtml;
    public Mock<IGlassHtml> GlassHtml
    {
      get
      {
        if (_mockGlassHtml == null)
          _mockGlassHtml = Mock.Get(_container.GetInstance<IGlassHtml>());
        return _mockGlassHtml;
      }
    }

    private MediaController _controller;
    public MediaController Controller
    {
      get
      {
        if (_controller == null)
          _controller = _container.GetInstance<MediaController>();
        return _controller;
      }
    }
```

```
public ControllerTestHarness()
{
  InitializeContainer();

  _fixture = new Fixture();

  ContextWrapper
     .SetupGet(rc => rc.Datasource)
     .Returns(Fixture.Create<string>());
}

protected void InitializeContainer()
{
  _container.Register<IContextWrapper>(() =>
    new Mock<IContextWrapper>().Object, Lifestyle.Singleton);

  _container.Register<IMediaContentService>(() =>
    new Mock<IMediaContentService>().Object, Lifestyle.Singleton);

  _container.Register<IGlassHtml>(() =>
    new Mock<IGlassHtml>().Object, Lifestyle.Singleton);

  _container.Register<MediaController>(Lifestyle.Transient);
  }
 }
}
```

2. Next, modify your HeroSliderTests class to inherit from TestBase, as shown in this code listing:

```
public class HeroSliderTests : TestBase<ControllerTestHarness>
```

3. Update HeroSliderSuccessful as shown in Listing 7-35.

Listing 7-35. Update Your Tests to Start Using the New Test Harness

```
[TestMethod]
public void HeroSliderSuccessful()
{
  //Arrange
  var content = _testHarness.Fixture
    .Build<HeroSlider>()
    .With(x => x.Slides,
      _testHarness.Fixture.CreateMany<HeroSliderSlide>().ToList())
    .Create();

  _testHarness.ContentService.Setup(x => x.GetHeroSliderContent(It.IsAny<string>()))
    .Returns(content)
    .Verifiable();
```

231

```
_testHarness.ContextWrapper.Setup(x => x.GetParameterValue(It.IsAny<string>()))
    .Returns("500")
    .Verifiable();
_testHarness.ContextWrapper.SetupGet(x => x.IsExperienceEditor)
    .Returns(true)
    .Verifiable();
_testHarness.ContextWrapper.SetupGet(x => x.Datasource)
    .Returns(Guid.NewGuid().ToString())
    .Verifiable();

_testHarness.GlassHtml.Setup(x => x.Editable(
    It.IsAny<IHeroSliderSlide>(),
    It.IsAny<Expression<Func<IHeroSliderSlide, object>>>(),
    It.IsAny<object>()))
    .Returns("test")
    .Verifiable();

//Act
var result = _testHarness.Controller.HeroSlider();

//Assert
result.Should().NotBeNull();
result.Model.Should().BeOfType<HeroSliderViewModel>();
var viewModel = result.Model as HeroSliderViewModel;
viewModel.Should().NotBeNull();
viewModel.HasImages.Should().BeTrue();
viewModel.ImageCount.Should().Be(content.Slides.Count());
viewModel.SlideInterval.Should().Be(500);
viewModel.IsSliderIntervalSet.Should().BeTrue();
viewModel.IsInExperienceEditorMode.Should().BeTrue();
viewModel.ParentGuid.Should().Be(content.Id.ToString());
}
```

4. Finally, update HeroSliderEmptyDatasource as shown in Listing 7-36.

Listing 7-36. Update Your Tests to Start Using the New Test Harness

```
[TestMethod]
public void HeroSliderEmptyDatasource()
{
  //Arrange
  _testHarness.ContextWrapper.Setup(x =>
      x.GetParameterValue(It.IsAny<string>()))
    .Returns("500")
    .Verifiable();
  _testHarness.ContextWrapper.SetupGet(x => x.IsExperienceEditor)
    .Returns(true)
    .Verifiable();
  _testHarness.ContextWrapper.SetupGet(x => x.Datasource)
    .Returns(String.Empty)
    .Verifiable();
```

```
//Act
var result = _testHarness.Controller.HeroSlider();

//Assert
result.Should().NotBeNull();
result.Model.Should().BeOfType<HeroSliderViewModel>();
var viewModel = result.Model as HeroSliderViewModel;
viewModel.Should().NotBeNull();
viewModel.HasImages.Should().BeFalse();
viewModel.ImageCount.Should().Be(0);
viewModel.SlideInterval.Should().Be(500);
viewModel.IsSliderIntervalSet.Should().BeTrue();
viewModel.IsInExperienceEditorMode.Should().BeTrue();
viewModel.ParentGuid.Should().BeNullOrEmpty();
}
```

Run your tests and all should still be good and passing!

Sitecore FakeDb

We have a problem: the System Under Test (SUT) code calls some other code, such as code in a different class, and it becomes impossible to test only the class you want to test. Your test is no longer atomic. A good example of this is Sitecore itself. You may at some point have code that calls the Sitecore API. How do you ensure your code is working when the code has these external dependencies you can't remove? Can anything be done?

Using "fakes" and creating test doubles are a way to remove these dependencies and isolate just your code. A NuGet package called Sitecore.FakeDb helps you do exactly this! Sitecore.FakeDb is a data provider for your tests which fakes the presence of a Sitecore database. This enables you to test your code against a fake database, ensuring no external dependencies are influencing whether your tests pass or fail. With Sitecore.FakeDb, you once again can have an atomic test. Without it, your tests get nasty, complex, and really are "integration tests" and not unit tests at all; you're testing multiple systems at once.

■ **Note** Whenever possible, abide by the single responsibility principle and pass dependencies as parameters of your constructors (as discussed in Chapters 3, 4, and 5). You can then mock up these dependencies in your Arrange phase. You use FakeDb as a last resort because you *cannot* influence the design and remove dependencies. Our repository examples in previous chapters actually do not need Sitecore.FakeDb because even they, with the sole purpose of getting Sitecore data, have been abstracted away with an ORM/Glass. Mapper. In a nutshell, you only use FakeDb in situations where you don't have control over the design and you need to get around limitations of that design, or when, in the case of code that uses the Sitecore API directly, where it can't be abstracted with an ORM. If you are customizing Glass.Mapper with delegates or data handlers, FakeDb could be beneficial as well.

After installing the Sitecore.FakeDb NuGet package, you must add references to the following DLLs within your Tests project:

- Lucene.Net.dll

- Sitecore.Analytics.dll

- Sitecore.Kernel.dll

- Sitecore.Logging.dll

- Sitecore.Nexus.dll

Lastly, you also need to copy your Sitecore license.xml file into the root of your Tests project. Only thereafter can you start using FakeDb to fake your Sitecore databases. As an example, check out the SitecoreHelpers class in Listing 7-37. This class has a method called GetItemTitle, where you pass in the path of the item and it should return the Title of that item. Sitecore.FakeDb can help remove the dependency on Sitecore itself and test your code in isolation.

Listing 7-37. Example Class We'd Want Sitecore.FakeDb to Help With

```
public class SitecoreHelpers
{
    public string GetItemTitle(string path)
    {
        Sitecore.Data.Database masterDb =
            Sitecore.Configuration.Factory.GetDatabase("master");
        Sitecore.Data.Items.Item item = masterDb.Items[path];
        return item["Title"];
    }
}
```

Now check out the test in Listing 7-38, which validates that you can get an item out of the Sitecore content tree and confirm that item's Title field is set to the expected result.

Listing 7-38. Uses FakeDb to Remove the Sitecore Dependency from the GetItemTitle Method

```
[TestMethod]
public void TestGetItemTitle()
{
    // Arrange
    string expectedTitle = "Hello World!";
    using (Db db = new Db
    {
        new DbItem("Home") { { "Title", expectedTitle } }
    })
        SitecoreHelpers sut = new SitecoreHelpers();

        // Act
        var result = sut.GetItemTitle("/sitecore/content/home");

        // Assert
        result.Should().Be(expectedTitle);
}
```

Let's talk a bit what this test is doing. First we are setting up our system under test in the arrange phase. We create a value for our expected title (Hello World!), and then we create a new mocked connection to the Sitecore database using `Sitecore.FakeDb`. This is done in the using brackets. It is essential to understand you must dispose of your databases or you can get memory issues with tests stepping on each other. You'll want to always wrap your database tests within using statements.

You'll also notice in the Arrange phase that we're creating a new item within the database. Without these new items you'll essentially be working with an empty Sitecore content tree. The code `new DbItem("Home") { { "Title", expectedTitle } }` is creating a new item named Home at the root of / sitecore/content. Additionally, we're assigning the Title field to our expected title. Lastly, we instantiate the System Under Test, in this case, our `SitecoreHelpers` class. This forms the basic data construct we'll run our test against and completes the Arrange phase.

Next, is the Act phase where we run our test against the faked database. We call the `GetItemTitle` method on our `SitecoreHelpers` class, which as you remember opens a connection to the Sitecore database. However, since we're running under the umbrella of our `Sitecore.FakeDb` database that call is injected with our faked object. The `GetItemTitle` method gets the item out of "Sitecore" and returns the title, which we inspect in the Assert phase. Since we're using FakeDb, it passes! Without FakeDb it would fail because we have no context to Sitecore; we wouldn't be able to open the database.

To take this a step further, notice the test in Listing 7-39. In this test we're starting to create a hierarchy of items. We have a parent item called Home and a child of that item called Child. Similarly, we test to ensure both title fields are as we expect them to be.

Listing 7-39. You Can Create Hierarchies of Items with FakeDb

```
[TestMethod]
public void TestChildItems()
{
    // Arrange
    string expectedParentTitle = "Hello Son!";
    string expectedChildTitle = "Hello Dad!";
    using (Db db = new Db
    {
        new DbItem("Home")
        {
            { "Title", expectedParentTitle },
            new DbItem("Child") { { "Title", expectedChildTitle } }
        }
    })
        SitecoreHelpers sut = new SitecoreHelpers();

        // Act
        var result = sut.GetItemTitle("/sitecore/content/home");
        var childResult = sut.GetItemTitle("/sitecore/content/home/child");

        // Assert
        result.Should().Be(expectedParentTitle);
        childResult.Should().Be(expectedChildTitle);
}
```

■ **Note**   Up to this point, all the new items we've been creating have fallen below the `/sitecore/content` path. This is the default location. If you want to place new items elsewhere, user the following convention (for example, to place an item below the `/sitecore/system path`): new `DbItem("home") { ParentID = ItemIds.SystemRoot }`.

There may be times when you want to create items using a specific template. Listing 7-40 shows you how to create a new template first, and then to create a new item using that template. Notice how we call the `SitecoreHelper's GetItem` method which just returns the item specified. Nothing new there. The point of Listing 7-40 is to demonstrate how that item's template has the expected `templateID` we injected into the faked database.

Listing 7-40. When Creating Items You Can Also Explicitly Set Their Templates

```
[TestMethod]
public void TestCreateItemWithTemplate()
{
    // Arrange
    var templateId = ID.NewID;
    using (Db db = new Db
    {
        new DbTemplate("My Template", templateId),
        new DbItem("Home", ID.NewID, templateId)
    })
        SitecoreHelpers sut = new SitecoreHelpers();

        // Act
        var result = sut.GetItem("/sitecore/content/home");

        // Assert
        result.TemplateID.Should().Be(templateId);;
}
```

Templates bring us to another point. You'll have noticed in earlier listings that we could create a title field without explicitly defining a template with a title field in it. When you instantiate an item without a template associated with it this works fine. However, if the new item has a template associated with it, it will need that title field explicitly defined or it breaks. The code in listing 7-41 would break if we tried to access a title field, because our item has a defined template without that title field. In this example we're completely relying on the explicit template as defined. So, to add title support you would want to add a second field into the template, in addition to the `CustomField` you see.

Listing 7-41. You Can Set Standard Values When Adding Fields to a Template

```
[TestMethod]
public void TestStandardValues()
{
    // Arrange
    var templateId = ID.NewID;
    var someData = "Some data";
```

```
using (Db db = new Db
{
    new DbTemplate("My Template", templateId) {
        { "CustomField", someData } },
    new DbItem("Home", ID.NewID, templateId)
})
    SitecoreHelpers sut = new SitecoreHelpers();

    // Act
    var result = sut.GetItem("/sitecore/content/home");

    // Assert
    result["CustomField"].Should().Be(someData);
}
```

Listing 7-41 also shows you how to set standard values on a template. When you declare that a template has a field, you can optionally also add a standard value onto that field, e.g., { "CustomField", someData }. Additionally, the listing demonstrates that the result Item has all the same properties you'd expect a Sitecore. Data.Items.Item would have, as seen by how we're accessing the CustomField item field and its value.

■ **Note**   Sitecore.FakeDb also supports tokens in the standard values just like within standard values on an item with Sitecore. For example, in Listing 7-41, instead of a string with "Some data" we could use "$name", in which case the $name token is replace with the item name. In this example, $name would resolve to "Home".

One thing you may need to work with is versions and languages. Check out the test in Listing 7-42 to see how to work with versions and languages within FakeDb.

Listing 7-42. Sitecore FakeDb Also Supports Languages and Versions

```
[TestMethod]
public void TestVersions()
{
    // Arrange
    var templateId = ID.NewID;
    var enusText = "I fell while organizing my cookie jar";
    var enus2Text = "I fell whilst organising my biscuit jar";
    var frText = "I ate all my cookies";

    using (Db db = new Db
    {
        new DbItem("Home")
        {
            new DbField("CustomField")
            {
                {"en", 1, enusText },
                {"en", 2, enus2Text },
                {"fr", 1, frText }
```

```
            }
        }
    })
        // Act
        var en1 = db.GetItem("/sitecore/content/home", "en", 1);
        var en2 = db.GetItem("/sitecore/content/home", "en", 2);
        var fr = db.GetItem("/sitecore/content/home", "fr", 1);

        // Assert
        en1["CustomField"].Should().Be(enusText);
        en2["CustomField"].Should().Be(enus2Text);
        fr["CustomField"].Should().Be(frText);
}
```

In this example, we first set up a few strings to test. Then, as we create our new DbField objects within the Home node, we specify which language and version combinations we want to set. Next, when we get the item out of the Sitecore fake we also include the language and version numbers as parameters. Lastly, we run our assertions to ensure the values come back as expected.

This was a whirlwind tour of Sitecore FakeDb. There's a ton of other things you can do, such as:

- Site context

- Authorization

- Authentication

- Roles

- Membership

- Pipelines

- Media provider

- Link database

- Content search

- Settings

To check out FakeDb resources or to pull down the source, go to http://Github.com/ sergeyshushlyapin/Sitecore.FakeDb. There is also an AutoFixture plugin for FakeDb this is worth checking out.

■ **Note**   It's finally safe to try writing a unit test of our repository code, now that you have a basic understanding of Sitecore FakeDb. However, we're not actually going to give you any additional steps to do it! The problem is, our book's solution is already so well designed (abstraction, DI, etc.) that adding a unit test for our repository actually isn't necessary! We don't need to test Sitecore's API, and we don't need to test Glass. Mapper. There's no business logic whatsoever in our repository—one less test to write! However, the code samples earlier are plenty to get you off to the races when you do have code directly calling Sitecore's API—a situation where you definitely *need* unit tests!

Summary

Well, there you have it, no more excuses to not write unit tests! They are easy, they save you time, and they build your confidence in the quality and integrity of the solution. Why wouldn't you, after reading this chapter, immediately start writing unit tests for your Sitecore code? We can think of no good reason.

This chapter walked you through how to create your first ever unit test, for those newbies out there without previous experience. We then built unit tests for the services and controllers we created in Chapters 3, 4, and 5. Next we discussed how AutoFixture can save you a ton of time. AutoFixture is a tool you can use to perform your data generation; no more hard-coding dummy data!

Lastly, we discussed Sitecore FakeDb. FakeDb can be used when you need to test your code that interacts with the Sitecore object model directly. Hopefully, as we discussed in Chapter 5, this isn't very often. Through abstraction and the use of generics you can reduce/eliminate the need for native Sitecore code. However, when you do need it, you don't want excuses for skipping unit tests, and with FakeDb you have none! FakeDb will fake a Sitecore database to ensure your code is tested in isolation from any external dependencies, Sitecore included.

CHAPTER 8

■ ■ ■

Search-Driven Solutions

Up until this point all of our code has been hitting the Sitecore database directly whenever we've needed Sitecore data. This, however, isn't always the best practice. For one it can put a lot of CPU pressure on your SQL server. For another, it doesn't perform well. Full-text search is a great example of where, if it were a SQL query, you would need to inspect every single row.

A better way is to index your data in such a way to enable it to be searched, accessed quickly and at scale. Fortunately, Sitecore has thought of this already; Sitecore comes out of the box with a Lucene index. Lucene is an open source index provider that makes it is easy to build solutions. Also, Sitecore uses Lucene for all the searches you see in the /sitecore administrative interfaces. All you need to do is add your data into this index and you can start searching against it!

■ **Warning**   Before you dig into code you need to consider your search architecture. This is beyond the scope of this book, but out-of-the-box Lucene is not configured in a highly-available architecture. To do that, you need Solr to partition your index and distribute it across multiple servers. Additionally, you need Zookeeper to "watch" your Solr servers for failure and to failover the index to another server in the event of a failure. For more information, see https://lucene.apache.org/solr/.

However, searching the index is just the beginning. There are a lot of other bells and whistles we need to build around our results to provide a great user experience. These include type-ahead results, search suggestions, and search facets. Code examples of all these and more are covered in this chapter!

■ **Note**   The examples in this chapter leverage concepts from Chapters 4 and 5, in particular a "modular architecture." Don't bother reading this chapter if you don't have a good handle on those previous concepts or you may have difficulty understanding the code.

Setting Up Your Index

Fortunately for you there isn't much you *need* to do to get your Lucene index set up—when you install Sitecore the installation also installs a Lucene index you can use immediately.

All item changes in Sitecore get logged to a history table (see Figure 8-1). An event fires after each change to ensure the index is updated with the new data. This process is called *indexing*, where new content is added to the search index and old content is updated or removed.

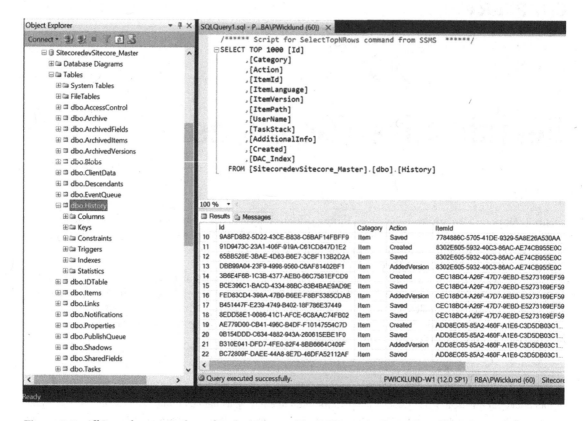

Figure 8-1. *All item changes get logged in the history table so Sitecore knows to keep the index fresh*

Sitecore stores most of the system fields in the index automatically, such as _id, _creator, and urllink. The list of fields stored in the index can be found in the Sitecore.ContentSearch.Lucene. DefaultIndexConfiguration.config file below WebSite->App_Config->Include. You'll see a <field> element below its parent <fieldNames> element with the following schema:

- *fieldname*: Name of the field you want indexed.

- *storageType*: Whether or not the original value of the field is stored in the index. Useful if you want to retrieve the value from the index instead of the database.

- *indexType*: Whether the default or the specified analyzer is run over the field value.

- *vectorType*: Whether or not to store the term vectors, i.e. the term frequency. Possible values include:

  - NO: Do not store the term vectors.

  - WITH_OFFSETS: Store the term vector and word offset information.

  - WITH_POSITIONS: Store the term vector and word position information.

  - WITH_POSITIONS_OFFSETS: Store the term vector and word position and offset information.

  - YES: Store the term vectors of each document.

- *boost*: Globally indicates the relative importance of this field at index and query time.

- *type*: The type to cast the value back to in the API.

- *settingType*: The class implementation to store the information specified in all other fields.

Additionally, field types can also be added into the index, enabling all fields of a given type to be automatically indexed (instead of needing to specify each field individually). Below the <fieldNames> element you'll see a <fieldTypes> element with a similar schema as fields.

■ **Note**   By default, all the field types are set to not be stored in the index. This means you'll need to query the database. Set the storageType value to Yes when you know you'll need to use search.

Our example site needs some extra fields in the index so we can use a Lucene search when searching it. Use the following steps as an example of how to add/change fields in the index. Let's start by creating a new project in the Foundation section.

1. Right-click on the Foundation folder and create a new folder named Indexing. In this new Indexing folder, create a new ASP.NET Web Application called SitecoreDev.Foundation.Index, selecting the empty template and checking the MVC box for adding core references. Once the project has been created, you can delete the Global.asax file and the Views, Controllers, App_Start, and App_Data folders.

2. Create a new folder called App_Config. In that folder, create one called Include, then a folder called Foundation in that one. In the new Foundation folder, add a new configuration file called Foundation.Indexing.config, with the contents found in Listing 8-1.

Listing 8-1. Lucene Configuration

```
<configuration xmlns:patch="http://www.sitecore.net/xmlconfig/"
xmlns:set="http://www.sitecore.net/xmlconfig/set/">
  <sitecore>
    <contentSearch>
      <indexConfigurations>
        <defaultLuceneIndexConfiguration>
          <fieldMap type="Sitecore.ContentSearch.FieldMap, Sitecore.ContentSearch">
            <fieldNames hint="raw:AddFieldByFieldName">
              <!-- Blog Entry Fields -->
              <field fieldName="title" storageType="YES" indexType="TOKENIZED"
              vectorType="NO" boost="1f" type="System.String" settingType="Sitecore.
              ContentSearch.LuceneProvider.LuceneSearchFieldConfiguration, Sitecore.
              ContentSearch.LuceneProvider" />
              <field fieldName="body" storageType="YES" indexType="TOKENIZED"
              vectorType="NO" boost="1f" type="System.String" settingType="Sitecore.
              ContentSearch.LuceneProvider.LuceneSearchFieldConfiguration, Sitecore.
              ContentSearch.LuceneProvider" />
            </fieldNames>
          </fieldMap>
```

```
        </defaultLuceneIndexConfiguration>
      </indexConfigurations>
    </contentSearch>
  </sitecore>
</configuration>
```

3. Build your solution and publish your site using the Publish-Site Gulp task. Once the publish has completed, navigate to `http://sitecore8/sitecore`, then click on Control Panel.

4. In the Indexing section, click on the Indexing Manager link (see Figure 8-2). This will open the Indexing Manager dialog. In the Indexing Manager dialog, select the `sitecore_master_index`.

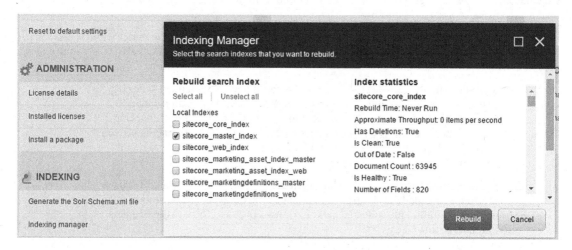

Figure 8-2. *Rebuild an index to throw it away and start fresh, which is necessary when you add new fields*

5. Click Rebuild.

6. Now, using a tool like the Index Viewer from Sitecore PowerShell Extensions (more on installing SPE in Chapter 10), you can view the contents of the `sitecore_master_index`. To launch the Index Viewer, click on the Desktop icon from the Launchpad (see Figure 8-3).

Figure 8-3. *The Index Viewer report allows you to view the contents of an index for testing/validation purposes*

7. Click on the Sitecore logo in the bottom left, then PowerShell Toolbox->Index Viewer. Then select the `sitecore_master_index` and click OK.

8. In the Index View Report dialog (see Figure 8-4), type in the title of your blog entry created in Chapter 4, then click OK. You should see one item returned.

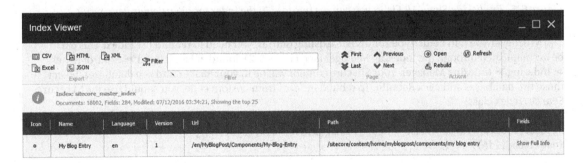

Figure 8-4. *Confirm the blog post is in the index*

9.   If you click on the Show Full Info link on the right, you can view the fields
     indexed for that item. As you can see in Figure 8-5, we have our two new fields,
     Title and Body!

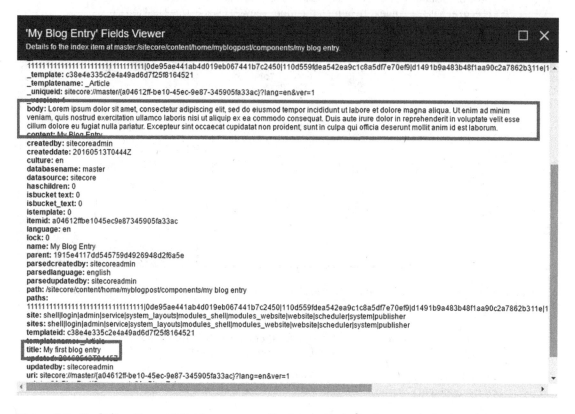

Figure 8-5. By clicking Show All Fields you can see the data in the index for a particular item/result

Whenever you add fields/types or update existing entries, you need to rebuild the index. This can
be accomplished through the Indexing Manager (see Figure 8-2), found at Launchpad ➤ Control Panel
➤ Indexing ➤ Indexing Manager. Your Sitecore content will be in your Master and Web databases. Select
those two databases and click Rebuild. To rebuild indexes from custom code, you should use the Sitecore.
Search.Index class:

```
Sitecore.Search.Index index = SearchManager.GetIndex("system");
index.Rebuild();
```

Searching Your Index

With your index in place with all the fields within it that you need to search, it's time to write some search
code! Notice the following code. The first thing you need to do is get the index context you want to search.
Next, you search the index using a Linq query. In this simple example we're searching the index for items
where the Title field contains the text "Hello World", which should bring back our Hello World item from
Chapter 2.

```
var context = ContextSearchManager
    .GetIndex("sitecore_master_index").CreateSearchContext()
var results = context.GetQueryable<SearchResultItem>().Where(q => q.Title.Contains("Hello World"))
```

This, however, is a very simple example. Check out the following steps to build a more robust example of using search to search our blog posts in our example project. We'll begin by adding a control for the search box for a user to type their query, and before the end we'll have another control to render the search results. All of this will be built within the "modular" architecture, as presented in Chapters 4 and 5.

Earlier, we created a single blog post page called MyBlogPost. That was at the root of the site. For this example, we'll need a few more. But rather than creating all the posts at the root of the site, let's create a blog page, then put all of the blog pages underneath it, as children.

1. In the Content Editor, start by navigating to /sitecore/content/home. Right-click on Home and select Insert ➤ Insert from template and select the /Branches/ Sitecore8Dev/Basic Empty Page branch template (see Figure 8-6). Name this new item Blog.

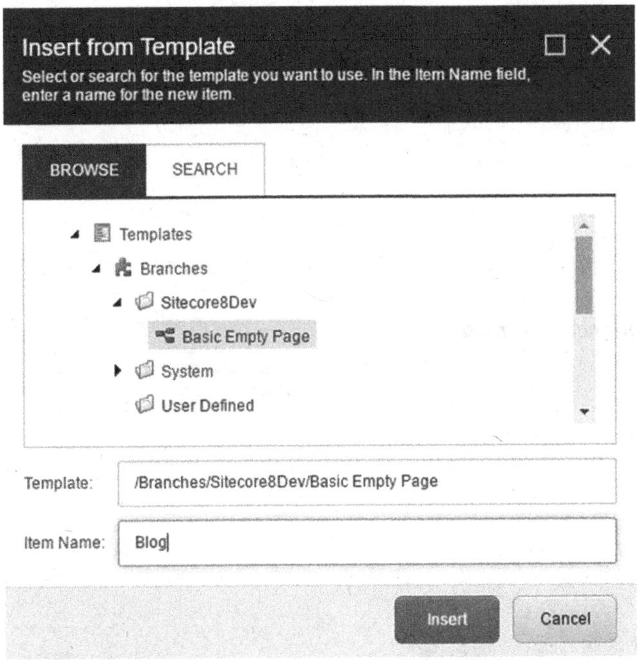

Figure 8-6. *Create a new page to house our blog*

2. Click Insert.

3. Next, right-click on the MyBlogPost page and select Copying ➤ Move To (see Figure 8-7). Select the new blog page.

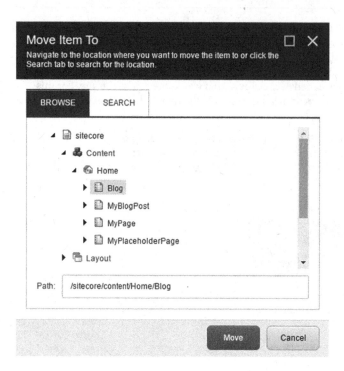

Figure 8-7. *Move the blog post page to below our new blog node*

4. Click Move.

5. Now, right-click on MyBlogPost and select Duplicate. Name it MySecondBlogPost. Change the title to My Second Blog Post. Do this a few more times to create a handful of posts (see Figure 8-8).

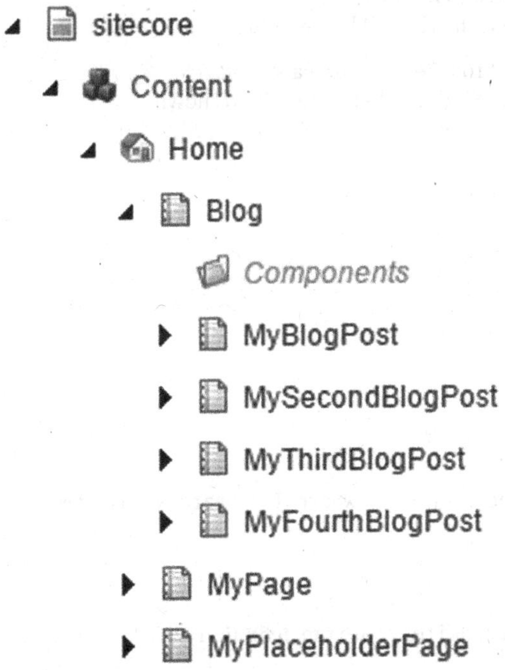

◢ ▤ sitecore

   ◢ 🎲 Content

      ◢ 🏠 Home

         ◢ ▤ Blog

            📁 *Components*

            ▶ ▤ MyBlogPost

            ▶ ▤ MySecondBlogPost

            ▶ ▤ MyThirdBlogPost

            ▶ ▤ MyFourthBlogPost

         ▶ ▤ MyPage

         ▶ ▤ MyPlaceholderPage

Figure 8-8. *Create a few more duplicate blog posts so we have some good content to search*

Now that we have a few posts with content, let's head back to Visual Studio.

6. In the Feature solution folder, create another folder called Search. In that folder, let's create another Empty ASP.NET MVC Web Application called SitecoreDev. Feature.Search. Once the project has been created, you can delete the Global. asax file and the App_Start and App_Data folders.

7. In this new SitecoreDev.Feature.Search project, add references to the Sitecore.Kernel.dll and Sitecore.Mvc.dll assemblies, then, through NuGet Package Manager, add references to Glass.Mapper.Sc and SimpleInjector. You'll also want project references to SitecoreDev.Foundation.Ioc, SitecoreDev.Foundation.Model, and SitecoreDev.Foundation.Repository.

8. After adding the reference to Glass.Mapper.Sc, you can delete the App_Config and App_Start folders and their contents.

9. Two more assemblies we'll be using that we haven't used before are the
    Sitecore.ContentSearch.dll and Sitecore.ContentSearch.Linq.dll
    assemblies. Locate these two assemblies in the %webroot%/bin folder and
    copy them to the %devroot%/libs/Sitecore folder. Once they're copied, add a
    reference to them in the SitecoreDev.Feature.Search project.

10. Next, we need to modify the SitecoreDev.Foundation.Repository project
    to support searching. In that project, add references to the Sitecore.
    ContentSearch.dll and Sitecore.ContentSearch.Linq.dll assemblies.

11. Now, add a new folder to SitecoreDev.Foundation.Repository called Search.
    In that folder, add a new file called ISearchRepository with the definition shown
    in Listing 8-2.

Listing 8-2. Create a Repository Interface to Hold Search Results

```
using System;
using System.Collections.Generic;
using System.Linq.Expressions;
using Sitecore.ContentSearch.SearchTypes;

namespace SitecoreDev.Foundation.Repository.Search
{
  public interface ISearchRepository
  {
    IEnumerable<T> Search<T>(Expression<Func<T, bool>> query) where T : SearchResultItem;
  }
}
```

12. Next, add a new class named SitecoreSearchRepository with the definition
    shown in Listing 8-3.

Listing 8-3. Implement the Repository to Query the Index

```
using System;
using System.Collections.Generic;
using System.Linq;
using System.Linq.Expressions;
using Sitecore.ContentSearch;
using Sitecore.ContentSearch.SearchTypes;

namespace SitecoreDev.Foundation.Repository.Search
{
  public class SitecoreSearchRepository : ISearchRepository
  {
    public IEnumerable<T> Search<T>(Expression<Func<T, bool>> query)
    where T : SearchResultItem
    {
      IEnumerable<T> results = null;
```

```
var index = String.Format("sitecore_{0}_index", Sitecore.Context.Database.Name);

using (var context = ContentSearchManager.GetIndex(index).CreateSearchContext())
{
   results = context.GetQueryable<T>().Where(query).ToList();
}

return results;
    }
  }
}
```

Since we're following the same pattern that we laid out with our IContentRepository, we want to make our ISearchRepository as generic as possible so it can be leveraged across multiple feature modules. In Listing 8-3, we use the Sitecore.Context.Database.Name property to identify which index should be used for searching. That way, we're not hardcoding sitecore_web_index, for instance. Then, using a using statement for the disposable IProviderSearchContext (returned by the CreateSearchContext() method), we pass the query, as defined in the service layer of a given Feature module (after all, building the search query would be considered business logic that belongs in the service layer), to the GetQueryable<T> method of IProviderSearchContext. This will return a list of items matching the criteria. Calling ToList() actually executes the query.

13. Now, in SitecoreDev.Foundation.Repository.Pipelines. InitializeContainer.RegisterDependencies, add this line to the Process method:

    args.Container.Register<ISearchRepository, SitecoreSearchRepository>();

14. In the Context folder, add this line to IContextWrapper

    string CurrentItemPath { get; }

15. And this line to the SitecoreContextWrapper.

    public string CurrentItemPath => Sitecore.Context.Item.Paths.FullPath;

16. Now, back in the SitecoreDev.Feature.Search project, in the Models folder, create a new class named BlogSearchResult and add the definition shown in Listing 8-4.

Listing 8-4. Create a BlogSearchResult Class

```
using Sitecore.ContentSearch.SearchTypes;

namespace SitecoreDev.Feature.Search.Models
{
  public class BlogSearchResult : SearchResultItem
  {
    public string Title { get; set; }
  }
}
```

251

17. Now create a new folder called Services. In this folder, create an interface named ISearchService, using the definition shown in Listing 8-5.

Listing 8-5. Create a New Interface for the New Search Service

```
using System.Collections.Generic;
using Sitecore.ContentSearch.SearchTypes;

namespace SitecoreDev.Feature.Search.Services
{
    public interface ISearchService
    {
        IEnumerable<BlogSearchResult> SearchBlogPosts(string searchTerm,
        string searchStartPath);    }
}
```

18. Next, create a new class in the Services folder called SitecoreSearchService, with the definition shown in Listing 8-6.

Listing 8-6. Implement the Search Service by Calling the Repository

```
using System.Collections.Generic;
using SitecoreDev.Feature.Search.Models;
using SitecoreDev.Foundation.Repository.Search;

namespace SitecoreDev.Feature.Search.Services
{
  public class SitecoreSearchService : ISearchService
  {
    private readonly ISearchRepository _searchRepository;

    public SitecoreSearchService(ISearchRepository searchRepository)
    {
      _searchRepository = searchRepository;
    }

    public IEnumerable<BlogSearchResult> SearchBlogPosts(string searchTerm)
    {
      return _searchRepository.Search<BlogSearchResult>(
        q => q.Title.Contains(searchTerm) && q.Path.StartsWith("/sitecore/content/Home"));
    }
  }
}
```

Now that we've created the service that will hold the logic for searching, let's register that dependency so it can be injected into our controller.

19. At the root of SitecoreDev.Feature.Search project, add a folder called Pipelines. Inside Pipelines, add a folder called InitializeContainer. In the InitializeContainer folder, add a class called RegisterDependencies with the definition shown in Listing 8-7.

Listing 8-7. Register the New Search Service as a Dependency for the Controllers by Adding It to the Pipeline

```
using SitecoreDev.Feature.Search.Services;
using SitecoreDev.Foundation.Ioc.Pipelines.InitializeContainer;

namespace SitecoreDev.Feature.Search.Pipelines.InitializeContainer
{
    public class RegisterDependencies
    {
        public void Process(InitializeContainerArgs args)
        {
            args.Container.Register<ISearchService, SitecoreSearchService>();
        }
    }
}
```

Now, let's create the config to patch in for our dependency registration.

20. Create a folder called App_Config at the root of SitecoreDev.Feature.Search. Then create a folder called Include. Finally, create one more named Feature. Inside the Feature folder, create a configuration file named Feature.Search. config with the definition shown in Listing 8-8.

Listing 8-8. Patch in the Dependency with a New Config File

```
<configuration xmlns:patch="http://www.sitecore.net/xmlconfig/"
xmlns:set="http://www.sitecore.net/xmlconfig/set/">
  <sitecore>
    <pipelines>
      <initializeContainer>
        <processor type="SitecoreDev.Feature.Search.Pipelines.InitializeContainer.
        RegisterDependencies, SitecoreDev.Feature.Search" />
      </initializeContainer>
    </pipelines>
  </sitecore>
</configuration>
```

Now that our service is built, let's create a few ViewModel classes before creating the controller.

21. In the ViewModels folder, create three new classes—BlogSearchViewModel, SearchResultViewModel, and SearchResultsViewModel—with the definitions shown in Listings 8-9, 8-10, and 8-11, respectively.

Listing 8-9. BlogSearchViewModel to Store the Term Used in the Search

```
namespace SitecoreDev.Feature.Search.ViewModels
{
    public class BlogSearchViewModel
    {
        public string SearchTerm { get; set; }
    }
}
```

Listing 8-10. SearchResultViewModel to Store a Search Result

```
namespace SitecoreDev.Feature.Search.ViewModels
{
  public class SearchResultViewModel
  {
    public string Id { get; set; }
    public string Title { get; set; }
    public string Url { get; set; }
  }
}
```

Listing 8-11. SearchResultsViewModel to Store a List of Search Results

```
using System.Collections.Generic;

namespace SitecoreDev.Feature.Search.ViewModels
{
  public class SearchResultsViewModel
  {
    public List<SearchResultViewModel> Results = new List<SearchResultViewModel>();
  }
}
```

Now, let's move on to the controller.

22. In the Controllers folder, create a new controller named SearchController with the definition shown in Listing 8-12.

Listing 8-12. Create a new Search Controller to Call the Search Service and Pass Results to the View

```
using System.Web.Mvc;
using SitecoreDev.Feature.Search.Services;
using SitecoreDev.Feature.Search.ViewModels;
using SitecoreDev.Foundation.Repository.Context;

namespace SitecoreDev.Feature.Search.Controllers
{
  public class SearchController : Controller
  {
    private readonly ISearchService _searchService;
    private readonly IContextWrapper _contextWrapper;

    public SearchController(ISearchService searchService, IContextWrapper contextWrapper)
    {
      _searchService = searchService;
      _contextWrapper = contextWrapper;
    }
```

```
public ViewResult BlogSearch()
{ .
  return View(new BlogSearchViewModel());
}

[HttpPost]
public PartialViewResult SubmitSearch(BlogSearchViewModel viewModel)
{
  var resultsViewModel = new SearchResultsViewModel();

  var results = _searchService.SearchBlogPosts(viewModel.SearchTerm);

  foreach (var result in results)
  {
    resultsViewModel.Results.Add(new SearchResultViewModel()
    {
      Id = result.ItemId.ToString(),
      Title = result.Title,
      Url = result.Url
    });
  }

  return PartialView("~/Views/Search/_SearchResults.cshtml", resultsViewModel);
  }
 }
}
```

23. In the Views\Search folder, create two new views—BlogSearch and _
    SearchResults—with the markup shown in Listings 8-13 and 8-14, respectively.

Listing 8-13. Create a BlogSearch View to Display the Search Box and Button

```
@model SitecoreDev.Feature.Search.ViewModels.BlogSearchViewModel

<div>
  <form id="blog-search">
      <div class="form-group">
        <label class="sr-only" for="search-field">Search:</label>
        <input id="search-field" type="text" class="form-control" style="width:300px;"
placeholder="Search Text">
      </div>

      <button type="submit" class="btn btn-primary ">Search</button>
    </form>

    <div class="search-results">

    </div>
</div>
```

255

```
<script type="text/javascript">
    (function ($) {
        'use strict';
        (window.BlogSearch = {
            initialize: function () {
                console.log('initializing blogsearch');
                var _this = this;

                $('#blog-search').submit(function (event) {
                    console.log('submitting');
                    _this.searchBlog();
                    event.preventDefault();
                });
            },

            searchBlog: function () {
                var searchText = $('#search-field').val();

                $.ajax({
                    url: "/search/submitsearch",
                    type: "POST",
                    data: {
                        SearchTerm: searchText
                    },
                    context: this,
                    success: function (html) {
                        $('.search-results').html(html);
                        success();
                    },
                    error: function (data) {
                        $('.search-results').html('');
                    }
                });
            }
        });
        $(function () {
            BlogSearch.initialize();
        });

    })(jQuery);

</script>
```

───

■ **Note**   There are certainly a number of ways to create and submit forms in ASP.NET MVC. In this example, we're submitting the form through an AJAX call.

───

Listing 8-14. Create a View that Renders the Search Results

```
@model SitecoreDev.Feature.Search.ViewModels.SearchResultsViewModel

@foreach (var result in Model.Results)
{
  <div style="width:300px;">
    <div style="float:left;width:200px;">@result.Title</div>
    <div style="float:right;width:100px;text-align:center">
      <a href="@result.Url">View</a>
    </div>
  </div>
}
```

Once final thing we need to do is register the route to our `SearchController.SubmitSearch` controller action. Since we are submitting this request through AJAX, we don't want Sitecore to attempt to handle routing that request. So we need to register the route ourselves.

   · 24.   In the `Pipelines` folder, create a new folder called `RegisterRoutes`. In that folder, create class named `RegisterRoutes` with the definition shown in Listing 8-15.

Listing 8-15. Register the Custom Route so an AJAX Call Can Hit Our Controller

```
using System.Web.Mvc;
using System.Web.Routing;
using Sitecore.Pipelines;

namespace SitecoreDev.Feature.Search.Pipelines.RegisterRoutes
{
  public class RegisterRoutes
  {
    public void Process(PipelineArgs args)
    {
      RouteTable.Routes.MapRoute("SubmitSearch", "Search/SubmitSearch",
      new { controller = "Search", action = "SubmitSearch" });
    }
  }
}
```

   25.   Next, we need to patch it in to our configuration. In the `App_Config\Include\` `Sitecore.Feature.config` file, add the configuration shown in Listing 8-16 to the `<pipelines>` node.

Listing 8-16. Patch in Our Custom Route into the Sitecore Pipeline with a New Config File

```
<initialize>
  <processor type="SitecoreDev.Feature.Search.Pipelines.RegisterRoutes.RegisterRoutes,
SitecoreDev.Feature.Search" patch:before="processor[@type='Sitecore.Mvc.Pipelines.Loader.
InitializeRoutes, Sitecore.Mvc']" />
</initialize>
```

That's it! Build your solution, then publish it using the Publish-Site Gulp task. Once your build completes, navigate to http://sitecore8/blog. You should see a form like the one shown in Figure 8-9.

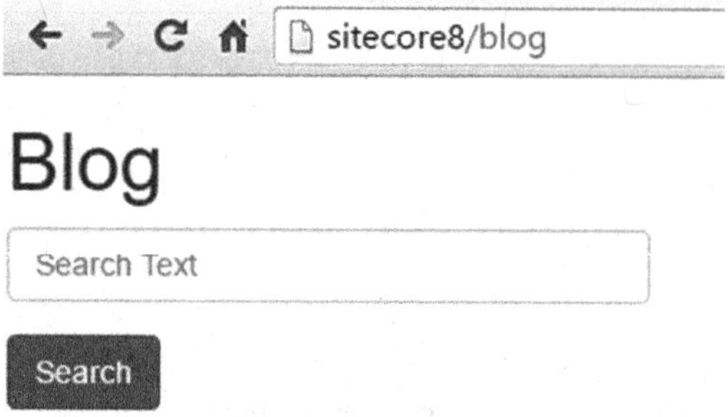

Figure 8-9. *Our simple search box!*

If you type something in the search box and click Search, you should get a result similar to the one shown in Figure 8-10.

Figure 8-10. *Results!*

You might notice more items than just our blog posts. They are the content items that hold the content. In the next section, we'll explain how to handle this.

Creating a Computed Field

Computed fields are a great way to store data in the index that is calculated at index time versus on the fly with each request. This means the computation is done once, not potentially thousands of times an hour. A good example of when this would be helpful would be our blog's categories. It is easy enough to pull the categories themselves out of the database, but what if we want a count next to the category of how many blog posts are in that category? This is similar to faceted search (covered later in this chapter). Notice the following steps on how to create a computed field for this purpose:

1. Before we dig in to the computed fields, let's add support for categorizing the content of our blog posts. In the Sitecore Content Editor, navigate to `/sitecore/templates/Sitecore8Dev/Feature/Articles`. Create a new template called `_Article Category`.

2. Next, navigate to `/sitecore/content/Home`. Right-click on Home and select Insert ➤ Folder. Name this folder `Shared Content`. In the `Shared Content` folder, add a new folder named `Blog Categories`.

3. In the `Blog Categories` folder, using the new `_Article Category` template we created in Step 1, create the categories shown in Figure 8-11.

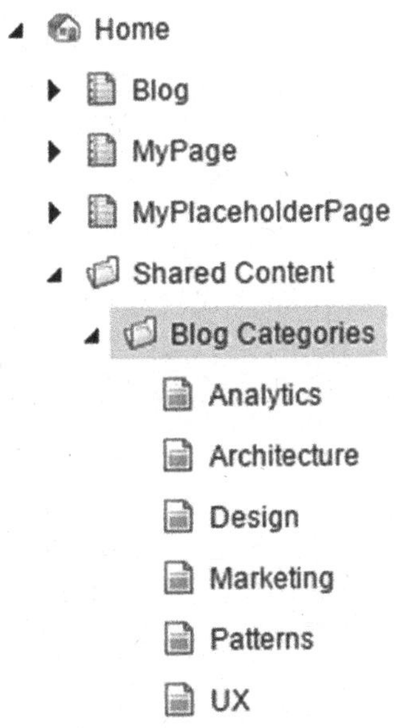

- ⊿ 🏠 Home
  - ▶ 📄 Blog
  - ▶ 📄 MyPage
  - ▶ 📄 MyPlaceholderPage
  - ⊿ 🗁 Shared Content
    - ⊿ 🗁 Blog Categories
      - 📄 Analytics
      - 📄 Architecture
      - 📄 Design
      - 📄 Marketing
      - 📄 Patterns
      - 📄 UX

Figure 8-11. *Create some new categories for our blog search*

4. Next, navigate back to the /sitecore/templates/Sitecore8Dev/Feature/
    Articles folder and select _Article. Add a new field called Categories, select
    Multilist as the Type, and enter /sitecore/content/Home/Shared Content/Blog
    Categories as the Data Source.

5. To complete the setup for blog categories, go through the content tree, assigning
    various categories to the _Article content items in the Components folder of our
    blog posts (see Figure 8-12).

Figure 8-12. Assign some categories to the posts, _Article content items

Now that we have the categories set up, let's move on to the computed fields. Let's start in the
SitecoreDev.Foundation.Indexing project.

6. In the Models folder, create a new class named HasPresentationComputedField
    with the definition shown in Listing 8-17.

Listing 8-17. Create a New Class that Extends IComputedIndexField Which Gets Computed at Index Time

```
using Sitecore.ContentSearch;
using Sitecore.ContentSearch.ComputedFields;

namespace SitecoreDev.Foundation.Indexing.Models
{
  public class HasPresentationComputedField : IComputedIndexField
  {
    public string FieldName { get; set; }

    public string ReturnType { get; set; }

    public object ComputeFieldValue(IIndexable indexable)
    {
      var indexItem = indexable as SitecoreIndexableItem;
      if (indexItem == null)
        return null;

      var item = indexItem.Item;
      if (item?.Visualization.Layout != null)
      {
        return true;
      }
      return null;
    }
  }
}
```

The `ComputeFieldValue` method runs for each item analyzed during the index process. This code is simply getting the Item and returning true if the `Visualization.Layout` field is not null. This will allow us to avoid displaying non-navigable content items in the results of a search.

7. Then, in the `App_Config\Include\Foundation\Foundation.Indexing.config` file, add the configuration shown in Listing 8-18 to the end of the `defaultLuceneIndexConfiguration` node.

Listing 8-18. Register Your New Computed Field with Lucene

```
<fields hint="raw:AddComputedIndexField">
  <field fieldName="haspresentation" storageType="no" indexType="untokenized">SitecoreDev.
  Foundation.Indexing.Models.HasPresentationComputedField, SitecoreDev.Foundation.Indexing</
  field>
</fields>
```

8. Now, let's move back to the SitecoreDev.Feature.Search project. In the Models folder, create a new class named BlogBodyComputedField with the definition shown in Listing 8-19.

Listing 8-19. Create Another New Computed Field for the Blog Post Body

```
using System.Linq;
using Sitecore.ContentSearch;
using Sitecore.ContentSearch.ComputedFields;
using Sitecore.Data;

namespace SitecoreDev.Feature.Search.Models
{
  public class BlogBodyComputedField : IComputedIndexField
  {
    public string FieldName { get; set; }

    public string ReturnType { get; set; }

    public object ComputeFieldValue(IIndexable indexable)
    {
      var indexItem = indexable as SitecoreIndexableItem;
      if (indexItem == null)
        return null;

      var item = indexItem.Item;
      var children = item.GetChildren();

      var componentsFolder = children.FirstOrDefault(x => x.TemplateID ==
      ID.Parse("{B0A97186-187F-4DCB-BABA-4096ABCD70B2}"));
      if (componentsFolder == null)
        return null;

      var childContent = componentsFolder.GetChildren();
      var blogContent = childContent.FirstOrDefault(x => x.TemplateID == ID.Parse {D45EAC17-
      5DC2-4AF2-8FCD-A4896E5CA07F}"));
      if (blogContent == null)
        return null;

      return blogContent.Fields["Body"]?.ToString();
    }
  }
}
```

The ComputedFieldValue method is simply querying the children of an item to find the first item matching the Article template type and grabbing the content of the Body field. Since this is where the actual content for the blog entry is held, making it available to the SearchResultItem will allow us to display a preview of the text, for instance, in the search results.

9. Add another class named BlogCategoriesComputedFields with the definition shown in Listing 8-20.

Listing 8-20. Create Another Computed Field for the Blog Post Categories

```csharp
using System.Collections.Generic;
using System.Linq;
using Sitecore.ContentSearch;
using Sitecore.ContentSearch.ComputedFields;
using Sitecore.Data;
using Sitecore.Data.Fields;

namespace SitecoreDev.Feature.Search.Models
{
  public class BlogCategoriesComputedField : IComputedIndexField
  {
    public string FieldName { get; set; }

    public string ReturnType { get; set; }

    public object ComputeFieldValue(IIndexable indexable)
    {
      var indexItem = indexable as SitecoreIndexableItem;
      if (indexItem == null)
        return null;

      var item = indexItem.Item;
      var children = item.GetChildren();

      var componentsFolder = children.FirstOrDefault(x => x.TemplateID ==
      ID.Parse("{B0A97186-187F-4DCB-BABA-4096ABCD70B2}"));
      if (componentsFolder == null)
        return null;

      var childContent = componentsFolder.GetChildren();
      var blogContent = childContent.FirstOrDefault(x => x.TemplateID == ID.Parse
      {D45EAC17-5DC2-4AF2-8FCD-A4896E5CA07F}"));
      if (blogContent == null)
        return null;

      MultilistField categories = blogContent.Fields["Categories"];
      var categoryNameList = new List<string>();
      foreach(var id in categories.TargetIDs)
      {
        var category = blogContent.Database.GetItem(id);
        if (categories != null)
          categoryNameList.Add(category.DisplayName);
      }

      return categoryNameList;
    }
  }
}
```

The `ComputeFieldValue` method here is querying the `Categories` field of the first descendent of our blog page matching the `Article` template type and returning it as a list of string values.

10. Add one more class named `BlogTitleComputedField` with the definition shown in Listing 8-21.

Listing 8-21. Add a Third Computed Field for the Blog Post Title

```
using System.Linq;
using Sitecore.ContentSearch;
using Sitecore.ContentSearch.ComputedFields;
using Sitecore.Data;

namespace SitecoreDev.Feature.Search.Models
{
  public class BlogTitleComputedField : IComputedIndexField
  {
    public string FieldName { get; set; }

    public string ReturnType { get; set; }

    public object ComputeFieldValue(IIndexable indexable)
    {
      var indexItem = indexable as SitecoreIndexableItem;
      if (indexItem == null)
        return null;

      var item = indexItem.Item;
      var children = item.GetChildren();

      var componentsFolder = children.FirstOrDefault(x => x.TemplateID ==
      ID.Parse("{B0A97186-187F-4DCB-BABA-4096ABCD70B2}"));
      if (componentsFolder == null)
        return null;

      var childContent = componentsFolder.GetChildren();
      var blogContent = childContent.FirstOrDefault(x => x.TemplateID == ID.Parse {D45EAC17-
      5DC2-4AF2-8FCD-A4896E5CA07F}"));
      if (blogContent == null)
        return null;

      return blogContent.Fields["Title"]?.ToString();
    }
  }
}
```

As with the other computed fields, this field is getting the value of the title field from the first descendent of the blog page, matching the `Article` template, to store with the `SearchResultItem`, making it available for display in the search results.

11. Next, let's add these new computed fields to the index configuration. In App_ Config\Include\Feature.Search.config, add the configuration from Listing 8-22 to the `<sitecore>` node.

Listing 8-22. Register Those Three Computed Fields so They Are Added to the Index Next Time We Rebuild

```
<contentSearch>
  <indexConfigurations>
    <defaultLuceneIndexConfiguration type="Sitecore.ContentSearch.LuceneProvider.
    LuceneIndexConfiguration, Sitecore.ContentSearch.LuceneProvider">
      <fields hint="raw:AddComputedIndexField">
        <field fieldName="blogbody" storageType="no" indexType="untokenized">SitecoreDev.
        Feature.Search.Models.BlogBodyComputedField, SitecoreDev.Feature.Search</field>
        <field fieldName="blogtitle" storageType="no" indexType="untokenized">SitecoreDev.
        Feature.Search.Models.BlogTitleComputedField, SitecoreDev.Feature.Search</field>
        <field fieldName="blogcategories" storageType="no" indexType="untokenized">SitecoreD
        ev.Feature.Search.Models.BlogCategoriesComputedField, SitecoreDev.Feature.Search
        </field>
      </fields>
    </defaultLuceneIndexConfiguration>
  </indexConfigurations>
</contentSearch>
```

12. In the `BlogSearchResult` class in the `Models` folder, make the modifications shown in Listing 8-23 to include the new computed fields.

Listing 8-23. Extend the BlogSearchResult Class to Include the New Fields

```
public class BlogSearchResult : SearchResultItem
{
  [IndexField("blogtitle")]
  public string Title { get; set; }

  [IndexField("blogbody")]
  public string Body { get; set; }

  [IndexField("haspresentation")]
  public bool HasPresentation { get; set; }

  [IndexField("blogcategories")]
  public IEnumerable<string> Categories { get; set; }
}
```

13. Next, in the `ViewModels` folder, modify the `SearchResultViewModel` class as shown in Listing 8-24.

Listing 8-24. Expand the View Models

```
public class SearchResultViewModel
{
  public string Id { get; set; }
  public string Title { get; set; }
  public string Body { get; set; }
  public string Url { get; set; }
  public string CategoryList { get; set; }
}
```

14. Now, in SearchController, modify the SubmitSearch controller action to match Listing 8-25.

Listing 8-25. Modify the Controller Created Earlier to Include New Fields

```
[HttpPost]
public PartialViewResult SubmitSearch(BlogSearchViewModel viewModel)
{
  Func<IEnumerable<string>, string> stringify = (list) =>
  {
    StringBuilder sb = new StringBuilder();
    foreach (var item in list)
      sb.Append(String.Format("{0}; ", item));
    return sb.ToString();
  };

  var resultsViewModel = new SearchResultsViewModel();

  var results = _searchService.SearchBlogPosts(viewModel.SearchTerm);

  foreach (var result in results)
  {
    resultsViewModel.Results.Add(new SearchResultViewModel()
    {
      Id = result.ItemId.ToString(),
      Title = result.Title,
      Url = result.Url,
      Body = result.Body,
      CategoryList = stringify(result.Categories)
    });
  }

  return PartialView("~/Views/Search/_SearchResults.cshtml", resultsViewModel);
}
```

15. Finally, modify the Views\Search_SearchResults.cshtml view as shown in Listing 8-26.

Listing 8-26. Update the View to Render the New Fields

```
@model SitecoreDev.Feature.Search.ViewModels.SearchResultsViewModel

<style type="text/css">
  .blog-post {
    float:left;
    width:700px;
    border:1px solid #808080;
    padding:7px;
  }
  .blog-title {
    font-weight:bold;
    font-size:16px;
```

```
    }
    .blog-categories {
      color:#aaaaaa;
      padding-top:7px;
    }
</style>

@foreach (var result in Model.Results)
{
  <div class="blog-post">
    <a href="@result.Url" class="blog-title">@result.Title</a>
    <div>@result.Body</div>
    <div class="blog-categories">Categories: @result.CategoryList</div>
  </div>
}
```

Now, build your solution and publish the changes using the Publish-Site Gulp task! Once the task completes, navigate to http://sitecore8/blog. If you perform a search, your results should now look something like Figure 8-13.

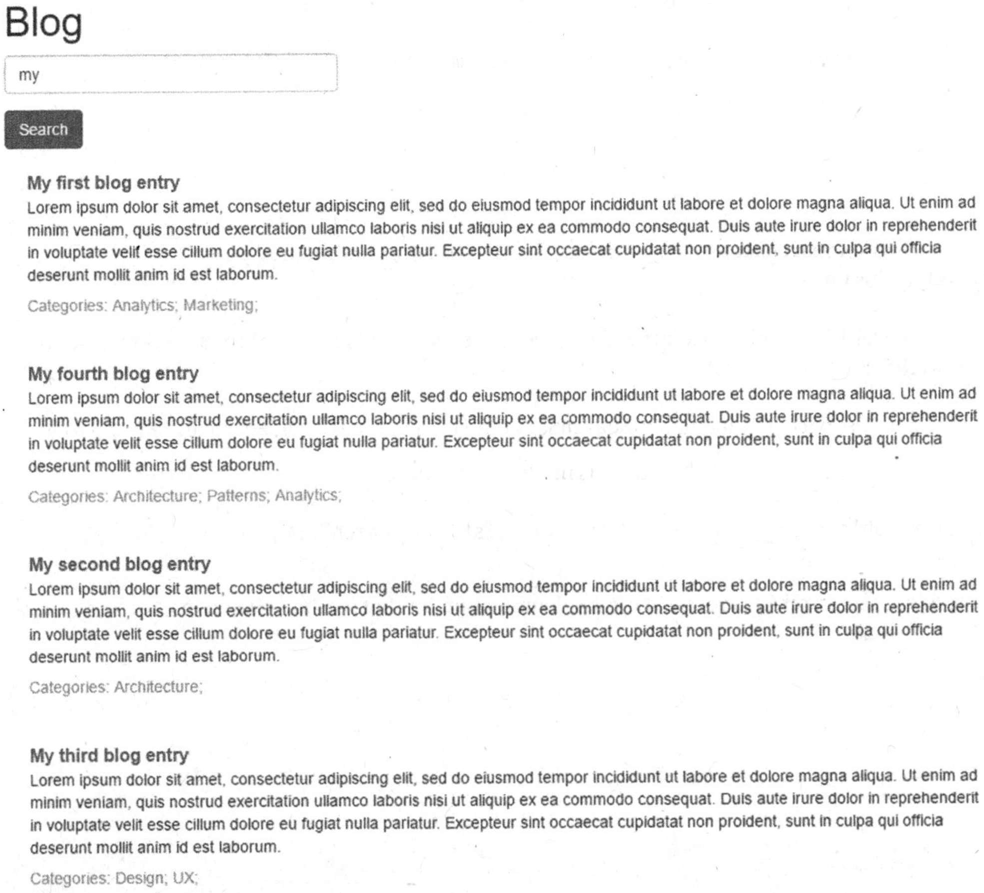

Blog

| my |

Search

My first blog entry
Lorem ipsum dolor sit amet, consectetur adipiscing elit, sed do eiusmod tempor incididunt ut labore et dolore magna aliqua. Ut enim ad minim veniam, quis nostrud exercitation ullamco laboris nisi ut aliquip ex ea commodo consequat. Duis aute irure dolor in reprehenderit in voluptate velit esse cillum dolore eu fugiat nulla pariatur. Excepteur sint occaecat cupidatat non proident, sunt in culpa qui officia deserunt mollit anim id est laborum.

Categories: Analytics; Marketing;

My fourth blog entry
Lorem ipsum dolor sit amet, consectetur adipiscing elit, sed do eiusmod tempor incididunt ut labore et dolore magna aliqua. Ut enim ad minim veniam, quis nostrud exercitation ullamco laboris nisi ut aliquip ex ea commodo consequat. Duis aute irure dolor in reprehenderit in voluptate velit esse cillum dolore eu fugiat nulla pariatur. Excepteur sint occaecat cupidatat non proident, sunt in culpa qui officia deserunt mollit anim id est laborum.

Categories: Architecture; Patterns; Analytics;

My second blog entry
Lorem ipsum dolor sit amet, consectetur adipiscing elit, sed do eiusmod tempor incididunt ut labore et dolore magna aliqua. Ut enim ad minim veniam, quis nostrud exercitation ullamco laboris nisi ut aliquip ex ea commodo consequat. Duis aute irure dolor in reprehenderit in voluptate velit esse cillum dolore eu fugiat nulla pariatur. Excepteur sint occaecat cupidatat non proident, sunt in culpa qui officia deserunt mollit anim id est laborum.

Categories: Architecture;

My third blog entry
Lorem ipsum dolor sit amet, consectetur adipiscing elit, sed do eiusmod tempor incididunt ut labore et dolore magna aliqua. Ut enim ad minim veniam, quis nostrud exercitation ullamco laboris nisi ut aliquip ex ea commodo consequat. Duis aute irure dolor in reprehenderit in voluptate velit esse cillum dolore eu fugiat nulla pariatur. Excepteur sint occaecat cupidatat non proident, sunt in culpa qui officia deserunt mollit anim id est laborum.

Categories: Design; UX;

Figure 8-13. *Our results have categories!*

Adding an Autocomplete

Autocomplete has become a standard expectation for users these days when searching. With each letter you type, an asynchronous search is executed to retrieve results on the fly and populate those results in a drop-down below the search box. Let's extend the search box we created earlier with similar type-ahead functionality. Use the following steps:

First of all, we need to add a new method to our `SitecoreSearchRespository`.

1. In the `Search.SitecoreSearchRepository` class in the `SitecoreDev.Foundation.Repository` project, add a new method called `GetTermsByFieldName` with the definition from Listing 8-27.

Listing 8-27. Add a New Repository Method to Get Search Terms by a Field Name

```
public IEnumerable<SearchIndexTerm> GetTermsByFieldName(string fieldName, string searchTerm)
    {
    IEnumerable<SearchIndexTerm> results = null;

    var index = String.Format("sitecore_{0}_index", Sitecore.Context.Database.Name);

    using (var context = ContentSearchManager.GetIndex(index).CreateSearchContext())
    {
        results = context.GetTermsByFieldName(fieldName, searchTerm).ToList();
    }

    return results;
}
```

2. Next, in the `ISearchRepository` interface, let's expose this new method by adding this line:

```
IEnumerable<SearchIndexTerm> GetTermsByFieldName(string fieldName, string searchTerm);
```

Next, create a new service method in our `SearchService` in the `SitecoreDev.Feature.Search` project.

3. In `Services.ISearchService`, add this method definition:

```
IEnumerable<string> GetSearchSuggestions(string searchTerm);
```

4. In `SitecoreSearchService`, add the implementation for that method shown in Listing 8-28.

Listing 8-28. Implement the GetSearchSuggestions Method in the Search Service, Which Calls the Repo

```
public IEnumerable<string> GetSearchSuggestions(string searchTerm)
{
  var suggestions = new List<string>();
  var results = _searchRepository.GetTermsByFieldName("title", searchTerm);
  foreach (var result in results)
  {
    suggestions.Add(result.Term);
  }
  return suggestions;
}
```

5.   Next, create a new controller action in the SearchController of SitecoreDev.
     Feature.Search called GetSuggestions with the definition shown in Listing 8-29.

Listing 8-29. Create a New Controller Action to Return Search Suggestions

```
[HttpPost]
    public JsonResult GetSuggestions(BlogSearchViewModel viewModel)
    {
      var suggestions = new List<string>();

      if (!String.IsNullOrEmpty(viewModel?.SearchTerm))
      {
        return Json(_searchService.GetSearchSuggestions(viewModel.SearchTerm));
      }

      return Json(new { });
}
```

6.   In Pipelines.RegisterRoutes.RegisterRoutes, add the following line to map
     an MVC route to allow our AJAX call to go around the Sitecore render pipeline:

```
RouteTable.Routes.MapRoute("GetSuggestions", "Search/GetSuggestions", new { controller =
"Search", action = "GetSuggestions" });
```

Now that we have our code, let's configure the title field of our post to be tokenized. This will allow the index to store "My First Blog Post" as a single token rather than four separate tokens.

7. Add the configuration from Listing 8-30 to the `<defaultLuceneIndexConfiguration>` node in `Feature.Search.config`.

Listing 8-30. Enable the Title Field To Be Tokenized

```
<fieldMap type="Sitecore.ContentSearch.FieldMap, Sitecore.ContentSearch">
  <fieldNames hint="raw:AddFieldByFieldName">
    <field fieldName="title" storageType="YES" indexType="TOKENIZED" vectorType="NO"
    boost="1f" type="System.String" settingType="Sitecore.ContentSearch.LuceneProvider.
    LuceneSearchFieldConfiguration, Sitecore.ContentSearch.LuceneProvider">
      <analyzer type="Sitecore.ContentSearch.LuceneProvider.Analyzers.
      LowerCaseKeywordAnalyzer, Sitecore.ContentSearch.LuceneProvider" />
    </field>
  </fieldNames>
</fieldMap>
```

■ **Note**   For more information about tokenization, see these two posts: `http://bit.ly/2aHf1Cu` and `http://bit.ly/2amrvAt`.

There are a number of ways to add autocomplete behavior to textboxes, but in this example, we'll be using autocomplete from jQuery UI.

8. In the `SitecoreDev.Foundation.Styling` project, using the NuGet Package Manager, add a reference to `jQuery.UI.Combined`.

9. In `SitecoreDev.Foundation.Layouts`, update `Views\Shared\DefaultMVCLayout.cshtml` to include these lines, including the jQuery UI functionality in our site:

    ```
    <link rel="stylesheet" href="~/Content/themes/base/jquery-ui.css" />
    <script type="text/javascript" src="~/Scripts/jquery-ui-1.12.0.js"></script>
    ```

10. Finally, back in `SitecoreDev.Feature.Search`, update `Views\Search\BlogSearch.cshtml` by adding the code from Listing 8-31 to the initialize method of our `BlogSearch` JavaScript object.

Listing 8-31. Initialize the Auto Complete JavaScript and Configure It to Post to Our Custom Route

```
$('#search-field').autocomplete({
  source: function (request, response) {
    $.ajax({
      url: "/search/getsuggestions",
      type: "POST",
      dataType: "json",
      data: {
        searchTerm: request.term
      },
```

```
      success: function (data) {
        response(data.length === 1 && data[0].length === 0 ? [] : data);
      }
    });
  },
});
```

That should be it! Build your solution and publish the site using the Publish-Site Gulp task. Once the publish completes, navigate to `http://sitecore8/blog` and type something into the search box. You should see something similar to Figure 8-14.

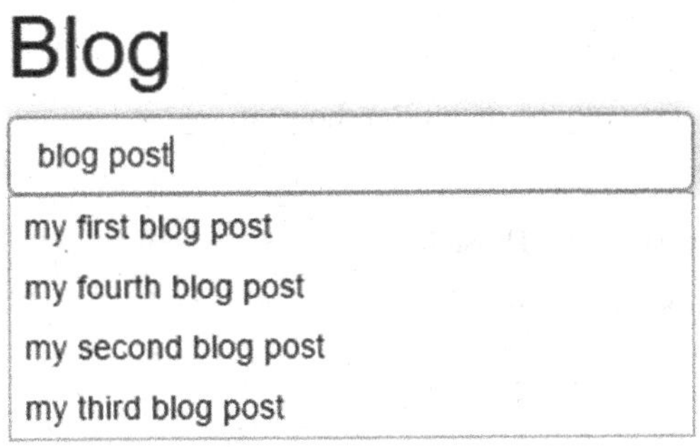

Blog

blog post|
my first blog post
my fourth blog post
my second blog post
my third blog post

Figure 8-14. *Type ahead made easy!*

Refining Results with Faceted Search

Last, but certainly not least, we need faceted search on our search results page. Search facets help your users refine their results. In all likelihood, when they search they are going to get thousands of results. The top 10 results may or may not be too good depending on how broadly they searched, and these facets help them narrow their results.

Search facets should be dynamically generated based on the metadata on the results themselves. So if I have a total of 50 possible facet categories (aka, "Brand") and 200 possible facet items (aka, "Sony", "LG", etc.), but after a search, only three categories and 20 facets are applicable, so I should only display those 20 below those three categories.

■ **Note**   Amazon.com provides a great example of the power of numbering on facet items. Every time you select a facet item, the facet list updates.

Check out the following steps for how to add faceted search into your site. Let's start by adding a few new classes in SitecoreDev.Foundation.Model.

1. Create a new folder called Search. In this Search folder, create a new class named Facet with the definition shown in Listing 8-32.

Listing 8-32. Create a Facet Class

```
public class Facet
{
  public string Name { get; set; }
  public int Count { get; set; }
}
```

2. Create an interface named IFacetedSearchResults with the definition shown in Listing 8-33.

Listing 8-33. Create an Interface to Hold the Results and the Facets for Those Results

```
public interface IFacetedSearchResults<T> where T : SearchResultItem
{
  IEnumerable<T> Results { get; set; }
  IEnumerable<Facet> Facets { get; set; }
}
```

3. Next, create an implementation class named FacetedSearchResults with the definition shown in Listing 8-34.

Listing 8-34. Implement the Interface

```
public class FacetedSearchResults<T> : IFacetedSearchResults<T> where T : SearchResultItem
  {
    public IEnumerable<T> Results { get; set; }
    public IEnumerable<Facet> Facets { get; set; }
}
```

4. Now, in the SitecoreDev.Foundation.Repository project, modify Search.ISearchRepository by adding a new method signature, shown here:

   ```
   IFacetedSearchResults<T> SearchWithFacets<T, TFacetKey>(Expression<Func<T,
    bool>> query, Expression<Func<T, TFacetKey>> facetOn) where T :
   SearchResultItem;
   ```

5. In SitecoreSearchRepository, add the implementation of that method as shown in Listing 8-35.

Listing 8-35. Add a SearchWithFacets Method in the Search Repository

```
public IFacetedSearchResults<T> SearchWithFacets<T, TFacetKey>(
  Expression<Func<T, bool>> query, Expression<Func<T, TFacetKey>> facetOn)
    where T : SearchResultItem
  {
    var results = new FacetedSearchResults<T>();
    List<T> searchResults = new List<T>();
    List<Facet> facets = new List<Facet>();

    var index = String.Format("sitecore_{0}_index", Sitecore.Context.Database.Name);

    using (var context = ContentSearchManager.GetIndex(index).CreateSearchContext())
    {
      var searchHits = context.GetQueryable<T>().Where(query).FacetOn(facetOn).
      GetResults();

      foreach(var hit in searchHits)
      {
        searchResults.Add((T)hit.Document);
      }
      foreach(var category in searchHits.Facets.Categories)
      {
        foreach(var facet in category.Values)
        {
          facets.Add(new Facet()
          {
            Name = facet.Name,
            Count = facet.AggregateCount
          });
        }
      }

      results.Results = searchResults;
      results.Facets = facets;
    }

    return results;
  }
```

The method from Listing 8-35 gets an instance of the IProviderSearchContext and executes the criteria from the service layer (Listing 8-36). Once it executes the query, it builds a list of hits based on the facetOn predicate passed in. Once it gets these hits, we can loop through the results and the values, assembling the facet item and the count for that facet item.

6. Going back up to `SitecoreDev.Feature.Search`, modify `ISearchService` by adding the method signature shown here:

```
IFacetedSearchResults<BlogSearchResult> SearchBlogPostsWithFacets
(string searchTerm, string[] facets);
```

7. In `SitecoreSearchService`, add the implementation for this method, as shown in Listing 8-36.

Listing 8-36. Implement a SearchBlogPostsWithFacets Method in the Service Layer

```
public IFacetedSearchResults<BlogSearchResult> SearchBlogPostsWithFacets(
    string searchTerm, string[] facets)
    {
      var predicate = PredicateBuilder.True<BlogSearchResult>();
      predicate = predicate.And(i => i.Title.Contains(searchTerm) &&
        i.Path.StartsWith("/sitecore/content/Home"));

      if (facets != null)
      {
        foreach (var facet in facets)
        {
          predicate = predicate.And(i => i.Categories.Contains(facet));
        }
      }

      return _searchRepository.SearchWithFacets<BlogSearchResult,
      IEnumerable<string>>(predicate, q => q.Categories);
    }
```

This service layer method is building the logic of the query itself and passing it to `ISearchRepository` for execution.

8. Now that we have our service layer returning more data, we need to update our `ViewModel` to carry this data to the View. In the `ViewModels` folder, create a new class named `FacetViewModel` with the definition shown in Listing 8-37.

Listing 8-37. Create a View Model for Our Facets

```
public class FacetViewModel
  {
    public string Name { get; set; }
    public int Count { get; set; }
  }
```

9. Next, modify the `SearchResultsViewModel` by adding a new property, as shown here:

```
public List<FacetViewModel> Facets { get; set; } = new List<FacetViewModel>();
```

10. Now that our ViewModels are up to date, let's go into the SearchController and populate them. Modify the SubmitSearch controller action as shown in Listing 8-38.

Listing 8-38. Modify the SubmitSearch Controller Action to Also Populate Our Facets

```
[HttpPost]
public PartialViewResult SubmitSearch(BlogSearchViewModel viewModel)
{
  Func<IEnumerable<string>, string> stringify = (list) =>
  {
    StringBuilder sb = new StringBuilder();
    foreach (var item in list)
      sb.Append(String.Format("{0}; ", item));
    return sb.ToString();
  };

  var resultsViewModel = new SearchResultsViewModel();

  var facetedResults = _searchService.SearchBlogPostsWithFacets
  (viewModel.SearchTerm, null);

  foreach (var result in facetedResults.Results)
  {
    resultsViewModel.Results.Add(new SearchResultViewModel()
    {
      Id = result.ItemId.ToString(),
      Title = result.Title,
      Url = result.Url,
      Body = result.Body,
      CategoryList = stringify(result.Categories)
    });
  }

  foreach(var facet in facetedResults.Facets)
  {
    resultsViewModel.Facets.Add(new FacetViewModel()
    {
      Name = facet.Name,
      Count = facet.Count
    });
  }

  return PartialView("~/Views/Search/_SearchResults.cshtml", resultsViewModel);
}
```

11. Next, in the Views\Search folder, modify _SearchResults as shown in Listing 8-39.

Listing 8-39. Update the _SearchResults View to Display the Facets

```
@model SitecoreDev.Feature.Search.ViewModels.SearchResultsViewModel
<div class="result-list">
  @foreach (var result in Model.Results)
  {
    <div class="blog-post">
      <a href="@result.Url" class="blog-title">@result.Title</a>
      <div>@result.Body</div>
      <div class="blog-categories">Categories: @result.CategoryList</div>
    </div>
  }
</div>

<div class="categories">
  <div class="category-title">Categories</div>
  <div class="facet-list">
    @foreach (var facet in Model.Facets)
    {
      <div class="facet-item">
        <span class="facet-name">@facet.Name</span>
        <span class="facet-count">@facet.Count</span>
      </div>
    }
  </div>
</div>
```

12. The final step is to add a little bit of styling to the SitecoreDev.Foundation. Styling project. In Content\foundation.styling.css, add the CSS shown in Listing 8-40.

Listing 8-40. Add Some Styling to Float the Posts Left and the Facets Right

```
.result-list {
  width:900px;
  float:left; }
  .result-list .blog-post {
    float:left;
    width:900px;
    padding:20px; }
    .result-list .blog-post .blog-title {
      font-weight:bold;
      font-size:16px;
      color: #337ab7;
  }

.categories {
  float:left;
```

```
margin-left:20px; }
.categories .category-title {
  font-weight:bold;
  font-size:16px;
  color: #337ab7; }
.categories .facet-list {
  float:left; }
  .categories .facet-list .facet-item {
    width:200px; }
    .categories .facet-list .facet-item .facet-name {
      width:175px;
      float:left; }
    .categories .facet-list .facet-item .facet-count {
      width:25px;
      float:right; }
```

That's it! Build your solution and publish it using the Publish-Site Gulp task. Once the publish is complete, navigate to http://sitecore8/blog and perform a search. You should see something resembling Figure 8-15.

Blog

| my |

Search

My first blog entry
Lorem ipsum dolor sit amet, consectetur adipiscing elit, sed do eiusmod tempor incididunt ut labore et dolore magna aliqua. Ut enim ad minim veniam, quis nostrud exercitation ullamco laboris nisi ut aliquip ex ea commodo consequat. Duis aute irure dolor in reprehenderit in voluptate velit esse cillum dolore eu fugiat nulla pariatur. Excepteur sint occaecat cupidatat non proident, sunt in culpa qui officia deserunt mollit anim id est laborum.
Categories: Analytics; Marketing;

My fourth blog entry
Lorem ipsum dolor sit amet, consectetur adipiscing elit, sed do eiusmod tempor incididunt ut labore et dolore magna aliqua. Ut enim ad minim veniam, quis nostrud exercitation ullamco laboris nisi ut aliquip ex ea commodo consequat. Duis aute irure dolor in reprehenderit in voluptate velit esse cillum dolore eu fugiat nulla pariatur. Excepteur sint occaecat cupidatat non proident, sunt in culpa qui officia deserunt mollit anim id est laborum.
Categories: Architecture; Patterns; Analytics;

My second blog entry
Lorem ipsum dolor sit amet, consectetur adipiscing elit, sed do eiusmod tempor incididunt ut labore et dolore magna aliqua. Ut enim ad minim veniam, quis nostrud exercitation ullamco laboris nisi ut aliquip ex ea commodo consequat. Duis aute irure dolor in reprehenderit in voluptate velit esse cillum dolore eu fugiat nulla pariatur. Excepteur sint occaecat cupidatat non proident, sunt in culpa qui officia deserunt mollit anim id est laborum.
Categories: Architecture;

My third blog entry
Lorem ipsum dolor sit amet, consectetur adipiscing elit, sed do eiusmod tempor incididunt ut labore et dolore magna aliqua. Ut enim ad minim veniam, quis nostrud exercitation ullamco laboris nisi ut aliquip ex ea commodo consequat. Duis aute irure dolor in reprehenderit in voluptate velit esse cillum dolore eu fugiat nulla pariatur. Excepteur sint occaecat cupidatat non proident, sunt in culpa qui officia deserunt mollit anim id est laborum.
Categories: Design; UX;

Categories

analytics	2
architecture	2
design	1
marketing	1
patterns	1
ux	1

Figure 8-15. Now our results show our categories off to the right as facets!

Summary

What a whirlwind tour of site search with Lucene on Sitecore! Sitecore provides a Lucene index out-of-the-box; all you need to do is add your custom fields and field types into the configuration for your data to get included in the index. From there, it is simple enough to query the index. However, providing a great user experience is not quite as easy. To do that you should consider including autocomplete and search suggestions. Additionally, you can use faceted search into your site provides a ton of value to the users. Facets help the users narrow their searches when too many results are presented to them.

CHAPTER 9

■ ■ ■

Programming the Customer Journey

Up until this point in the book you have been growing as a Sitecore Developer. However, in this chapter you'll start to learn how to be an Experience Developer. There is a subtle nuance between the two; the first is focused on building web sites, whereas the second, while good at the first, is also concerned with building great user experiences. These experiences are heavily reliant on and driven by deep analytics, personalization, automation, and business objectives.

■ **Note** Most of the "strategy" behind Sitecore's digital marketing capabilities can be found in the sister book, *Practical Sitecore 8 Configuration and Strategy*. Most of the end-user configuration can be found there as well. As such, this chapter attempts to extend those discussions by adding advanced concepts only accomplishable by a developer with code. As a result, there won't be a deep introduction into the capabilities themselves and you are encouraged to get the sister book for that broader perspective (after all, it took an entire book to cover that material).

A great place to start our tour of Sitecore's marketing capabilities is by showing you how to extend Web Forms for Marketer's (WFFM) with custom actions that can be fired as a result of a form submission. I'd wager most forms created in WFFM will require this sort of extension; it is helpful when needing to submit data to an external data source, for example. After all, getting data from your customers is the most basic form of "programming the customer journey."

We'll next go a bit deeper by discussing how to programmatically fire goals, events, and outcomes. If you recall, goals, events, and outcomes form the foundation of measuring user engagement and interactions within Sitecore. They are a cornerstone of Sitecore's Experience Analytics capabilities. There are many out-of-the-box configurable ways to fire them, but often you require programmatic means to fire them as well.

We then will move into customer personalization rules to help accommodate unique personalization requirements, again beyond the out-of-the-box rules described elsewhere. The conversation around personalization dovetails nicely with a discussion on how to extend the out-of-the-box engagement plans to help drive marketing automation in your digital experience. For engagement plans, this means developing custom actions and conditions.

From there we'll move into learning how to extend the out-of-the-box xDB contact. This contact is where all interactions get traced back to a particular user or anonymous contact. It is the focal point of all things analytics within Sitecore. Extending this contact is a key, fundamental activity of any Experience Developer. Beyond this, a marketer will obviously want/need to see all that data around each customer or user. As such, it becomes immediately necessary to extend the Experience Profile interface to present that custom data.

© Phil Wicklund and Jason Wilkerson 2016
P. Wicklund and J. Wilkerson, *Professional Sitecore 8 Development*, DOI 10.1007/978-1-4842-2292-8_9

Lastly we'll discuss Sitecore's Federated Experience Manager (FXM). FXM allows you to track your customers' journeys even when they are not interacting with a site built on Sitecore! It also allows for other helpful tricks, such as sharing content between Sitecore and non-Sitecore sites.

Well, let's begin!

Extending Web Forms for Marketers

WFFM helps a marketer do what marketers often do the most when it comes to digital experiences; WFFM makes it easy to set up lead capture pages. Are you creating an e-mail campaign through Email Experience Manager, but you want to link that customer to a digital experience where you hope to capture some data and a lead? This is a great use case for WFFM. Do you want a small Download Now button (see Figure 9-1) on your home page but have it connected to a textbox asking the users to enter their e-mail addresses first? Yet another creative WFFM use case.

WFFM forms are very simple to create. Simply create a page (or add one to an existing page), add the WFFM component to that page, configure the fields you want to gather, and lastly tell WFFM what to do with that data once it's submitted. Very simple indeed! In fact, most things you can do in WFFM don't require a developer and are very easy for non-technical marketers. However, some things are more complex and a developer may be required.

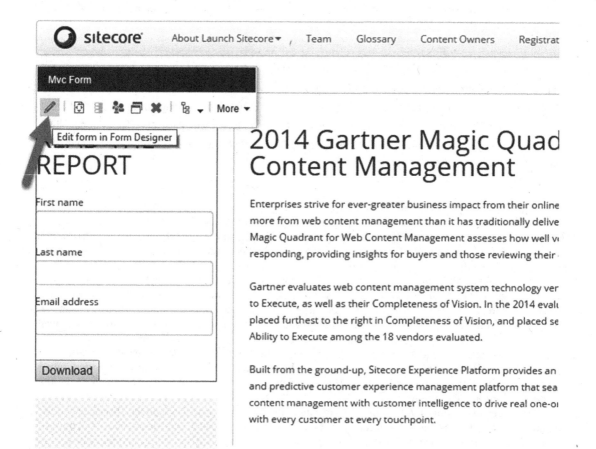

Figure 9-1. *WFFM comes with its own component that you simply add to your page*

Save actions, for example, commonly require developer involvement when custom actions are needed. However, as you can see in Figure 9-2, there are many, many out-of-the-box form save actions to choose from. Most are quite self-explanatory. However, here are some important actions you will likely be using a lot:

- *Add the contact to a contact list*: Lists can be set up in the List Manager, used primarily in conjunction with Email Experience Manager. WFFM can help you administer these lists when customers submit their contact information.

- *Account management (create user, change password, user login, logout, update contact details, edit role membership)*: Need to build registration/login capabilities? This is a great use case for WFFM due to a broad swath of save actions that help you create users, assign them to roles, and provide password management capabilities.

- *Enroll in engagement plans*: Engagement plans can be set up to help drive your customers to a desired outcome. A form submission is often the catalyst to enroll a customer in an engagement plan.

- *Register a conversion/campaign*: You will most likely want to associate the form submission to a campaign and/or conversation to feed into your analytics reporting.

- *Create CRM account/contact/entity*: CRM and digital web experiences are almost always integrated. There are two very important modules (one for Microsoft Dynamics and one for Salesforce) separately installable to help you integrate with your CRM system.

- *Send an e-mail message*: A very common task when completing a form online is sending an e-mail. Using this save action, you can configure an e-mail message to be sent, configurable through the properties on the save action, using all of the fields available on that particular form.

■ **Note**   CRM add-ins for Sitecore can be found here: `http://bit.ly/1T8ULto` (Microsoft Dynamics) and here: `http://bit.ly/1KT4SNk` (Salesforce).

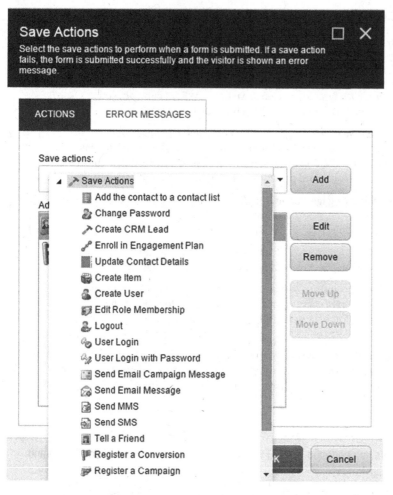

Figure 9-2. *There are many, many out-of-the-box save actions! However, you likely will run into a situation where you need to roll your own*

Do you not see an action you wish was there? It is very easy for a developer to create custom actions for your forms. The basic process is to create a new Action item to register your action, then create a .NET class that is executed when the action is executed. The rest of this section will walk you through how to do exactly this. By building custom actions, you can empower marketers to interface with back-end proprietary systems, integrate with other marketing tools where a connector is not available, and many other possibilities. Use the following steps to create, publish, and test a custom save action that writes some form data to a custom database (as an example).

WFFM INSTALLATION

WFFM is a module that you install over the top of your existing Sitecore instance. Like just about anything with Sitecore, the process involves installing a package and then manually changing a few config settings.

The process is elaborate and thoroughly documented for each release. As such, it makes the most sense simply to direct you to the installation instructions for the most recent update, which can be found at http://bit.ly/1HHKsmz.

---

1. The first step we should take is to add another feature to our solution. In Visual Studio, create a new solution folder called Marketing inside the Feature folder.

2. In this new folder, create a new ASP.NET Web Application called SitecoreDev. Feature.Marketing, selecting the empty template and checking the MVC folders and core references checkbox. Once the new project has been created, delete the App_Data and App_Start folders, and the Global.asax file.

3. Add a reference to Sitecore.Kernel.dll, Sitecore.Logging.dll, Sitecore. Wffm.Actions.dll, and Sitecore.Wffm.Abstractions.dll. You'll need to copy Sitecore.Logging.dll, Sitecore.Wffm.Actions.dll, and Sitecore.Wffm. Abstractions.dll from the %webroot%\bin folder to the %devroot%\libs\ sitecore folder.

4. In the SitecoreDev.Feature.Marketing project, add a new folder called Wffm. Inside that folder, create another called Actions.

5. In the Actions folder, add a new class named SaveToCommentDatabase and the definition shown in Listing 9-1.

Listing 9-1. Custom Save Action Code that Can Be Used to Write to a Database

```
using System.Configuration;
using System.Data.SqlClient;
using System.Web;
using log4net;
using Sitecore.Data;
using Sitecore.WFFM.Abstractions.Actions;
using Sitecore.WFFM.Actions.Base;

namespace SitecoreDev.Feature.Marketing.Wffm.Actions
{
  public class SaveToCommentDatabase : WffmSaveAction
  {
    private ILog _log;

    public override void Execute(ID formId, AdaptedResultList adaptedFields,
        ActionCallContext actionCallContext = null, params object[] data)
```

```
    {
        _log = Sitecore.Diagnostics.LoggerFactory.GetLogger("LogFileAppender");

        var name = adaptedFields.GetEntryByName("Name");
        var email = adaptedFields.GetEntryByName("Email");
        var comment = adaptedFields.GetEntryByName("Comment");

        _log.Info("Writing comment to database");
        //Let's store the e-mail in session. We'll use this in a later example.
        HttpContext.Current.Session["Email"] = email;

        var connectionString = ConfigurationManager
            .ConnectionStrings["<comment db connection>"].ConnectionString;
        using (var connection = new SqlConnection(connectionString))
        {
            //Insert whatever code is necessary to write to your custom database that stores
comments
        }
    }
  }
 }
}
```

6. Next, build your solution and publish it using the Publish-Site Gulp task.

Now that we have created our custom save action, let's add it to Sitecore so it can be used with a WFFM form.

7. In the Content Editor, navigate to /sitecore/system/Modules/Web Forms for Marketers/Settings/Actions/Save Actions. Right-click on the Save Actions item and select Insert->Save Action. Name this item Save to Comment Database.

8. In the Data section of the new Save to Comment Database action, configure the fields as shown in Figure 9-3.

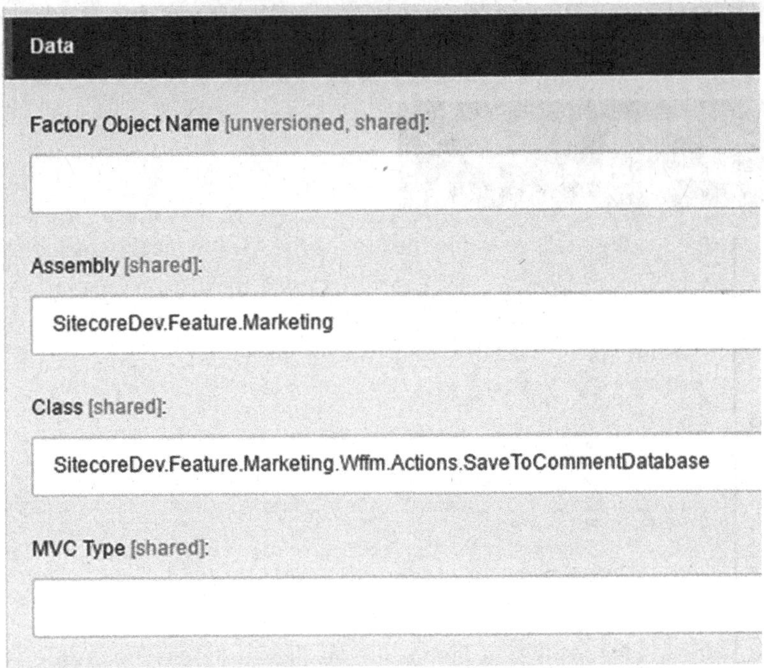

Data

Factory Object Name [unversioned, shared]:

Assembly [shared]:

SitecoreDev.Feature.Marketing

Class [shared]:

SitecoreDev.Feature.Marketing.Wffm.Actions.SaveToCommentDatabase

MVC Type [shared]:

Figure 9-3. *Register your save action within Sitecore*

9. Click Save.

10. Now, let's go add a form to the page! From the Content Editor, navigate to
    /sitecore/content/Home/Blog/MyBlogPost. From the Publish tab, click on the
    Experience Editor button to launch the Experience Editor.

11. Once Experience Editor has finished loading, from the Home tab, click on the
    Component button. This will activate the Add Here buttons for our placeholders.
    Click the Add Here button below our blog post rendering.

In the Select a Rendering dialog (see Figure 9-4), select Renderings\Modules\Web Forms for Marketers\Mvc Form.

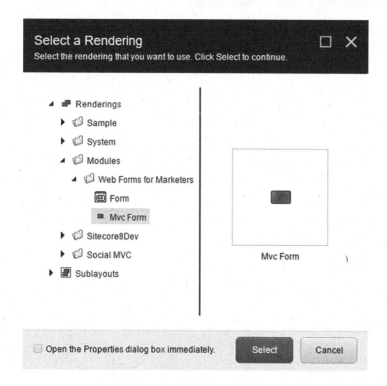

Figure 9-4. Select MVC Form and create a new WFFM form

12. Click Select. This will launch the wizard to walk you through creating the form.

13. Select the Create a Blank Form option and click Next.

14. For the Form Name, insert Add a Comment (see Figure 9-5).

Figure 9-5. *Name the form Add a Comment*

15. For Analytics, leave Create a New Goal selected and name the goal Comment Added (see Figure 9-6).

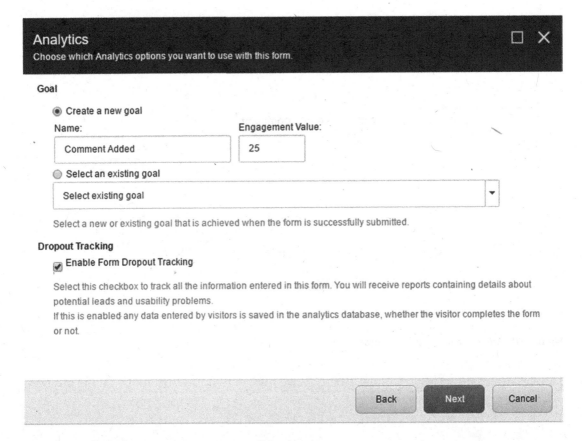

Figure 9-6. *Register a new goal when the form is submitted*

16. Click Next, then Create on the Confirmation dialog.

17. Once the form has been created, it will render on the page. Once it's been rendered, click the pencil all the way to the left on the toolbar to edit the form (see Figure 9-7).

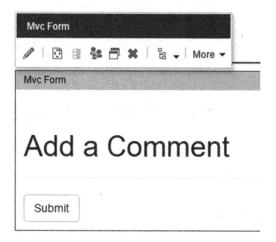

Figure 9-7. *Click on the pencil to design and edit the form*

18. Configure three fields on this form, as shown in Figure 9-8: Name, Email, and Comment.

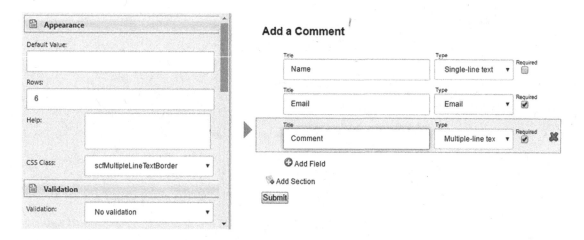

Figure 9-8. *Add three new fields to the form*

These three fields correspond to the fields referenced in Listing 9-1 as `adaptedFields`. `GetEntryByName("Name")`, etc.

19. Click the Save button.

20. Next, select the Submit button at the bottom. On the left side of the Form Designer, there is a section called Save Actions. Click the Edit link to the right of that section.

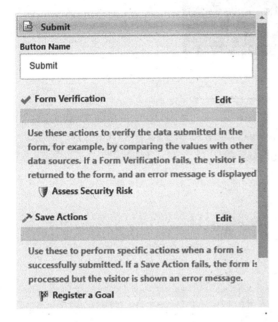

Figure 9-9. *Click Edit next to Save Actions to specify what happens when the form is submitted*

21. This will launch the Save Actions dialog.

22. In the Save Actions drop-down list, you should see the new Save to Comment Database save action we created in Steps 7 and 8 (see Figure 9-10). Select that save action and click Add.

Figure 9-10. Select our customer save action

23. Click OK and then click Save/Close in the Form Designer.

24. Finally, click Save in the top-left corner of Experience Editor to save the changes we've made to this page.

Close Experience Editor and navigate to `http://sitecore8/blog/myblogpost`. You should see the new form at the bottom of the page. Fill out the information and click Submit. If you provided code to write to a database, you should see the information in your database. If not, check the log file and you should see an entry from our custom save action!

Programing Goals, Events, and Outcomes

Events, failure events and goals are all customer behaviors recorded by Sitecore during a customer's journey across your channels. Events, failure events, and goals are amazingly more valuable from an analytics perspective than, say, page clicks or other pretty, yet less useful, anonymous data you might get in Google Analytics without customization. The reason events, failure events, and goals are so important to a marketer is twofold: they can be tied directly to your user personas and they track occurrences *and* value.

■ **Note** By "value" we mean "engagement value," a key way to measure the business value being provided by your digital experiences back to your business. Engagement value is a numeric measurement of the value any given interaction may have to the business and is a core report marketer's track.

Outcomes are used to track the lifelong value a particular customer is to your business over time. An outcome in its most basic form is just a tag on the customer's profile. That tag name can be whatever you want it to be and it can represent whatever you want it to represent. Typically, outcomes represent some combination of events, goals, and/or campaign interactions. Outcomes, unlike goals, often have a direct monetary value to the business (such as a purchase) and can be configured with that monetary value.

For example, you may have goals around social media sharing. Perhaps a customer is sharing a lot of your content on social media and has reached 10 "shares". In this case you may use this milestone to tag that customer with the Promoter outcome so you can segment your promoters for an e-mail campaign down the road, such as a new product launch.

It is simple enough to log goals, events, and failure events directly from the user interface (see Figure 9-11, the Goals and Attributes buttons). It's equally simple enough to log them with code.

Before you programmatically register a goal, event, or failure event you need to configure a goal to be registered within Sitecore. This can be done in the Marketing Control Panel found on the Launchpad and is discussed elsewhere.

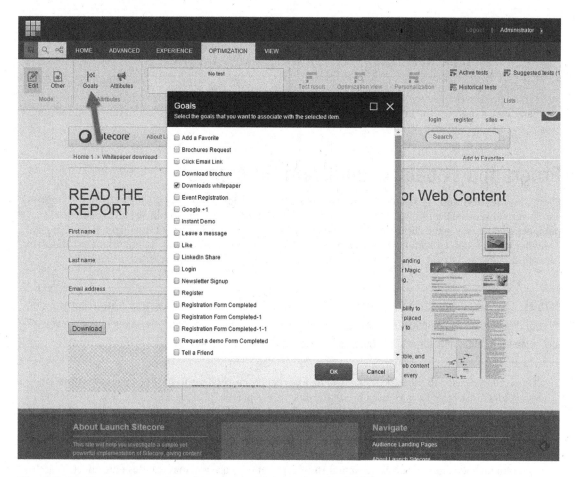

Figure 9-11. *Goals can be registered to a page with just a few simple clicks*

Typically, a goal is associated with a page. For example, if you have a goal to get people to download a whitepaper, the page that kicks off the download would be the page the goal would be associated with. This can be seen in the `Sitecore.Analytics.Tracker.Current.CurrentPage.Register()` method found in Listing 9-2.

■ **Tip** You can also trigger a goal via the query string, for example `http://www.yoursite.com/page1?sc_trk=[GOAL NAME]`, where `[GOAL NAME]` is the display name of the goal. Registering goals by their GUID is a best practice, but the query string is undoubtedly the easiest.

Listing 9-2. Registering a Goal/Event Programmatically

```
if (Sitecore.Analytics.Tracker.IsActive && Sitecore.Analytics.Tracker.Current.
CurrentPage != null)
{
    var goalItem = Sitecore.Context.Database.GetItem(goalOrEventID);
    var goalPageEvent = new PageEventItem(goalItem);
    var pageEventsRow = Sitecore.Analytics.Tracker.Current.CurrentPage.
    Register(goalPageEvent);

    pageEventsRow.Text = goalItem.Name + " has been fired at " + DateTime.Now.ToString("F");
    pageEventsRow.Data = somedata; // some data you may want to save with the event
    pageEventsRow.ItemId = Sitecore.Context.Item.ID.Guid;
    pageEventsRow.DataKey = Sitecore.Context.Item.Paths.Path;
    Sitecore.Analytics.Tracker.Submit();
}
```

In Listing 9-2, we first get access to the Analytics Tracker. This tracker is a static class that provides access into all Analytics within Sitecore. We first check to ensure the tracker has an active session and an active page, the result of which is a tracking context we can use to fire our goals, events, etc. Next, we get the item that is the goal/event which is then passed in as a parameter to create a new `PageEventItem` object. This is the object registered within the tracker, as seen in line 5. Beyond this, other data is associated with the event, such as a helpful message, some custom data, the current page's item ID and path.

Outcomes are registered similarly to goals. You also create and define outcomes in the Marketing Control panel, just like goals, which also contains several predefined outcome types and definitions. To register any outcome, whether predefined or custom, you must use the API to register the outcome event in xDB when it is triggered by a visitor on your web site. Registering an outcome ensures that the outcome is attached to an existing contact in xDB. Unlike goals and events, there are no out-of-the-box mechanisms to register outcomes. It must be done in code.

There are two API classes you can use to register outcomes (available from the `Sitecore.Analytics.Outcome.dll` assembly):

- *TrackerExtensions*: Just like with goals/events, Tracker Extension methods on the `Tracker` abstract class enable you to register outcomes in visitor sessions on a Sitecore web site. For example:

```
decimal valueOfOutcome = 100.0;
var outcome = new ContactOutcome(outcomeID, outcomeDefinitionID, xDBcontactID);
outcome.MonetaryValue = valueOfOutcome;
Tracker.Current.RegisterContactOutcome(outcome);
```

■ **Note** When you register a goal, event, or outcome using the TrackerExtensions API, it is not saved directly to the xDB collection database, instead it is stored in session. This means that while the session is active it is still possible to cancel or modify the outcome, for example, if a contact changes their delivery address during the purchase process. The outcome is only registered and written to the collections database when the session ends. To do this, use the `DeleteContactOutcome` method on the `Tracker.Current` session.

- *OutcomeManager*: Enables you to register outcomes from external data sources and save them directly to your database (for example, an event in CRM may need to register an outcome into Sitecore).

```
var manager = Factory.CreateObject("outcome/outcomeManager", true) as OutcomeManager;
var outcome = new ContactOutcome(outcomeId, outcomeDefinitionId, contactId);
manager.Save(outcome);
```

■ **Note** When updating information about a contact "out of session" or from an external source, contact locking (and session state, in general) needs to be considered. Session management is a key topic to understand, when talking about xDB contacts. Martina Wehlander has a fantastic post describing session state and all that it entails at `http://bit.ly/2dvnrS5`.

Using the OutcomeManager API does not ensure data consistency or improve performance. When you register an outcome using the OutcomeManager, it is saved directly to the xDB collection database. The outcome is still saved even if the contact ID you use does not correspond to a known contact in the xDB.

---

outcomeID in these cases is the GUID of the outcome item within Sitecore, outcomeDefinitionID is the GUID of the outcome definition item within the marketing control panel, and the contactID is the GUID of the contact within xDB.

Custom Personalization Rules

Personalizing a digital experience with Sitecore is incredibly easy and powerful. Sitecore provides two main ways to personalize: rules-based personalization and behavioral-based personalization. Rules-based is simply using "if X, then Y" types of rules you can associate to content. The most common practice is to use a rule to replace one piece of content for another depending on the outcome of the rule. Behavior-based personalization is a bit different, where the contacts' browsing habits can be used to personalize the experience based on which persona/profile the user happens to best match over the course of the browsing session. Even in this case, however, a rule is used to match the current user to the profile, from which the content can be personalized. You can see this rule in action in Figure 9-12.

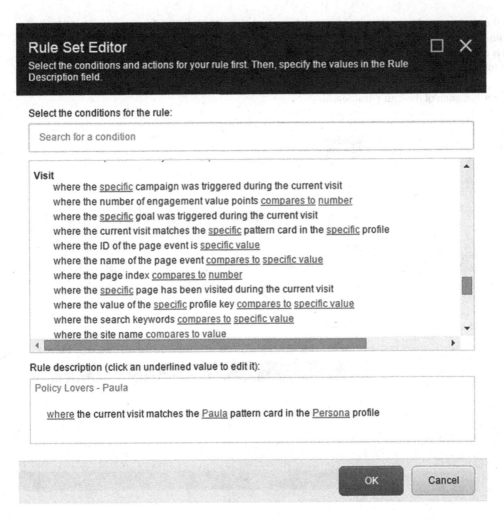

Figure 9-12. Custom personalization rules enable your marketer to configure any kind of experience your customer might need.

Fortunately, Sitecore provides many out-of-the-box rules you can use to personalize content. However, it is a fairly common development task to build your own rules to meet your unique requirements. The goal of this section is to describe how to do just that.

Rules appear in the Rules Editor (see Figure 9-12) only if they are registered with Sitecore. Rules should be added into the master database below /sitecore/system/settings/rules/definitions/elements (see Figure 9-13). You'll add your custom rule below the rule category or a custom category that makes sense. A rule is based on the Condition data template, found below /sitecore/templates/system/rules/condition. The Condition template has five fields, where the Text and Type fields are of most importance. Type, as you guessed, is the namespace and assembly name of your assembly containing your condition. Simply type in the following format: "namespace, assembly". Note the steps later on in this section for a walkthrough of how to create a custom condition.

Notice the sentence in Figure 9-12: "where the current visit matches the Paula pattern card...". This sentence comes from the value you put in the Text field of the condition. The Area Code example in Figure 9-13 is also helpful. Note the brackets [, , ,] with three commas. There are four possible parameters you can use to make the selectable "where", "Paula", and "Persona" values you saw in the rule example. Whenever a [, , ,] is used, Sitecore replaces that with whatever instructions you provide in the parameters. Table 9-1 describes each of the four parameters.

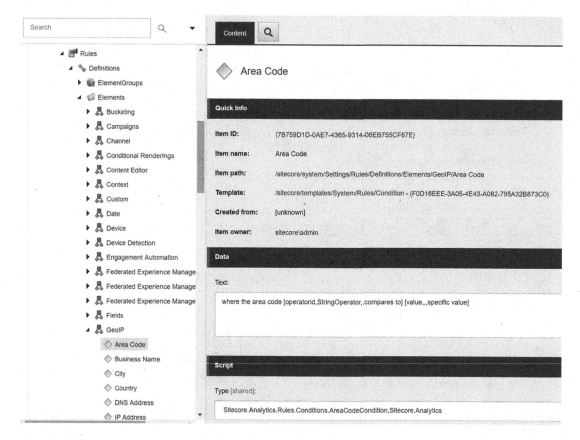

Figure 9-13. *Register your custom personalization rules, paying special attention to the Text and Type fields*

Table 9-1. Table of Parameters

Parameter Position	Description
First, e.g., `Country`	Your rule will have a corresponding C# class. This parameter is the name of the `public` property within that class which is being set.
Second, e.g., `Tree`	Set the type of display/popup helper the content author uses when configuring the rule (e.g., a tree view, textbox, and date picker). See the "Options for the Second Parameter" sidebar.
Third, e.g., `root=/sitecore/system/ Settings/Analytics/ Lookups/Countries`	This parameter is used to pass some path onto the previous, macro parameter. The following macros use the third parameter: • `PositiveInteger`: For this macro the third parameter is not used as a path. Instead, a default value can be written which will appear in the text field that pops up. • `Tree` and `TreeList`: Limits the tree that the editor can choose from. The notation has to be as explained above, `root=/sitecore/subitem/ subitem/etc.` If the name of the second parameter does not match any macros or the second parameter is blank, the third parameter is passed into the text field of the textbox that pops up when using the condition.
Fourth, e.g. `specific country`	This parameter is the word that will appear as the clickable text the editor can select when using the condition (placeholder text).

OPTIONS FOR THE SECOND PARAMETER

The following is a list of macros available to be used in conditions. These are stored below `/sitecore/ system/Settings/Rules/Common/Macros` and you can add your own if you need to. The out-of-the-box macros are:

`DateTime`: Loads a date picker when clicked.

`Operator`: Loads a dialog where the user can select an operator (e.g., "is equal to", "is greater than", etc.).

`Pattern`: Loads available pattern cards (items that match a session to a profile/persona).

`PositiveInteger`: Shows a textbox, but if anything entered is not a positive integer an error will display.

`Profile`: Loads available profile cards (e.g., personas); between Profile and Pattern an ProfileKey, Profile will be used most frequently.

`ProfileKey`: Loads available profile/persona "facets", e.g., characteristics of a persona.

`Script`: Opens a dialog where the editor can choose a script item.

`StringOperator`: The same as Operator but the options available are defined in `/sitecore/system/ Settings/Rules/Common/String Operators.`

`Template`: Shows a dialog where a user can select from among the data templates.

`Tree`: Shows a tree of items at the root. The third parameter can be used to limit the node specified.

`Treelist`: The same as the Tree macro, but allows the editor to choose multiple items from the tree list. The third parameter must be used to define the tree list. The condition will give the editor an error if the third parameter is left blank.

`Empty`: If the parameter name does not match any of the macro above, or if you leave the parameter blank, a standard text input box will pop up when the editor clicks the clickable word. The value of the textbox that the editor writes will set the property corresponding to the first parameter.

The high-level steps to creating a custom rule are:

1. Create a C# class for the rule.

2. Create the rule item in Sitecore and configure the Text property that gets presented as a sentence.

Let's create a custom rule which checks to see if the current user's e-mail address is in session or not. If yes, the rule will return true; otherwise, it will return false. If it is present, we want to show a special call to action to ask the user to provide their e-mail address. It's kind of a silly example, but it demonstrates a common need for personalization: if the user has accomplished a goal or two, we want to drive them toward other, more valuable goals or outcomes through personalized content. Note the following steps, showing you this process end-to-end:

1. In the earlier example where we created a custom save action for WFFM, we set the value of the Email field to a key in session called Email. We're going to create a rule that checks to see if that session key exists and if it has a value. In the `SitecoreDev.Feature.Marketing` project, create a new folder called `Rules`. In that folder, create another called `Conditions`.

2. In the new `Conditions` folder, create a new class named `SessionHasValueForKey` with the definition shown in Listing 9-3.

Listing 9-3. A Custom Condition Used Without Our Custom Personalization Rule

```
using System;
using System.Web;
using Sitecore.Rules;
using Sitecore.Rules.Conditions;

namespace SitecoreDev.Feature.Marketing.Rules.Conditions
{
  public class SessionHasValueForKey<T> : WhenCondition<T> where T : RuleContext
  {
    public string SessionKeyName { get; set; }

    protected override bool Execute(T ruleContext)
    {
      try
      {
        return HttpContext.Current.Session[SessionKeyName] != null &&
            !String.IsNullOrEmpty(HttpContext.Current.Session[SessionKeyName].ToString());
      }
```

```
    catch (Exception ex)
    {
      //Write the exception to whatever logging mechanism you're using
    }
  }
 }
}
```

3. Build your solution then deploy it using the Publish-Site Gulp task.

4. Once the solution has been deployed, open the Content Editor and navigate to /sitecore/system/Settings/Rules/Definitions/Elements/Conditional Renderings.

5. Right-click on Conditional Renderings and select Insert->Condition. Name this new condition Session Has Value for Key. Configure this condition as shown in Figure 9-14.

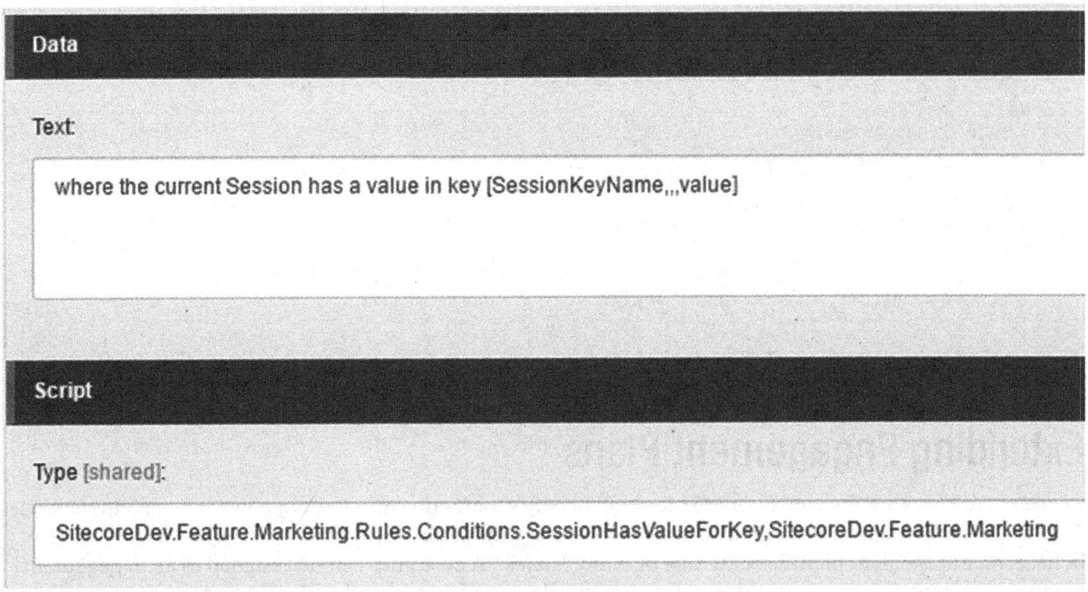

Data

Text:

where the current Session has a value in key [SessionKeyName,,,value]

Script

Type [shared]:

SitecoreDev.Feature.Marketing.Rules.Conditions.SessionHasValueForKey,SitecoreDev.Feature.Marketing

Figure 9-14. *Complete the fields in the personalization rule item*

6. Click Save.

Now, if you were to set personalization on a particular rendering, this rule would be available under Conditional Renderings, as shown in Figure 9-15.

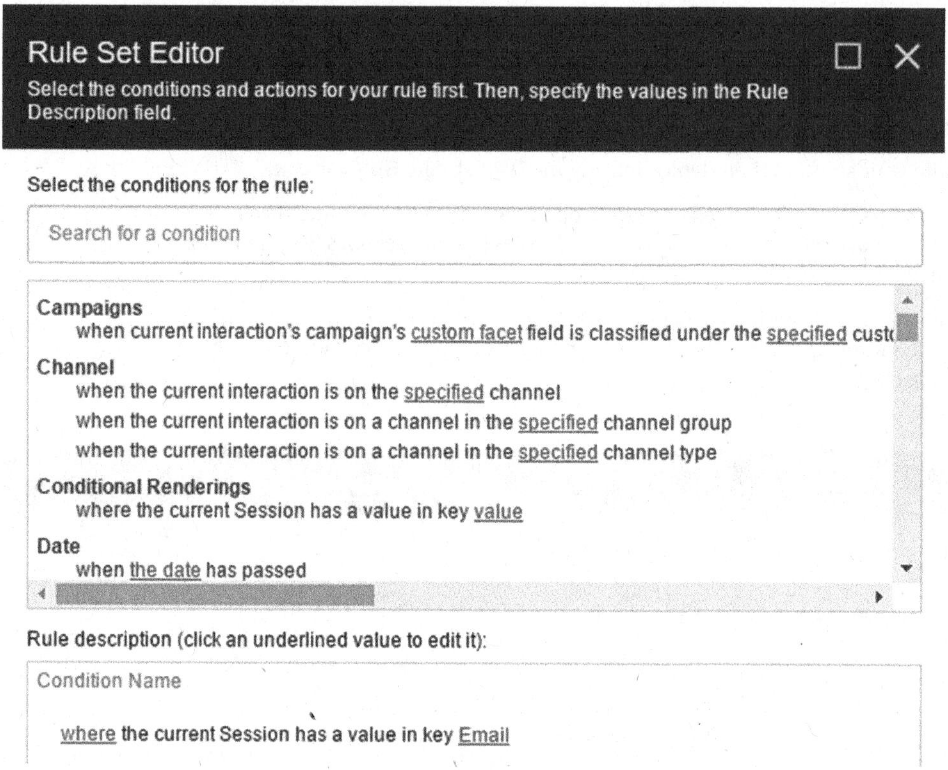

Figure 9-15. *Our custom personalization rule in action!*

Extending Engagement Plans

Engagement plans are the core building block of Sitecore's marketing automation engine. Engagement plans might be better named "Engagement Workflows" because they behave just like you'd expect a workflow to behave. An engagement plan can have one or many "states." A customer can be assigned to an engagement plan and into one of those states. Most engagements plans have a start and end state, such as the case when you are trying to sequentially move the customer through a sales funnel, for example. However, the states need not be sequential and a customer can be assigned to any state as their first state. It really depends on your business requirements.

The point is, engagement plans help you *move* your customer from one state to another; where the goal is to advance them toward a more desirable state. This often results in an outcome that you're trying to help the customer achieve. Engagement plans can be viewed from the Engagement Plans node within the Marketing Control Panel (see Figure 9-16). They are very easy to configure a well; Sitecore provides an intuitive drag-and-drop like experience to configure the flow. Square shapes represent states, and diamond shapes represent conditions. You can see an example Engagement Plan design surface in Figure 9-17. The design surface is loaded when you click the Design button in the middle of the screen near Options. (Sitecore 8.1 and below require Silverlight; Sitecore 8.2 removed this requirement.)

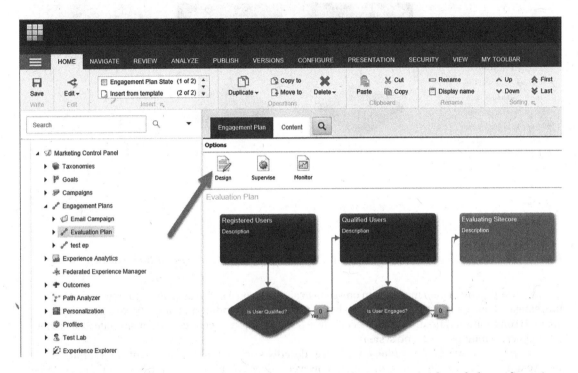

Figure 9-16. *Engagement plans are where you automate your marketing strategies through the configuration of simple marketing workflows*

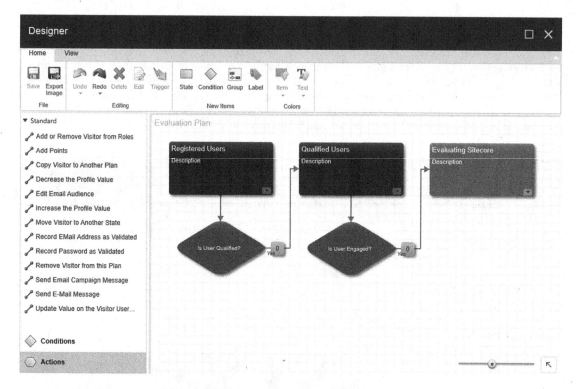

Figure 9-17. *The Engagement Plan workflow designer is a simple to use, drag-and-drop experience*

As an engagement plan moves from one state to another, you can fire off actions to respond to that movement. There are quite a few out-of-the-box actions, such as sending an e-mail, however, a custom action is commonly required. This is especially true because engagement plans often facilitate a customer journey across multiple back-end systems.

Practical Sitecore 8 Configuration and Strategy describes how to build engagement plans through these out-of-the-box actions, rules, and states; however, it does not describe how to build your own custom actions. The following steps show a simple example of a custom action which writes to a back-end SQL table. This is a simple, but useful starting place for you to build your own, more complex actions later. Check out the following steps for how to do this:

1. Start by adding a reference to `Sitecore.Analytics.Automation.dll` in the `SitecoreDev.Feature.Marketing` project. This assembly should be copied from `%webroot%\bin` to `%devroot%\bin`.

2. Add a new folder called `Automation`. In that folder, create another named `Actions`.

3. In the new `Actions` folder, create a new class called `AddInfoToCustomerTable` with the definition shown in Listing 9-4.

Listing 9-4. Custom Action for Our Engagement Plans

```
using System.Data.SqlClient;
using Sitecore.Analytics.Automation;
using Sitecore.Diagnostics;

namespace SitecoreDev.Feature.Marketing.Automation.Actions
{
  public class AddInfoToCustomerTable : IAutomationAction
  {
    public AutomationActionResult Execute(AutomationActionContext context)
    {
      Assert.ArgumentNotNull(context, "context");

      using (var connection = new SqlConnection("<your connection string>"))
      {
        //Add code to insert information into database table
      }

      return AutomationActionResult.Continue;
    }
  }
}
```

4. Build your solution and publish using the Publish-Site Gulp task.

5. Once the publish is complete, open Content Editor and navigate to /sitecore/
    system/Settings/Analytics/Engagement Automation/Predefined items/
    Actions.

6. Right-click on Actions and select Insert➤Engagement Automation Action. Name
    this new action Add Info to Customer Table.

7. Configure this action as shown in Figure 9-18.

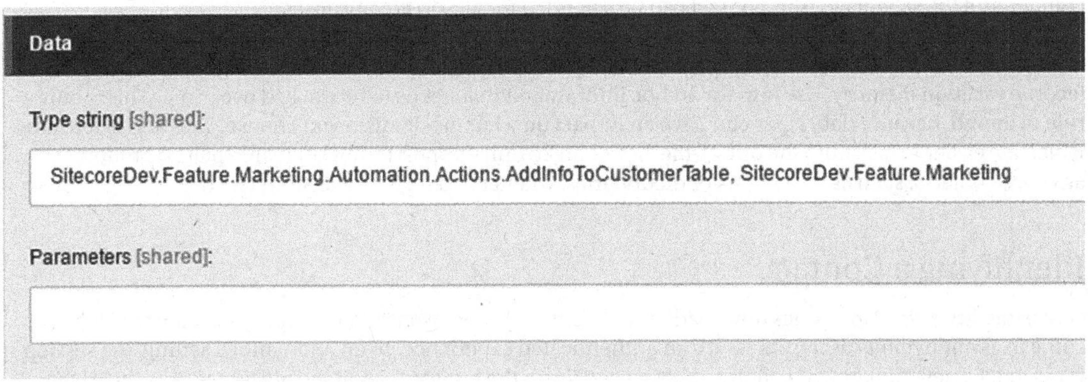

Data

Type string [shared]:

    SitecoreDev.Feature.Marketing.Automation.Actions.AddInfoToCustomerTable, SitecoreDev.Feature.Marketing

Parameters [shared]:

Figure 9-18. *Create a new Engagement Automation action to register your action code*

Now, if you create a new engagement plan, you'll see this custom action available in the Actions pane (see Figure 9-19)!

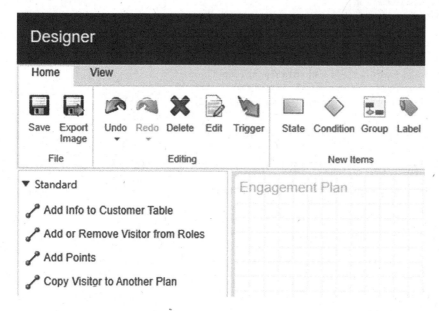

Figure 9-19. *Our custom Engagement Automation action!*

Programming the xDB Contact

Goals, events, outcomes, and many other data types are stored in a customer's xDB contact out-of-the-box. It is common to need to programmatically interact with this data about a customer. Additionally, you often get to a point where you need additional proprietary data to be added to the contact. You may need this data in Sitecore because you want to personalize your site based on data from your CRM or an ERP back-end, for example. Basically every user who comes into contact with your Sitecore experiences will get their own contact, and the schema for this contact can be extended for all sorts of purposes.

There are a number of ways to add more information to a contact. Use **facets** for permanent, business-critical information, such as a loyalty card number. Use **extensions** for more ad hoc information, such as a favorite vacation memory. Use **tags** for ad hoc information that needs to be tracked over time. This is only a rule of thumb, because data types can have an impact on what mechanism you choose. Tags and extensions, which are easier to tack onto the out-of-the-box contact, only support string key/value pairs. For more advanced objects, such as collections or dictionaries, you need to register a custom facet.

Identifying a Contact

One of the first things to learn is how to identify a contact. When users first visit your site, they typically come in as anonymous users, unless it's an authenticated experience. In an anonymous setting, the session is assigned a new "unknown" contact, unless a cookie on the browser can associate that user to an existing unknown contact. There are times, however, when your code will need to convert the current session's contact from unknown to known. The code in Listing 9-5 shows you how to accomplish this.

Listing 9-5. Code to Identify an Unknown Contact and Convert It to a Known

```
var contact = Tracker.Current.Session.Contact;

if (contact.Identifiers.IdentificationLevel != ContactIdentificationLevel.Known)
    contact.Identifiers.IdentificationLevel = ContactIdentificationLevel.Known;

contact.Identifiers.Identifier = someModel.EmailAddress;
```

The first thing the code does is retrieve the contact in the current session. Next, it checks to see if the current contact is known or unknown. If unknown, it sets it to known and then establishes an identifier. E-mail addresses are a common way to establish a contact's identifier. Hereafter, the contact is converted to known and established for that customer.

MERGING CONTACTS

There's a bit of a problem with the code in Listing 9-5. The issue is we may end up with more than one contact in xDB for that e-mail address. The Session contact might be unknown until the user fills out a form, for example. At that point they become known. However, if they jump back on the experience at a different time but from a different device they'll go back to being an unknown contact. If they fill out another form from that other device, we'll have created a second contact for the same person. These two contacts needed to be merged to ensure we don't end up with duplicate information. The simple solution for this is to use the .Identify() method, as seen here:

```
Tracker.Current.Session.Identify(emailAddress);
```

The Identify method basically does the same thing as the code in Listing 9-5; however, it checks to ensure an existing contact for that e-mail address doesn't already exist first. If it does exist, the current Session contact will be merged with the existing contact. If a contact for that e-mail address doesn't exist, the session contact is converted much like in Listing 9-5.

If it sounds too good to be true, it is! The problem with Identify() is it is resource intense, since it goes through the MergeContacts pipeline. You don't want to use it for heavy loads. For light loads or one-offs, however, its simplicity makes it a compelling and popular option.

So how do you merge contacts when you have heavy loads? You merge them yourself, preferably behind the scenes, through the API. The following MergeContacts method is an example of how to do this:

```
ContactRepository ContactRepository = Sitecore.Configuration.Factory.CreateObject(
    "tracking/contactRepository", true) as ContactRepository;

ContactRepository.MergeContacts(survivingContact, dyingContact);
```

In this example you get the Contacts out of xDB or Session and pass in the surviving contact as the first parameter and the dying contact as the second. Jonathan Robbins has a great blog post featuring a GetContact factory you can use to retrieve your contacts from xDB before merging. He also shares some extra tidbits on merging when you have custom facet data, a situation requiring some custom code to tell Sitecore *how* to do the merge. Custom facet data is discussed later in this chapter. You can find his post at http://bit.ly/2d1KbnR.

Using Custom Tags

Tags are just a tag you put on a contact, along with a timestamp. They're a simplistic way to track the status of a contact over time. This is helpful when you want to quickly search for all contacts with a given tag applied. The following steps show you how to add a `CommentCounter` tag onto all contacts, incremented from our WFFM save action. In the future, one could create e-mail campaigns targeting this segment, or perhaps personalize content unique for those who have commented a lot. This could also build some cheap gamification into the blog, showing top followers.

1. In the `SaveToCommentDatabase` save action we created earlier, add the code from Listing 9-6 to the bottom of the `Execute` method to initialize or increment the `CommentCounter` tag.

Listing 9-6. Code to Add Our Custom Tags to Each User's xDB Profile

```
var contact = Tracker.Current?.Contact;
if (contact != null)
{
  var commentCounterTag = contact.Tags.Find("CommentCounter");
  if (commentCounterTag == null)
    contact.Tags.Set("CommentCounter", "1");
  else
  {
    var counter = commentCounterTag.Values.FirstOrDefault();
    if (counter != null)
    {
      int originalValue = 0;
      int newValue = 0;
      if (Int32.TryParse(counter.Value, out originalValue))
      {
        newValue = originalValue + 1;
        contact.Tags.Remove("CommentCounter", originalValue.ToString());
        contact.Tags.Set("CommentCounter", newValue.ToString());
      }
    }
  }
}
```

2. Build your solution and deploy it using the Publish-Site Gulp task.

Once the solution has been deployed, navigate to `http://sitecore8/blog/myblogpost` and submit the form a number of times. After submitting the form, if you look at the collections database in MongoDB (see Figure 9-20), you should see the new tags and their values!

```
/* 2 */
{
    "_id" : LUUID("a659acec-5318-8e45-925b-4faf173e99f0"),
    "System" : {
        "Classification" : 0,
        "OverrideClassification" : 0,
        "VisitCount" : 1,
        "Value" : 250
    },
    "Tags" : {
        "Entries" : {
            "CommentCounter" : {
                "Values" : {
                    "0" : {
                        "Value" : "8",
                        "DateTime" : ISODate("2016-08-21T03:40:15.304Z")
                    }
                }
            }
        }
    },
    "Lease" : null
}
```

Figure 9-20. *You can see our custom tag within MongoDB!*

Using Custom Extensions

Extensions are a simple and easy way to stick custom data into an xDB contact without all the fuss of registering a custom facet via config files. You simply start registering custom key/value pairs into the SimpleValues property. Note the code sample in Listing 9-7. In this example, like always, we get a handle on our tracker, which stores state for all our analytics tracking. We then check to ensure the tracker is not null, nor its handle on the xDB contact of the current visitor. We then simply stick some additional data within this key/value pair to persist it across sessions.

Listing 9-7. Example Setting a Value to a Custom Extension Key

```
var tracker = Sitecore.Analytics.Tracker.Current;
if (tracker != null && tracker.IsActive && tracker.Contact != null)
{
    tracker.Contact.Extensions.SimpleValues["SomeKey"] = "Some Value";
}
```

A simple extension example for our example site would be to add an extension that tracks the total number of comments a poster has submitted and sets a ContributorLevel. This gives us the ability to add some quick and dirty gamification into our blog. Note the following steps, as a guide, on how to add this nice little enhancement into our example:

1. As in the last example, let's extend the SaveToCommentDatabase custom save action to add a value to the Extensions property. Modify the code from the last example to match the code shown in Listing 9-8.

Listing 9-8. Example Setting a Contributor Level to "Fanboy" When a User Leaves >10 Comments

```
 var contact = Tracker.Current?.Contact;
if (contact != null)
{
  var commentCounterTag = contact.Tags.Find("CommentCounter");
  if (commentCounterTag == null)
    contact.Tags.Set("CommentCounter", "1");
  else
  {
    int originalValue = 0;
    int newValue = 0;

    var counter = commentCounterTag.Values.FirstOrDefault();
    if (counter != null)
    {
      if (Int32.TryParse(counter.Value, out originalValue))
      {
        newValue = originalValue + 1;
        contact.Tags.Remove("CommentCounter", originalValue.ToString());
        contact.Tags.Set("CommentCounter", newValue.ToString());
      }
    }

    if (originalValue < 10 && newValue >= 10)
      contact.Extensions.SimpleValues["ContributionLevel"] = "Fanboy";
  }
}
```

2. Build your solution and deploy it using the Publish-Site Gulp task.

Once the solution has been deployed, navigate to http://sitecore8/blog/myblogpost and submit the form more than 10 times. After submitting the form, if you look at the collections database in MongoDB, you should see the new Extensions value (see Figure 9-21)!

```
/* 4 */
{
    "_id" : LUUID("9fb3039c-742c-0c4e-9182-e0d29a176d4c"),
    "System" : {
        "Classification" : 0,
        "OverrideClassification" : 0,
        "VisitCount" : 1,
        "Value" : 300
    },
    "Tags" : {
        "Entries" : {
            "CommentCounter" : {
                "Values" : {
                    "0" : {
                        "Value" : "12",
                        "DateTime" : ISODate("2016-08-21T04:09:34.397Z")
                    }
                }
            }
        }
    },
    "Extensions" : {
        "Groups" : {
            "SimpleValues" : {
                "Entries" : {
                    "ContributionLevel" : {
                        "Value" : "Fanboy"
                    }
                }
            }
        }
    },
    "Lease" : null
}
```

Figure 9-21. *You can see our custom extension within MongoDB!*

Programing the Out-of-the-Box Facets

As was earlier stated, an xDB contact comes out-of-the-box with quite a bit of goodies you can explore with code. Before you jump on the custom facet bandwagon, it's worth spending a bit of time exploring some of these facets to be sure you can't simply use them for your basic contact information needs. The following lists out what out-of-the-box facets will be immediately available to you:

- *Personal*: Stores the personal name, nickname, age, gender, and the job title of the contact. Interface = IContactPersonalInfo (see Listing 9-9).

- *Addresses*: Implements a dictionary of named postal addresses associated with the contact. The postal address consists of the country, state, or province, city, postal code, and the street. It also supports storing geographic coordinates. Interface = IContactAddresses (see Listing 9-10).

- *Emails*: Implements a dictionary of named e-mail addresses associated with the contact. The facets support storing a bounce count with each e-mail address. Interface = IContactEmailAddresses (see Listing 9-11).

- *Phone Numbers:* Implements a dictionary of named phone numbers associated with the contact. Each phone number includes a country code, phone number, and extension (if relevant). Interface = IContactPhoneNumbers (see Listing 9-12).

- *Picture*: Stores a binary stream that contains the profile picture associated with the contact. Interface = IContactPicture (see Listing 9-13).

- *Communication Profile:* Stores the communication preferences of the contact, including whether the contact has revoked their consent to be contacted. Interface = IContactCommunicationProfile.

- *Preferences*: Stores preferences such as the contact's preferred language. Interface = IContactPreferences (see Listing 9-14).

Listing 9-9. Example Writing Data into a Contact's "Personal" Facet

```
Contact contact = Tracker.Current.Contact;
IContactPersonalInfo personal = contact.GetFacet<IContactPersonalInfo>("Personal");
personal.FirstName = firstName;
personal.Surname = surename;
personal.BirthDate = birthDate;
```

Listing 9-10. Example Updating a Customer's Home City

```
Contact contact = Tracker.Current.Contact;
IContactAddresses addresses = contact.GetFacet<IContactAddresses>("Addresses");
if (!addresses.Entries.Contains("Home"))
{
   IContactAddress home = addresses.Entries.Create("Home");
   home.City = "Minneapolis";
}
```

Listing 9-11. Example Updating a Customer's E-Mail Address and Setting the Preferred Address

```
Contact contact = Tracker.Current.Contact;
IContactEmailAddresses emails = contact.GetFacet<IContactEmailAddresses>("Emails");
if (!emails.Entries.Contains("Work"))
{
    IEmailAddress email = emails.Entries.Create("Work");
    email.SmtpAddress = "phil@sitecoreconfig.com";
    emails.Preferred = "Work";
}
```

Listing 9-12. Example Creating a New Phone Number Entry Called "Cell" and Setting It as the Preferred Phone

```
Contact contact = Tracker.Current.Contact;
IContactPhoneNumbers phone = contact.GetFacet<IContactPhoneNumbers>("Phone Numbers");
if (!phone.Entries.Contains("Cell"))
{
   IPhoneNumber cell = phone.Entries.Create("Cell");
   cell.CountryCode = "001";
   cell.Number = "555-555-5555";
   cell.Extension = "12345";
   phone.Preferred = "Cell ";
}
```

Listing 9-13. Example Updating a Contact's Profile Picture

```
Contact contact = Tracker.Current.Contact;
IContactPicture picture = contact.GetFacet<IContactPicture>("Picture");
MediaItem pic = Sitecore.Context.Database.GetItem("{Guid of the media item}");
var stream = pic.GetMediaStream();
var memoryStream = new MemoryStream();
if (stream != null)
    stream.CopyTo(memoryStream);
picture.Picture = memoryStream.ToArray();
picture.MimeType = mediaItem.MimeType;
```

Listing 9-14. Example Updating a Contact's Preferences

```
Contact contact = Tracker.Current.Contact;
IContactPreferences preferences = contact.GetFacet<IContactPreferences>(" Preferences ");
preferences.Language = "en"; // item names below system/Languages
```

Building Custom Facets

Tags aren't enough? Extensions don't support your complex object? Out-of-the-box facets not what you need? Time to build your own! Building a custom facet involves the following high-level steps:

1. Define your facet interface.

2. Implement the interface.

3. Register the interface in the `Sitecore.Analytics.Model.config` file (patch config recommended).

4. Read/write data into the facet.

For our example site, we want to provide readers the ability to subscribe to specific categories on the blog. That way, they get e-mails/promotions only related to topics they've told us they are interested in being notified about. This collection of topics is a great case for a custom facet. The following steps walk you through the four high-level steps, but this time, with all the detail you'll need to implement something similar yourself.

■ **Warning**　Be careful how much data to store in a contact. A customer's entire contact gets pulled into session as a JSON object, which could be a memory concern or data transfer time concern if you have a *huge* schema. That entire object has to come over the wire to the delivery cluster when the session begins, so if it's large, it will affect the initial page load time, too.

---

1. In SitecoreDev.Feature.Marketing, add a new folder called Contacts. In that folder, add another called Facets.

2. In the new Facets folder, add a new interface named ITopicSubscriptionElement and a new class named TopicSubscriptionElement with the definitions shown in Listings 9-15 and 9-16, respectively.

Listing 9-15. ITopicSubscriptionElement, Definition of a Topic Element that Can Be Subscribed To

```
public interface ITopicSubscriptionElement : IElement
{
  string Topic { get; set; }
}
```

Listing 9-16. TopicSubscriptionElement, Implementation of the Topic Element

```
public class TopicSubscriptionElement : Element, ITopicSubscriptionElement
{
  private const string _topic = "Topic";
  public string Topic { get { return GetAttribute<string>(_topic); } set { SetAttribute(_
topic, value); } }

  public TopicSubscriptionElement()
  {
    EnsureAttribute<string>(_topic);
  }
}
```

3. Next, add a new interface named ISubscriptionsFacet and a class named SubscriptionsFacet with the definitions shown in Listings 9-17 and 9-18, respectively.

Listing 9-17. ISubscriptionsFacet, Defines Our Facet (Collection of Topics)

```
public interface ISubscriptionsFacet : IFacet
{
  IElementCollection<ITopicSubscriptionElement> Subscriptions { get; }
}
```

Listing 9-18. SubscriptionsFacet, Implementation of Our Facet

```
[Serializable]
public class SubscriptionsFacet : Facet, ISubscriptionsFacet
{
  public static readonly string EntryCollectionName = "Subscriptions";

  public IElementCollection<ITopicSubscriptionElement> Subscriptions {
    get { return GetCollection<ITopicSubscriptionElement>(EntryCollectionName); } }
```

```
public SubscriptionsFacet()
{
   EnsureCollection<ITopicSubscriptionElement>(EntryCollectionName);
}
}
```

4. Now that we have created our elements and facets, we need to patch them into Sitecore's configuration. At the root of SitecoreDev.Feature.Marketing, add a new folder named App_Config. In that folder, add another named Include. Finally, inside Include, add a folder named Feature.

5. In the Feature folder, add a new web configuration file named Feature. Marketing.config with the definition shown in Listing 9-19.

Listing 9-19. SubscriptionsFacet

```
<configuration xmlns:patch="http://www.sitecore.net/xmlconfig/">
  <sitecore>
    <model>
      <elements>
        <element interface="
          SitecoreDev.Feature.Marketing.Contacts.Facets.ITopicSubscriptionElement,
          SitecoreDev.Feature.Marketing"
          implementation="SitecoreDev.Feature.Marketing.Contacts.Facets.
          TopicSubscriptionElement,
          SitecoreDev.Feature.Marketing" />
        <element interface="
          SitecoreDev.Feature.Marketing.Contacts.Facets.ISubscriptionsFacet, SitecoreDev.
          Feature.Marketing"
          implementation="SitecoreDev.Feature.Marketing.Contacts.Facets.SubscriptionsFacet,
          SitecoreDev.Feature.Marketing" />
      </elements>
      <entities>
        <contact>
          <facets>
            <facet name="Subscriptions" contract="
              SitecoreDev.Feature.Marketing.Contacts.Facets.ISubscriptionsFacet,
              SitecoreDev.Feature.Marketing" />
          </facets>
        </contact>
      </entities>
    </model>
  </sitecore>
</configuration>
```

Build your solution and deploy it using the Publish-Site Gulp task. Now, you're ready to start adding data to your custom facet, just like the out-of-the-box facets!

EXTENDING EXPERIENCE PROFILES WITH SPEAK

In the previous section we expanded the xDB contact with some custom data. This data can be used all over your site, such as personalization, routing to CRM, and many other applications. Another common practice is to extend the out-of-the-box Experience Profile to also render this data within the profile. This way, marketers and sales people can browse profiles and get a fuller picture of that customer's behaviors across Sitecore or any back-end system that might be represented within their xDB contact. Jonathan Robbins has an excellent set of posts on this advanced topic (extending Sitecore's SPEAK interface):

http://bit.ly/2bB5r5k

http://bit.ly/2bMf68Q

Federated Experience Manager

Sitecore's federated experience manager (FXM) is the last leg in our quest to program the customer journey. FXM enables a marketer to see customer behavioral data and share Sitecore content across all their digital properties, regardless of their technology stack. No matter where the customer's journey takes them, Sitecore will know about it!

This enables you to maintain a single view of the customer and a single source of content no matter if you've upgraded/migrated all your digital properties to Sitecore, or if you plan to take a more gradual approach to your migration. Examples might be Sitecore sites, non-Sitecore sites, or native mobile apps.

Additionally, FXM enables better collaboration with partners. You and your partners may want to collaborate on customer data. You can ask your partners to deploy the necessary page scripts on their properties to send a feed of customer data back to your xDB instance to create a consolidated view. Here are a few more examples where FXM can create value for your marketers:

- A company hosts sites that cannot be managed by Sitecore (e.g., non-.NET sites or apps, such as WordPress or PHP sites).

- A company wants to better collaborate with their partners.

- A company is in process of migrating their properties; however, they don't want to wait until they are all migrated before taking advantage of xDB's capabilities.

- You are in acquisition mode and need to take control of new properties and quickly integrate them into your overall marketing objectives.

To get started using FXM, open FXM from the Launchpad->Federated Experience Manager tile. The page, by default, looks pretty empty. Click on Add External Website to get started.

Figure 9-22 shows the new site form. There are basically two pieces of information you need to add: the site name and the URL to the site. The name is just a token and can be anything descriptive that make sense. The URL needs to be the root path to your site. Fill in this data and click Save.

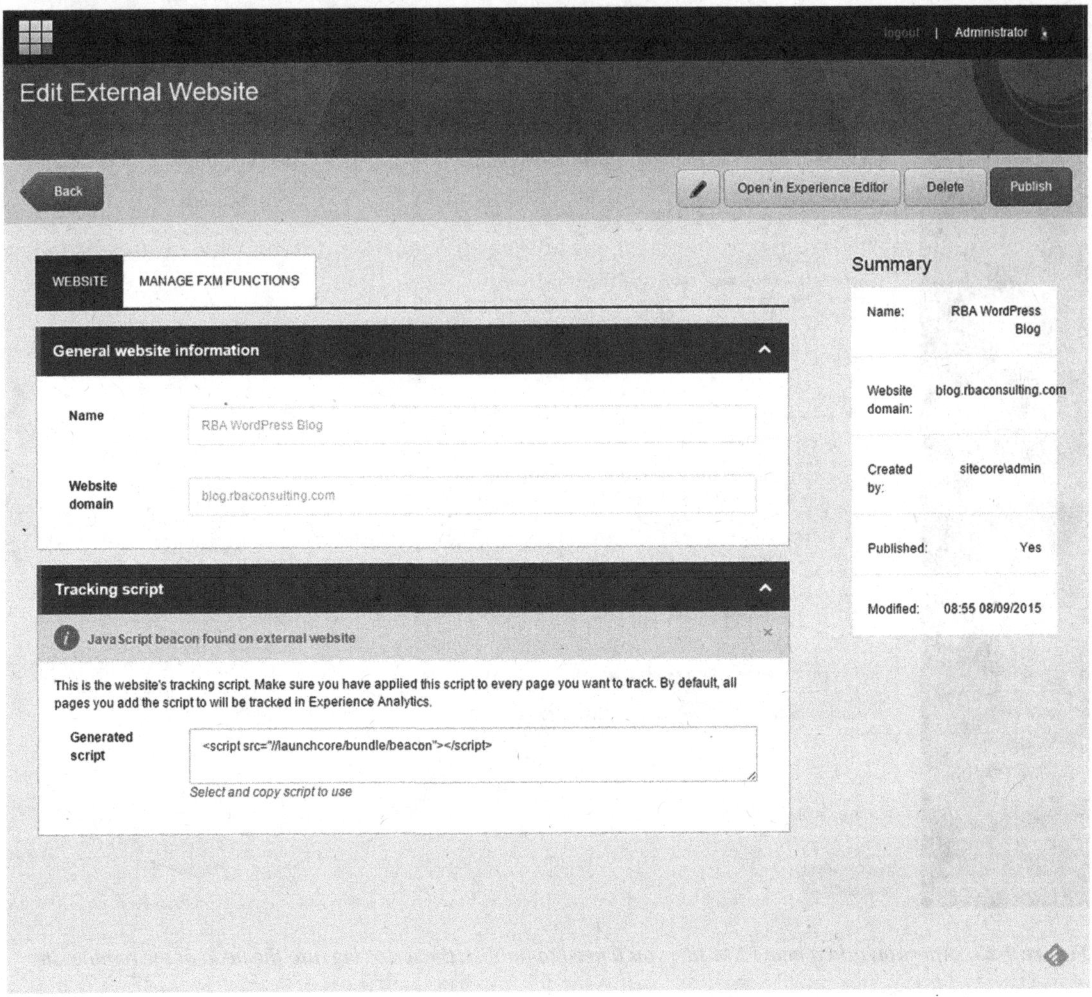

Figure 9-22. *You can add a site into FXM from the FXM button on the Launchpad*

After you click Save, you'll notice the save button is updated and now shows Publish. Before you publish, however, there are a couple more steps to take. First, you need to paste in the script tag into the head of your remote site (found in the Generated Script textbox). Second, you need to enable cross-site scripting for your remote site.

Figure 9-23 shows an example of pasting in the script tag into a WordPress site. Simply paste it in directly before the </head> tag, wherever that might be in your remote site's solution.

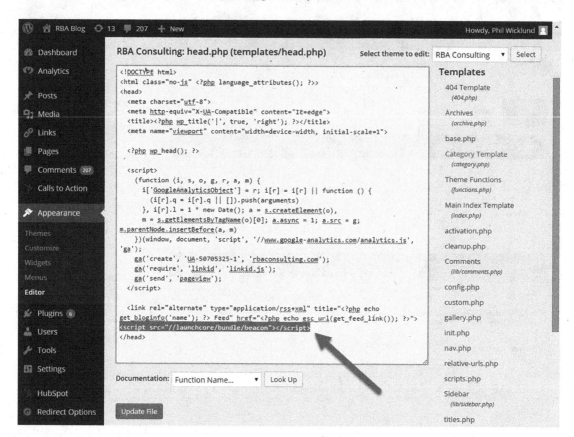

Figure 9-23. *After you add a new FXM site, you'll need to publish the script tag into the head of the remote site*

Finally, you need to enable cross-site scripting for the remote site, otherwise all the JavaScript callbacks will be prevented and FXM won't work. Navigate to the site's node within the Marketing Control Panel ➤ Federated Experience Manager. Add a rule similar to what you see in Figure 9-24 by clicking Edit Rule below Matching Rule. When this is complete, you can go back to the site in FXM and click the Publish button.

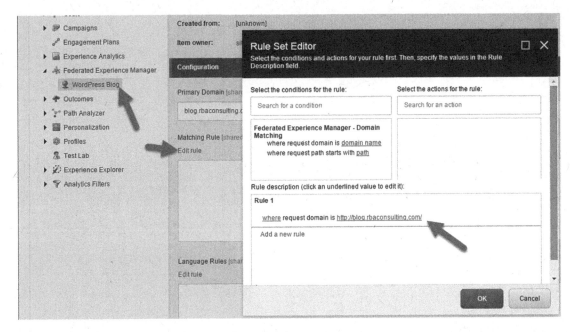

Figure 9-24. *Because of cross-site scripting rules, you'll need to explicitly grant access to allow scripts from the remote site*

This is all it takes to get FXM up and running for your marketers! The rest of the configuration details of FXM are covered in *Practical Sitecore 8 Configuration and Strategy,* so be sure to check that out if you want more information on how to add content or track analytics on external sites. But for now, we'll assume that's the marketer's job.

Summary

There you have it, if you worked through the exercises within this chapter you can start calling yourself an *Experience Developer,* because you now know how to program the customer journey, not just web pages. The customer journey requires programmatically registering key events, such as goals, events, failure events, and outcomes, to enable your marketers to gain better insight into customer behaviors.

These insights enable the marketer or content author the ability to personalize the experience and deliver the most relevant content to the right person, at the most appropriate time. Your custom personalization rules empower the marketer to personalize across all kinds of data sources, such as back-end systems or user profiles. This personalization might feed into your custom engagement plans, where marketing automation comes to life.

But what is a customer journey if we aren't tracking customer details within Sitecore, such as preferences? Preferences, or other insights, are commonly stored in xDB within custom facets. This enables the data to stay close to the digital experience, often being a source of personalization.

CHAPTER 10

■ ■ ■

Sitecore PowerShell Extensions

This chapter was generously contributed by Michael West. Michael is a Sitecore MVP and a chief contributor to the Sitecore PowerShell Extensions module.

At this point you may have mixed feelings about learning Sitecore. On the one hand, you have been exposed to a wonderful and solid platform for building a wide array of web sites and applications. On the other hand, you've realized how much more there is to learn. Well, I have some great news for you! There just so happens to be a Sitecore module that can help you go from "Zero to Hero" in no time flat!

While you may not get a cape, you'll still convince those around you that you have super powers. In this chapter I'll introduce you to Sitecore PowerShell Extensions (SPE), a community built module for Sitecore which incorporates Windows PowerShell and the Sitecore API.

SPE provides a command line and scripting interface for automating the hell out of all sorts of things. Need a confirmation dialog? Easy. How about accepting information from the user? No problem. What about deleting all of the wasted space in the media library because the content authors felt like uploading cat pictures along with all the other corporate documentation? Kittens are cute so we'll leave those alone; however, the unreferenced PDFs and images can be deleted. Easy peasy.

I'll break down the chapter into a few keys areas to help you focus on what matters the most to you. So before you decide to skip the chapter because you don't know PowerShell, you'll be happy to know that the module does not require any experience with it. In fact you can simply use all of the out-of-the-box features without writing a single line of code.

First we have integration points that tap into features like the Content Editor (Ribbons, Gutters, Content Editor Warnings, Context Menus, etc.). These integration points provide you with the ability to save a ton of time in both prototyping and delivering the solution. Did somebody say, "No downtime"? We'll cover the tools that require no coding then move on to how you can add your own.

Second, we have maintenance tasks that can be authored and performed through the command-line interface (known as the "console"), the integrated scripting environment (known as the "ISE"), run automatically from a scheduled task, or perhaps through one of the integration points previously mentioned.

Finally, we have a Windows PowerShell module (available for any Windows desktop or server) that allows you to interact with the Sitecore instance remotely. This is most commonly used in a Continuous Integration (CI) setup where you need to deploy packages to your Sitecore instance from a remote machine. You may even use this module to download/upload media items, migrate content, or anything else you can think up.

© Phil Wicklund and Jason Wilkerson 2016
P. Wicklund and J. Wilkerson, *Professional Sitecore 8 Development*, DOI 10.1007/978-1-4842-2292-8_10

■ **Note**   In 2010 Adam Najmanowicz had a brilliant idea to bring the power of Windows PowerShell to
the Sitecore platform and in 2013 Michael West joined the team. Through years of late hours and numerous
contributions from the community, the module has grown to be a powerful module that many Sitecore
developers incorporate into their development toolset.

Installing the PowerShell Extensions

Getting started, there are a few items you'll want to verify before we can dig into the details of the module.

Prerequisites

There are three prerequisites you must have before you can get started:

1. Module downloaded from the Sitecore marketplace:

    `https://marketplace.sitecore.net/Modules/Sitecore_PowerShell_console`

    There are a number of packages available to choose from which support Sitecore 7 and 8. This book will
use the latest and greatest Sitecore 8 packages. Be sure to unblock all of the newly download ZIP files.

    - *Standard*: Sitecore PowerShell Extensions-4.0 for Sitecore 8.zip (download now)

    - *Lightweight*: SPE Minimal-4.0 for Sitecore 8.zip

    - *Remoting*: SPE Remoting-4.0.zip (download now)

2. Windows PowerShell 3.0 or newer is installed (Windows 10 comes
    preloaded with 5.0+):

    `http://bit.ly/1OzPYfe`

3. Sitecore 7 or newer installed and ready for use.

    For the remainder of the chapter, we'll cover usage with Sitecore 8. If you are still using Sitecore 7, the
steps will pretty much be identical. Installation of SPE is just like any other module found on the Sitecore
marketplace. If you haven't already, set aside some time later to explore the marketplace where you'll find
modules built by some smart people.

Installation Wizard

If you haven't already, download the standard installation package listed in the prerequisites section named
Sitecore PowerShell Extensions-4.0 for Sitecore 8.zip. If a newer version is available download that instead.

1. Beginning with the Sitecore desktop, navigate to the Installation wizard by selecting Sitecore ➤ Development Tools ➤ Installation Wizard (see Figure 10-1).

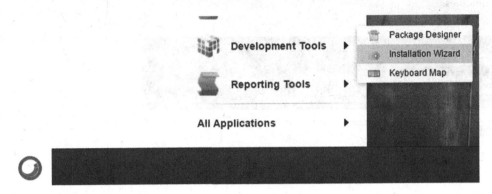

Figure 10-1. *Installation wizard*

2. Once you're presented with the wizard, choose to upload a package (see Figure 10-2).

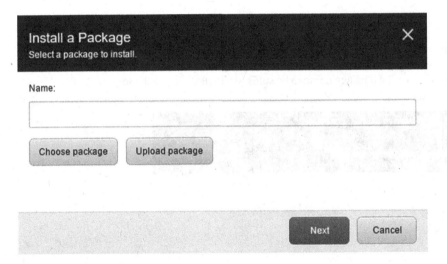

Figure 10-2. *Installing a package*

3. The Upload Files dialog (see Figure 10-3) gives you the option of uploading one or more packages. This can be a time-saver when you're setting up several modules.

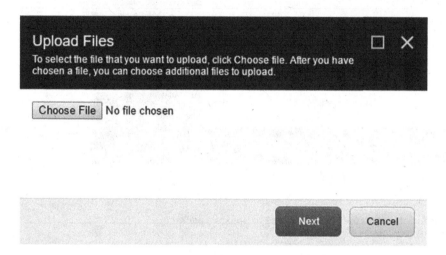

Figure 10-3. *Upload Files window*

4. After selecting all the files you want uploaded, decide whether or not to overwrite existing packages that have matching filenames (see Figure 10-4). Not selecting this option will force the package name to be suffixed with 001, 002, 003, etc.

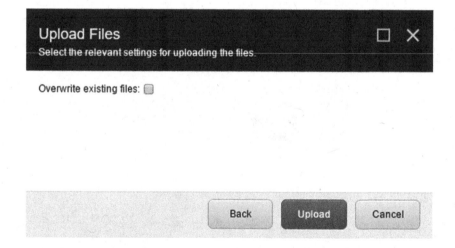

Figure 10-4. *Upload files with overwrite*

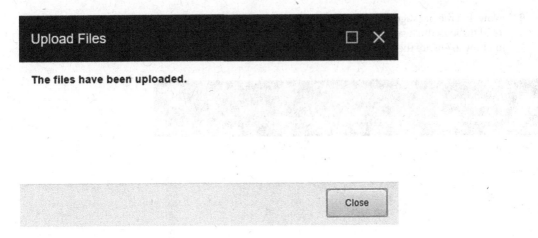

Upload Files □ ✕

The files have been uploaded.

Close

Figure 10-5. *Upload files confirmation*

5. Selecting the Choose Package option provides a list of packages that have been previously uploaded. Since we just uploaded the SPE package, you'll see in the list (see Figure 10-6).

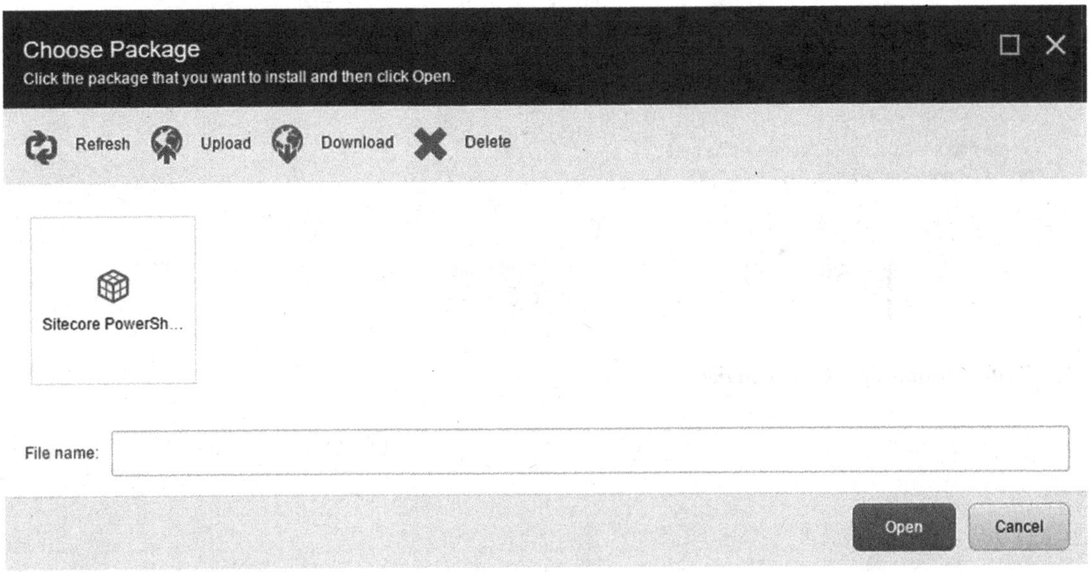

Choose Package □ ✕
Click the package that you want to install and then click Open.

🔄 Refresh   🎗 Upload   🌐 Download   ✖ Delete

📦
Sitecore PowerSh...

File name:

Open   Cancel

Figure 10-6. *Choose the package*

6. Now that the package is uploaded, we can begin the installation. Make sure you read through the Read Me (see Figure 10-7), as it contains very important details on how to ensure the modules works as expected. Click Install (see Figure 10-8).

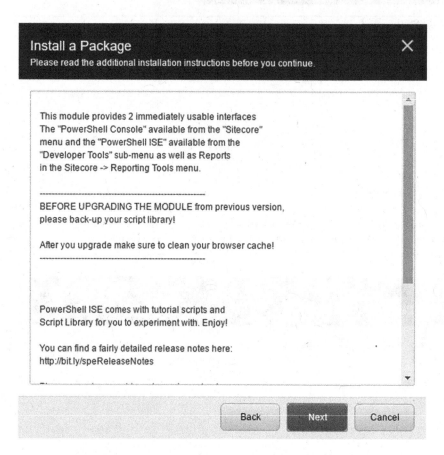

Figure 10-7. Install a package read me

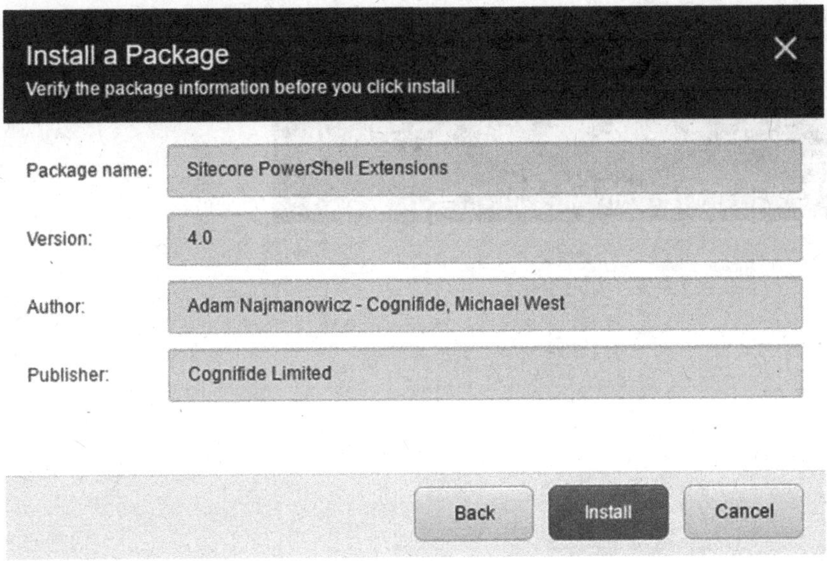

Install a Package   ✕
Verify the package information before you click install.

Package name:	Sitecore PowerShell Extensions
Version:	4.0
Author:	Adam Najmanowicz - Cognifide, Michael West
Publisher:	Cognifide Limited

Back   Install   Cancel

Figure 10-8. *Install a package version*

In the event of a package upgrade or reinstallation, you may encounter a few dialogs that prompt for overwriting files and items. Figure 10-9 is an example of particular file that previously exists. There is another dialog not shown which allows you to overwrite, skip, or merge items.

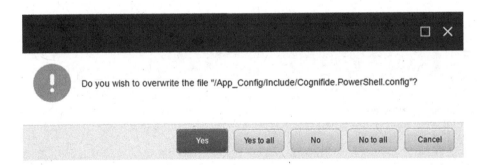

!   Do you wish to overwrite the file "/App_Config/Include/Cognifide.PowerShell.config"?

Yes   Yes to all   No   No to all   Cancel

Figure 10-9. *Overwrite file confirmation*

Don't be alarmed if you see the installation progress screen spin until you get dizzy (see Figure 10-10). Some packages may have many files and items that take the server a while to process.

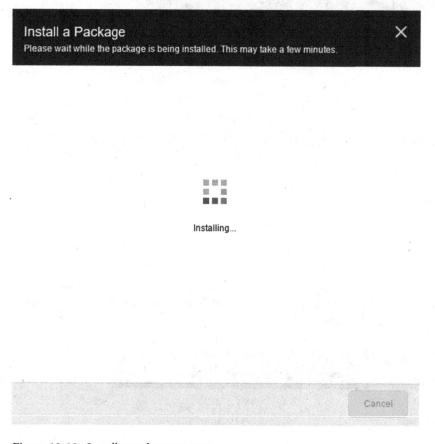

Figure 10-10. *Install a package progress*

7. Finally the package is installed. The last dialog prompts you to restart the Sitecore client, which pretty much refreshes the page. Any open windows such as the Content Editor are closed. See Figure 10-11.

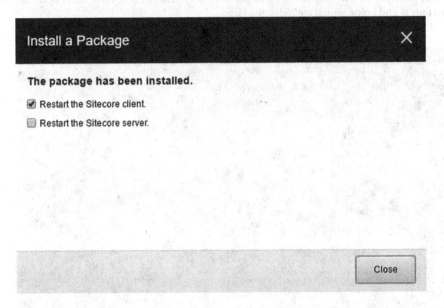

Figure 10-11. Install a package restart

Don't forget to follow any of the post installation steps outlined in the module documentation shown in the read me. If you are curious about where the uploaded packages went, a default Sitecore installation puts it somewhere on the server outside the Website folder. If you know where that is, check out the sibling folder, Data, which contains a Packages folder.

■ **Note** The SPE team has put together a user guide and developer cookbook. If you run into any issues during the installation or want to explore more of the nitty gritty details of SPE, you can check out the links at the end of the chapter.

Module Highlights

Let's have a look at some of the features that come out of the box. The following new shortcuts have been added to the Sitecore menu:

- Sitecore ➤ PowerShell Console
- Sitecore ➤ PowerShell Toolbox
- Sitecore ➤ Development Tools ➤ PowerShell ISE
- Sitecore ➤ Reporting Tools ➤ PowerShell Reports

Take a few moments after reading each of the following sections to view the interfaces for yourself.

PowerShell Console

Let's first have a look at the PowerShell Console (see Figure 10-12). I went ahead and increased the font size from the default for my user profile in SPE to help when I give presentations. There are several other options configurable such as font family and color, which we'll discuss later.

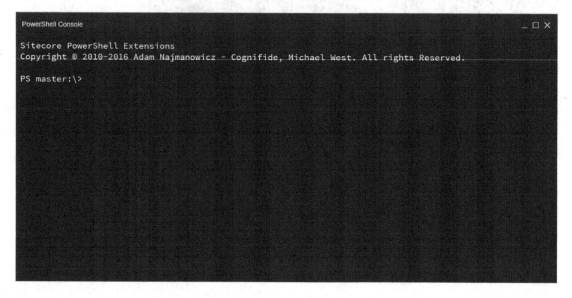

Figure 10-12. *The PowerShell console*

The PowerShell Console is a command-line interface (CLI) that many power users find helpful when needing to quickly run commands. While running PowerShell commands are at the heart of SPE, we won't dive too deep right away since this is still an introduction to the module.

PowerShell ISE

Next we have the integrated scripting environment commonly referred to as the PowerShell ISE (see Figure 10-13). You essentially get a fancy text editor with syntax highlighting, autocomplete, and many other nice features. Most SPE users developing scripts will go straight here for their scripting needs. You open, save, and execute saved scripts through this interface.

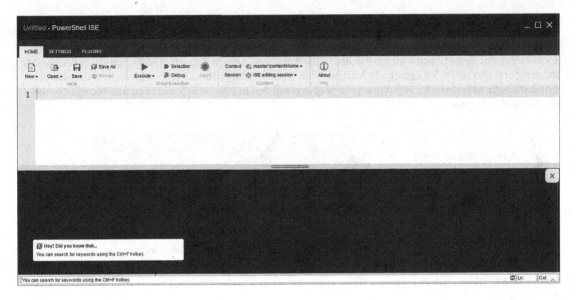

Figure 10-13. *PowerShell ISE*

PowerShell Toolbox

Moving on to the next item of interest is the PowerShell Toolbox (see Figure 10-14). These shortcuts offer a convenient way to run tools built on the SPE platform. At a glance, you can see that these may come in handy.

Figure 10-14. *PowerShell Toolbox*

PowerShell Reports

Last but not least we have a series of PowerShell Reports bundled and made visible through the Reporting Tools menu. For those of you who have heard of the Advanced System Reporter (ASR), you know how handy those reports can be. We've essentially built our own reporting tool within Sitecore, giving you the ability to tweak the logic as you see fit. The reports are of course written in PowerShell and even pair nicely with the Sitecore Rules Engine.

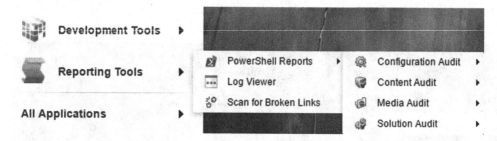

Figure 10-15. *PowerShell Reports*

Out-of-the-Box SPE Features

Earlier I made claims that you can get some quick wins after installing SPE; therefore, in this section I'll do my best to back those claims up.

Bundled Tools

The PowerShell Toolbox is a convenient way to expose tools for power users and content editors. The tools bundled with SPE are both useful and a great example for those whom desire to create their own. Let's have a look at a few of those tools.

Index Viewer

Have you found yourself needing to quickly query the Sitecore index but would rather avoid installing any special applications on your workstation or on the server? The Index Viewer runs in your Sitecore instance and takes advantage of the Content Search API.

After selecting the Index Viewer shortcut, you'll be prompted (see Figure 10-16) with a dialog for selecting which index to query. The master index is typically a good place to start since Content Editors are managing their content there.

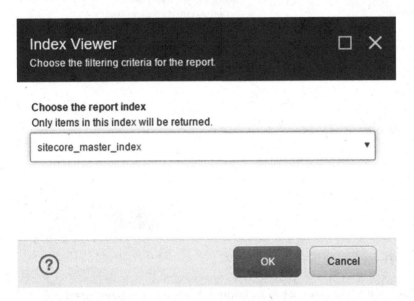

Figure 10-16. Index Viewer report index

The criteria section (see Figure 10-17) is a little busy but shows merely a subset of available options to a developer when querying the index. Using the default settings, you'll receive the top 25 entries with a paged result.

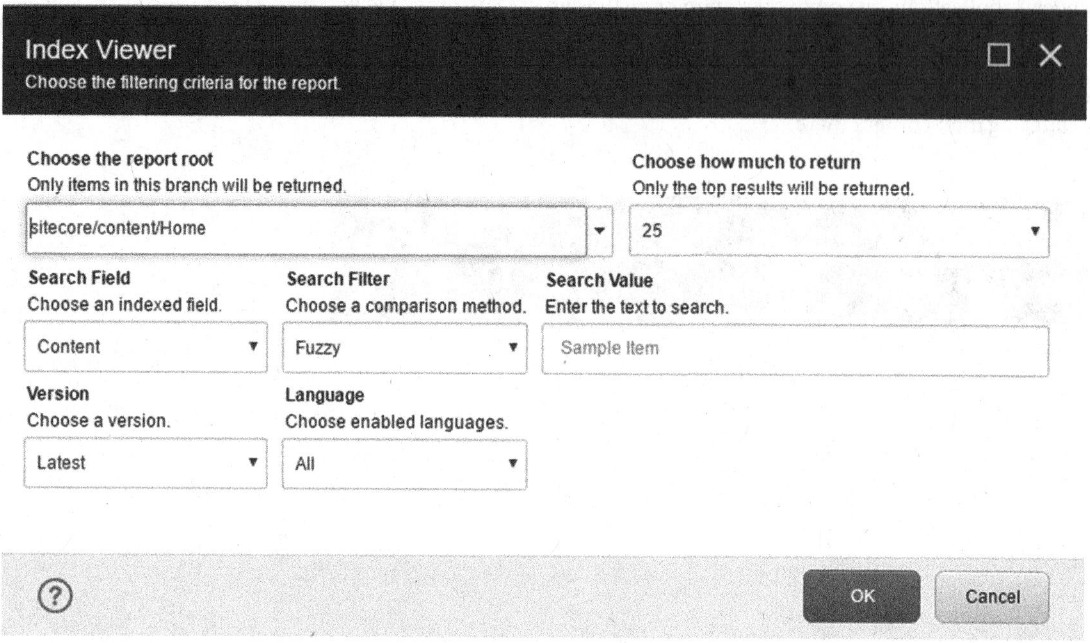

Figure 10-17. *Index Viewer report criteria*

The report reviewer (see Figure 10-18) has several helpful features. The results can be exported and downloaded into a variety of formats, open the indexed item, or even rebuild the index.

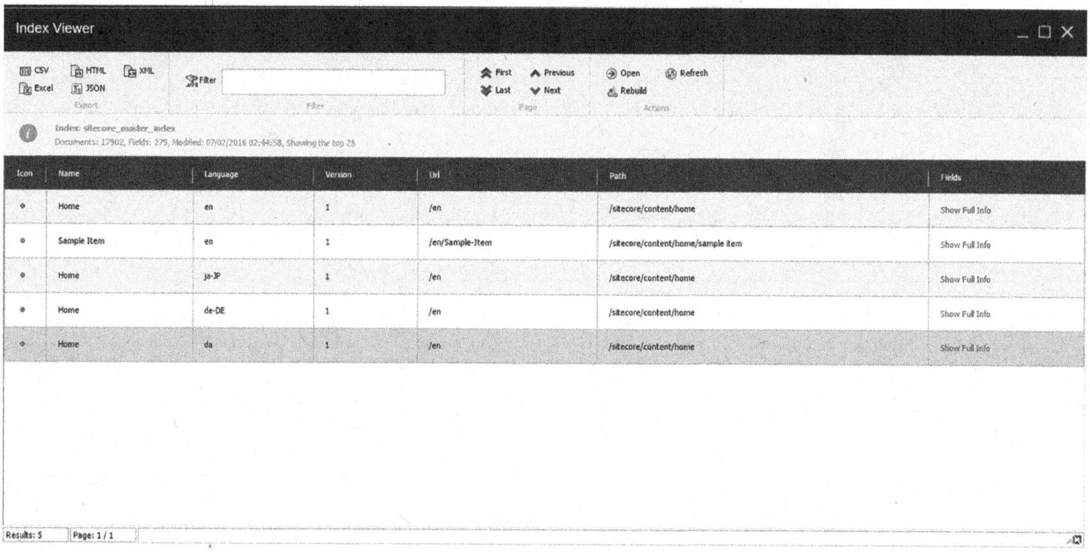

Figure 10-18. *Index Viewer report results*

Double-click an item in the table to see the Content Editor open and navigate to the item in the tree. If you just want to see some of the indexed data for the item, click the Show Full Info link (see Figure 10-19).

Figure 10-19. *Index Viewer report fields viewer*

You may not be too familiar with what all this data is but it won't be long before you need to know it. The dialog displays all of the fields stored in the search index and may prove helpful when troubleshooting search queries.

Rules Based Report

The Sitecore Rules Engine is one of the many powerful features built into Sitecore. The simplicity of the Rules Engine made building the Rules Based Report fairly straight forward. After selecting the Rules Based Report shortcut, you'll be prompted with a dialog (see Figure 10-20) for selecting the starting point for the search and an option to specify the rules.

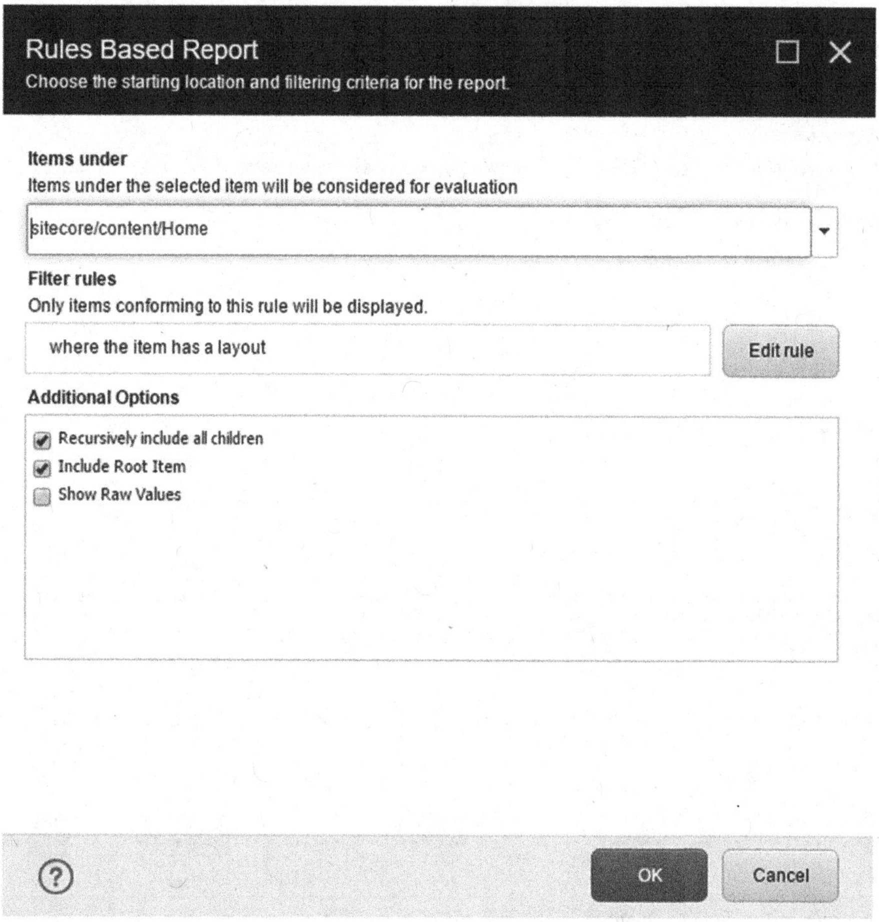

Figure 10-20. *Rules Based Report filter*

By default, the rule filters all items that have a layout. Edit the rule if you want to use different filtering criteria (see Figure 10-21).

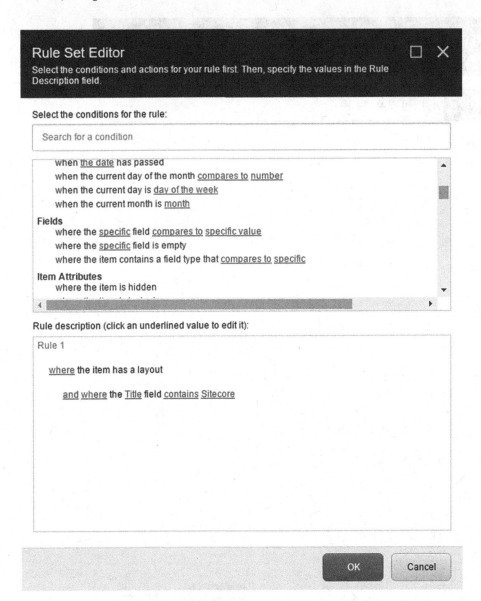

Figure 10-21. *Rules based report rule editor*

In Figure 10-21, you can see that I added a filter based on the title field. Continuing on, we can see more of the options available for the report (see Figure 10-22).

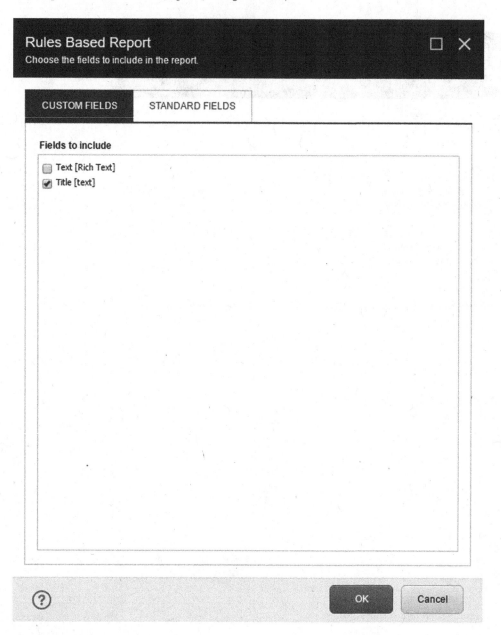

Figure 10-22. *Rules based report fields*

As you can see, I've elected to include the title field in the report. Continuing from here, we finally get our reports back (see Figure 10-23). Simple yet powerful.

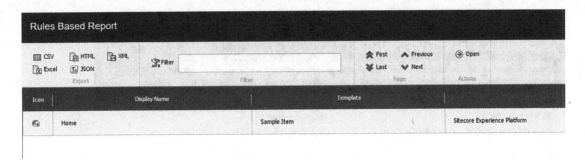

Figure 10-23. *Rules based report results*

Task Manager

The Task Manager tool provides an interface (see Figure 10-24) for running scheduled tasks on-demand as well as configuring the execution frequency.

Icon	Name	Last Run	Command	Start Date	End Date	Days of the Week	Frequency
	__Task Schedule	Never		Beginning of Time	Forever		
	Calculate Statistical Relevancy	Never	Calculate Statistical Relevancy	Beginning of Time	1/1/1900 12:00:00 AM	Everyday	1.00:00
	Rebuild Suggested Tests Index	7/2/2016 2:44:57 AM	Rebuild Suggested Tests Index	1/1/2014 12:00:00 AM	1/1/9999 12:00:00 AM	Everyday	1.00:00
	Suspend Corrupted Tests	7/2/2016 2:44:57 AM	Suspend Corrupted Tests	1/1/2015 12:00:00 AM	1/1/9999 12:00:00 AM	Everyday	1.00:00
	Try Finish Test	7/2/2016 2:44:58 AM	Try Finish Test	1/1/2014 12:00:00 AM	1/1/9999 12:00:00 AM	Everyday	1.00:00

Figure 10-24. *The Task Manager*

You can edit or execute any selected entry right from the Task Manager. Choosing to edit will produce the configuration dialog (see Figure 10-25). The schedule field in Sitecore is stored as a single line text, so SPE provides a nice improvement over 20140101|99990101|127|1.00:00.

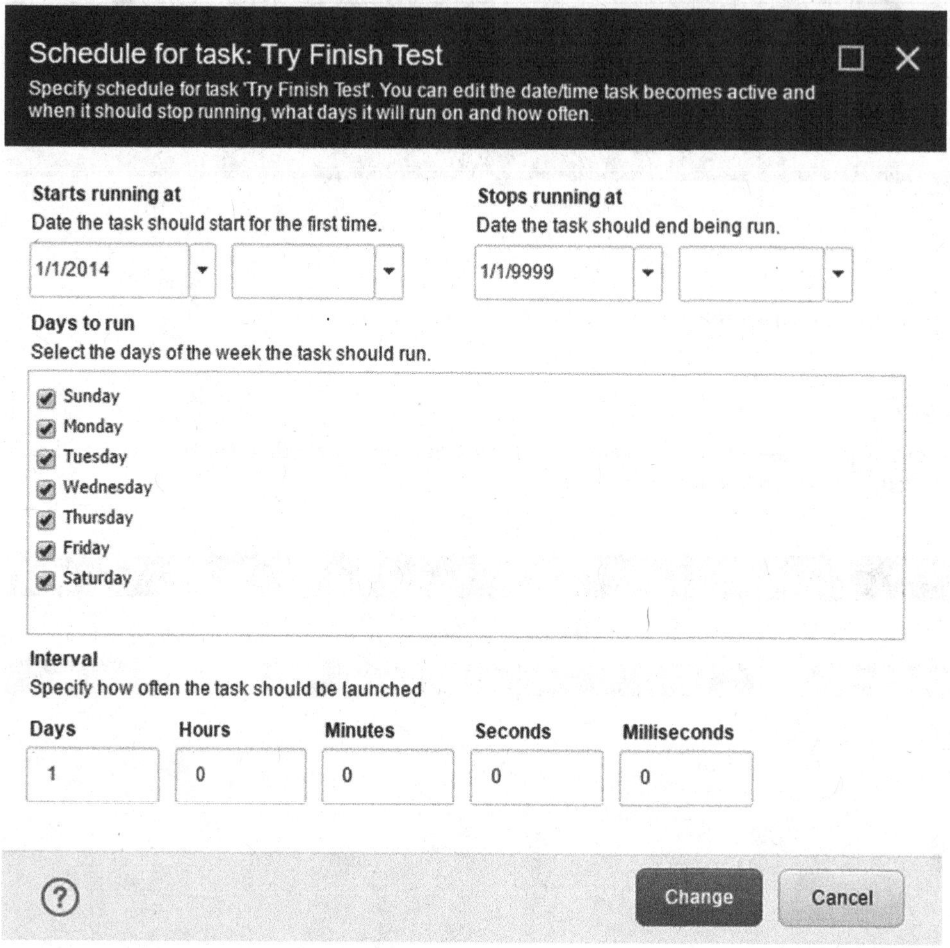

Figure 10-25. *Task Manager schedule configuration*

Audit Reports

There will no doubt be a need to audit your Sitecore solution so any help you can get will avoid unnecessary headaches. The SPE audit reports help Content Editors and Admins with some of the maintenance tasks that without them would not be cost effective. Many of the bundled reports provide information that would be nearly impossible to do manually. There are far too many reports to cover in this section, so we'll take a look at the top two.

Locked Items

The Locked Items report (see Figures 10-26 and 10-27) helps in locating items that are checked out by all users or a specified user. The title of the report dialog can be whatever custom text you choose. Without specifying a title the dialog will simply say PowerShell Scripts Results.

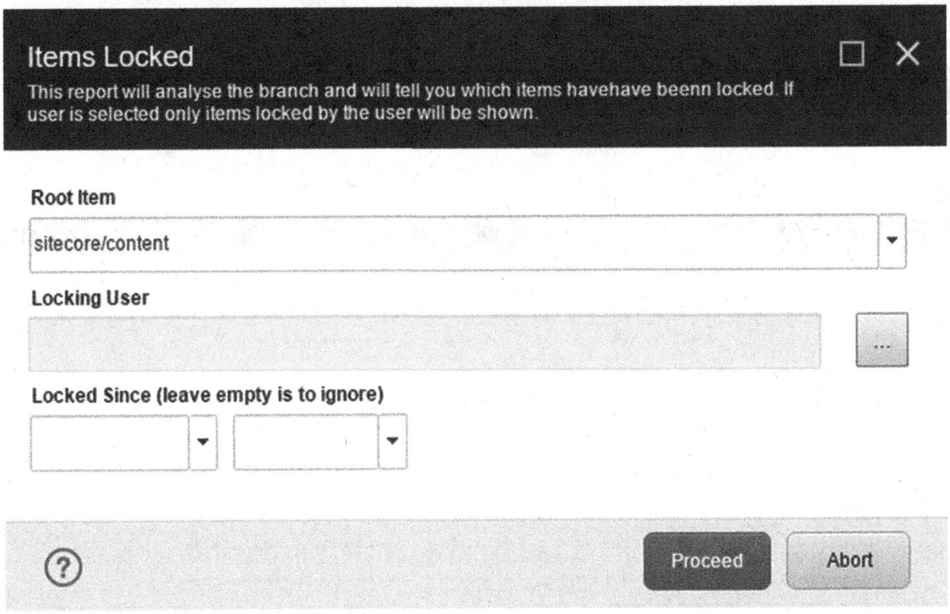

Figure 10-26. *Locked items filter*

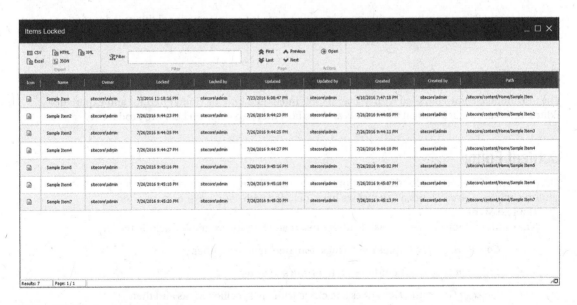

Figure 10-27. *Locked items report*

Unused Media Items

The Unused Media Items report locates items contained in the media library that are not referenced by any other items. You can save quite a bit of space in your database when using this report. The report makes some assumptions about where to start in the media library. In a multi-tenant solution you may have a need to duplicate the report and include a filter for the tenants. You may also decide to filter for types, sizes, or age of the unused items.

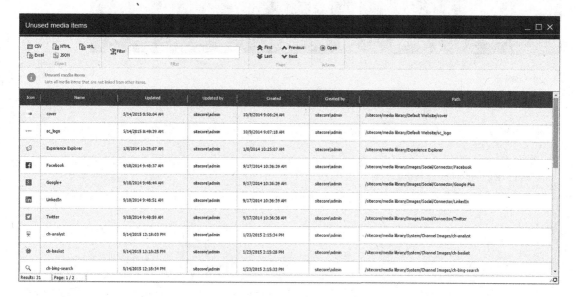

Figure 10-28. *Unused media items*

In this report, not only has the title been specified, but also an informational title and description as can be seen beneath the export commands.

Bonus Features

The SPE module comes bundled with a several tools integrated into the Content Editor and Experience Editor. Let's take a quick tour on those tools and see how they can help you be more productive.

Content Editor

The CE is one of the most utilized applications in Sitecore. There are so many integrations possible that we couldn't help ourselves. Here's a few that we have included with your free purchase of SPE.

Context Menu

The Context Menu entries are visible under Insert and Scripts. Examples include the following:

- *Copy Renderings*: Copies renderings from one item to another.

- *Index On Demand*: Reindexes an item and subitems.

- *Package Generator*: Generates a package with the specified items and then downloads them.

Gutter

The Gutter notifications are visible on the far left column of the tree just like any other Gutter integration. Examples include the following:

- *Publishing Status Gutter*: Provides an indicator of whether an item has been publish in all, some, or none of the publishing targets. The flag colors specify the publishing status.

Content Editor Warning

The warning is visible on the selected item just like any other warning just above the Quick Info section. Examples include the following:

- *License Expiration*: Notifies the user that their Sitecore license is about to expire.

Experience Editor

The EE is a powerful application that Sitecore is investing considerable amount of development time on. Here we will cover the available integrations bundled in SPE.

Notification

Like the CE warning we have a similar notification for page designers. Examples include the following:

- *License Expiration*: Notifies the user that their Sitecore license is about to expire.

Programming Sitecore with PowerShell

The following sections describe how SPE solves whole classes of problems for the developer. Each of the integration points with Sitecore can be implemented in a fraction of the time that traditional development would take. Dare I say hours and not days! All ye who keep reading will no longer be the same.

We covered some clever features included in the default installation of SPE and while reading you may have also thought of a few ways that they could be altered to better meet the needs of your projects. First we'll go over some of the basic concepts of Windows PowerShell and then dive right into building a custom module in SPE.

Learning PowerShell as a Language

Since you have come this far in the chapter, I'll assume that you have a good understanding of the Microsoft .Net Framework and how to write code in C#. PowerShell really isn't all that different. Sure, the syntax is a little different but at the end of the day you can basically perform all of the same tasks.

Language Syntax

Table 10-1 shows a side-by-side comparison of code written in C# and PowerShell in order to give you a basic comparison of syntaxes. As you can see, the language syntaxes are not all that different. Within a few minutes you might even be able to translate code from your library classes into SPE scripts.

Table 10-1. *Side-By-Side Comparison of C# and PowerShell*

Microsoft .NET C#	Windows PowerShell
`// Assign data to a new variable` `var name = "Michael";`	`# Assign data to a new variable` `$name = "Michael"`
`// Perform simple math` `var total = 1 + 1;`	`# Perform simple math` `$total = 1 + 1`

`// Create a new list of strings`
`var names = new List<string>();`
`names.Add("Michael");`
`names.Add("Adam");`
`// Create a hashtable of data`
`var table = new Hashtable();`
`table["Name"] = "Michael";`
`table["Age"] = 33;`
	`# Create a new list of strings`
	`$names = @()`
	`$names += "Michael"`
	`$names += "Adam"`
	`# Create a new hashtable of data`
	`$table = @{}`
	`$table["Name"] = "Michael"`
	`$table["Age"] = 33`

`// Check if the string is null or empty`
`using a static method`
`if(string.IsNullOrEmpty(name)) { ... }`
	`# Check if the string is null or empty using a`
	`static method`
	`if([string]::IsNullOrEmpty($name)) { ... }`

`/*`
`Create a comment block`
`*/`
	`<#`
	`Create a comment block`
	`#>`

`// Loop through a list of strings` `foreach(var name in names) { ... }`	`# Loop through a list of strings` `foreach($name in $names) { ... }`

`// Compare values`
`name == "Michael"`
`total <= 3`
`names.Count() > 2 && name[0] != "Adam"`
	`# Compare values`
	`$name -eq "Michael" # case-insensitive`
	`$total -le 3`
	`$names.Count() -gt 2 -and $name[0] -ne "Adam"`

`// Negate value`
`var isTrue = !false;`
	`# Negate value`
	`$isTrue = !$false`
	`$isTrue = -not $false`

`// String interpolation` `var message = $"Hello, {name}";`	`# String interpolation` `$message = "Hello, $($name)"`
`// Access static property` `var today = DateTime.Today;`	`# Access static property` `$today = [datetime]::Today`

Commands

Another interesting thing about Windows PowerShell is the use of commands, often called cmdlets ("command-lets") or functions. Let's have a look at some basic usage syntaxes for commands. For example, the following provides an example syntax for a fake command:

```
Get-Something [[-SomeParameter] <sometype[]>] [-AnotherParameter <anothertype>]
[-SomeSwitch]
```

PowerShell commands follow a verb-noun syntax. Notice that all properly named commands start with a verb such as Get, Set, or Remove and end with a noun such as Item, User, or Role.

The verbs are considered "approved" if they align with those that Microsoft recommends. See https://msdn.microsoft.com/en-us/library/ms714428(v=vs.85).aspx for a list of approved verbs and a brief explanation on why they were chosen. They are intended to be pretty generic so they apply for multiple contexts like the file system, registry, and even Sitecore!

The noun in the command should be singular even if the command returns more than one object.

The parameters follow the command and usually require arguments. In the previous example, we have a parameter called SomeParameter followed by an argument of type SomeType. The final parameter, called SomeSwitch, is called a switch. The switch is like a flag that enables or disables behavior for the command. The example in Listing 10-1 provides possible permutations of the fake command.

■ **Note**   The brackets surrounding the parameter and the brackets immediately following a type have different meanings. The former has to do with optional usage whereas the latter indicates the data can be an array of objects.

Listing 10-1. Example Issuing Some Commands

```
<#
All of the parameters in the command are surrounded by square brackets indicating they are
optional.
#>
Get-Something


<#
SomeParameter has double brackets around the parameter name and argument indicating the name
is optional and when an argument is passed the name can be skipped.
#>
Get-Something  "data"


<#
AnotherParameter has single brackets indicating that the parameter is optional. If the
argument is used so must the name. The same reasoning can be applied to the switch.
#>
Get-Something "data","data2" -AnotherParameter 100 –SomeSwitch
```

■ **Tip**   Allow scripts to be written with the full command and parameter names. Avoid relying on positional or optional parameters. Avoid abbreviating parameter names. Avoid using command aliases (e.g., dir and cd).

Some of the most useful commands to learn are shown in Table 10-2.

Table 10-2. *Common PowerShell Commands You Should Familiarize Yourself With*

Command	Description
Get-Item	Returns an object at the specified path.
Get-ChildItem	Returns children at the specified path. Supports recursion.
Get-Help	Returns the help documentation for the specified command or document.
Get-Command	Returns a list of commands.
ForEach-Object	Enumerates over the objects passed through the pipeline.
Where-Object	Enumerates over the objects passed through the pipeline and filters objects.
Select-Object	Returns objects from the pipeline with the specified properties and filters objects.
Sort-Object	Sorts the pipeline objects with the specified criteria; usually a property name.
Get-Member	Returns the methods and properties for the specified object.

■ **Note** PowerShell was designed so that after learning a few concepts you can get up and running. Once you get past the basics, you should be able to understand most scripts included with SPE.

Pipelines

PowerShell supports chaining of commands through a feature called "pipelines" using the pipe symbol |. This is similar to Sitecore in that you can short-circuit the processing of objects using Where-Object. Let's have a look at a few examples. Listing 10-2 queries a Sitecore item and removes it.

Listing 10-2. Example Querying an Item and Removing It

```
# The remove command accepts pipeline input.
Get-Item -Path "master:\content\home\sample item" | Remove-Item

# If multiple items are passed through the pipeline each are removed individually.
$items | Remove-Item
```

PowerShell also comes with a set of useful commands for filtering and sorting. Let's see those in action. Listing 10-3 queries a tree of Sitecore items and returns only those that meet the criteria. The item properties are reduced and then sorted.

Listing 10-3. Example Querying for Items, Filtering Down the Results

```
# Use variables for parameters such as paths to make scripts easier to read.
$path = "master:\content\home\"

Get-ChildItem -Path $path -Recurse |
    Where-Object { $_.Name -like "*Sitecore*" } |
    Select-Object -Property Name, ItemPath, ID
    Sort-Object -Property Name
```

■ **Tip**   A best practice in PowerShell is to reduce the number of objects passed through the pipeline as far left as possible. While the example would work if the Sort-Object command came before Where-Object, we will see a performance improvement because the sorting has fewer objects to worry about. Some commands such as Get-ChildItem support additional options for filtering, which further improves performance.

Listing 10-4 demonstrates how commands can be written clearly with little confusion on the intent, then how aliases and abbreviations can get in the way. Always think about the developer that comes after you to maintain the code.

Listing 10-4. Example Simplifying Some Commands to Reduce Code and Complexity

```
# Longhand
Get-Command -Name ForEach-Object -Type cmdlet | Select-Object -ExpandProperty ParameterSets

# Shorthand
gcm -na foreach-object -ty cmdlet | select -exp parametersets
```

Windows PowerShell is bundled with a ton of documentation that could not possible be included with this book; we can however show you how to access it. Listing 10-5 demonstrate ways to get help...with PowerShell.

Listing 10-5. Example Getting Help with Commands You're Unfamiliar With

```
# Displays all of the about help documents.
help about_*

# Displays help documentation on the topic of Splatting.
help about_Splatting

# Displays help documentation on the specified command.
help Get-Member
```

■ **Tip**   PowerShell does not include the complete help documentation by default on Windows. Run the command update-help from an elevated prompt to update the help files to the latest available version. See help update-help for more information on the command syntax and details of its use. All of the SPE help documentation is available regardless of running update-help.

Providers

The provider architecture in PowerShell enables a developer to make a command like Get-Item interact with the file system files and folders, and then interact with the Sitecore CMS items. The SPE module implements a new provider that bridges the Windows PowerShell platform with the Sitecore API. Table 10-3 demonstrates the use of Get-Item for a variety of providers.

345

Table 10-3. *The Many Uses of Get-Item*

Name	Drives	Example
Alias	Alias	`Get-Item -Path alias:\dir`
CmsItemProvider	core, master, web	`Get-Item -Path master:\`
Environment	Env	`Get-Item -Path env:\HOMEPATH`
FileSystem	C, D, F, H	`Get-Item -Path c:\Windows`
Function	Function	`Get-Item -Path function:\prompt`
Registry	HKLM, HKCU	`Get-Item -Path hklm:\SOFTWARE`
Variable	Variable	`Get-Item -Path variable:\PSVersionTable`

The default provider used by the PowerShell Console and ISE is the `CmsItemProvider` with the drive set to the master database. Listing 10-6 demonstrates switching between providers using the function `cd`, an alias for `Set-Location`, while in the Console.

Listing 10-6. Example Switching Between Providers

```
PS master:\> cd c:\
PS C:\> cd hklm:
PS HKLM:\> cd env:
PS Env:\>
```

■ **Note**   You may have noticed that the C drive is the only path in which a backslash was used before changing drives. Leaving off the backslash will result in the path changing to `C:\windows\system32\inetsrv`. This similar behavior can be experienced while in the Windows PowerShell Console, where the path is changed to `C:\Windows\System32`.

Moving forward, we'll focus on the provider used to access Sitecore content, since that is what this book is all about.

Components of SPE

Now that you have seen an overview of Windows PowerShell we can take a deeper dive into how PowerShell is incorporated into Sitecore through integration points. Think of these integration points as a generic implementation of each major feature (e.g. Context Menu, Gutter, and Warning), which calls a PowerShell script.

The SPE module stores its settings and scripts under the System Modules root. Let's have a quick look at the top level elements distributed by the package.

- *PowerShell*: Root node for SPE.

  - *Console Colors*: Provides the options for background and foreground colors in the UI.

  - *Fonts*: provides The options for the font family in the UI.

  - *Script Library:* Root node for the SPE modules.

  - *Settings*: Container for the user settings applied in the UI.

Now let's break down the structure of an SPE module.

- *Module*: Container for the PowerShell script libraries and scripts.

  - *PowerShell Script Library:* Container for more PowerShell script libraries and scripts.

    - *PowerShell Script:* Container for executable code.

Modules

The module structure allows for developers to package up self-contained bundles of PowerShell scripts. Modules are portable and can be disabled. Later on in the chapter we will see how disabling the module impacts the user experience. The term module is shared between Sitecore module packages and SPE modules; while in the context of SPE a module will be the root node.

Script Libraries

After modules come the script libraries. Many of the script libraries seen in SPE are generated as part of the integration points mentioned earlier. For example, the script library "Toolbox" is tied to an integration point made visible through the Sitecore shortcut menu. When you follow the conventions outlined by the integration points, you get some really cool behaviors without much effort. Script libraries are Rules Engine-aware, allowing you to show and enable scripts contained in a library wherever they are used.

Scripts

Scripts makeup the building blocks for SPE because they contain the executable code. Whenever we talk of running scripts in Sitecore through SPE, there is usually an item in a script library that corresponds with the script.

Scripts are Rules Engine-aware, allowing you to skip execution when the conditions are not met. The rules are configured just like those in the script library but less about visibility and more about execution. Integration points that impact the user experience can see a dramatic performance improvement when rules are configured to limit the scope of execution.

Building Your First Module

The previous sections have prepared you for this moment. You are about to embark on a journey to build your own SPE module. We will cover a few interesting integration points and leave you to explore the rest. The following integration points will be covered:

- Content Editor:

- Context Menu: Display a message to the user that gives the number of immediate children of the selected item.

- Ribbon: Display a ribbon command to the user that triggers a download of the latest log file. The command should only appear when the current user is an administrator.

- Reports: Provide a report that audits the content for unprocessed tokens in the title and text fields. The report should be displayed to the user while logged into Sitecore.

- Tasks: Configure a scheduled task for running, exporting, and e-mailing the token report.

In order to get things going you'll want to navigate to the location where Sitecore modules store their content. Beginning inside the Content Editor, navigate through the content tree to the System Modules item at the path /sitecore/system/Modules (see Figure 10-29). Most community modules found on the Sitecore marketplace add items here as well.

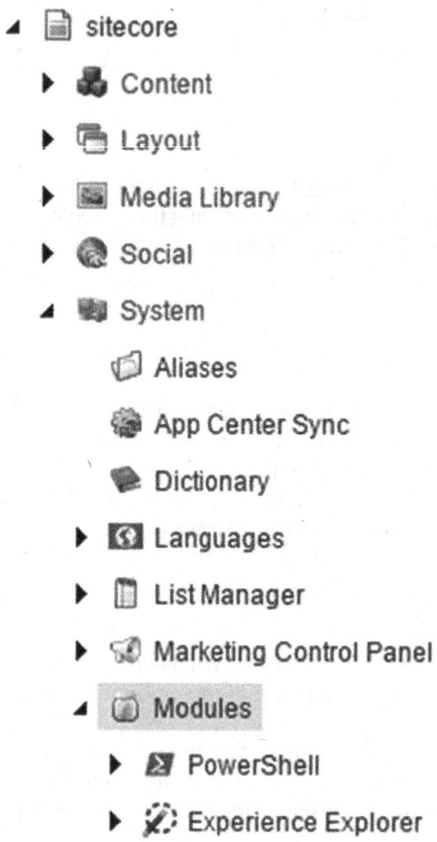

▲ 🗋 sitecore

   ▶ 🎲 Content

   ▶ 🗐 Layout

   ▶ 🖼 Media Library

   ▶ 🌐 Social

   ▲ 🗄 System

       🗇 Aliases

       🗐 App Center Sync

       📚 Dictionary

       ▶ 🇸 Languages

       ▶ 📋 List Manager

       ▶ 📢 Marketing Control Panel

       ▲ 📦 Modules

          ▶ ⚡ PowerShell

          ▶ 🌀 Experience Explorer

Figure 10-29. *Modules tree*

As you can see from Figure 10-19, SPE has provided an item called PowerShell. Expanding the tree further, we can see some of the key areas of configuration for SPE (see Figure 10-31).

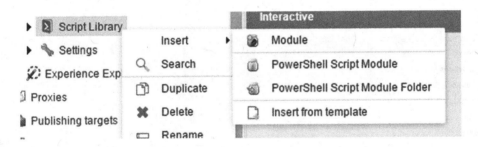

Figure 10-30. *PowerShell module tree*

The Console Colors, Fonts, and Settings items pertain to visual configuration settings for the PowerShell Console, PowerShell ISE, and PowerShell Results dialogs; these settings can be managed while in the ISE. For now we'll focus on the Script Library item to create our SPE module.

Right-click the Script Library and Insert a new module (see Figure 10-31).

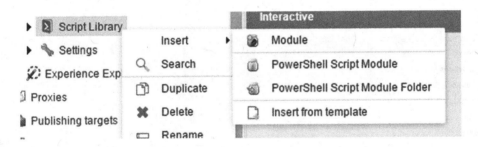

Figure 10-31. *Insert module*

■ **Note**   Some of the integration points selected in the wizard take longer than others to complete due to the number of items needed in the tree. The Event Handlers integration may be the most time consuming.

In Figure 10-32, you can see that modules can be disabled at the time of creation. Each integration is aware of this flag. When modules are disabled the associated shortcuts, context menu commands, ribbon commands, and other features are also disabled.

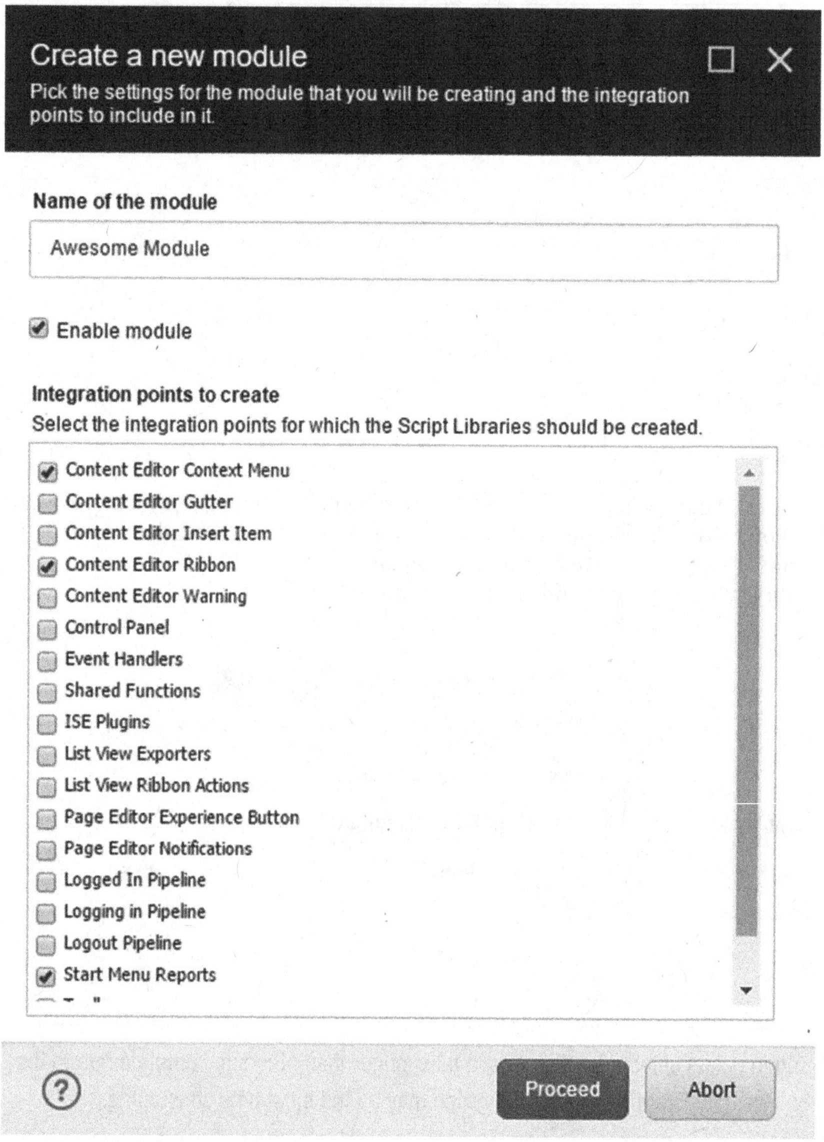

Create a new module

Pick the settings for the module that you will be creating and the integration points to include in it.

Name of the module

Awesome Module

☑ Enable module

Integration points to create

Select the integration points for which the Script Libraries should be created.

- ☑ Content Editor Context Menu
- ☐ Content Editor Gutter
- ☐ Content Editor Insert Item
- ☑ Content Editor Ribbon
- ☐ Content Editor Warning
- ☐ Control Panel
- ☐ Event Handlers
- ☐ Shared Functions
- ☐ ISE Plugins
- ☐ List View Exporters
- ☐ List View Ribbon Actions
- ☐ Page Editor Experience Button
- ☐ Page Editor Notifications
- ☐ Logged In Pipeline
- ☐ Logging in Pipeline
- ☐ Logout Pipeline
- ☑ Start Menu Reports

Proceed   Abort

Figure 10-32. *Create a new module*

The wizard creates items that follow a standard naming convention supported by SPE. While creating them manually is possible, we recommend you use the wizard to help speed it up and avoid typos. Now that the wizard has completed you'll want to expand the tree to /sitecore/system/Modules/PowerShell/Script Library/Awesome Module.

Context Menu

Let's go ahead and create our fancy menu for counting the number of immediate children.

1. Right-click on the /Awesome Module/Content Editor/Context Menu item and Insert a new PowerShell Script named Count Immediate Children.

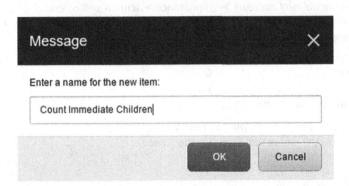

Figure 10-33. Create a new PowerShell script

2. Expand the Context Menu item to reveal the new script. If you were to right-click on it, you'll see the option appear under Scripts.

Figure 10-34. Awesome module scripts menu

■ **Note**   If you were to create nested PowerShell Script Library items, the context menu would duplicate the structure.

In this integration point even the icon of the item will be used in the context menu. Feel free to change that now using a command found in the ribbon Configure ➤ Appearance ➤ Icon. It's often said that the hardest part about Sitecore projects is choosing the right icon. I went ahead and chose the icon Office/32x32/sum.png because we are trying to sum up a number.

3. Copy and paste the code from Listing 10-7 into the Script body field for the Count Immediate Children item.

Listing 10-7. Example Getting the Item Count Below a Certain Path

```
# Within the context of the menu, get the items from the current path.
# In this case the period "." symbolizes the selected item in the tree.
$items = Get-ChildItem -Path .

# There may be zero or more items returned by the Get-ChildItem command.
Show-Alert -Title "The total number of immediate children is: $($items.Count)"

# Dialogs rendered by SPE are automatically closed when using this command.
Close-Window
```

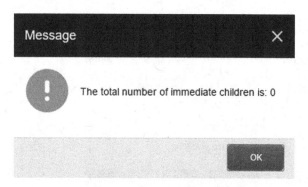

Figure 10-35. *Show context menu alert*

4. Save the item and then right-click on any of the items in the Sitecore tree. After SPE runs the code, you should see a dialog appear showing the number of immediate children.

A powerful part of the SPE module is the interactive dialogs bundled that can be displayed with short bits of code like in this example. The visibility of the context menu may also be controlled using rules saved on the script item. There is a rule field to control button enablement and another rule to control visibility. In the next section, you'll see how to configure a rule to control the visibility for non-administrators.

Ribbon

The ribbon provides a convenient way to interact with Sitecore in both a global and local way. Global in the sense that your ribbon commands can appear all the time and apply to the running instance; as can be seen under Developer ➤ Indexing Tools in which you can rebuild the search index. Local in a way that allows the selected item provide context to the command behavior, as can be seen under Developer ➤ Serialize, in which you can serialize and deserialize items.

Right-click on the /Awesome Module/Content Editor/Ribbon/Developer item and Insert a new PowerShell Script Library named Logging. Then Insert a new PowerShell Script named Download Latest Log.

Expand the Developer item to reveal the new script. To make managing the script library easier, the empty libraries have been removed. To do this, you can right-click on Ribbon then Scripts ➤ Purge Empty Libraries.

▲ 🔵 Awesome Module

  ▲ 🔷 Content Editor

   ▶ 🔷 Context Menu

   ▲ 🔷 Ribbon

    ▲ 🔷 Developer

     ▲ 🔷 Logging

        🔷 Download Latest Log

Figure 10-36. *Awesome module download log ribbon*

This integration point requires an extra step for things to work. Let's begin by opening up the script in the PowerShell ISE. Right-click on the script then choose Edit with ISE.

Once in the PowerShell ISE, select Settings ➤ Integration ➤ Rebuild All to generate the appropriate items in the "core" database to make the button appear in the ribbon. If a new dialog appears describing the script executing results, you can go ahead and close that.

Figure 10-37. *PowerShell ISE ribbon rebuild*

Before we exit the PowerShell ISE, let's go ahead and save the script from Listing 10-8 in the editor.

Listing 10-8. PowerShell to Download a Log

```
$date = Get-Date -Format "yyyyMMdd"
# Skip the first file because the latest is likely locked by the worker process.
$log = Get-ChildItem -Path $SitecoreLogFolder\log.$($date)*.txt |
    Sort-Object -Property LastWriteTime -Descending |
    Select-Object -Skip 1 -First 1
$log | Send-File
```

To save the script changes, either press Ctrl+S or select Home ➤ Write ➤ Save in the ISE ribbon.

Figure 10-38. PowerShell ISE ribbon save

After you change the icon of the script item to Office/32x32/document_notebook.png, the command is now ready for testing.

Figure 10-39. Download latest log ribbon command

Running the command will execute a script to locate the most recently modified log file and prompt downloading right from the Content Editor. Figure 10-40 only displays the filename but can optionally include the full path through configuration in the script.

Figure 10-40. *Download log file*

We should go ahead and configure rules around the visibility of the download command since you may not want all users to have access to the log files.

1. Click on the Download Latest Log item and look for the Interactive field section with the rules.

2. Add a rule to the script by following clicking Edit Rule and searching for administrator.

3. The filtered results should present you with a Security Editor category and a rule that applies only when the current user is an administrator; choose that rule.

4. Click OK to acknowledge the new rule.

5. Save the script item.

6. Confirm the changes by logging into Sitecore with a non-admin user and verifying that the command does not appear.

The example places the command on the Developer tab, which implies that the non-admin user is in the Sitecore\Developer group.

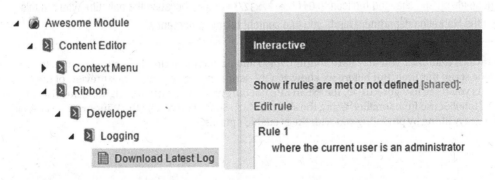

Figure 10-41. *Ribbon command visibility rule*

Now would be a good time to disable the module to see how the context menu and ribbon commands become hidden. The setting is available on the module item under the field section Module Activation; uncheck Enabled and save the item. If you decide to package up the module and distribute on the Sitecore marketplace, consider filling out the other fields such as Author, Description, and What's New!

■ **Note**   Be sure to re-enable the module before proceeding to the next section.

Reports

The reports included with SPE audit content items, media items, and analyzes based on Sitecore recommendations.

Every once in a while you may find that your content contains tokens (e.g., $name, $date) that are not replaced and therefore rendered on the web site. This may happen when a field is reset to the default value configured in the Standard Values template. A web site with hundreds or thousands of pages would require quite a bit of time to locate and replace these tokens with the appropriate information. Fortunately, SPE makes this a more trivial task.

Right-click on the /Awesome Module/Content Editor/Ribbon item and Insert a New PowerShell Script named Items still containing tokens (see Figure 10-42). Now expand the Ribbon item to reveal the new script and then right-click to Edit with ISE (see Figure 10-43).

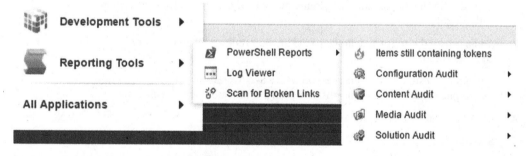

Figure 10-42. *PowerShell report for tokens*

■ **Tip**   If you were to navigate through the Sitecore shortcuts immediately the new report is available. Out of habit I've gone ahead and changed the icon to Office/32x32/fire.png because the only time you run this report is when the Marketing department alerts you to a content related emergency.

In the previous examples, you may have simply copied and pasted the script. I encourage you to try and type out the script this time. But before we show you the script, we'll give you a quick preview of the ISE interface. As you'll see in Figure 10-43, the ISE in SPE not only provides syntax highlighting but also an autocomplete/IntelliSense functionality. Using the shortcut Ctrl+Space you can let the Windows PowerShell engine do the heavy lifting by providing you with the available options.

```
1  $homeRoot = "master:\content\home"
2  $items = Get-ChildItem -Path $homeRoot -R
                                             -Recurse
                                             -ReadOnly
```

Figure 10-43. PowerShell ISE autocomplete

A really cool feature in the ISE is the ability to execute only a portion of the script. As you may have noticed, there is a button labeled Selection that helps make this possible in the ISE. To test it out, highlight the line(s) you want to execute and then click the button shown in Figure 10-44.

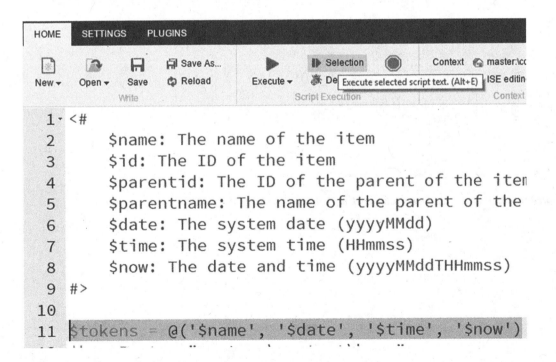

```
1· <#
2      $name: The name of the item
3      $id: The ID of the item
4      $parentid: The ID of the parent of the item
5      $parentname: The name of the parent of the
6      $date: The system date (yyyyMMdd)
7      $time: The system time (HHmmss)
8      $now: The date and time (yyyyMMddTHHmmss)
9  #>
10
11  $tokens = @('$name', '$date', '$time', '$now')
```

Figure 10-44. PowerShell ISE execute selection

Once the script completes, you can now mouse over the variable for tokens to see what it contains. We call this feature "variable peek" (see Figure 10-45).

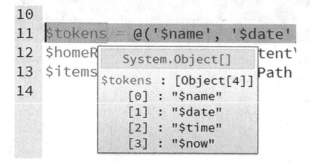

```
10
11  $tokens = @('$name', '$date'
12  $homeR                        tent'
              System.Object[]
13  $items  $tokens : [Object[4]]  Path
14              [0] : "$name"
                [1] : "$date"
                [2] : "$time"
                [3] : "$now"
```

Figure 10-45. *PowerShell ISE variable peek*

■ **Note** The script surrounds the variable names using a single quote. Doing this tells PowerShell to treat it as written (string literal) rather than evaluating the variable before assigning to the array.

Figure 10-46 shows an example when using the double quotes, with the cursor over the variable name.

```
10
11  $tokens = @('$name', '$date',
12  $tokens = @("$name", "$date",
13  $homeRo                       ent\
              System.Object[]
14  $items  $tokens : [Object[4]]  ath
15              [0] : ""
                [1] : ""
                [2] : ""
                [3] : ""
```
You can find more docume...s book.

Figure 10-46. *PowerShell ISE variable peek with double quotes*

Let's have a look at the final report (see Figure 10-47), and then walk through some of the key points of interest in the provided code.

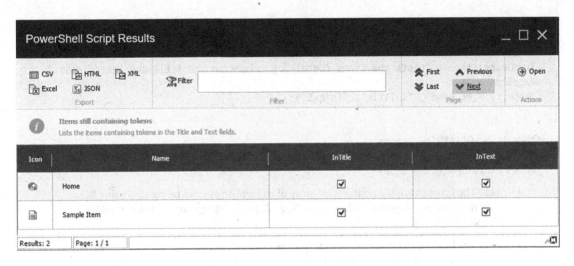

Figure 10-47. *PowerShell report for tokens*

■ **Tip**   The item can be opened in the Content Editor by double-clicking the row. The report title by default shows "PowerShell Script Results." When using Show-ListView, you can modify this title to meet your needs.

Finally, we have the completed report script, as shown in Listing 10-9.

Listing 10-9. PowerShell to Replace Tokens in Title or Text Fields

```
$tokens = @('$name', '$date', '$time', '$now')                              #1
$homeRoot = "master:\content\home"                                          #2
$items = Get-ChildItem -Path $homeRoot -Recurse -WithParent                 #3
$matches = @()                                                              #4
foreach($item in $items) {                                                  #5
    $item | Add-Member -Name InTitle -Value $false -MemberType NoteProperty #6
    $item | Add-Member -Name InText -Value $false -MemberType NoteProperty
    $foundMatch = $false                                                    #7
    foreach($token in $tokens) {                                            #8
        if($item.Title.Contains($token)) {                                  #9
            $item.InTitle = $true
            $foundMatch = $true
        }
        if($item.Text.Contains($token)) {
            $item.InText = $true
            $foundMatch = $true
        }
    }
```

```
        if($foundMatch) {
            $matches += $item                                          #10
        }
    }
}

$props = @{                                                            #11
    InfoTitle = "Items still containing tokens"
    InfoDescription = "Lists the items containing tokens in the Title and Text fields."
    PageSize = 25
    Property = @("Name", "InTitle", "InText")
}

$matches | Show-ListView @props
```

Here's a walkthrough line by line:

- (#1) The tokens variable contains an array of strings. Arrays can be created using @( ) and then comma-separating the values. The values are string literals as denoted by the single quotes.

- (#2) The home root variable is assigned a path with the provider drive specified, which in this case is the master database.

- (#3) The items variable is populated with a command used to query children items recursively. A special feature of the Get-ChildItem command in SPE is the WithParent switch, which will include the root item in the results. Optionally use the Where-Object command to further filter the results before investigating the properties.

- (#4) An empty array is instantiated and assigned to the matches variable.

- (#5) The items variable is enumerated using a foreach loop.

- (#6) The Add-Member command provides a way to dynamically add properties to an object. Here we add a custom property to contain a true/false value.

- (#7) The found match flag is preset with a value of false.

- (#8) The tokens variable is enumerated using a foreach loop.

- (#9) If the item property Title contains the token, then set the custom property InTitle to true and toggle the flag. Repeat for the item property Text.

- (#10) If a match is found then add the extended item to the match array.

- (#11) The props variable is a new hashtable to be used for the Show-ListView command that generates the report.

- The matches are piped to the report command Show-ListView and the props variable is "splatted" on the command. Splatting is the technique where a hash table is unwrapped and mapped to each parameter on a command.

There you have it, a new report for finding tokens in fields. You can always export the results and e-mail to your manager, where you'll be thanked by an offer to take the rest of the day off. In the next section, we'll see how to automate the report e-mail.

Tasks

Scheduled tasks in Sitecore is a powerful feature that's often overlooked. You can think of them like the Task Scheduler in Windows where an agent at some frequency checks to see if any tasks need to be executed. The Sitecore instance must be running and may require some interval tuning to meet your needs. We won't cover too much about the core feature here, but we will see how SPE can help make creating and maintaining them less complex with no downtime.

From the Content Editor, navigate to /sitecore/system/Tasks, where you will be presented with the available commands and schedules (see Figure 10-48).

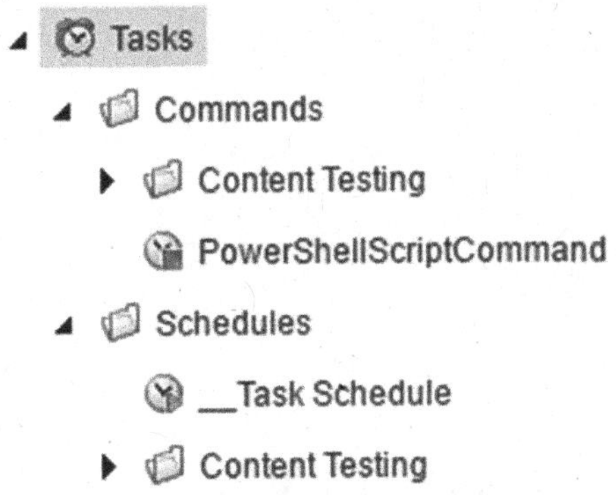

▲ ⊘ Tasks

    ▲ 🗀 Commands

        ▶ 🗀 Content Testing

        🕮 PowerShellScriptCommand

    ▲ 🗀 Schedules

        🕘 __Task Schedule

    ▶ 🗀 Content Testing

Figure 10-48. *Sitecore task commands and schedules*

As you can see in Figure 10-48, SPE includes a custom command for executing PowerShell scripts; later we will see how that command is used. In order to create our new PowerShell Task, we should first go back to /Awesome Module/ and insert a new PowerShell Script Library named Tasks and a new PowerShell script named Send Content Report (see Figure 10-49).

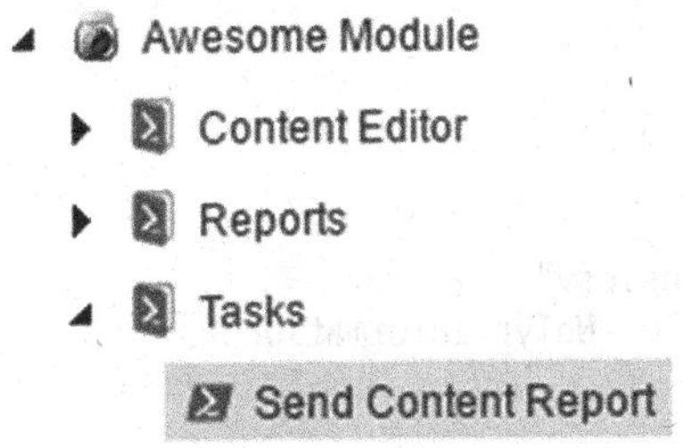

▲ 🕮 Awesome Module

    ▶ ▶ Content Editor

    ▶ ▶ Reports

    ▲ ▶ Tasks

        ▶ Send Content Report

Figure 10-49. *PowerShell Tasks Library with script*

This script is not made visible through the Content Editor with any special interface; changing the icon is optional. Edit the script in the ISE and save the code found in Listing 10-10.

Listing 10-10. Send a Report Automatically Via E-Mail on a Scheduled Basis

```
$tokens = @('$name', '$date', '$time', '$now')
$homeRoot = "master:\content\home"
$items = Get-ChildItem -Path $homeRoot -Recurse -WithParent
$matches = @()
foreach($item in $items) {
    $item | Add-Member -Name InTitle -Value $false -MemberType NoteProperty
    $item | Add-Member -Name InText -Value $false -MemberType NoteProperty
    $foundMatch = $false
    foreach($token in $tokens) {
        if($item.Title.Contains($token)) {
            $item.InTitle = $true
            $foundMatch = $true
        }
        if($item.Text.Contains($token)) {
            $item.InText = $true
            $foundMatch = $true
        }
    }
    if($foundMatch) {
        $matches += $item
    }
}

# The code from here on is where the walk through line by line begins

$props = @{
    Property = @("Name", "InTitle", "InText", @{n="Updated by";e={$_."__Updated by"}},
    @{n="Updated";e={$_."__Updated"}}, "ItemPath")
}

$reportsFolder = "$($SitecoreDataFolder)\reports"
if(-not(Test-Path -Path $reportsFolder)) {
    New-Item -Path $reportsFolder -ItemType Directory | Out-Null
}

$reportFile = "$($reportsFolder)\Items-still-containing-tokens.csv"
$matches | Select-Object @props | Export-Csv -Path $reportFile -NoTypeInformation

$email = @{
    To = "pointy.haired.boss@spe.demo.com"
    From = "guy.with.glasses@spe.demo.com"
    Subject = "Items still containing tokens report"
    Body = "Good afternoon,<br/>Please see the attached report for content items still
    containing tokens.<br/><br/>Guy with Glasses"
    BodyAsHtml = $true
    Attachments = $reportFile
    SmtpServer = "localhost"
}
Send-MailMessage @email
```

■ **Note**   The example uses a convenient tool called Papercut found on Codeplex here: `https://papercut.codeplex.com/`. The command `Send-MailMessage` contains additional parameters for configuring the appropriate mail servers.

Here's a walk through line by line where the new example code begins:

- More parameters have been added using a notation the command `Select-Object` understands. The n represents the new name for property. The e represents an expression that will be evaluated for each item passed through the pipeline. This is very helpful when the property has an unfriendly name or complex evaluations are required to generate the new property.

- SPE provides automatic variables like `$SitecoreDataFolder` and `$SitecoreLogFolder` that map to the settings found in the Sitecore configuration files.

- The command `Test-Path` provides a method of verifying the existing of a file, folder, or Sitecore item. In the case of needing to "negate" the result the operator `-not` can be used, similar behavior can be seen in C# using the character ! (commonly referred to as bang or exclamation point).

- The command `New-Item` creates an item based on the provider used. In this example, the `Filesystem` provider is used which makes `Directory` a valid value. Commands that generate output to the pipeline may be suppressed using `Out-Null`.

- The matches are processed to contain fewer properties then exported to a comma-separated file. By default the `Export-Csv` command generates a file with .Net type information; in this case that information is unnecessary and can be excluded.

- `Send-MailMessage` requires a few parameters before sending such as the `SmtpServer` and the `To` address.

Before setting up the scheduled task we must first validate that the script generates the report and that the e-mail is sent successfully. Run the script in the ISE to confirm that the file is generated on the server (or local workstation). The location of the new report may be something like `C:\[SITECORE_INSTANCE_PATH]\Data\reports`.

In Figure 10-50, we can see the generated file from our script and an e-mail successfully sent to Papercut.

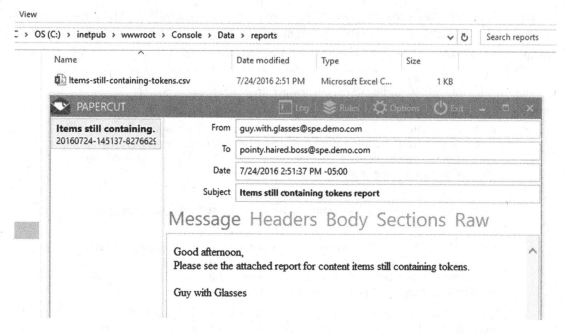

Figure 10-50. *Papercut e-mail received*

Here you can also see that the attachment is available in the e-mail (see Figure 10-51).

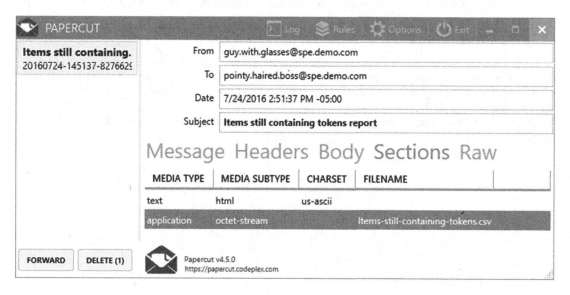

Figure 10-51. *Papercut e-mail with attachment*

One really cool feature in the ISE is its convenient feature of finding the help documentation. Try placing the cursor immediately after the Send-MailMessage command or completely highlight the command. Use the shortcut Ctrl+Enter to display the SPE generated help (see Figure 10-52).

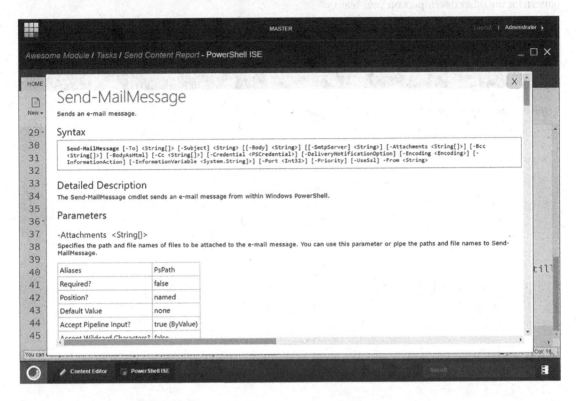

Figure 10-52. Command help dialog

Try scrolling the help dialog all the way to the bottom to see what is available. One great thing about SPE is that each command comes packed with a few examples to help you get started.

Continuing with the setup, we now need to configure the scheduled task. Navigate to /sitecore/system/Tasks/Schedules, right-click on the Schedules folder, then insert a new PowerShell scripted task schedule (see Figure 10-53) named Send Content Report.

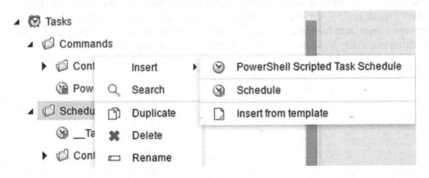

Figure 10-53. PowerShell scripted task schedule

Immediately after clicking on the insert option you will be presented with a series of SPE dialogs (see Figure 10-54). The first dialog requests a name for the new scheduled task and one or more scripts to execute when triggered. Saving scripts under the Tasks Library helps to keep things organized and establishes a good pattern for the other developers on your team.

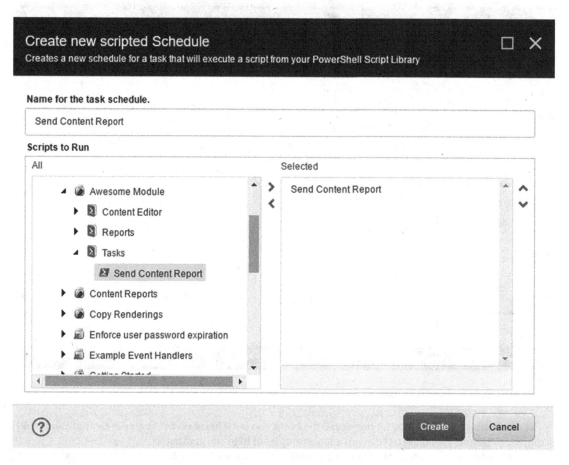

Figure 10-54. Create a new PowerShell schedule

Click the Create button to continue to the next dialog. Next enter the appropriate start date, end date, and frequency of the task (see Figure 10-55). The schedule is broken into four components: start date-time, end date-time, days of the week to run, and frequency each day. Since the Sitecore schedule format can get a bit complicated and configuring manually is prone to error, it's best to let the dialog do the work for you.

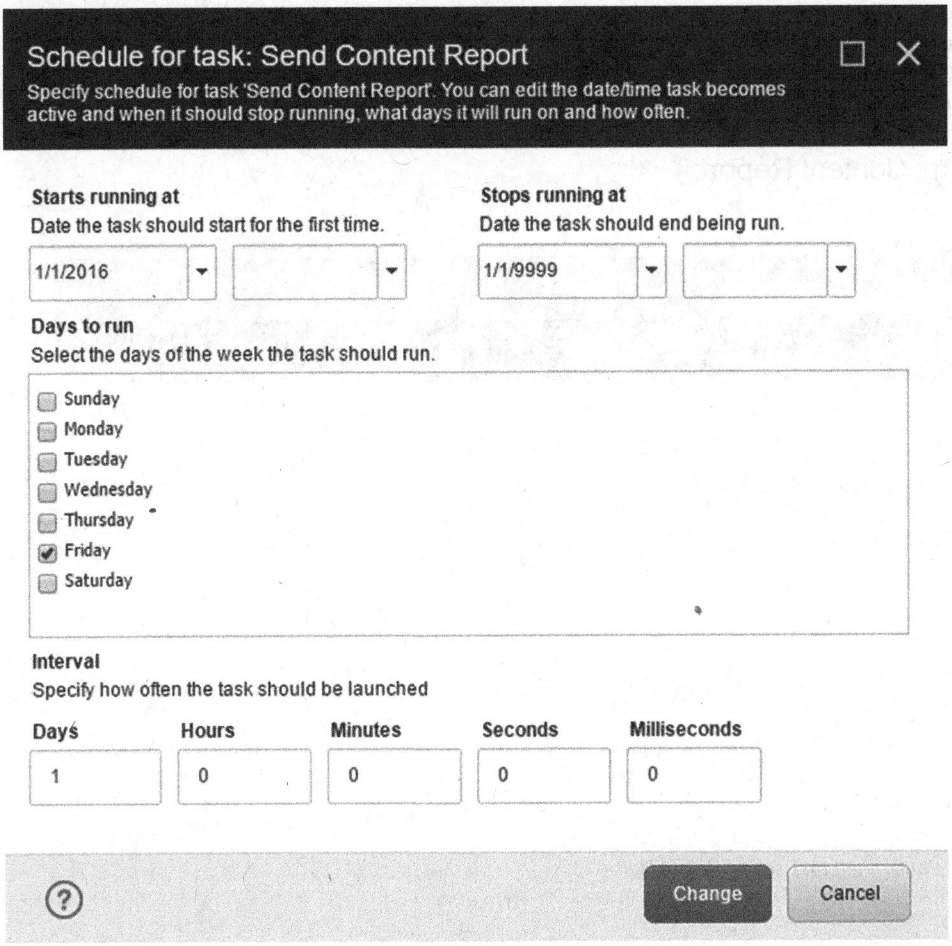

Schedule for task: Send Content Report   □ ✕

Specify schedule for task 'Send Content Report'. You can edit the date/time task becomes active and when it should stop running, what days it will run on and how often.

Starts running at
Date the task should start for the first time.

| 1/1/2016 | ▼ | | ▼ |

Stops running at
Date the task should end being run.

| 1/1/9999 | ▼ | | ▼ |

Days to run
Select the days of the week the task should run.

- ☐ Sunday
- ☐ Monday
- ☐ Tuesday
- ☐ Wednesday
- ☐ Thursday
- ☑ Friday
- ☐ Saturday

Interval
Specify how often the task should be launched

Days	Hours	Minutes	Seconds	Milliseconds
1	0	0	0	0

⑦   Change   Cancel

Figure 10-55. *Edit new PowerShell schedule*

Click the Change button to update the schedule for the newly created task. Refresh the Schedules folder in the tree to reveal the new scheduled task. In the event you want to change the schedule for the task, simply right-click on the task and select Scripts ➤ Edit Task Schedule.

Take a quick look at the fields on the scheduled task to see how SPE maps from the dialog to the item. Notice that the custom command distributed with SPE mentioned earlier is configured as the command for the scheduled task (see Figure 10-56). SPE can pretty much eliminate the need for you to create your own custom command!

Figure 10-56. *PowerShell task schedule fields*

Finally, we test the scheduled task using a feature SPE provides in the context menu (see Figure 10-57). Right-click on the Send Content Report schedule item then select Scripts ➤ Run Task Schedule. You've got mail!

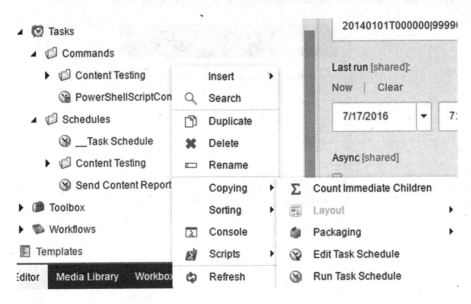

Figure 10-57. *PowerShell run and edit task schedule*

With your automated report set up for your boss, feel free to take the rest of the day off.

UI Settings

The UI configuration settings in SPE provide a way to customize the font family, size, and colors without much hassle. These settings can found under the Settings item as depicted in Figure 10-58.

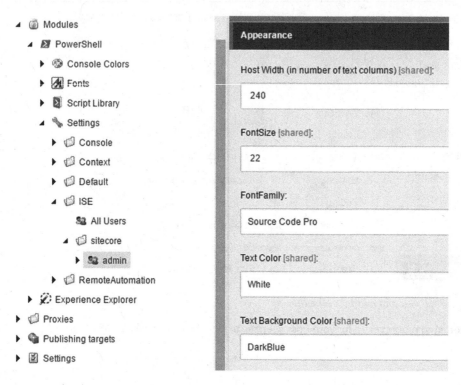

Figure 10-58. *UI settings*

The two most popular settings to change are the font size and family. Create new child items under the Fonts node to teach SPE about other font types available on the system. Figure 10-58 shows Source Code Pro as a configured font which may not be available on a system you are working with. SPE will use an existing system font as a fallback if the specified font is unavailable.

The UI settings for PowerShell Console, ISE, and Results dialogs are configured independently. One convenient way to manage them is through the ISE. With the ISE open, go to Settings ➤ Settings. Clicking the Settings button will reveal an option for each of the interfaces (see Figure 10-59).

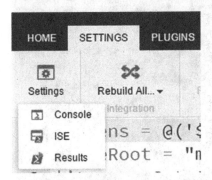

Figure 10-59. *UI settings for interfaces*

Selecting one of the options will reveal a Field Editor dialog (see Figure 10-60) with the current configured values.

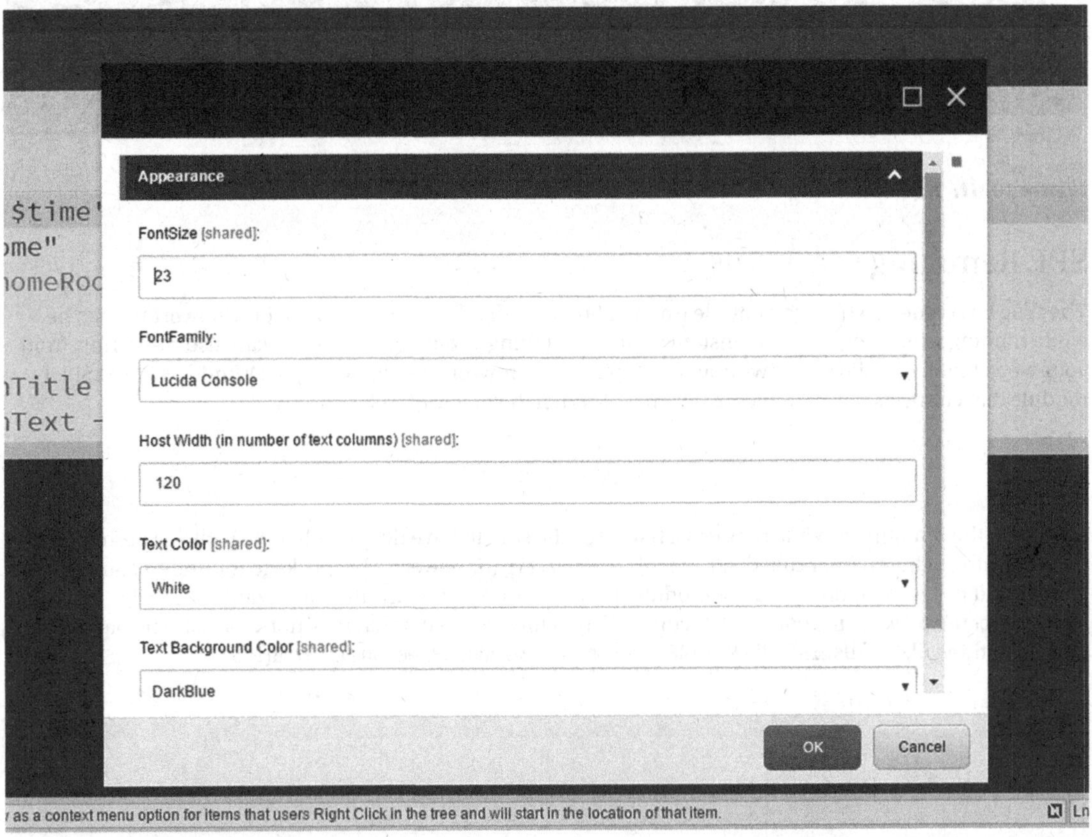

Figure 10-60. *UI settings configuration*

When the command Show-Result is used in a script the data output in the script session can be written to a result window like Figure 10-61.

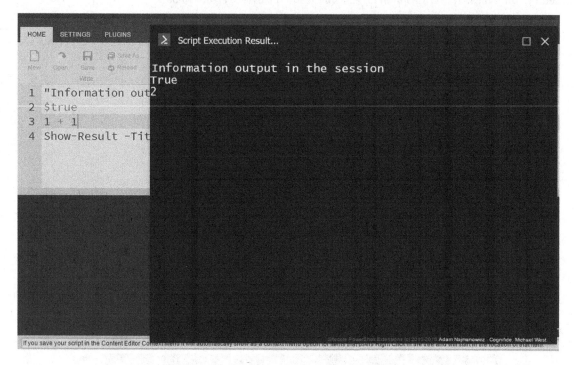

Figure 10-61. Results dialog

SPE Remoting

The time has come in which you have learned enough about SPE that you can see how powerful it can be while running within your Sitecore instance. One great thing about SPE is that you can also run scripts from your workstation or build server without ever opening a browser. SPE Remoting is a Windows PowerShell module that connects to your Sitecore instance through the magic of web services.

Setup

Setting up the remoting module requires a few steps. Be sure to have downloaded the package described at the beginning of the chapter called SPE Remoting-4.0.zip (or newer). This package is purely a compressed archive and has no relationship to the module packages used by the Installation wizard.

Extract the package to your local documents directory to a folder that may not yet exist. The path should look something like C:\Users\[USER_NAME]\Documents\WindowsPowerShell\Modules\.

Once the package is extracted, the Modules folder should contain a new directory called SPE (see Figure 10-62).

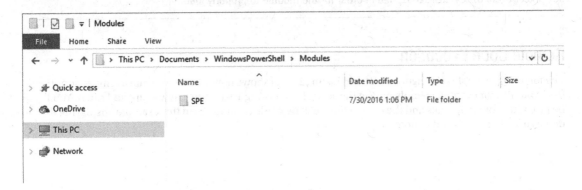

Figure 10-62. *Remoting module path*

Now open the Windows PowerShell ISE by searching the Start menu or navigating to it directly. In Windows 10, you can navigate to Start ➤ All Apps ➤ Windows PowerShell ➤ Windows PowerShell ISE (see Figure 10-63).

Figure 10-63. *Windows 10 Search*

■ **Note** You may need to launch the Windows PowerShell ISE with elevated privileges and run the command Set-ExecutionPolicy RemoteSigned in order for the module to properly load.

Remote Code Execution

The following example (see Figure 10-64 and Listing 10-11) shows how you can execute a remove script, from your PC, for example. Simply type in the script from Listing 10-11 into a new script and run it. You'll be prompted for credentials and the connections will be made to Sitecore (in this example, displaying the details of an item retrieved remotely).

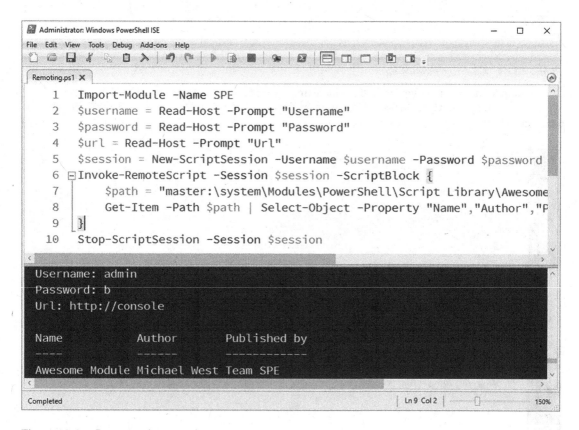

Figure 10-64. *Remote script execution*

Listing 10-11. Example Invoking Some Remote PowerShell

```
Import-Module -Name SPE                                                              #1
$username = Read-Host -Prompt "Username"                                             #2
$password = Read-Host -Prompt "Password"
$url = Read-Host -Prompt "Url"
$session = New-ScriptSession -Username $username -Password $password -ConnectionUri $url  #3
Invoke-RemoteScript -Session $session -ScriptBlock {                                 #4
    $path = "master:\system\Modules\PowerShell\Script Library\Awesome Module"
    Get-Item -Path $path | Select-Object -Property "Name","Author","Published by"    #5
}
Stop-ScriptSession -Session $session                                                 #6
```

Here's a walk through line by line on what the script is performing:

- (#1) Windows PowerShell modules can be imported into the session using the Import-Module command. The folder we extracted earlier during the setup must match the name argument; in this case, it's SPE.

- (#2) Rather than storing the username, password, and URL in the script, we prompt the user for the information. Another option would be to store these values in a configuration file/database.

- (#3) The New-ScriptSession command creates a new session object for communicating with the remote Sitecore instance. This session should be reused, but once completed, it should be disposed of using the Stop-ScriptSession command.

- (#4) The Invoke-RemoteScript command takes the provided session and script, then executes on the remote Sitecore instance. The script block is a piece of code intended to be executed at a later time; it can even be saved to a variable for reuse.

- (#5) Code is executed remotely and gets an item at the specified path. It selects only the relevant properties before returning the data. Any code written inside the script block is only evaluated on the remote Sitecore instance.

- (#6) Finally, the script session on the remote Sitecore instance is disposed.

There are a number of wonderful things made possible through the use of SPE Remoting. Check out the user guide described in the resources section for more details on what features are supported. The guide also provides details on how to enable those features such as remote file upload/download.

Resources

After reading through this book, you will no doubt have additional questions. One easy way to find the links described next is to open up the Sitecore PowerShell ISE and click the About button. Figure 10-65 happens to be using a prerelease of the next version of SPE!

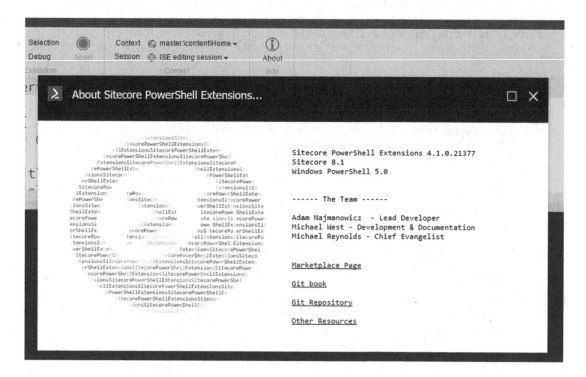

Figure 10-65. *About Sitecore PowerShell Extensions dialog*

Here are some other resources you should check out:

- *Sitecore Marketplace:* Primary download location for the module. http://marketplace.sitecore.net/en/Modules/Sitecore_PowerShell_console.aspx

- *Gitbook:* Definitive user guide and cookbook for the module. https://sitecorepowershell.gitbooks.io/sitecore-powershell-extensions/

- *GitHub:* Source code and issue log for the module. https://github.com/SitecorePowerShell/Console

- Other resources:

  - http://blog.najmanowicz.com/sitecore-powershell-console/

  - http://michaellwest.blogspot.com/

  - *Official SPE channel:* https://www.youtube.com/playlist?list=PLCI6BDk45U s9f7LW7m74zdcXNd-d6HtvK

  - *Community playlist:* https://www.youtube.com/playlist?list=PLph7ZchYd_ nCypVZSNkudGwPFRqf1naOb

Summary

What a whirlwind tour! Special thanks to Michael West for this invaluable content! As you are convinced by now, PowerShell is a tool every Sitecore developer should have in their tool belt. It's incredibly helpful for automating any manual, repeatable work, such as running reports, updating item metadata, or uploading thousands of documents into Sitecore with one click of the button. Certainly more could be said on this important topic, however, we only have so much space in a book such as this. Check out the resources Michael suggested for more PowerShell goodness.

CHAPTER 11

▪ ▪ ▪

Extending the Experience Editor

All front-end Sitecore developers must have a deep understanding of how their front-end code affects a content author's ability to administer content. Specifically, they need to optimize their code for the Experience Editor, and likely, even extend the Experience Editor to help authors manage content easily.

The Experience Editor is one of the most important tools within Sitecore. It's where your content authors are going to spend most of their time, so it's important their experience within the Experience Editor is a good one. Sitecore doesn't know what components you are going to build. As such, the Experience Editor can sometimes become clunky and hard to use if your components start getting rather complex.

This chapter will help you optimize the Experience Editor with some tips to help improve the content editing experience within Sitecore. Without these tips your users might be forced to jump between the Experience Editor for some tasks, and the Content Editor for others. The Content Editor is much harder to use and understand for a non-technical audience, so it's important to ensure their experience in the Experience Editor is a good one.

Three tips that we'll explore are:

- Enabling dynamic placeholders so authors can configure any style of page they need.

- Adding chrome around components so that the relationship between nested components is more clear.

- Using custom buttons and properties, reducing the need for content authors to jump between the Experience Editor and the Content Editor.

All of these extensions are optional, but are helpful in explaining how one might customize the Experience Editor.

Configuring Dynamic Placeholders

As we discussed in the introduction to this chapter, dynamic placeholders are a very powerful and important topic in Sitecore. They enable a marketer to design a page in any way, shape, or form they want. Dynamic placeholders make this possible by allowing placeholders to be added within placeholders at design time. A "two-column 50/50" placeholder could be added into the left column of a two-column 75/25 placeholder to create a two-column page with a right rail. This is just one example out of infinite possibilities. The alternative is to have pre-canned page templates for every layout combination you need. The con of this is two-fold:

- If you create 10 layouts, your marketers will always be asking for an 11th that meets some unforeseen need.

- The risk of code duplication goes up if many of the layouts are more similar than they are different.

© Phil Wicklund and Jason Wilkerson 2016

P. Wicklund and J. Wilkerson, *Professional Sitecore 8 Development*, DOI 10.1007/978-1-4842-2292-8_11

Nine times out of 10 we recommend having a single layout and leverage dynamic placeholders to accommodate each page's unique layout needs. The con might be each page must be built from scratch. However, that can be mitigated with the use of branch templates, which we covered in Chapter 3. Use the following steps to add support for dynamic placeholders into our new layout.

■ **Note**   Technically, dynamic placeholders are not natively supported by the Sitecore platform, but nearly every Sitecore implementation uses them. There are two community solutions that are the most popular—one is a GUID-based approach, taking the unique xid field from the parent component and the other adds a number to the end of the placeholder name. The GUID-based approach seems to be the most popular, so it's the one we use.

---

1. In Visual Studio, open the `SitecoreDev.Foundation.SitecoreExtensions` project in the `Foundation\Extensions` folder.

2. In the NuGet Package Manager window, search for `DynamicPlaceholders.Mvc` by Jason Bert (see Figure 11-1).

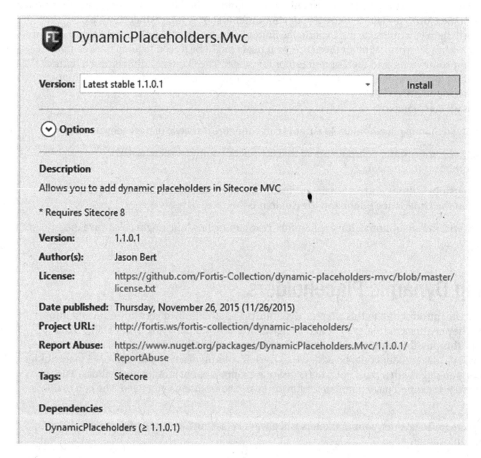

Figure 11-1. *Jason Bert has created a NuGet package to add support for dynamic placeholders to help you get started*

3. Click Install.

4. Once the NuGet package is installed, add a reference to `Sitecore.Mvc.dll` from the `libs\Sitecore` folder, then create a new folder in `SitecoreDev.Foundation.SitecoreExtensions` called `Extensions`.

5. In this new `Extensions` folder, create a new static class named `HtmlHelperExtensions` with the definition from Listing 11-1.

The `DynamicPlaceholder` static method provides a wrapper to the rest of the solution so that the `DynamicPlaceholders.Mvc` NuGet package only needs to be installed in the `SitecoreDev.Foundation.SitecoreExtensions` project.

Listing 11-1. Extension Method Enables Dynamic Placeholder Support Across the Solution

```
using System.Web;
using DynamicPlaceholders.Mvc.Extensions;
using Sitecore.Mvc.Helpers;

namespace SitecoreDev.Foundation.SitecoreExtensions.Extensions
{
    public static class HtmlHelperExtensions
    {
        public static HtmlString DynamicPlaceholder(
            this SitecoreHelper helper, string placeholderName)
        {
            return SitecoreHelperExtensions.DynamicPlaceholder(
                helper, placeholderName);
        }
    }
}
```

IS YOUR EXPERIENCE EDITOR SLOOOOOW?

Clearly the Experience Editor is a great tool that makes content entry in Sitecore a snap. However, depending on page size or how many components you have on the page, the Experience Editor at times can feel rather slow and clunky. The good thing is there are a few ways to speed things up. This is especially true for developers who are building frequently; the start-up times for the Experience Editor can be quite awful.

The SPEAK interface (what the Experience Editor is built from) is compiled at runtime. That first hit to the Experience Editor, as a result, can take a rather long time to load. The benefit of precompilation is that all subsequent requests should be much faster. However, if you build often this first hit can be a killer. Developers especially will benefit from disabling precompilation. To disable precompilation, create a new config file below `Website\App_Config\Include` that modifies the settings in `Sitecore.Speak.Config`, such as can be seen in Listing 11-2.

▓ **Note**   This, and all other config changes, should ideally be in a separate config file, stored in source control with the rest of your solution and deployed just like any other file that needs to go into your Sitecore site's web root. *You should never edit sitecore config files directly!* Rather, you should use Sitecore's patching mechanism to patch in your changes.

Listing 11-2.   Improve Performance of the Experience Editor by Disabling SPEAK Precompilation

```
<configuration xmlns:patch="http://www.sitecore.net/xmlconfig/">
  <sitecore>
    <pipelines>
      <initialize>
        <processor
type="Sitecore.Pipelines.Initialize.PrecompileSpeakViews, Sitecore.Speak.Client">
          <patch:delete />
        </processor>
        <processor            type="Sitecore.Pipelines.Initialize.PrecompileSpeakViews,
Sitecore.Speak.Client">
          <patch:delete />
        </processor>
      </initialize>
    </pipelines>
  </sitecore>
</configuration>
```

John West wrote a great blog post that discusses many other good tips for developers to speed up their development time. Check it out at `http://bit.ly/1QbyIDZ`. Kam Figy also has a patch file that has a ton of impact on performance of Sitecore and the Experience Editor in your local dev environment. It can be found at `http://bit.ly/2cYKUpT`.

Customizing Renderings in the Experience Editor

One of the (many) key differentiating factors that sets Sitecore apart from many other CMS platforms is the Experience Editor. The Experience Editor is quite a powerful tool. That being said, there is always room for improvement. As with everything else within the platform, Sitecore provides a method to customize the Experience Editor to make it more useful to content authors.

For example, a layout developer can specify regions of the page into which authors can place a variety of components. This can be very helpful, but as you start adding more and more components to placeholders on a given page, it becomes confusing where you're placing what, especially if you're nesting placeholders.

Take a scenario, for example. In Figure 11-2 you'll notice we have added three layers of placeholders to subdivide my page. When you click on Component in the ribbon, to pop up the +Add Here button, you get some stacking of buttons. When the +Add Here button stacks, it's nearly impossible to know what you might actually be adding the component into. It gets even worse if you have small blocks of content! Of course, you can always select the placeholder and use the Parent button (see Figure 11-3) to traverse back up the ancestor placeholders/components tree but, visually, it could be way better.

Figure 11-2. *Out of the box, the Experience Editor doesn't visually handle a hierarchy of components and placeholders well, making it difficult to manage complex pages*

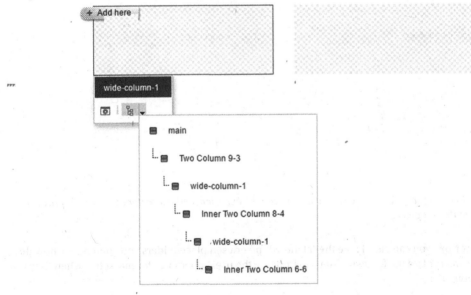

Figure 11-3. *You can see the hierarchy when you click the Parent button, but it still doesn't provide many helpful visual cues into what you're managing*

An alternative is to inject a little CSS into the Experience Editor, through a custom pipeline extension, to define some custom styling rules. This will add some helpful separation between the various components and their placeholders. It will also better define, visually, the layering and hierarchy of components within placeholders. Once we're done, it'll look more like Figure 11-4.

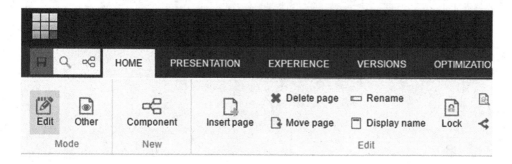

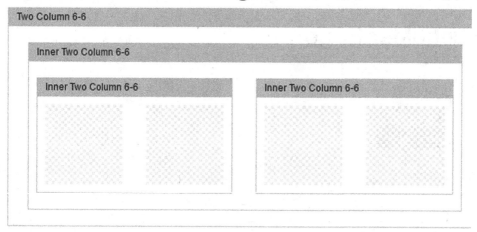

Figure 11-4. By injecting some custom CSS we have made the experience much better by adding separation between components and placeholders

Better, right? Now, you can clearly see the relationship between placeholders and content. So, how do we achieve this sorcery? Use the following steps to improve the user experience for marketers when they are managing components:

1. Start by copying `Sitecore.Mvc.ExperienceEditor.dll` assembly from the `%webroot%\bin` folder to the `%devroot%\libs\Sitecore` folder.

2. In the `SitecoreDev.Foundation.SitecoreExtensions` Foundation project, add a reference to the `Sitecore.Mvc.ExperienceEditor.dll` assembly you just copied into the `libs\Sitecore` folder, then add a new folder called `RenderingWrapper`. In that folder, add another folder named `Markers`.

3. In the `Markers` folder, create a new class named `EditorComponentRenderingMarker` with the definition from Listing 11-3. The HTML code in this class wraps the placeholders to draw the boxes.

Listing 11-3. Create a New IMarker to Wrap Placeholders with Additional HTML

```
using Sitecore.Mvc.ExperienceEditor.Presentation;

namespace SitecoreDev.Foundation.SitecoreExtensions.RenderingWrapper.Markers
{
    public class EditorComponentRenderingMarker : IMarker
    {
        private string _componentName;
        public EditorComponentRenderingMarker(string componentName)
        {
            _componentName = componentName;
        }

        public string GetStart()
        {
            string formatstring =
                "<div class=\"component-wrapper {0}\"><span class=\"wrapper-
                header\">{1}</span><div class=\"component-content clearfix\">";
            return string.Format(formatstring, _componentName.Replace(
                " ", string.Empty), _componentName);
        }

        public string GetEnd()
        {
            return "</div></div>";
        }
    }
}
```

4. In the RenderingWrapper folder, add a new class named EditorRenderingWrapper with the definition from Listing 11-4.

Listing 11-4. Create a Wrapper

```
using Sitecore.Mvc.ExperienceEditor.Presentation;
using System.IO;

namespace SitecoreDev.Foundation.SitecoreExtensions.RenderingWrapper
{
    public class EditorRenderingWrapper : Wrapper
    {
        public EditorRenderingWrapper(TextWriter writer, IMarker marker)
            : base(writer, marker)
        {
        }
    }
}
```

5. Next, also in the RenderingWrapper folder, create a new class named AddEditorRenderingWrapper with the definition from Listing 11-5. This class's Process method is called from the Sitecore pipeline during rendering processes, with the Marker added to the rendering collection.

Listing 11-5. Add a New Pipeline Processor to Add the Marker into the Rendering Collection

```
using Sitecore;
using Sitecore.Mvc.ExperienceEditor.Presentation;
using Sitecore.Mvc.Pipelines.Response.RenderRendering;
using Sitecore.Mvc.Presentation;
using SitecoreDev.Foundation.SitecoreExtensions.RenderingWrapper.Markers;

namespace SitecoreDev.Foundation.SitecoreExtensions.RenderingWrapper
{
    public class AddEditorRenderingWrapper : RenderRenderingProcessor
    {
        public override void Process(RenderRenderingArgs args)
        {
            if (args.Rendered || Context.Site == null ||
                !Context.PageMode.IsExperienceEditorEditing ||
                args.Rendering.RenderingType == "Layout")
            {
                return;
            }

            var marker = GetMarker(args);
            if (marker == null)
            {
                return;
            }

            args.Disposables.Add(new EditorRenderingWrapper(args.Writer, marker));
        }

        public IMarker GetMarker(RenderRenderingArgs args)
        {
            var renderingContext = RenderingContext.CurrentOrNull;
            IMarker marker = null;
            var renderingItem = args.Rendering.RenderingItem;

            if (renderingItem != null)
            {
                marker = new EditorComponentRenderingMarker(renderingItem.Name);
            }

            return marker;
        }
    }
}
```

6. One final class to add to the RenderingWrapper folder is
   EndEditorRenderingWrapper with the definition from Listing 11-6.

Listing 11-6. Create an End Wrapper to Dispose the Marker in the Collection

```
using System;
using System.Linq;
using Sitecore.Mvc.Pipelines.Response.RenderRendering;

namespace SitecoreDev.Foundation.SitecoreExtensions.RenderingWrapper
{
    public class EndEditorRenderingWrapper : RenderRenderingProcessor
    {
        public override void Process(RenderRenderingArgs args)
        {
            foreach (IDisposable wrapper in
                args.Disposables.OfType<EditorRenderingWrapper>())
            {
                wrapper.Dispose();
            }
        }
    }
}
```

7. Now that we've added the code for our rendering wrappers, let's patch
   them into the config. In the App_Config\Include\Foundation folder of the
   SitecoreDev.Foundation.SitecoreExtensions project, open the Foundation.
   SitecoreExtensions.config file and add the config from Listing 11-7 to the
   sitecore\pipelines configuration node.

Listing 11-7. Register Your Processors in the Web.Config

```
<!-- Rendering Wrappers -->
<mvc.renderRendering>

    <processor  patch:after="processor[@type='Sitecore.Mvc.ExperienceEditor.Pipelines.
Response.RenderRendering.AddWrapper, Sitecore.Mvc.ExperienceEditor']" type=" SitecoreDev.
Foundation.SitecoreExtensions.RenderingWrapper.AddEditorRenderingWrapper, SitecoreDev.
Foundation.SitecoreExtensions"/>

    <processor  patch:before="processor[@type='Sitecore.Mvc.Pipelines.Response.
RenderRendering.AddRecordedHtmlToCache, Sitecore.Mvc']" type=" SitecoreDev.Foundation.
SitecoreExtensions.RenderingWrapper.EndEditorRenderingWrapper, SitecoreDev.Foundation.
SitecoreExtensions"/>

</mvc.renderRendering>
```

8. Now that we've patched in our new config, we need to throw in a little CSS. In the `SitecoreDev.Foundation.SitecoreExtensions` project, create a new folder called `Content`. In that folder, add a new CSS Style Sheet named `foundation.sitecoreextensions.css` with the contents from Listing 11-8.

■ **Note** Typically, in a modular architecture, all CSS for a site goes into a module in the Project layer. However, since this markup is only applicable to chrome that's added to markup within Experience Editor, it belongs in the Foundation module.

Listing 11-8. Add Some CSS to Draw Boxes Around the Components

```
body.edit-mode .component-wrapper {
  border: 1px solid #9dd;
  border-top: none;
  box-sizing: border-box;
  margin: 10px;
  overflow: hidden; }
  body.edit-mode .component-wrapper span.wrapper-header {
    display: block;
    color: #111;
    background-color: #9dd;
    height: 24px;
    line-height: 24px;
    padding: 0 10px;
    font-size: 12px;
    font-family: Arial, sans-serif;
    }
  body.edit-mode .component-wrapper .component-content {
    padding: 10px;
    min-height: 50px; }
    body.edit-mode .component-wrapper .component-content .component-wrapper {
      margin: 10px 0; }

body.edit-mode .mdl-container .mdl-locations-container .scEmptyImage {
  display: none; }
```

9. Lastly, in the `SitecoreDev.Website` project, in the `Views\Shared` folder, modify the `DefaultMVCLayout.cshtml` file. Modify the `<body>` tag to match this line of code:

```
<body class="@(Sitecore.Context.PageMode.IsExperienceEditor ?
"edit-mode" : string.Empty)">
```

10. Finally, build your solution and then publish all of the changes using the Publish-Site Gulp task in the Task Runner.

That's it! Now whenever you open the page in the Experience Editor, you'll have helpful boxes around your components!

■ Tip This example only adds chrome to renderings in the Experience Editor. Ken McAndrew extended this concept to also wrap empty placeholders. His contribution can be found at `http://bit.ly/1Tadqao`.

Custom Experience Editor Buttons and Properties

At this point our Experience Editor is getting really easy to use by our non-technical content authors. It's easy for them to assemble page layouts anyway they like, and they can nest components within one another and not lose them in a sea of hierarchical components due to the helpful chrome we added between them. However, if you recall the Hero Slider from Chapter 2, you'll remember that many components still rely on the Content Editor for their configuration. The Hero Slider got its data from a series of images added into a list of items. That list of items was associated with the component as its data source. This is unfortunate because it leaves the content authors in a state where it's necessary to manage related content using two separate tools, the Content Editor and the Experience Editor. The Content Editor doesn't have the user interface preview, leaving non-technical folks unsure that their changes are resulting in what they want.

So what options do have to enable this deeper configuration to be done from the Experience Editor? Luckily, as with everything else in Sitecore, the Experience Editor is almost infinitely extensible. We can add custom toolbar buttons and rendering parameters to components or we can add new buttons to our component altogether, only for use in the Experience Editor, to further enable the content authors to manage and own their content.

Here, we'll show three examples of how to extend the Experience Editor. Notice in Figure 11-5 we have added a custom button into the component menu. Clicking that button will load a modal dialog with configuration options directly from the Experience Editor (the same interface you might see in the Content Editor but without needing to switch user interfaces).

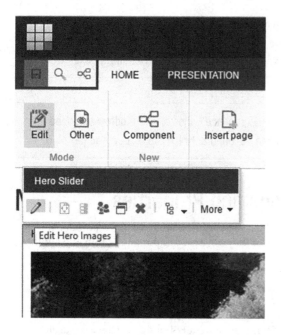

Figure 11-5. *Custom toolbar buttons paired with a modal dialog provide a helpful way to manage the content for a component without needing to leave the Experience Editor*

Additionally, you can set component properties by extending the properties dialog of the component itself (see Figures 11-6 and 11-7). Even though the interface is not very elegant, these properties provide a quick-and-dirty way for a content author to customize a component within the Experience Editor.

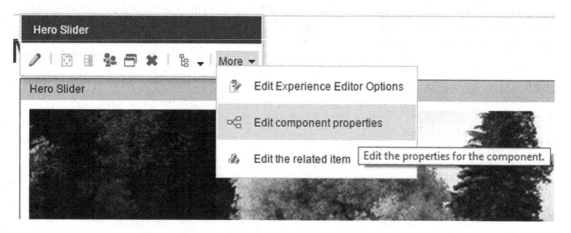

Figure 11-6. *Custom component properties can be accessed from the More button while a component is selected within the Experience Editor*

■ **Note** "Edit the Related Item" links the user to the item set as the component's data source. This is helpful if that item contains all the data/settings that need to be configured. However, most of the time a data source item will have descendent child items that are not accessible through this link, in which case of these three options may be necessary so the user doesn't have to go to the Content Editor.

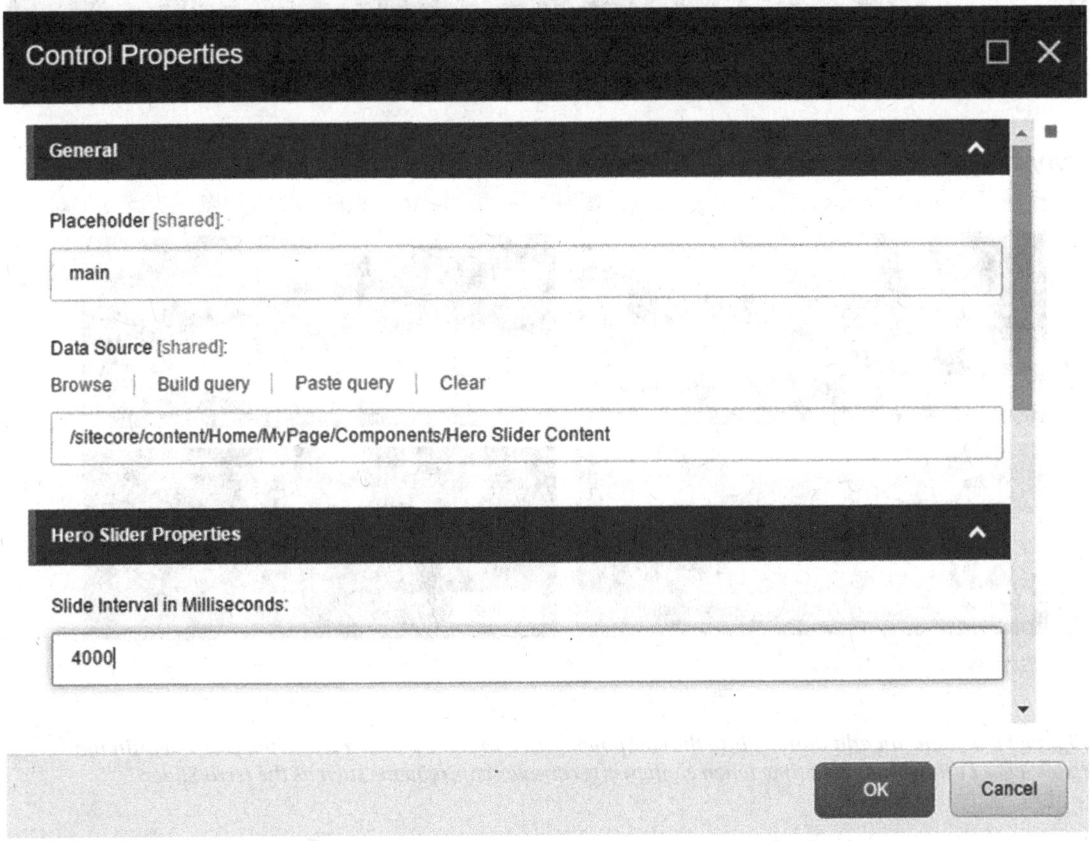

Figure 11-7. Custom component properties are a quick-and-dirty way for a content author to configure options on a component directly within the Experience Editor

Lastly, we can really take things to the extreme by adding custom markup into our views when (and only when) the author is within the Experience Editor. Notice how in Figure 11-8 we have a bunch of buttons within the component itself that provide an administrative user interface for authors to use to administer that component. In the case of our Hero Slider, we've added buttons to add or edit an image, as well as resize them so that all images in the slider are visible at once. This puts the administration of the Hero Slider directly within the Experience Editor without any foreign interfaces for the content author user.

Figure 11-8. *You can add buttons into the component itself that only render while the user is within the Experience Editor. This saves time when configuring complex components such as the Hero Slider*

So how do you do all this? The follow sections contain all the steps you need to set up custom buttons with modal dialogs, custom property windows, and custom buttons on the Experience Editor design surface itself.

Configuring Custom Component Toolbar Buttons

The following steps show how to add custom buttons into your components editor toolbar when they are selected within the Experience Editor:

1. Custom toolbar buttons are stored and configured in the Core database. Navigate to http://sitecore8/sitecore to open the Launchpad. Click on the Desktop button, then in the bottom right, click on the database icon. Select the Core database (see Figure 8-9).

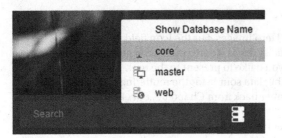

Figure 11-9. *Switch to the Core database to add your toolbar items*

2. Now, launch the Content Editor, either through the Launchpad or from the Sitecore menu in the bottom-left of the desktop. Navigate to /sitecore/ content/Applications/WebEdit/Custom Experience Buttons.

3. First, like we've done many places where we've defined custom items, let's organize things a bit by creating a folder under Custom Experience Buttons called SitecoreDev.

4. Right-click on the SitecoreDev folder and select Insert ➤ Insert from template. In the Insert from Template dialog, select the /System/WebEdit/Field Editor Button (see Figure 11-10). Name it Edit Hero Images.

Insert from Template

Select or search for the template you want to use. In the Item Name field, enter a name for the new item.

BROWSE   SEARCH

▶ 🗁 Validation

◢ 🗁 WebEdit

  🗁 Edit Frame Button Folder

  📄 Edit Frame Small Button

  🌀 Field Editor Button

  ⬤ WebEdit Button

  📄 WebEdit Texts

▶ 🗁 Workflow

Template: /System/WebEdit/Field Editor Button

Item Name: Edit Hero Images|

Insert   Cancel

Figure 11-10. *Add a new toolbar item below the WebEdit folder*

5. Click Insert.

6. In the Header and Tooltip fields, enter Edit Hero Images. For the Icon field, select People/32x32/pencil2.png. In the Fields field, this is where you enter a pipe-separated list of fields on the content item you'd like to present to the user. These fields are from the template being used as the data source for the rendering/component that was selected. If you remember back from Chapter 2, our _Hero Slider template had a single field called Hero Images. This is the field we'd like to present to the user to edit. When you're done, your new field editor button should look like Figure 11-11.

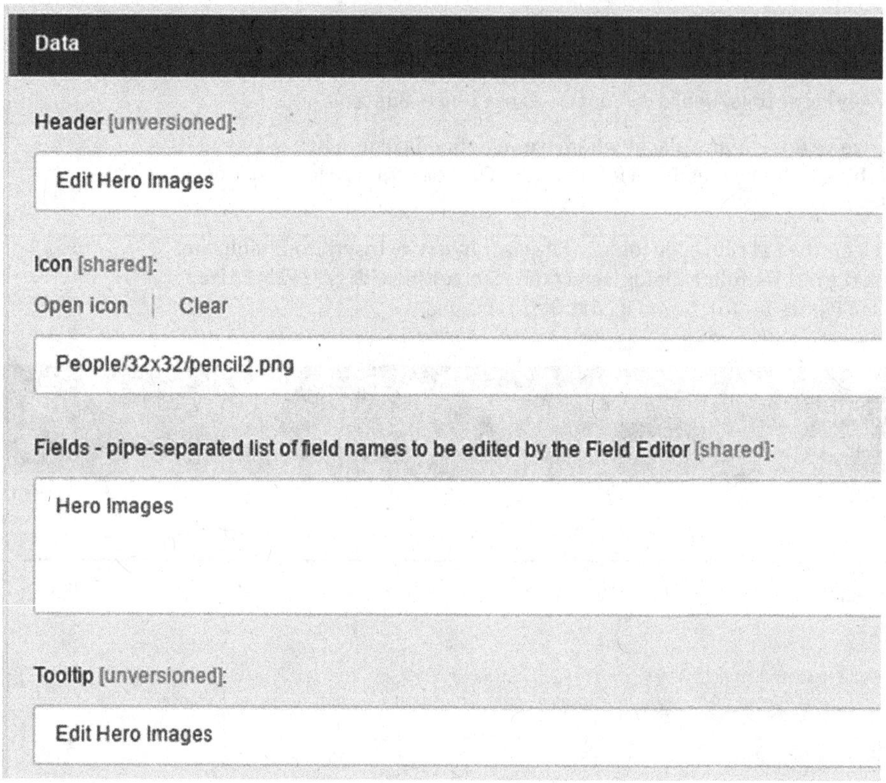

Data

Header [unversioned]:

    Edit Hero Images

Icon [shared]:

Open icon | Clear

    People/32x32/pencil2.png

Fields - pipe-separated list of field names to be edited by the Field Editor [shared]:

    Hero Images

Tooltip [unversioned]:

    Edit Hero Images

Figure 11-11. *Fill out the applicable fields for the new toolbar item*

7. Click Save.

8. Now that we've configured our new field editor button, we need to add it to the toolbar of our Hero Slider rendering/component. From the Launchpad, click the Desktop button and let's switch back to the master database using the database icon in the bottom-right. Once you're back into the master database, launch the Content Editor and navigate to /sitecore/layout/Renderings/Sitecore8Dev/ Feature/Media/Hero Slider.

9. On the item, scroll down to the Editor Options section. The last field in this section is called Experience Editor Buttons. In this field, select the new Edit Hero Images button, as shown in Figure 11-12.

Figure 11-12. *Add your toolbar item into the Editor Options selector*

10. Click Save.

11. That's it! Now, in the Content Editor, if you navigate to /sitecore/content/Home/MyPage and select the Publish tab and click the Experience Editor button, selecting our Hero Slider component should bring up a toolbar with our custom button (see Figure 11-13)!

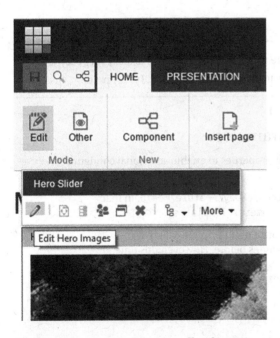

Figure 11-13. *Notice your new toolbar button!*

12. Clicking on the pencil icon will open a modal dialog with the appropriate fields presented for editing (see Figure 11-14).

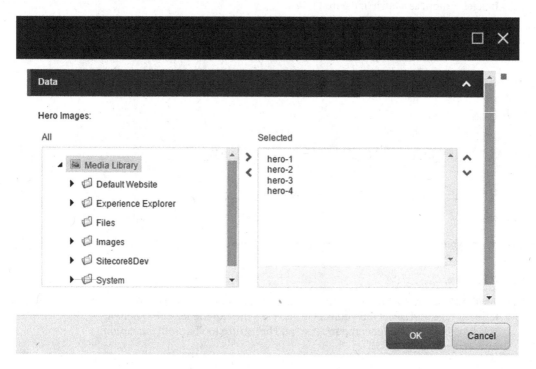

Figure 11-14. This is much easier to administer

■ **Note**   Now that we've shown you the long way, if you're using Glass.Mapper, it is actually very easy to add custom edit frame buttons using GlassHtml. You can view more info at http://bit.ly/2cErw5e.

Configuring Custom Component Parameters

The following steps show how to use custom component properties to enable additional configuration within the Experience Editor:

1. First, navigate to /sitecore/templates/Sitecore8Dev/Feature/Media. In that folder, create a new template folder called Parameter Templates.

2. In the new Parameter Templates folder, create a new template called Hero Slider Properties, as we have done many times before. However, this time, change the base template to be /Templates/System/Layout/Rendering Parameters/Standard Rendering Parameters. Configure this template as shown in Figure 11-15.

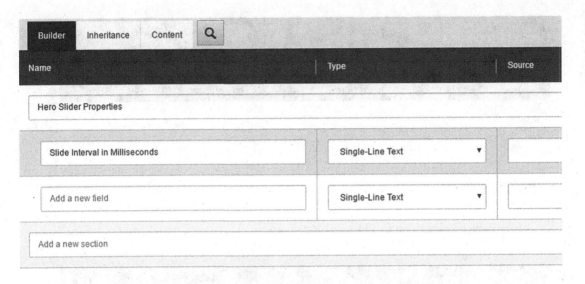

Figure 11-15. Create a new template to store our Hero Slider properties

3. Click Save.

4. Click on the Options tab, then the Standard Values button to create a __Standard Values item for this parameter template. In the Slide Interval in Milliseconds field of the __Standard Values item, insert 1000 to set the interval to 1 second. This will be the default value. Click Save.

5. Next, navigate to the Hero Slider rendering, located in /sitecore/layout/ Renderings/Sitecore8Dev/Feature/Media. In the Editor Options section, there is a Parameters Template field. Using the drop-down, select Templates/ Sitecore8Dev/Feature/Media/Parameter Templates/Hero Slider Properties. Click Save.

6. Now, if you load MyPage from the Experience Editor (by navigating to /sitecore/ content/Home/MyPage in the content tree, selecting the Publish tab and clicking the Experience Editor button) and select the Hero Slider component, the Component Toolbar will pop up. Click the More button, then select Edit Component Properties (see Figure 11-16). In the Control Properties dialog, you should now see the new Hero Slider Properties section with our Slide Interval in Milliseconds field.

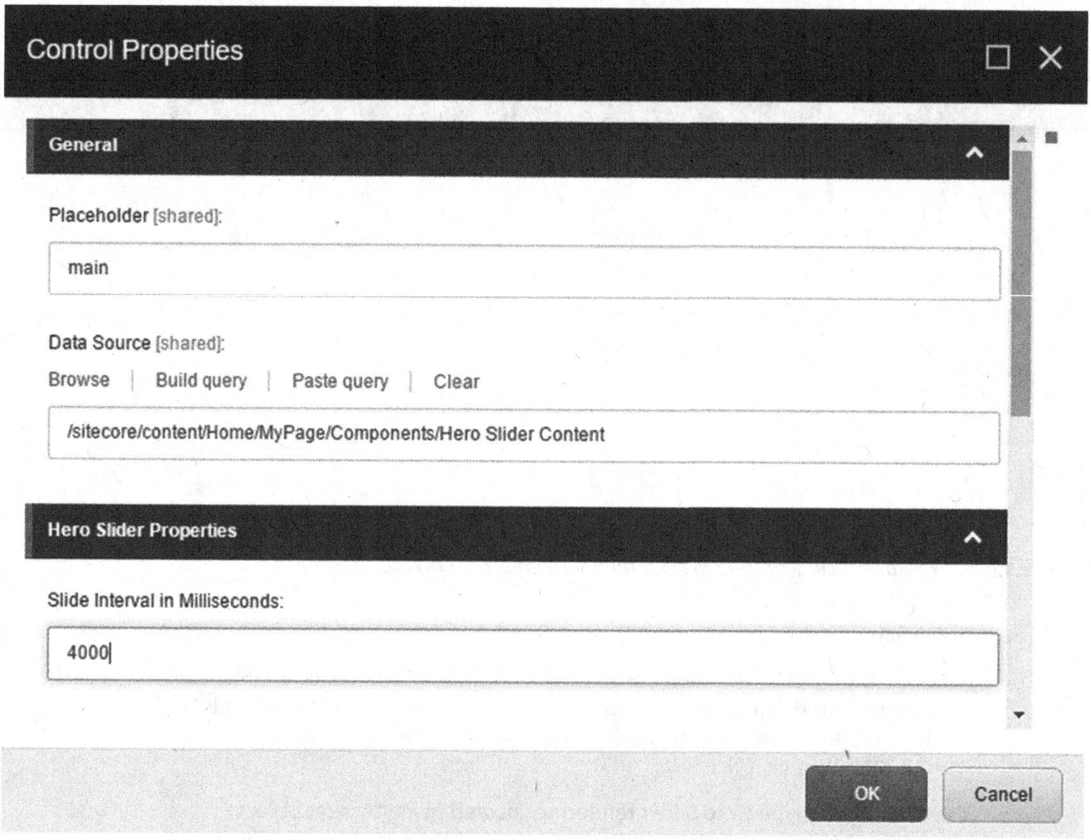

Figure 11-16. *This is much easier to administer*

7. Next, let's wire up that property so that we're actually leveraging that value. In Visual Studio, navigate to the SitecoreDev.Feature.Media project. Let's start by adding a value to the view model used by the Hero Slider component. Open ViewModels\HeroSliderViewModel and the property from this code:

```
public int SlideInterval { get; set; }
public bool IsSliderIntervalSet { get { return SlideInterval > 0; } }
```

8. In the Views\Media\HeroSlider.cshtml file, add the code from Listing 11-9 between the last </div> and the closing } bracket.

Listing 11-9. Check If an Interval Is Set and If So Sets that Parameter on the JavaScript Carousel Object

```
@if (Model.IsSliderIntervalSet)
{
    <script type="text/javascript">
    $(document).ready(function () {
        $(".carousel").carousel({
            interval: @(Model.SlideInterval),
        });
    });
    </script>
}
```

Now that we have our view and ViewModel ready to leverage this new setting, let's wire it up in the controller. Open the Controllers\MediaController.cs. There are two methods that will be illustrated here: directly calling the Sitecore API to get the value (tightly coupling our code in Step 9) and accessing the value through abstraction (loosely coupling our code; skip to Step 10).

9. Calling the Sitecore API directly, insert the code from Listing 11-10 just above return View(ViewModel) in the HeroSlider controller action, Controllers\ MediaController.cs class. This approach gets the property out of the component directly through tightly coupled API Code within the controller (not a best practice, but certainly the fastest approach).

Listing 11-10. Get the Property Out of the Component Directly Through Tightly Coupled API Code Within the Controller

```
int interval = 0;
if (int.TryParse(RenderingContext.Current?.Rendering?.Parameters["Slide Interval in
Milliseconds"], out interval))
    viewModel.SlideInterval = interval;
```

10. To accomplish this through abstraction, we need to do a little bit more setup. In the SitecoreDev.Foundation.Repository project, create a folder in the root of the project called Context. In that folder, create an interface called IContextWrapper with the definition from Listing 11-11.

Listing 11-11. We'll Use This Interface to Abstract Our Parameter Dependency

```
using System.Collections.Specialized;

namespace SitecoreDev.Foundation.Repository.Context
{
    public interface IContextWrapper
    {
        string GetParameterValue(string key);
    }
}
```

11. Also in the Context folder, create a new class called SitecoreContextWrapper with the definition from Listing 11-12. This method is used instead of directly within the controller as we saw in Listing 11-10.

Listing 11-12. Our Context Wrapper Implementation Has the Code to Hit the API

```
using System.Collections.Specialized;
using Sitecore.Mvc.Presentation;

namespace SitecoreDev.Foundation.Repository.Context
{
    public class SitecoreContextWrapper : IContextWrapper
    {
        public string GetParameterValue(string key)
        {
            var value = String.Empty;
            var parameters = RenderingContext.Current.Rendering.Parameters;
            if (parameters != null && parameters.Count() > 0)
                value = parameters[key];
            return value;
        }
    }
}
```

12. Finally, in the Pipelines\InitializeContainer\RegisterDependencies class, add this code to inject the implementation of our wrapper:

    ```
    args.Container.Register<IContextWrapper, SitecoreContextWrapper>();
    ```

13. Moving back to the SitecoreDev.Feature.Media project, in Controllers\ MediaController.cs, add this field right after private readonly IMediaRepository _repository:

    ```
    private readonly IContextWrapper _contextWrapper;
    ```

14. Next, modify the constructor to match Listing 11-13.

Listing 11-13. Modify the Constructor to Take a Dependency (Injected from Our Pipeline Addition from Step 12)

```
public MediaController(IContextWrapper contextWrapper)
{
    _repository = new SitecoreMediaRepository();
    _contextWrapper = contextWrapper;
}
```

15. Replace the tightly-coupled code we used in Step 9, Listing 11-10 with the code in Listing 11-14. This updated listing will set the view's internal parameter from our context wrapper instead of hitting the API directly.

Listing 11-14. Replace the Code in the HeroSlider Action to Get the Parameter from the Context Rather than the API Directly

```
var parameterValue = _contextWrapper.GetParameterValue("Slide Interval in Milliseconds");

int interval = 0;
if (int.TryParse(parameterValue, out interval))
    viewModel.SlideInterval = interval;
```

Finally, build your solution, then publish the site using the Publish-Site Gulp task. Now, you should be able to repeat Step 5, change the value of the Slide Interval in Milliseconds, and see your change reflected in the behavior of the component.

Configuring Custom Component Experience Editor Buttons

The following steps show how to add custom buttons into the Experience Editor design surface to improve the authoring experience for complex components. In order to effectively demonstrate in a more reusable manner, we need to refactor our Hero Slider component a little. If you recall, back in Chapter 2, we created a Hero Slider template that had a single field called Hero Images. It was a treelist with a data source pointing directly at the Media Library. This worked well for the simple example we were illustrating at the time. However, the following refactoring steps, while they may seem a little overly complicated for a "carousel of images," will serve to illustrate a better example of how to handle and work with more complex components that contain child content items.

Use the following refactoring steps to update the hero slider to use "slide" items instead of one treelist field. This will provide greater flexibility within the Experience Editor.

1. Let's start by navigating to /sitecore/templates/Sitecore8Dev/Feature/Media in the Content Editor. Create a new interface template named _Hero Slider Slide and configure it as shown in Figure 11-17.

Builder	Inheritance	Content	Q
Name		**Type**	**Source**
Image			
Image		Image ▼	/sitecore/media library/Sitecore8Dev/Hero Images
Add a new field		Single-Line Text ▼	
Add a new section			

Figure 11-17. Create a new template for our hero image slide

401

2. In the _Hero Slider template, remove the entire Hero Slider Content field section. Expand _Hero Slider, then right-click on Hero Slider Content, and select Delete. Click OK to confirm that you'd like to delete all the subitems as well.

3. Next, in /sitecore/templates/Sitecore8Dev/Project/SitecoreDev/Content Types, add a new template called Hero Slider Slide. This is a datasource template. Using the Content tab, in the Data section, select /Templates/ Sitecore8Dev/Feature/Media/_Hero Slider Slide as a base template.

4. Next, select the Hero Slider template. Click the Options tab and click the Standard Values button to create a __Standard Values item for the Hero Slider. Now, click the Configure tab, then the Assign button in the Insert Options ribbon section. This will open the Insert Options dialog. In the tree on the left, navigate to /templates/Sitecore8Dev/Project/Sitecore8Dev/Content Types and select the Hero Slider Slide template, as shown in Figure 11-18.

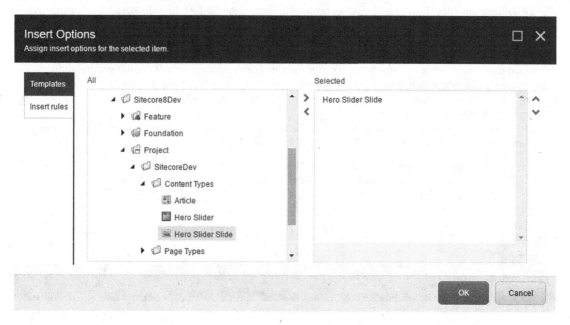

Figure 11-18. *Configure insert options to allow only Hero Slider Slide items to be created below the Hero Slider component*

5. Click OK then Save.

6. Now, let's update our content items. Navigate to /sitecore/content/Home/ MyPage/Components. If you select the Hero Slider Content content item, you'll notice that the Hero Images field is gone. Right-click on Hero Slider Content, select Insert ➤ Hero Slider Slide. This option appears because we set the Insert Options on the __Standard Values item of the Hero Slider template. Name this new content item Slide 1.

7. In the Image field of Slide 1, click Browse to browse the Media Library for the image you want. Select hero-1, then click the Select button. Repeat Steps 4 and 5 for the other three images that will appear in our carousel.

8. If you were to visit http://sitecore8/mypage right now, you will see an error page. That's because we have quite a bit of code to refactor as well. Head on over to Visual Studio. In the SitecoreDev.Foundation.Orm project, use the NuGet Package Manager to add SimpleInjector.

9. Next, create a folder called Pipelines in the root of the project. In the Pipelines folder, add another folder called InitializeContainer. Finally, in the InitializeContainer folder, add a new class called RegisterDependencies with the definition from Listing 11-15.

Listing 11-15. Use a Pipeline to Inject Our SitecoreContext and GlassHTML Dependencies

```
using Glass.Mapper.Sc;
using SimpleInjector;
using SitecoreDev.Foundation.Ioc.Pipelines.InitializeContainer;

namespace SitecoreDev.Foundation.Orm.Pipelines.InitializeContainer
{
    public class RegisterDependencies
    {
        public void Process(InitializeContainerArgs args)
        {
            args.Container.Register<ISitecoreContext>(() =>
                new SitecoreContext(), Lifestyle.Transient);
            args.Container.Register<IGlassHtml, GlassHtml>();
        }
    }
}
```

10. In this step, we're registering a couple of dependencies from Glass.Mapper that will be injected into our MediaController in the SitecoreDev.Feature.Media project.

11. Now that we've registered our dependencies, we need to patch that into the initializePipeline. In the App_Config\Include folder, create a new folder called Foundation. Inside that folder, add a new configuration file called Foundation.Orm.config with the contents from Listing 11-16.

Listing 11-16. Add Our RegisterDependencies Injector to the Sitecore Pipeline

```
<configuration xmlns:patch="http://www.sitecore.net/xmlconfig/"
xmlns:set="http://www.sitecore.net/xmlconfig/set/">
  <sitecore>
    <pipelines>
      <initializeContainer>
        <processor type="SitecoreDev.Foundation.Orm.Pipelines.InitializeContainer.
RegisterDependencies, SitecoreDev.Foundation.Orm" />
      </initializeContainer>
    </pipelines>
  </sitecore>
</configuration>
```

That's all that's needed for the SitecoreDev.Foundation.Orm project. Next, let's refactor the Foundation.Model project a bit.

12. In the SitecoreDev.Foundation.Model project, modify the ICmsEntity interface to include a new property shown in this code:

```
Guid Id { get; }
```

■ **Note** Because we're adding this Id property to the base ICmsEntity interface, that property needs to be removed from the IArticle interface in the Models folder of the SitecoreDev.Feature.Articles project.

---

13. Moving on to the SitecoreDev.Feature.Media project, use NuGet Package Manager to add Glass.Mapper and SimpleInjector, then add a new folder to the root of the project called Models. Then, in the Models folder, create a folder called Configuration.

14. Add a new interface to the Models folder called IHeroSliderSlide with the definition from Listing 11-17.

Listing 11-17. Create a New Interface for Our Hero Image Slide

```
using Glass.Mapper.Sc.Fields;
using SitecoreDev.Foundation.Model;

namespace SitecoreDev.Feature.Media.Models
{
    public interface IHeroSliderSlide : ICmsEntity
    {
        Image Image { get; }
    }
}
```

15. Also in the Models folder, add a new interface named IHeroSlider with the definition from Listing 11-18.

Listing 11-18. Create a New Interface for the Hero Slider Itself

```
using System.Collections.Generic;
using SitecoreDev.Foundation.Model;

namespace SitecoreDev.Feature.Media.Models
{
    public interface IHeroSlider : ICmsEntity
    {
        IEnumerable<IHeroSliderSlide> Slides { get; set; }
    }
}
```

16. In the Models\Configuration folder, add a new class called IHeroSliderSlideMap with the definition from Listing 11-19.

Listing 11-19. Add a Class to Map Each Sitecore Slide Item into the Interface

```
using Glass.Mapper.Sc.Maps;

namespace SitecoreDev.Feature.Media.Models.Configuration
{
    public class IHeroSliderSlideMap : SitecoreGlassMap<IHeroSliderSlide>
    {
        public override void Configure()
        {
            Map(config =>
            {
                config.AutoMap();
                config.Id(f => f.Id);
                config.Field(f => f.Image).FieldName("Image");
            });
        }
    }
}
```

17. Also in the Models\Configuration folder, add a class named IHeroSliderMap with the definition from Listing 11-20.

Listing 11-20. Add a Class to Map the Sitecore Slider Item to the Interface

```
using Glass.Mapper.Sc.Maps;

namespace SitecoreDev.Feature.Media.Models.Configuration
{
    public class IHeroSliderMap : SitecoreGlassMap<IHeroSlider>
    {
        public override void Configure()
        {
            Map(config =>
            {
                config.AutoMap();
                config.Id(f => f.Id);
            });
        }
    }
}
```

■ **Note** The IHeroSlider interface has a Slides property that can hold children. We could configure Glass.
Mapper to load children with a statement like config.Children(f => f.Slides);. In this particular case, one
could argue that it's not a problem and doesn't violate the single responsibility principle in SOLID. However,
in other cases, you might only want children of a certain type. Glass.Mapper can certainly handle that as
well through configuration; however, at that point, you are mixing business logic with configuration, definitely
violating the single responsibility principle! Because of this, we will save the loading of children for our Service
layer, where the rest of our business logic lives.

---

18. Next, let's add a new folder to the root of SitecoreDev.Feature.Media called
    Services. In that folder, create a new interface named IMediaContentService
    with the definition from Listing 11-21.

Listing 11-21. Add a New Service to Get the Hero Slides

```
using SitecoreDev.Feature.Media.Models;

namespace SitecoreDev.Feature.Media.Services
{
    public interface IMediaContentService
    {
        IHeroSlider GetHeroSliderContent(string contentGuid);
    }
}
```

19. Before we create the implementation for IMediaContentService, we need to
    add a new method to our IContentRepository to retrieve the slides out of the
    Sitecore database. In SitecoreDev.Foundation.Repository, open the Content\
    IContentRepository interface. Add this line of code:

    ```
    IEnumerable<T> GetChildren<T>(string parentGuid) where T : class, ICmsEntity;
    ```

20. In SitecoreContentRepository, add the method from Listing 11-22.

Listing 11-22. Implement the New Service that Retrieves the Slides Out of the Sitecore Database

```
public virtual IEnumerable<T> GetChildren<T>(string parentGuid) where T : class, ICmsEntity
{
    Assert.ArgumentNotNullOrEmpty(parentGuid, "parentGuid");

    var parentItem = _sitecoreContext.Database.GetItem(ID.Parse(parentGuid));
    var childrenItems = parentItem.GetChildren();

    if (childrenItems == null || childrenItems.Count == 0)
        return Enumerable.Empty<T>();
    else
        return childrenItems.Select(c => _sitecoreContext.Cast<T>(c));
}
```

21. Now that we've added a method to our generic repository to get the children of an Item, let's head back to the SitecoreDev.Feature.Media project to create the service that calls this repository. In the Services folder, create a new class called SitecoreMediaContentService with the definition from Listing 11-23.

Listing 11-23. Add a New Service to Retrieve the Slides from the Content Repository

```
using SitecoreDev.Feature.Media.Models;
using SitecoreDev.Foundation.Repository.Content;

namespace SitecoreDev.Feature.Media.Services
{
    public class SitecoreMediaContentService : IMediaContentService
    {
        private readonly IContentRepository _repository;

        public SitecoreMediaContentService(IContentRepository repository)
        {
            _repository = repository;
        }

        public IHeroSlider GetHeroSliderContent(string contentGuid)
        {
            var heroSlider = _repository.GetContentItem<IHeroSlider>(contentGuid);
            heroSlider.Slides = _repository.GetChildren<IHeroSliderSlide>
                (contentGuid);
            return heroSlider;
        }
    }
}
```

22. Now that we've created our service layer, let's register this new dependency with our IoC container so it can be injected into MediaController. Create a folder called Pipelines in the root of the project. In the Pipelines folder, add another folder called InitializeContainer. Finally, in the InitializeContainer folder, add a new class called RegisterDependencies with the definition from Listing 11-24.

Listing 11-24. Register the New Service as a Dependency To Be Injected into the MediaController

```
using SitecoreDev.Feature.Media.Services;
using SitecoreDev.Foundation.Ioc.Pipelines.InitializeContainer;

namespace SitecoreDev.Feature.Media.Pipelines.InitializeContainer
{
    public class RegisterDependencies
    {
        public void Process(InitializeContainerArgs args)
        {
            args.Container.Register<IMediaContentService,
                SitecoreMediaContentService>();
        }
    }
}
```

23. Now that we've registered our dependencies, we need to patch that into the initializePipeline. In the root of the project, create an App_Config folder and an Include folder as a subdirectory. Then create a folder called Feature. Inside the Feature folder, add a new configuration file called Feature.Media.config with the contents from Listing 11-25.

Listing 11-25. Patch the New Dependency Injector into the Sitecore Pipeline

```
<configuration xmlns:patch="http://www.sitecore.net/xmlconfig/"
xmlns:set="http://www.sitecore.net/xmlconfig/set/">
  <sitecore>
    <pipelines>
      <initializeContainer>
        <processor type="SitecoreDev.Feature.Media.Pipelines.InitializeContainer.
RegisterDependencies, SitecoreDev.Feature.Media" />
      </initializeContainer>
    </pipelines>
  </sitecore>
</configuration>
```

24. Next, we move back to MediaController. Replace private readonly IMediaRepository _repository with private readonly IMediaContentService _mediaContentService; so that the controller accesses the hero slides via the service instead of directly, as is best practice.

25. Replace the existing constructor with Listing 11-26.

Listing 11-26. Our New Controller Constructor Takes the Content Service as a Dependency, in Addition to the Context Wrapper

```
public MediaController(IContextWrapper contextWrapper, IMediaContentService
mediaContentService)
{
  _contextWrapper = contextWrapper;
  _mediaContentService = mediaContentService;
}
```

26. Next, replace the existing HeroSlider controller action with Listing 11-27.

Listing 11-27. Update the HeroSlider Action Method to Retrieve the Slides out of the Service and Add Them to the HeroImages ViewModel Object

```
public ViewResult HeroSlider()
{
  var viewModel = new HeroSliderViewModel();

  if (!String.IsNullOrEmpty(RenderingContext.Current.Rendering.DataSource))
  {
    var contentItem = _mediaContentService.GetHeroSliderContent(
      RenderingContext.Current.Rendering.DataSource);
```

```
    foreach (var slide in contentItem?.Slides)
    {
        viewModel.HeroImages.Add(new HeroSliderImageViewModel()
        {
            MediaUrl = slide.Image.Src,
            AltText = slide.Image.Alt
        });
    }
    var firstItem = viewModel.HeroImages.FirstOrDefault();
    firstItem.IsActive = true;
}

var parameterValue = _contextWrapper.GetParameterValue(
    "Slide Interval in Milliseconds");

int interval = 0;
if (int.TryParse(parameterValue, out interval))
    viewModel.SlideInterval = interval;

return View(viewModel);
}
```

■ **Note**   You can now delete the `Repositories` folder in `SitecoreDev.Feature.Media`, containing the
`IMediaRepository` and `SitecoreMediaRepository`. This functionality was replaced with the generic
`IContentRepository`.

Now, if you build your solution and publish it using the Publish-Site Gulp task, `http://sitecore8/`
`mypage` should still work! We've successfully refactored the hero slider to use slide items instead of a treelist.
Now, with all that refactoring complete, let's get to the real steps of actually extending the Experience Editor
with custom editor buttons!

27.   First things are first—we will need a couple of properties added to our
      `HeroSliderViewModel`, one to signify we're in Experience Editor mode and the
      other to indicate the ID of the parent content item. In `SitecoreDev.Feature.`
      `Media`, open `ViewModels\HeroSliderViewModel.cs` and add these properties:

      ```
      public bool IsInExperienceEditorMode { get; set; }
      public string ParentGuid { get; set; }
      ```

28.   We'll also need to store the ID of each slide, so in `HeroSliderImageViewModel`,
      add this property:

      ```
      public string Id { get; set; }
      ```

29.   Next, in `SitecoreDev.Foundation.Repository`, open the `Context\`
      `IContextWrapper` class and add this line:

      ```
      bool IsExperienceEditor { get; }
      ```

30. Now, add the implementation of this line in `SitecoreContextWrapper`, found here:

```
public bool IsExperienceEditor { get { return Sitecore.Context.PageMode.
IsExperienceEditor; } }
```

31. Now, back in the `MediaController` in `SitecoreDev.Feature.Media`, modify the `HeroSlider` controller action to match Listing 11-28. It will inform the view whether or not the page is being edited in the Experience Editor and add GUIDs for the slides (used when Edit Image is clicked).

Listing 11-28. Update the HeroSlider Controller Action

```
public ViewResult HeroSlider()
{
    var viewModel = new HeroSliderViewModel();

    if (!String.IsNullOrEmpty(RenderingContext.Current.Rendering.DataSource))
    {
        var contentItem = _mediaContentService.GetHeroSliderContent(
            RenderingContext.Current.Rendering.DataSource);

        foreach (var slide in contentItem?.Slides)
        {
            viewModel.HeroImages.Add(new HeroSliderImageViewModel()
            {
                Id = slide.Id.ToString(),
                MediaUrl = slide.Image?.Src,
                AltText = slide.Image?.Alt
            });
        }
        var firstItem = viewModel.HeroImages.FirstOrDefault();
        firstItem.IsActive = true;
        viewModel.ParentGuid = contentItem.Id.ToString();
    }

    var parameterValue = _contextWrapper.GetParameterValue(
        "Slide Interval in Milliseconds");

    int interval = 0;
    if (int.TryParse(parameterValue, out interval))
        viewModel.SlideInterval = interval;

    viewModel.IsInExperienceEditorMode = _contextWrapper.IsExperienceEditor;

    return View(viewModel);
}
```

32. Next, let's add a little CSS that will be applied to our custom buttons. In the `SitecoreDev.Website` project, add the classes from Listing 11-29 to `Content\sitecoredev.website.css`.

Listing 11-29. Add Some CSS to Style the Buttons When Editing in the Experience Editor

```
.imageContainer {
   float:left;
   min-height:100px;
   width:500px;
   background-color:#808080;
   margin:10px;
       position: relative;
   }
   .imageContainer img {
      height: 200px;
      width:500px;
   }
.editButton {
   position:absolute;
   bottom:15px;
   left:15px;
}
.carousel-inner img {
   height: 768px;
   width:1920px;
}
```

33. Finally, let's refactor the HeroSlider.cshtml view in the Views\Media folder of the SitecoreDev.Feature.Media project to use this new IsInExperienceEditorMode property. The refactored code is shown in Listing 11-30.

Listing 11-30. Add a Class to Map the Sitecore Slider Item to the Interface

```
@model SitecoreDev.Feature.Media.ViewModels.HeroSliderViewModel

@if (Model.HasImages)
{
   if (Model.IsInExperienceEditorMode)
   {
      <div>
         @foreach (var image in Model.HeroImages)
         {
            <div class="item imageContainer">
               <img src="@image.MediaUrl" alt="@image.AltText" />
                        <!-- We'll add a custom button here! -->
            </div>
         }
      </div>
      <div style="clear:both;">
         <!-- We'll add our custom buttons here! -->
      </div>
   }
```

```
else
{
    <div id="myCarousel" class="carousel slide" data-ride="carousel">
        <ol class="carousel-indicators">
            @for (int i = 0; i < Model.ImageCount; i++)
            {
                <li data-target="#myCarousel" data-slide-to="@i" class="@(Model.
                HeroImages[i].IsActive ? "active" : "")"></li>
            }
        </ol>

        <div class="carousel-inner" role="listbox">
            @foreach (var image in Model.HeroImages)
            {
                <div class="item @(image.IsActive ? "active" : "")">
                    <img src="@image.MediaUrl" alt="@image.AltText" />
                </div>
            }
        </div>
    </div>

    if (Model.IsSliderIntervalSet)
    {
        <script type="text/javascript">
            $(document).ready(function () {
                $("#myCarousel").carousel({
                    interval: @(Model.SlideInterval),
                });
            });
        </script>
    }
}
}
```

You can see that we have removed the carousel functionality while in Experience Editor mode. This will prepare us to better manage the content for this component while in the Experience Editor.

Before we add our custom buttons to the markup, we need to add a new Field Editor button in the Core database, just like we did earlier in the chapter, in the "Configuring Custom Toolbar Buttons" section.

34. From the Launchpad, click on the Desktop button, then in the bottom right, click on the Database icon. Select the Core database (see Figure 11-19).

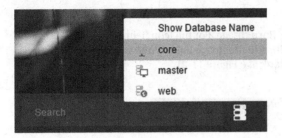

Figure 11-19. *Switch to the core database*

35. Now, launch the Content Editor, either through the Launchpad or from the Sitecore menu in the bottom-left of the desktop. Navigate to /sitecore/ content/Applications/WebEdit/Custom Experience Buttons.

36. Right-click on the SitecoreDev folder and select Insert ➤ Insert from template. In the Insert from Template dialog, select the /System/WebEdit/Field Editor Button. Name it Edit Hero Image, as shown in Figure 11-20.

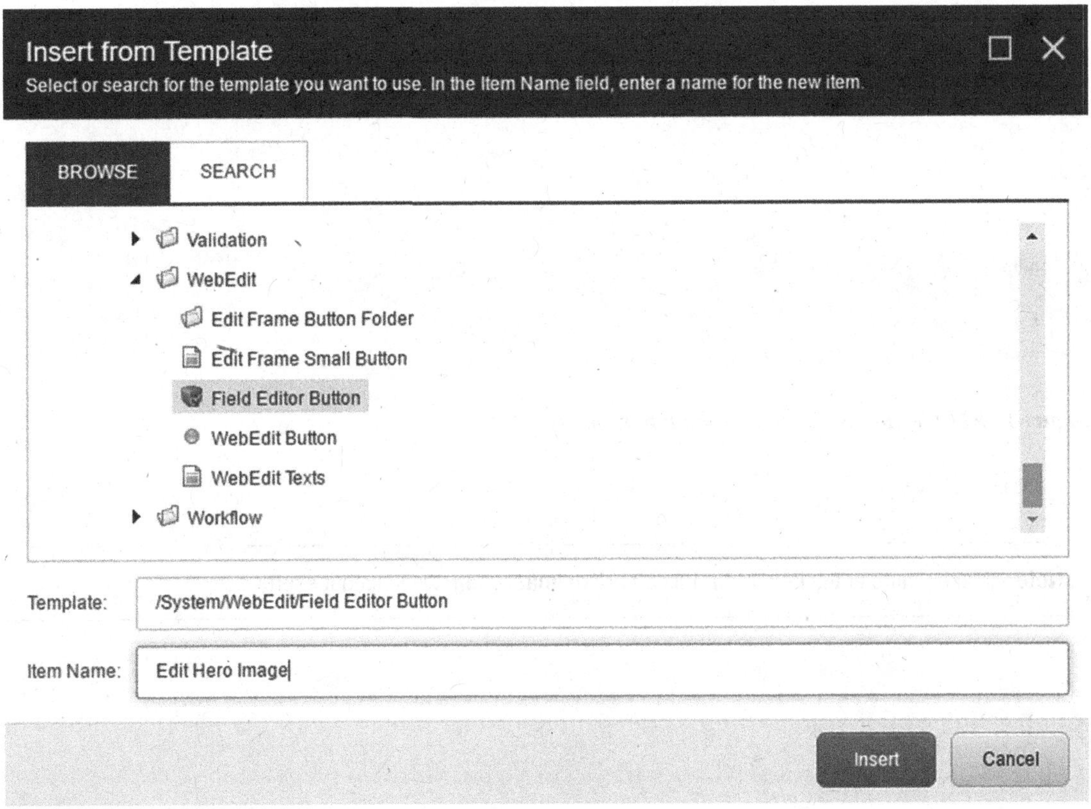

Insert from Template
Select or search for the template you want to use. In the Item Name field, enter a name for the new item.

☐ ✕

| BROWSE | SEARCH |

▶ 📁 Validation

▲ 📁 WebEdit

　　📁 Edit Frame Button Folder

　　📄 Edit Frame Small Button

　　🛡 Field Editor Button

　　⬤ WebEdit Button

　　📄 WebEdit Texts

▶ 📁 Workflow

Template: /System/WebEdit/Field Editor Button

Item Name: Edit Hero Image|

| Insert | Cancel |

Figure 11-20. *Add a new button to allow for editing the hero image*

37. Click Insert.

38. In the Header and Tooltip fields, enter Edit Hero Image. For the Icon field, select People/32x32/pencil2.png. In the Fields field, add the Image field. When you're done, your new Field Editor button should look like Figure 11-21.

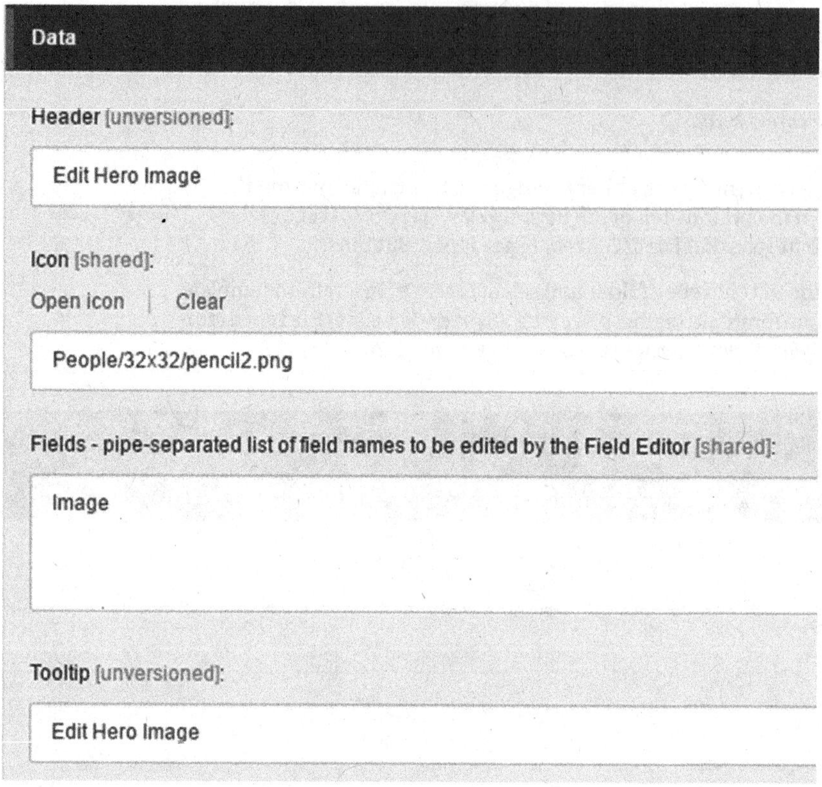

Data

Header [unversioned]:

Edit Hero Image

Icon [shared]:

Open icon | Clear

People/32x32/pencil2.png

Fields - pipe-separated list of field names to be edited by the Field Editor [shared]:

Image

Tooltip [unversioned]:

Edit Hero Image

Figure 11-21. *Fill out the new toolbar button properties*

39. Click Save.

■ **Note** Make a note of the item ID for this Edit Hero Image item. We'll need it shortly…

---

40. Now, let's go back to our HeroSlider.cshtml view and add our two new buttons. Replace the markup in the if (Model.IsInExperienceEditorMode) block with the markup from Listing 11-31.

Listing 11-31. Update the Hero Slider's View to Include Edit Image Buttons and a Add New Image Button

```
if (Model.IsInExperienceEditorMode)
{
    <div>
        @foreach (var image in Model.HeroImages)
        {
            <div class="item imageContainer">
                <img src="@image.MediaUrl" alt="@image.AltText" />
                <!-- This button opens the Field Editor dialog to edit the field
                    specified in our Edit Hero Image command -->
                <a href="#" class="btn btn-default editButton"
                    onclick="javascript:Sitecore.PageModes.PageEditor.postRequest(
                        'webedit:fieldeditor(id=@(image.Id),
                        fields=Image,
                        command={19F37115-C98E-4EEE-9C2B-5FA732D14F03})')">
                    Edit Image</a>
            </div>
        }
    </div>
    <div style="clear:both;">
        <!-- This button calls the webedit:new command to add a
            new Item to the content tree -->
        <a href="#" class="btn btn-default"
            onclick="javascript:Sitecore.PageModes.PageEditor.postRequest(
                'webedit:new(id=@(Model.ParentGuid))')">
            Add new image</a>
    </div>
}
```

Notice the two <a> tags we inserted. The first one, inside the foreach loop, opens the Field Editor dialog, using the Edit Hero Image field editor command we just created. This command takes three parameters:

- *Id*: This is the Item ID of the content item containing the fields we want to edit.

- *Fields*: This is a pipe-delimited list of fields to display in the field editor dialog.

- *Command*: This is the item ID of the command we just created. You will want to insert the item ID for your Edit Hero Image field editor command.

The second button, inside the <div> tag after the foreach loop, calls the webedit:new command to add a new content item as a child to the parent specified in the ID field.

41. Last, but not least, build your solution and publish your changes using the Publish-Site Gulp task.

42. Once the build completes, navigate to http://sitecore8/mypage. The Hero Slider should be operating as normal.

43. Opening this page in the Experience Editor will now render something different! You should see something more like Figure 11-22.

Figure 11-22. *This is much easier to administer!*

44. Clicking on the Add New Image button will open the Insert Item dialog (see Figure 11-23). Select the Hero Slider Slide template, name the new item Slide 5, and click OK.

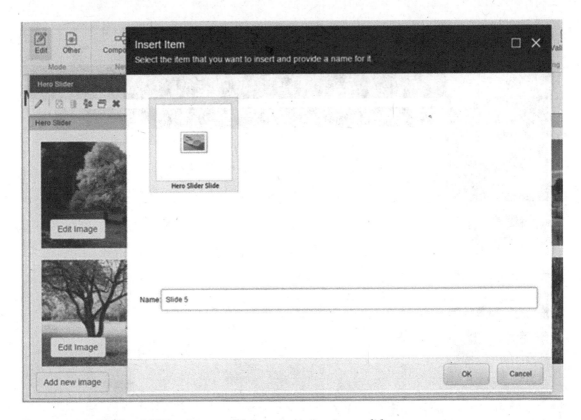

Figure 11-23. Clicking Add New Image will let you create new image slides

45. You should now see your new "empty image" in the list.

46. Clicking the Edit Image button on this empty image should open a dialog with the Image field (see Figure 11-24). From here you can select your image and click OK.

Figure 11-24. *It's very easy to click Edit Image to specify a different image for that slide*

Summary

Well that was a whirlwind tour of techniques to extend the Experience Editor! We launched into a discussion on how to extend the Experience Editor. Concepts such as dynamic placeholders, custom toolbar buttons, and custom properties can all help your content authors manage their content much more easily.

Index

A

Acrylic Dependency Principle, 125
AngularJS, 206–208
ASP.NET MVC, 115, 117, 119, 123
ASP.NET Web Forms, 115, 116
Autocomplete, 268–271

B

Branch templates, 103–104

C

Code rot, 123
Common Closure Principle, 125
Computed fields, blog posts
    BlogBodyComputedField, 262
    BlogCategoriesComputedFields, 262–263
    BlogSearchResult class, 265
    BlogTitleComputedField, 264
    categories, 259–260
    configuration, 261
    description, 259
    HasPresentationComputedField, 260–261
    index configuration, 264–265
    results, 267
    SearchController, 266
    SearchResultViewModel, 265
    Views\Search_SearchResults.cshtml, 266–267
configurations, 188
Content approval and publishing workflows, 112
Content cloning, 113
Content management fundamentals
    architect, content tree, 107–108
    Content Editor, 105
    content placeholder, 106
    database and file system, media storage, 109
    delete and archive, 112
    Experience Editor, 105
    rich media, 109
    translations, 113

Content management system (CMS), 51
Content optimization, 112
Content personalization, 110–111
Content versioning, 111
Controller rendering
    associated content dialog, 74
    coding, 70–75
    controller and action, 73
    fields, 73
    Hero Image components
        adding images, 70
        Bootstrap, 70
        components, 62
        ComponentsController, 70
        creating folder template, 64
        custom folder template and CSS, 67
        data template, 63
        helpful icons, 65
        Hero Slider Content, 62, 71
        media library, 69
        new content item, 68
        setting custom icons, data
            templates, 65
        standard values button, 66
        Tree Node Style dialog, 66
    sitecore component, 75
    vs. view renderings, 61
Custom personalization rules
    behavior-based, 294
    conditions, 298–300
    e-mail address, 298
    end-to-end process, 298
    macros, 297
    parameters, 296–297
    Rules Editor, 295
    text and type fields, 296

D

Data templates, 62
    branch templates and command templates, 97
    custom field types

P. Wicklund and J. Wilkerson, *Professional Sitecore 8 Development*, DOI 10.1007/978-1-4842-2292-8

Get the eBook for only $4.99!

Why limit yourself?

Now you can take the weightless companion with you wherever you go and access your content on your PC, phone, tablet, or reader.

Since you've purchased this print book, we are happy to offer you the eBook for just $4.99.

Convenient and fully searchable, the PDF version enables you to easily find and copy code—or perform examples by quickly toggling between instructions and applications.

To learn more, go to http://www.apress.com/us/shop/companion or contact support@apress.com.

Printed in the United States
By Bookmasters